W9-BXH-012

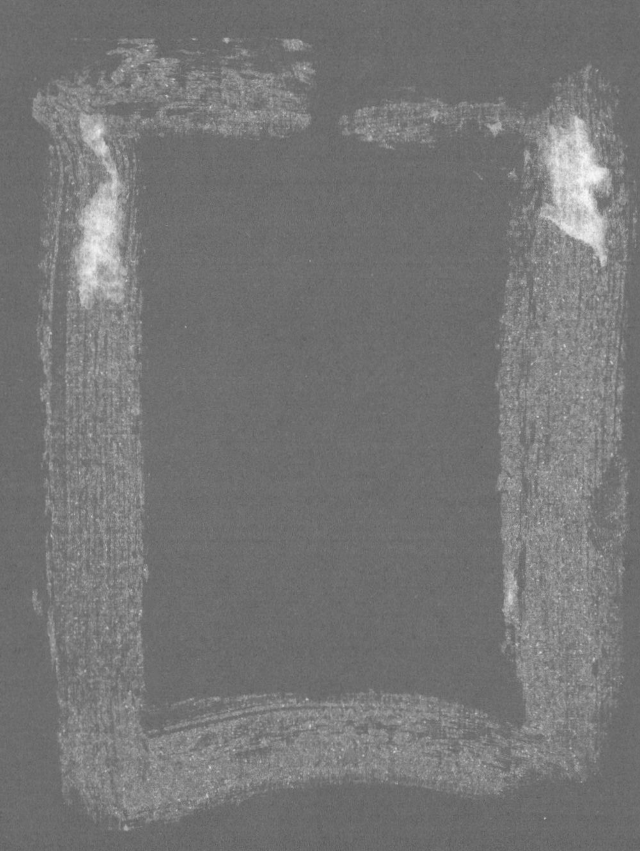

Heart of Stone

First published 2012 by
New Holland Publishers Pty Ltd
London • Sydney • Cape Town • Auckland

Garfield House 86–88 Edgware Road London W2 2EA United Kingdom
1/66 Gibbes Street Chatswood NSW 2067 Australia
218 Lake Road Northcote Auckland New Zealand
Wembley Square First Floor Solan Road Gardens Cape Town 8001 South Africa
www.newhollandpublishers.com
www.newholland.com.au

A record of this book is held at the National Library of Australia

ISBN 9781742572895

Publisher: Lliane Clarke
Editor: Bronwyn Phillips
Designer: Tracy Loughlin
Production Director: Olga Dementiev
Printer: Toppan Leefung Printing Ltd

10 9 8 7 6 5 4 3 2 1

Keep up with New Holland Publishers on Facebook and Twitter http://www.facebook.com/NewHollandPublishers

Heart of Stone

Justice for Azaria

MICHAEL CHAMBERLAIN

To Azaria Chantel Loren Chamberlain.
Born 11 June 1980.
Died 17 August 1980.
Dearly loved and cherished daughter of Lindy and Michael Chamberlain

and to my children Aidan, Reagan, Kahlia and Zahra.

Justice has a grave
In this country's heart of stone.
The soil of prejudice covered it
And tabloids bleached its bone.
Kath Fisher

And I will give them one heart, and shall put a new spirit within them. And I shall take the heart of stone out of their flesh and give them a heart of flesh.
Ezekiel 11:19 ASV

Acknowledgements

I would like to thank the following people who have significantly assisted in my journey to create this book: Ingrid Chamberlain, Professor Ray Watterson, Dr Belinda Middleweek, Dr Norman Young, Dr Ken Crispin, Trish Norris, Martyn Glanville, John Bright, Les Smith, Bert Hingley and John Bryson.

I would also like to pay particular acknowledgements to:

Stuart and Cherie Tipple and my legal teams headed by John Phillips QC (later Chief Justice of Victoria) and John Winneke QC (later President of the Appeals Court of Victoria), who worked tirelessly, courageously and in the spirit of the law.

Liz and Tony Noonan, Guy Boyd and the Chamberlain support groups around Australia and New Zealand, who, whether through evidence or by faith, stood up for a just cause during our terrible ordeal.

Those forensic scientists, who used their fine skills of logic without bias, fear or favour.

Retired legal personnel and parliamentarians noted in this work who demonstrated moral guts.

Those journalists, including Malcolm Brown, John Bryson and Ray Martin, who demonstrated integrity in reporting.

The members of the Seventh-day Adventist Church and other Christian believers who worked or were vigilant for our physical or moral security and who stood up and endured the indignity.

The true blue Australians who may not have had any belief at all but who stood up for a fair go in pubs, clubs and other meeting places.

Contents

Preface

Few Australians over the age of 40 would not have heard of the Azaria Chamberlain case. Thirty-two years ago, on the 17 August, 1980, our nine-week-old daughter, Azaria, disappeared from our tent during a family holiday at Ayers Rock, now named Uluru. It was obvious to us, and our fellow campers, that Azaria had been taken by a dingo. Aboriginal trackers confirmed this, as did the finding of the Coroner Denis Barritt at the inquest. How then did my wife Lindy come to be convicted of murder and to be sentenced to life imprisonment at a trial in Darwin two years later? And why did it take another six years for that verdict to be quashed by a Federal Royal Commission and a Federal Appeals Court?

The answers to these questions illuminate the most celebrated case in Australian legal history. This case has echoed in the halls of jurisprudence, setting new reforms nationally and legal ripples internationally, for many years since it happened. But the terrible saga has continued, despite the fact that Lindy and I were exonerated, declared legally innocent and compensated for false convictions. The prosecutors at the Darwin Supreme Court trial clearly stated that Azaria could only have died from two causes: either Lindy or a dingo killed her. Despite this, a 1995 Northern Territory Coronial inquest into our daughter's death, brought down an 'open' verdict.

Only my former wife, Lindy, Aidan, Reagan and I know what it was like to walk through the confusion and prejudice around Azaria's death. Many interpretations expressed in books and films have endeavoured to portray the real circumstances surrounding our daughter's disappearance. Some publications emerged as true and faithful representations. Others have been defamatory and predatory. There is little difficulty in discerning the differences in the two approaches. The vicious accounts dehumanise and depersonalise the life and memory of my daughter. In my first book, *Beyond Azaria: Black Light White Light,* written in 1999, I said that I would use 'a measure of discretion' in telling my story. *Heart of Stone* draws ever more deeply from memory explicitly anchored by 32 years of documentation. It is not about the moment but the tide of time.

My journey has shaped my thinking dramatically. The loss of Azaria catapulted Lindy and I into territory foreign to our experience. It contributed significantly to a divorce and her writing a book that reflected badly on me. The whole journey, in which the Australian media followed our every move with the scrutiny usually reserved for the royal family or celebrities, was like being dropped from a great height onto a new planet, with completely foreign air, water and food. Our environment was circumscribed by a goldfish bowl-like existence. The 'global village' sat around their television 'camp fires' and examined us almost every evening for dinner. For years we were a household name. It was a case of the Chamberlains versus the state, the Northern Territory of Australia. It slowly emerged, however, that we were pitted against self-serving guardians, intent on cutting corners, some of whom lied to us and failed to disclose significant evidence—all seemingly to protect the thrust for state recognition and the tourist dollar. The goldfish bowl that now held us captive seemed to have been dropped slap in the middle of a surreal, *Blade Runner*-like justice system where the government appeared to see us as a 'negative value statistic', perhaps with the potential to wipe millions from the coffers of a debt-ridden hotel development at Uluru that had to survive, regardless of the cost.

Amidst all this, I was on a steep learning curve to understand the workings of the state, confront the state and conquer the state. This, however, meant pitting myself against an almost absolute power. The truth must be ultimately told, regardless. If the conclusion about a death of a child is falsified, it must be corrected. The question must be asked: is there enough light to expose the dark side of the law when its face is turned away?

In a country that prides itself as a champion of democracy, as a direct representative of the Queen, justice cannot be sullied by dirty tricks. The effective administration of justice is the cornerstone of civilization; the basis for security, satisfaction and well-being in the community and the nation. Justice not done can cause destabilisation, distrust and the depreciation of a community's assets.

Police create problems and waste huge resources and sums of money when they start investigations with presuppositions based on misinformation or rumour. These are often driven by prejudice or are coloured by stereotypes of the persons or groups they are investigating. Typical targets include people belonging to minority, racial or religious groups, or those who happen to be in the wrong place at the wrong time. Political interference by people in high places is another effective means of obstructing or skewing justice. In this book I will not shy away from introducing or discussing these themes.

This book seeks to be more than an autobiographical recount. It is investigative and documented and in paying such attention to detail assists me in closure. John Bryson's 1985 book *Evil Angels* was a benchmark narrative and powerful coda about experts directing aberrant behaviour or authorities persuading others into black-hearted deeds in the name of the law. Bryson's task, as difficult as it was, came from the pen of a legal mind and gifted writer who was on the outside looking in. My task is to communicate the layers of meaning that expose error and enhance truth from the inside, looking out.

I have been variously portrayed by the media, and by my former wife, Lindy, as being too weak, pedantic, precious, lacking guts and lacking leadership. So badly equipped did I appear in my first media presentations that there was no buffer to prevent me from catapulting into notoriety, from the quashing of the second inquest to the finding of the Chamberlain Royal Commission. So ill equipped did I appear to many, that my shadow grew longer as a perceived inept male in contrast to the improved lighting created for Lindy by her book and media portrayal. Azaria now became the exclusive property of Lindy. Kahlia became the physical and emotional property of Lindy. Rick, her new husband, had come from heaven. I was the ex-husband from hell. That's okay, I can live with all that—now.

This book is not a self-conscious effort to change the reader's view of me, regardless of what that may be. I have deliberately written it with minimal help, but those who have helped me are persons of high value and wisdom. Through brief and succinct analysis they encouraged me to become more available in my work, to stand or fall accordingly. My story has the ingredients to surprise, the potential to shock some and it may even change minds. One highly experienced professor of coronial law made the bold prediction: 'Of all the people I've seen in a situation of serious and prolonged injustice, there is no one else I know apart from you that is equipped to take control and overcome this as the central authentic voice and catalyst to the final act of justice for Azaria.'

This book is about getting justice for a family, and coming full circle. It is about a father's quest to have the truth of his daughter's death told. It is about driving the endgame; a seemingly impossible mission, driven by me this time and against all odds, to open the fourth inquest. It is a quest that the truth, backed by the law, will finally be declared: that a dingo killed Azaria.

Time and the One behind the scaffold of truth has been the arbiter of this.

Editor's note: In 1985 the name of Ayers Rock was changed to Uluru and is now referred to as Uluru/Ayers Rock. As Azaria's death occurred when it was called Ayers Rock, that name is used consistently in this book.

The First Wave:
The Trial of the Century

1. *Annus Horribilis*

True, I never thought that in my wildest dreams I would become the victim of circumstances in the way my life was about to unfold. The main event I will describe and the experience following it would rock the nation and polarise the community for 32 years afterwards. The clock is still ticking.

Until August 1980 my life had been plain sailing. I was married to an attractive, petite young woman, and in many ways our match was one of chalk and cheese, and like many couples, we had to work at it. Lindy, my wife, had been brought up in a rigid but caring sectarian Seventh-day Adventist family. In contrast, I had experienced an evangelistic Christian upbringing as a Methodist. We married at the traditional age of the day; Lindy was 21, I was 25. We courted over 18 months but had spent only 19 days together before the knot was tied. Our first child, a son who we named Aidan, arrived four years later. By 1980 we had three beautiful children to our union, all planned for and dearly loved. I enjoyed work immensely and it was taking me around Australia, state by state.

We were now on vacation. Lindy and I arrived at Ayers Rock in the evening of Saturday August 16 with our three young children, Aidan six, Reagan four and Azaria nine weeks and four days. We had just travelled from Mount Isa, some 2000 kilometres east of our holiday destination. The Isa community was a large copper-mining town, 900 kilometres west of Townsville. I was a minister in the Seventh-day Adventist Church and was working hard to attract people to the Church. My tenure was for two years and I was going to make the most of it. I had already served the Church for ten years and was beginning to 'run' with my work. Mount Isa had a population of about 30,000 people, and was full of itinerants and miners, who earned good money underground, but there were also a great many people who were running away from something and here was a place for them to hide.

Some would later criticise our decision to bring a baby as young as nine-week-old Azaria to Ayers Rock/Uluru, but we had some knowledge of the outback, and were confident. An experienced camper, I selected a tent site close to the barbecue area where there was propane gas and toilets close by. We erected a compact four-man sleeping tent which faced a powerful 150-watt barbecue light.

On Sunday morning I was the first of our family to rise. It was just 30 minutes before sunrise and the light was still gloomy. As I peered out of the tent I was taken by surprise by two things. The water in a saucepan, heated the night before, was frozen. The temperature was cold enough to freeze a rat! There was also something quite odd about the barbecue fire grate where Lindy had stuffed one of Azaria's nappies. Some animal had clawed the cotton wool stuffing out of it; I imagined it to be a dingo and it had made a bit of a mess. I placed the nappy in a bin close by. It was my first omen but I thought nothing more about it. It was still early and the sun was almost up, so I rushed up to the top of the sand hill behind the tent with my tatty beloved camera bag, which contained two SLR cameras, an Olympus OM 1 and an OM 2 with motor drive, which I thought were pretty special. (at that time I hadn't used a Leica, a Canon or a Nikon) and decided to get some photos of the rising sun on the Rock. I had been in the habit for years carrying that old black bag given to me by a ministerial colleague. It had been high and low, down the shaft of the Mount Isa copper mine to the jagged peaks around the town. Even if I wasn't a great writer, I knew the power and emotion that a strong photograph could evoke. It would always galvanise the memory.

The sky was a deep purplish blue and the Rock blended beautifully into the half-lit landscape. Author James Simmons described it as an edifice that erupts from the red centre of Australia in 'shades of silver, black, crimson and purple. From the air, it looks like some gigantic mollusc dreamed up in the bizarre imagination of some pulp science fiction writer.' (*Wednesday's Child,* 1982). Uluru, its traditional owners' name, meant 'place of shade' but that was very much dependent which side of the Rock you found yourself on a particular time of the day. Something like 77,000 tourists visited this sacred place each year during 1980. At that time there was a $4.00 per car entry fee into the campsite.

I was satisfied, like the handful of fanatics with me, that I had got the pick of the morning photos. We were all clicked up and comfortable with our prize-winning shots. I used an array of different filters to highlight the colours and different lenses to capture the intensity and spaciousness of the giant monolith. I went back to the tent where the kids were all still slumbering. Azaria was being her usual good self. She hardly cried or fussed. She was still so tiny and delicate, but very strong and able to keep her head up quite well to look about. Lindy was talking to some tourists from Esperance, Western Australia, Mrs Judy West and her farmer husband, although I don't think he was up at the time. Mrs West was impressively serene. Her greying hair, neat facial features, smoothly modulated voice and well-considered words were nothing like the stereotypical ocker Territory outback characters. Her husband was less talkative, indicating a different wisdom. His craggy weather-beaten features belied a man who had worked extremely hard in the outdoors and had acquired his own farming intelligence with it.

The day soon warmed up, but not until 10 o'clock did it start to become comfortable. There was no wind to speak of and we all dressed as if it was a summer's day. We decided to go shopping for food and look for Aboriginal tourist items of the Rock at the one solitary shop. We entered the tourist shop and bought some souvenirs. I remember well the elegant if not rough-hewn golden brown wood lizard with circular burn marks around its body. That was the desert style. The northern coastal Aboriginal artists of Darwin and Yirkala went in for lines. It cost the handsome sum of $30 but was the best of its type there and I cheerfully, if not a little recklessly, abandoned my money without thinking it might be needed later on for more important things.

The packs of mangy dogs and the third world lifestyles of the local Aboriginals shocked me. It was not a romantic view. As I plied my way through the disadvantaged settlement, one old man with a seaman's cap, perched on his head, was the picture of ultimate sadness for me. Stunned by his appearance, I was compelled to take a couple of photos of him and then he asked for money. He called himself 'Captain Number Two'. I gave him two dollars but I should have given him more. What was really shocking was his unkempt appearance, the smell, the deeply wrinkled crows feet around his eyes and the green slimy conjunctivitis in his eyes. I decided these particular frames were too shocking to be seen. My compulsion had led to revulsion and I later destroyed them out of respect for the poor man and the little dignity he had left in his dreadful condition.

We then decided to explore the Rock itself. Lindy, the children and I wandered along the path that largely followed the base. The total trek around the perimeter I considered to be seven or eight kilometres. To run around the road I estimated about nine kilometres. I had planned to do that on Monday, a nice little jog to start the day.

At 36 years of age, I was still fit and healthy, with no known allergies or diseases. My love for middle-distance running had not abated. Rewards had come from a modest number of team trophies in competition 'fun runs' on the North Queensland coast. We had called ourselves 'The Good Life' team after a media outreach program I had dreamt up. Altogether about 15 ran, including Sylvana Pullom, Darry Thompson, Linda and Colin Lees, Lindy and myself and a few other very strong runners who were not attached to the SDA. I remember one local newspaper reporting on us as a vegetarian mob of runners, a bit tongue in cheek with the headline: 'Vegetables won the day'. Running certainly kept one slim; I could eat all I wanted and not put on weight.

Lindy was very health-conscious and had never allowed a morsel of flesh to enter her mouth. Nutmeat, Nutolene and Granola were our staple Sanitarium foods.

Not being brought up in the Adventist Church I hated them, but as a generational member she loved them. To me they tasted like wet straw, but with a bit of seasoning, some onion and salt in a fry pan they were tolerable. Until I became an Adventist at years of 21, and went directly to Avondale College to train as a minister, I preferred a good leg of fresh farm-killed lamb, crackling bacon and eggs. A high-fibre diet of raw and cooked vegetables, legumes and nuts knocked me about at the beginning, as did my adjustment to broccoli, spinach, brussels sprouts and capsicum, and the food ran through me for a while. But it was all good food and my health would never look back, I told myself.

I graduated with a Bachelor of Arts, majoring in theology, and entered into the ministry in 1969. I took pride in the way I stayed on top of things: positive thinking; positive processing. As an outreach into the community, I wrote, produced and presented my own health and lifestyle programs three days a week for the local radio station. The program usually went to air at around 10am, which I liked, as people listened when they were more relaxed at home or work at morning tea, and hopefully more receptive to the ideas. It was generally a two to five-minute segment, and I undertook the program as a way of presenting popular concepts about health for listeners to consider. I also wrote a column for the local newspapers including *The Cairns Post*, the city which was known as the gateway to the Great Barrier Reef. It was a weekly column that was occasionally controversial and attracted letters to the editor. One large corporation got a bit concerned when I attacked the nutritional worth of Coca Cola!

I believed that religious belief and lifestyle should coincide, and that I should practise what I preach. Adventists embraced a healthy lifestyle in every way—not only food and drink, but thoughts and actions too. Adventism was about striving for total health in an enjoyable way. The body is God's temple, so look after it and don't rubbish it. Adventism tried to be exactly that with its worldwide health food manufacturing groups, hospitals and schools. I was committed to acting as a role model in the community so this might attract people into taking seriously the faith I had embraced since age 21, and it was certainly working. People even stopped me in the street to ask questions about a number of Adventist programs that I coordinated, including the Five Day Plan to quit smoking;

the Health Quotient (HQ) which determined a rough score for a person's lifestyle; and vegetarianism. These programs included input from trained nurses and doctors, usually Church members. As the local minister I would invite people to become lifestyle members and join our social network every Sunday morning, when we would engage in some physical pursuit and get to know each other. It was a very informal and enjoyable way of making genuine friends, and as questions were asked I would attempt to provide answers. At that time I was outgoing and confident in my ability to get my views across to both strangers and people I knew.

Sometimes questions would be raised on healthy lifestyles that I couldn't answer which led me to think that further education on these topics would be very useful. Even though I had read widely and had a good working knowledge, I was becoming unnerved, knowing that I was not an authority. Even though it was comforting to know that the Church had already bought some of my radio scripts and had written my work up in their national PR papers, praising my efforts and innovative approach, that was a long way from being completely on top of my subject. Would the Church sponsor me to go to the United States, to Loma Linda University, a celebrated Adventist academic institution, and get a Doctorate of Health Science under my belt, I wondered. It was wishful thinking but the idea was growing. In the meantime, I was gathering more credibility in the community. In July 1980, the South Pacific Church Office in Wahroonga summoned me to audition for a pilot Southern New South Wales radio program where I would be doing my usual thing. I was confident of a bright future for myself and my young family.

I have always been interested and active in sport. Lincoln High School, a substantial country student mecca on the Canturbury Plains in New Zealand, provided most of my pre-university education. My education there was more physical than nerd-like I guess, although I was a senior school prefect. At the age of thirteen I was asked to play rugby union for Irwell, a rich farming community south of the Selwyn River, which had many woolsheds and amazing crops of wheat and barley. The farm boys there seemed to delight in knocking the stuffing out of any opposing rugby union teams on Saturdays. I was not as strong as the big boys however, and as a small boy I had nearly lost my life twice—once to a throat disease and once to tuberculosis. In my weakened state I was constantly under the gaze of the school bullies.

Irwell had been famous for its rugby power in the 1950s. Its senior team of 1958 had boasted two All Blacks forwards, the Heslop brothers, and when they played they would bring in a sizeable crowd to the sheep paddock rugby field to watch. In the same year, playing as a flank forward, my prolific try scoring and attacking play assisted in the team scoring 336 points, the opposition only managing a total of 6 points.

In 1961 I was privileged to play for Lincoln's First Fifteen Rugby Union team, its representative tennis team, the athletics team and its First Eleven cricket team which I captained. I loved my sport! It never occured to me in the rugby union forward pack that I would be taking on kids twice my size. I thought at least if I was light on my feet I could play as a flank forward and knock out the opposition's back line. But my rugby days were numbered. I eventually took a heavy hit to my face from an angry rugby boot when representing County Districts against Christchurch City at Lancaster Park, and suffered concussion and a bloodied nose. It slowed me down for a while.

I left Lincoln High and finished my schooling at Christchurch Boys High School, where both my father and grandfather had been. Its motto was *altiora peto*—I seek higher things. Here I tried to focus on those higher things and my future professional career. From this school oozed New Zealand All Blacks and cricket representatives, not to forget its much-vaunted Canterbury Crusaders Union Tri-Nation champions. Regrettably, the city life didn't suit this country boy and I got sick. Many late nights out socializing also destroyed my focus. I didn't get involved in sport and I didn't do too much study either.

* * * * * * * * * * * * * * * * *

Our walk on our first day to the Rock would be about two kilometres, quite long enough for our children in the early afternoon. Eerily, one of the canine inhabitants of the Rock already seemed to focus on us. Lindy remarked on the curious dingo silently watching the many walkers passing below as it looked down at us from 20 metres above, at a vantage point known as the Fertility Cave. Before I could photograph it, the creature had gone.

At that time tourists were allowed to climb the Rock. The boys and I wanted to see how far up we could climb, so following our exploratory walk we returned to the car to drive around to the climb parking bays. It was stinking hot inside and we nearly melted trying to get some cooler air into its dark interior before driving to the southern base, where the climb started. A few busloads of goggle-eyed people had stopped, a couple of other tourists' cars and perhaps one ranger's vehicle were in the parking bay. I was determined to conquer the 340-metre monolith and sign the register at the summit, keen to get a photo or two of myself as proof to show my grandchildren someday.

At the climb area I sprang out of our car, a brilliant-yellow Holden Torana V8 hatchback, hastily pulled out my black camera bag from the base of the front of my seat, and to give the day full meaning, prepared to run up this ancient 'abdomen' of stone. I had not realised that the climb, estimated to be nearly 1500 metres long, would be so daunting as I started to run up the smooth and well-worn path. I think it took about 15 minutes, stopping a few times to catch my breath. Carrying seven kilos of camera stuff also reminded me of my age! But I loved running and was determined to finish. A few others were on the trail but none seemed silly enough to run up in the heat of the day. It was an absolute blast to be at the top, though. I think two youthful weary climbers were present at the time. I asked one of them to give me the proof that I had done it and they obliged with a picture of me trying to look relaxed and surveying the Olgas, a conglomerate of scenic rocks perhaps 30 kilometres to the south of Ayers Rock.

Then, as quickly as I arrived, I darted back down to see how far the boys wanted to come up. The lactic acid in my leg muscles had already set in and when I got down almost to the base, my toes in the Puma rubber spiked runners felt like they were on fire. This had now become a real test of altruism and fatherly patience, as well as strength. I complained to

Lindy that my toenails were too long for my running shoes so she selected a pair of nail clippers she always carried in the car. I didn't like the things because my big toenail was rather robust and tough critters to cut. But the other small nail scissors were pathetically weak and couldn't cut much more than paper and the children's thin nails so I had to put up with the mild pain of the blunt scissors she carried.

I was worried to see Aidan and Reagan were already adventuring on the Rock, following in Dad's footsteps, as it was dangerous up there and I was concerned they might fall. Aidan was perhaps 100 metres up. Lindy, with Azaria firmly bound in her arms, had also climbed up about 50 metres and it was here I photographed our little girl a few times in the bright sunlight later in the afternoon; first Lindy and then me holding her. They were proud moments for us both, milestone photos that indicated our spirit of adventure and desire to explore Australia. It was quite deliberate that I wore a white cotton T-shirt with a stylized blue and red Union Jack imprinted on it and the Frank Byrne Innisfail travel logo. I was a patriotic citizen of the British Commonwealth, proud to be born a Kiwi, but enjoying the Australian lifestyle and the adventures it offered, and sharing that with my young family.

We were now all very tired and returned to our tent and to get some rest. It was around 4.30pm and the next exciting event was the sunset at 'Sunset Strip' where the best angle of the Rock could be viewed using a standard lens. Everyone from the camp and tourist buses would attend this ritual photographic event, which might last half an hour. We changed into warmer clothing as the chill winter air was beginning to bite.

On return to the Rock I took my fair share of 35mm frames, perhaps over 100 photos. We almost had to jostle for a position, as the area for the best vantage point was surprisingly quite small. Then we drove back to the camp to eat and have an early night. We decided on baked beans, mushrooms and toast. At the barbecue we met an interesting couple, Greg and Sally Lowe from Hobart, Tasmania. Greg was a joker, always quipping and laughing, with an occasional beer in his hand. I challenged him to guess my occupation, and he seemed fascinated to meet a minister of religion. Few people guessed my calling as it seemed I didn't fit the typical minister mould—until I opened my mouth when they would usually find I was quite passionate about my Christian beliefs.

There was an atmosphere of conviviality and goodwill around the barbecue. They were carefree moments, marred only by a strange occurrence. A mangy-looking dingo came within several metres of me and, feeling sorry for its sad state, I threw it a crust of bread. What came next from this silent night prowler caused a little shock. Ignoring my pathetic offering, the dingo suddenly pounced on a field mouse in the brush beside me. It did so in absolute silence. The stealth of the animal caused me to exclaim, 'Did you see that?' I had grown up with dogs all my life but they were domesticated or sheep-trained. I had a rapport with all of them, and they would linger around me for affection or scraps, but not this dog. The incident happened so quickly that I doubted anyone else witnessed it. It was my second omen and I had missed it, leaving me totally unprepared for what was about to happen.

2. A Cry in the Dark

On Sunday evening, 17 August, at about 7.45pm, Lindy put Reagan, Aidan and Azaria to bed in the green and gold tent which was just 20 metres away, and partially lit by the barbecue floodlight. Azaria was fast asleep in her mother's arms. We had just had one of the most enthralling days in the bush of our lives. All was well. I continued my evening meal and was beginning to clean up. It was about 8pm and now getting quite icy again. Lindy returned to the barbecue area, which afforded a little warmth for her.

There was a brief lull in the conversation when, coming from the direction of the tent, I heard a faint cry almost cut short in the middle of a breath. The sound unnerved me somewhat, and I asked Lindy if she'd heard anything. She hesitated for a second and said she'd heard nothing. I thought that Lindy ought to check the tent and told her to do so. Sally Lowe also heard the cry and was about to say something, but saw that Lindy had decided to check on the children anyway.

It was then that all hell broke loose.

Approaching the tent Lindy saw a dingo move through the open tent flap and leave, its head down and obscured by the shadows. It gave an impression that it had a load in its mouth, but nothing sinister had registered for her. She raced inside.

Reagan had his sleeping bag hood up and his face buried in a pillow.

'He never sleeps like that, not ever', Lindy thought, concern growing for her son.

Instinctively, she placed one hand on Reagan to feel for his heartbeat and check that he was alive. With her other hand she lifted the blankets that should have been covering Azaria, which were uncharacteristically scattered. Then she screamed. Springing out of the tent and running towards me, she yelled those now immortal words:

'THAT DINGO'S GOT MY BABY!'

'WHAT?' I yelled back in disbelief.

* * * * * * * * * * * * * * *

On 11 June, 1980 Lindy gave birth to our daughter Azaria in the Mount Isa Public Hospital. I arrived at the maternity room just slightly ahead of Dr Irene Milne, the attending doctor. We had consciously tried all the latest theories, according to Lindy, to have a girl, and I was excited about this birth, although I was a little sceptical as boys, in the Chamberlain family history, were well in the majority. When first told the baby was a girl, I could not believe it until I saw the proof. She was tiny, with very fine features and eyes a deep and alert brown. For Lindy and I, it was just what we had desired and prayed for. We named her Azaria; Azaria Chantelle Loren Chamberlain.

At around 3 kilograms, Azaria was a little smaller than the average birth weight, but many people remarked on her strength for her age. On hearing her name for the first time, my mother Greta was perplexed. 'Oh, is that a girl's name?' she asked, 'How unusual.'

Mum was right; it was unusual but we loved it. 'Azaria' was Hebrew in origin, being the feminine of Azariah in the Old Testament. For us, the best thing about our new daughter's name was the meaning, 'Blessed of God.'

It took a while for it to sink in that I had a daughter now, it was such an unexpected and beautiful feeling. In my very rushed existence in mount Isa, the frenetic life I was living through growing hte Mount Isa Church, pioneering new ways to reach out, I was still getting used to the change of life that Azaria had brought us, slowing down and smelling the roses with new my daughter. Lindy, like me, was extremely proud of our new prized possession. Everything she did for Azaria was precise and detailed and all Azaria's clothes and baby items were colour coded or colour matching. Lindy was fussy and adoring with her, and then I would get my turn to hold and hug her.

Some weeks later, Lindy and I decided we needed a break and a good rest. We thought that a fortnight in August would be the best time, and to go before the monsoon season began in the Northern Territory. The further north you travelled, the more acute the monsoon became. The question was, where should we go? I wanted to go to Darwin. There I could go on a grand mission to catch the celebrated barramundi, the best eating and fighting fish in Australia. A five-kilo fish would be just perfect, I dreamed.

Lindy, however, had other plans. As a 16-year-old, she had visited Ayers Rock, and even had a photo of herself there, with a live, cool brown python around her neck. I remember the picture well. In it she looked fearless and cocky. She reminded me of a young Aboriginal girl who had just shown she could catch dinner singlehandedly. This confidence was part of the initial attraction I felt for Lindy. Competitive and fun loving, she was also a woman who hated to lose.

Before leaving Mount Isa, I baptized my eighth new member for the year into the tiny Mount Isa Church. Six adults and two youngsters by immersion, just the way Jesus had it done in the river Jordan. They had now become our newest Church members. Gratified by the power of God's working in their hearts, I gave thanks regularly for the privilege of being a minister. Azaria, also, had been baptised by a Church representative from Townsville, Pastor Merv Kennaway. This event had crowned a magnificent celebration for the Church and also for us as a family.

Our lives felt so good. The only exception was that I was so tired! I wondered how I could drive the 2000 kilometres to the great heart of stone in the middle of Australia, Ayers Rock. With five on board I often wished I could buy a larger car but on a single income and as a minister of religion, money was scarce. I looked at our bare minimum camping accommodation, which consisted of two four-man tents and wished I could have afforded the magnificent six-man tent with a luxury heavy-duty four separate compartments, one for each of us, so that we could have stayed for a week comfortably. I was $30 short.

It was dry, warm and sunny the day we left Mount Isa and a hot copper blue sky beckoned us to seek early rest. As the afternoon wore on we entered the Devil's Marbles area on the Alice Springs to Darwin Highway. A golden sunset was approaching and, after being cooped up in the car, I remember the boys being exhilarated by their newfound freedom, to run around with abandon between the large and awesome rocks pointing starkly into the evening sky. A truly wondrous quirk of God's geology, this incredible conglomerate was a bizarre and chaotic collection of massive red granite boulders, looming and eerie. Standing among weeping spinifex and the ghostly sinuous boughs of stunted gums on this evening I felt as though I was on an alien planet, empty and waterless. But the Aborigines had survived here for thousands of years and the traditional owners of the land know differently. There is 'Plenty of life out here,' said one Aboriginal woman. 'You just gotta know where to look.'

In the winter the setting sun had lost its fierce heat, and provided cosy warmth on our backs enough to sleep on mattresses outside the car for the evening. There were no mosquitoes, no nasty flying bugs. It seemed the perfect thing to do. We were quite confident that nothing could harm us and deliberately bedded down where no passersby could see us unless they came looking. After a meal we all prepared for bed. After a minor squabble between the boys over a toy, we all went soundly to sleep at 6.30pm, even Lindy and I. I took the precaution of placing my powerful spotlight 'Big Jim' next to my pillow.

Around 11.30pm, something woke me. To this day I don't know what it was but I instinctively reached for my spotlight and flicked the switch. There, about 100 metres out into the dessert, I saw what seemed to be a dozen pairs of green glowing eyes, but it was hard to estimate. I thought for a moment they belonged to goats but the colour was wrong. It dawned on me that I might be looking at something I had never seen in the wild at night before, the eyes of dingoes. Feeling uneasy, I transferred Azaria and the boys to the car while Lindy and I remained outside. We slowly drifted back to sleep until daylight, and the chill air, awakened us. We needed warm clothes to keep from freezing, and once in the car with the heater on, we soon cheered up. We left at about 8am, and I soon realised why we had this 'campsite' all to ourselves. We hadn't noticed the 'No Camping' sign.

Our second day took us from the Marbles to an all too public campsite just below Alice Springs. It was an uneventful trip, the weather was fine as usual, not a cloud in the sky, and the boys, uncomfortable and irritable, fought some of the way. They were a bit too cramped for comfort. Azaria, on the other hand, seemed oblivious, drowsing between sucks of her mother's breast milk. We arrived at the campsite just before sundown Friday night. Our Christian Sabbath was about to commence from sundown Friday evening to Saturday evening. We felt a bit uncomfortable with the racket at the campground, which seemed like we had struck some rodeo or circus event. Somehow, we slept through the noise, only to find it even worse the next morning. Instead of staying, as would have been our custom on the Sabbath day, to rest from one's labours and become rejuvenated, we found no rest here. We packed up, got into our car and drove slowly down the bitumen highway towards Ayers Rock, some 700 kilometres away.

By midday we had reached another milestone. We were now on the hot dusty rutted road that would take us to Ayers Rock. The track was pretty straight but it was becoming the road from hell for cars like mine, with 13-inch tyres. My V8 Torana must have had every nut and bolt tested and every dust seal unsealed with these horrendous corrugations which stretched for hundreds of kilometres. Dozens of red-grey patches of bull dust lay hidden in the middle of the road, showering the unsuspecting driver with the worst form of talcum powder-like material imaginable. I first tried jumping the ridges at 120 km per hour, but that was beginning to feel like our bodies were parting company from the bones and sinews that fastened them. I then decided to travel at 40 km per hour and the rocking motion was putting us to sleep. Such was my desperation, I thought of going off road. In the end I reverted to speeding across the tops of the corrugations.

At various stages we were compelled to stop for toilet breaks as the Rock came closer and the urge to photograph it, stronger. The midday light did little for its beauty but as the afternoon sun descended behind us, the Rock began to change its hue and to light up, glowing against the azure-blue backdrop. As it happened, we only just arrived to see the magnificence of a setting sun on the Rock, a mystical and awesome experience that you don't ever forget.

The boys were sick of watching anything. All they wanted to do was run around crazily, burning off their pent-up energy. We signed in at the ranger's hut just minutes into the sunset. We paid our $16 for four nights, got our directions to pitch camp and drove over to the northern edge of the camp. The ranger didn't discuss dingos or recent dingo attacks with us, even though we had three children with us.

Once at the campsite, we saw not one warning about the fact that there had been recent dingo attacks on people. There was no notices or warning signs that a child had been attacked the night before we set up camp and in virtually the same place. There was no warning that this was the season for puppies and that dingoes were particular hungry at this time, or that not only were dingoes predatory they were also territorial. There were no warnings that as people had been asked to stop feeding these predatory animals, they would be increasingly hungry. There were no warnings that dingoes were entering tents and also buses looking for food. There was one sign which asked campers 'Please don't feed the dingoes'. That was it.

We pitched the tent. We were all exhausted and predictably a bit grumpy. We ate and dressed for the night, jumped into our warm sleeping bags in our winter pyjamas and were asleep very quickly. The tent was just large enough for the five of us. As I drifted off, I wondered what we would do if it rained, but rain at the Rock was not a common event. When it happened, it sent photographers scurrying to capture the waterfalls and other delightful views.

* * * * * * * * * * * * * * * *

My feet felt like lead as I cleared the low fence and dived into the tent headlong.

'Azaria, oh Azaria, what has happened to you? What is happening to you? Your bed is still warm and you're out there, somewhere! Oh God, Oh God, help me,' I cried in my heart.

Lindy turned and dived into the tent again, still in disbelief, then rushed out in the direction in which she had seen the dingo go. Chaos and pandemonium ruled. To chase that dingo, to get help. Lindy ran to the right where the dingo had probably headed, but there was nothing. Nothing! I rushed out into the scrub. I ran into a bush at full speed and into the sharp razor-like spinifex grass. I think Greg Lowe was behind me, perhaps others. It was all a blur. But the stabbing pain I felt was lost in the overwhelming task to find Azaria.

With no light and no torch, things were as black as pitch. Where is that dingo? Where is Azaria? I ran back to the car to get my torch. I found it, hidden under the children's clothes. I flicked the Big Jim switch. Nothing. The battery was dead.

I cursed under my breath. My main line of attack was dashed. No light in the bush means no hope, I thought. Suddenly someone was with me and put a torch in my hand. It was weak but it was a light. I ran again. Everywhere I went I told startled campers that my daughter had been taken by a dingo. They just sat there. But some moved and started to look. Where did the animal go, some asked. 'I have no idea, but probably over there,' I yelled, pointing to the direction where there was only a dark void. Stark panic, helplessness and horror crushed me as I prayed for a miracle, a miracle that wasn't happening. I thought of turning my car around and shining the high-powered spotlights into the bush. No good. I couldn't find my keys.

My little girl, who charmed all who looked upon her petal face, was now alone in the harsh desert night. She had shone as briefly as a Sturt Sweet Pea flower. Suddenly, it seemed that as quickly as Azaria had come, she was gone.

For two or more terrible hours we searched frantically. I saw a wave of torchlights moving like a chain of jiggling glowworms in the distance.

Later I was told that up to 300 people were out there. Aboriginal trackers were with them and had seen a clothing imprint of Azaria's tiny body having been put down in the sand and raised again. They traced dingo paw prints to an Ayers Rock ranger's house. After that they had been lost. One of the rangers, Ian Cawood, had a pet dingo called Ding, but, he claimed later he had shot it six weeks before the event and had placed it in a plastic bag on the rubbish tip.

On several occasions I returned to the tent to where some women were keeping vigil with Lindy. She was sobbing. The two boys had gone back to sleep in the tent, oblivious or too much in shock to comprehend the terror of the event which was unfolding. As I moved between the tent and the search area, I tried to offer a prayer of courage and hope but I was just mouthing words. The shock had emptied me. I was numb.

Unbeknown to me, before our arrival, the Head Ranger, Derek Roff, a former policeman in Rhodesia (now Zimbabwe) had been agonising over the possibility of a catastrophe like this happening. Roff had requested from the Northern Territory Conservation Commission .22 Hornet bullets to eradicate the troublesome dingoes, which had been attacking tourists for three months before Azaria's disappearance. A reasonable request, it had, however, been denied by the Commission, which was overseen by the Northern Territory legal system and the Chief Minister, Paul Everingham.

At around 10 o'clock, I had all but given up hope of finding Azaria alive. Despite my faith in God, and prayers for a miracle, I knew that even if she had survived a dingo attack, she would have been fatally injured and now exposed to the freezing night temperatures. We were told either by the police or the chief ranger to stay close to our tent and car and wait for any information about finding her. Earlier in the evening the police, Constable Frank Morris or Constable Noble, I'm not sure, had come to the tent and looked for any clues to her disappearance. They were very grave-faced on the matter. Later I prayed with a group of campers about Azaria's loss and for the strength to overcome the horrendous event, knowing that Azaria would be there on the Day of the Resurrection when Christians would arise from the dead and see Christ's return and triumph over evil. It was a prayer of last resort.

My faith in God and Jesus Christ had taken a huge hit. Yes, I was a minister of religion and more than anytime before had now to practise the peace and grace of God that I preached. But I was no zealot. A one-time Methodist youth mentor, I had a healthy respect for observing moderation in all things, although I was an avid researcher into the total health of our body and spirit. I had to keep reminding myself of the bigger picture above because the mental pain and pandemonium here was not doing any good. Whatever the outcome, the bottom line was my daughter's resurrection which she would await for the Second Coming of Jesus. My shock and grief had to be submerged in that hope. There was no other way of compensating. This was the only source of peace I knew and from it I summoned my courage.

Sometime after, nurse Bobby Elston, having comforted us both, took us to the Uluru motel and we were led to our room for the night, courtesy of the management. By now Lindy was feeling under pressure from the milk swelling her breasts and needed an expressing pump to alleviate the problem. I remember her crying as she left the campsite over not being able to feed Azaria. It was a truly unbelievable moment for both of us. We were both aware that by now, if she was alive, she would be freezing, and hungry. The night was very long and we slept fitfully with our boys waking up every hour, hoping, wondering if there was any news and if, perchance of a miracle, Azaria might be found alive, God knows where. But an overwhelming hopelessness pervaded our spirits.

We began to read the boys a children's story written by a Pentecostal minister, Ken Chant. We had no idea where the story would lead us. It started out about a baby kangaroo, which had been separated from its mother and had become distressed and oblivious to some ominous signs. Reading several pages on, we hit the brick wall. In the story a creature emerged that had been stalking the little Joey. It wasn't a crocodile or a wedge tail eagle. The creature that was eyeing it for food was a dingo. I looked at Lindy and then at the children and we burst into tears. I apologised to them, angry and confused. This bizarre experience had just rubbed toxic salt into our raw wounds.

We lay there shivering and silent. We were so stunned and our feelings were beyond words. We just lay there, half dazed, half weeping, holding onto each other. And as we waited and waited, the seconds ticked by. Would the dawn bring a policeman, or someone—just to please tell us something, anything? But no one came.

At about 6.30am Constable Morris knocked on our motel door.

'I'm sorry Mr and Mrs Chamberlain, there is no news about your daughter,' he said. The answer defied imagination. Emotionally, we were broken. The desert was so vast and nebulous, and foreboding. What if she were found now? What state would she be in? I could not bear to think about it. It would take more than believing in a miracle now to bring her back to us. It would be believing in the impossible.

The day wore on. Time seemed to have stopped. We ate little. We went nowhere except to our tent. Lindy gathered some sand. I watched, knowing that she needed something symbolic to cling to when we would eventually leave the next day. I remember ringing our parents about the dreadful news. Around mid-afternoon the press arrived at the motel from Adelaide and talked to us. Outwardly I must have exuded an eerie calm but beneath the surface was an unspeakable sadness and growing depression, as the loss was sinking in. For the boys and as the head of my family, I felt I had to project an outward demeanour of control and authority, while everything else was falling apart. I was the person to whom people normally turned in times of crisis, and now it was happening to me. I had to practise what I advised others: to be calm, to have faith and believe in God's merciful goodness, even in the darkest hours.

I remember well Geoff de Luca at this time, the Murdoch press' *Adelaide News* photographer and journalist. Mr de Luca unnerved me. He seemed not to believe our story and could not understand our demeanour. Apparently we were too serene and too assured for him and this would go against us in the future. I watched him trying to work out his spin and wondered why he was so cynical. He was a hard-bitten journalist, I concluded, but why had such a person been sent here to harangue us? It felt very strange.

We looked out from our motel to the Rock, friendless and frightening. We had no news, no updates, no information about our daughter. We felt we had no part in the search effort and saw no people out searching. We then met some key searchers, three Aboriginal women, a small child and an Elder, along with a man named Derek Roff. They told us that the searching was continuing but we were cordoned off from it, it seemed. We stayed in the motel with the two boys.

The following morning I saw the police again. Lindy and I were presented with a message of finality on our daughter. We were asked to sign a form for a coronial inquiry into her death. We slowly packed our tent and belongings. I took several photos of the police, Mr Roff and the Aboriginal trackers. I was deeply grateful for all their efforts and wanted never to forget them. I also took some photos of our boys at the campsite and Lindy, just before leaving. That was really tough, so painful in fact that to squeeze the trigger for these frames was like pressing thorns into our flesh. We had arrived with three children, our family intact; we were leaving one behind and our family was fractured. For me these were warning shots about going to Ayers Rock: 'Watch out, your child might be next.'

We were told by a senior policeman, Inspector Michael Shamus Gilroy, after a fairly casual 'record of interview' with him and a Sergeant John Lincoln, that there was nothing else we could do by staying around. It was suggested that we go home. Both officers were pleasant to us and I noted that Lincoln was deep in thought. He obviously felt more should be done at the Rock while we were there but I could not work out what. Before I left I spoke to the local (Alice Springs) Pastor Bert Cozens. I asked him to collect the tent and dispose of it, probably burn it because I did not wish to see it again. For me it felt like it was a morgue. On the following day, Bert Cozens discovered that the police had already taken the tent for a coroner's inquest. He photographed the campsite because as he said, 'I wanted to be able to illustrate to anyone I might be talking to about it, how hopeless it would be to find anything in that area in daylight, let alone in the dark!'

Inside I experienced an emotional numbness as if anaesthetised and alienated from all reality. Having lost our precious daughter in such horrible circumstances I had to somehow turn the wheel of my car towards Mount Isa.

The journey seemed purposeless. We were moving away from where we last saw Azaria. On leaving, we were encouraged to ring for any new information everywhere we stayed at on the way back.

At Tennant Creek we called in to stay with a Church member and local ambulance identity, Steve Piez, and his wife to see if there was any news of Azaria being found; a moment we dreaded. But it would turn out more distressing than this. There was no news: not a word, not a sound. No way could there be any hope now. Our daughter's life had been lent to us for such a short time—now snatched from us so quickly and cruelly. No time even for a goodbye.

The road home from Tennant Creek to Mount Isa was again a blur. At 'the Isa' there were flowers and food on the doorstep from Church members and we were enveloped in an overwhelming warmth. People were in shock. But I was unprepared for the sinister accusations of this copper-dusted outback town. The police were eerily quiet. Was a malign spirit at work here? I dismissed the thought as a nonsense.

3. The Fifth Column

The mood in Mount Isa over our daughter's death seemed to change from absolute sympathy, to perplexity, and then to suspicion. We entered the town to a barrage of national media headlines on Tuesday 19 and Wednesday 20 August:

Daily Telegraph, 'Anguished Mum Tells: 'I saw my baby stolen by a dingo'.'

Alice Springs Star, 'Ayers Rock Tragedy Baby Girl Taken by Wild Dingo.'

Townsville Daily Bulletin, 'Snatched from Basket in Tent: Baby Girl Taken by Wild Dog.'

The Melbourne Herald, 'Baby Snatched: Hunt for Dingo. Mother gave chase.' 'Guns out after Dingoes: 'The wild dog grabbed our baby' Father.'

North West (Mount Isa) Star, 'Dingo Stalks Mount Isa Baby.'

The Age (Melbourne), 'Marker Where Dingo Seen With Baby.'

Northern Territory News, 'Tragic Search Goes On For Azaria.'

Daily Mirror, (Sydney and Melbourne) 'Mother sees Dingo take Baby: Dogs Shot in Baby Hunt.'

The Sun, (Sydney and Newcastle) 'Tragic Tourist Couple: Baby Girl Snatched by Dingo.' 'Camp Raid, 200 in Hunt.'

(Brisbane) Telegraph, 'Dingo Tracks Found.'

This front page showed the photo I had taken of my children beside the empty tent on Monday.

Our first and most solemn task was to hold a memorial service for

Azaria. We invited our Townsville colleague, Pastor Merv Kennaway, to perform the ceremony as he had dedicated Azaria some six weeks before. But it failed to bring any closure. While it did not take much convincing for us, or the Aboriginal trackers, nor the tourist witnesses at Ayers Rock, that Azaria was killed by a dingo, we were still in limbo because of the Northern Territory police silence. The modern Mount Isa Church was packed but no media were present, nor were they invited. It was of some comfort that we were able to grieve in an atmosphere away from prying eyes.

But it was also apparent that the media's interest had not abated, despite their finding the distance from Sydney to Mount Isa, a little overwhelming. Already a fifth column was preparing its dissent to undercut our testimony. Vincent Serventy, describing himself as a naturalist author and editor of *Wildlife Australia* magazine, in *The Courier-Mail* (20/8/1980), suggested that 'everyone considers it most unlike a dingo in the wild to attack a small defenceless baby. His message was that dingoes would only 'sniff around scraps at tourist camps' and they only ever tugged at his sleeping bag while at Ayers Rock two years before. Lucky man. It was my first moment of rage.

The finding of Azaria's clothing a week later, outside a dingo lair, also brought little comfort to us. Lindy immediately noticed that the little matinee jacket Azaria had been wearing was missing from the clothing found. Tourist Wallace (Wally) Goodwin, a manager of a tyre company from Melbourne, stumbled upon the clothes a week after Azaria's disappearance. He summoned Constable Morris, who failed to photograph them in their original state. Instead, he picked the clothes up to examine them. Later he took photos, but of his own reconstruction of how the clothes had been positioned. It was an act that horrified Goodwin and caused him to disagree with Constable Morris on how the clothes looked when he found them. It appeared that Inspector Gilroy was out to dispute that a dingo had killed Azaria when he told the media that this find did not necessarily implicate a dingo. Even though Ayers Rock Ranger, Ian Cawood, stated that active dingo lairs were close to where Azaria's clothes were found, Morris and Gilroy provided confusing and inaccurate information.

The initial media magazine event was a *Woman's Day* feature. One of my 17 August photos of Azaria with Lindy on Ayers Rock appeared on the front cover of the September 1980 edition. The story evoked sad and painful memories. The storyline about Azaria and the tragic loss was sympathetic as one would expect, but contained some licence and terminology that Lindy never had used: this irked her. She was annoyed by the journalist's reference to her calling Azaria, 'Poppet'. I had never heard Lindy call her by that name nor anyone else.

Then came a front-page headline in the Sydney tabloid press that rang alarm bells. Lindy had spoken at some length to a journalist who had clearly upset her and had set her up for a sensational headline. In being asked if she might have in some way been complicit in Azaria's death, she exclaimed, 'I did not kill my baby!' Deaf Freddy would have heard that trap question coming a mile off. The headline, 'I DID NOT KILL MY BABY: Lindy' reverberated all around Australia and the doubt was sown in the public's mind. The question was now, 'Did she?' We both descended into deep anger and depression, with pounding headaches and stomach cramps brought on by the stress.

I found blood spots on our sleeping bags when we got home, and I rang the police with this information. Here was further confirmation that Azaria was not coming back. Oddly they showed little interest in this new evidence of dingo attack and gave us clearance for our bags to be cleaned at a Mount Isa dry cleaner. But when I arrived several days later to collect the sleeping bags I was rudely awakened by a police change of heart. The dry cleaners informed me that the Mount Isa police, under instruction from the Northern Territory police, had 'seized' them before they had been dry cleaned. I began to suspect that we had become the focus of their gaze.

The media started to publish false rumours. It began with the misinterpretation of Azaria's name. One Mount Isa resident said on outback radio (Citizen's Band) that her name did not mean 'Blessed of God' but 'sacrifice in the wilderness'. This was completely false, and was in fact the meaning given to 'Azazel', which appeared in a baby book of names three lines down from 'Azaria'.

The official report written by Inspector Michael Gilroy in Alice Springs (Police Report, Inspector Michael Gilroy, Alice Springs Police Station, 30 August 1980) records this along with his strange collection of points:

'Azaria Chamberlain was born at 1.16pm on Wednesday the 11th of June at Mt. Isa Hospital, at a weight of 2880 grams (6 pounds 5½ ounces). The mother was reported to have repeatedly complained about the child being sick, stated that she was suffering from pyloric stenosis, an ailment which closes the sphinctum (sic) and causes vomiting. She would not heed hospital staff when they told her the baby was completely normal.

She allegedly told the staff that her other children suffered from the same complaint and that she had cured it herself when she had fallen down a hole carrying them as babies.

It is reported that she appeared not to have cared for the baby and at one stage did not feed it for over eight hours. Registration of the baby was never completed.

When bringing the baby in for a check-up she astounded the Sisters by having the baby dressed in black. A doctor who treated the baby said that she did not react like a normal mother.

The same doctor said that he looked up the name Azaria in a Dictionary of Names and Meanings and found that it means 'sacrifice in the wilderness.'

On visiting the library on Saturday morning, I found that this book is in stock but it has been mislaid. It is believed it should be available on Monday.

The parents appeared on the TV show 'This Day Tonight' on Channel Seven, on Friday evening 29 August 1980. Mrs Chamblerlain (sic) allegedly made the comment that the blanket which covered Azaria was a strong one and difficlt to cut with a knife. (The blanket which we took possession of at Ayers Rock had numerous small cuts in it which, even to the layman, looked more like cuts from a sharp instrument than punctures one would expect from a dog's teeth.)

To date we have actually not one witness who can say they saw the baby at Ayers Rock, but people who have assumed she was holding a baby when they have seen her holding a white bundle to her breast.

The impression given in her statement to me was that the two boys climbed the Rock with their father and she was left at the bottom with the baby in the car. Later on in her statement, she states when she was at the Fertility Caves with the baby (when the dingo 'cased' it). The two boys were with her but the husband was not. They would appear to have descended by themsevles. Where the clothes were found was not more than four hundred metres from there. Constable Morris was instructed to check out the floor of the caves for patches of soft earth etcetera. Many tourists have been visited them since, and he has, no doubt, contacted them. He is also reinterviewing the ranger who saw Mrs Chamberlain at the bottom of the climb that Sunday afternoon, who saw her holding the apparel of the baby.'

On 4 September, 1980 the Brisbane *Courier-Mail* published various rumours about events surrounding Azaria. It had turned on Lindy and was calling Azaria, insultingly, 'the dingo baby'. I could never forgive the feral reporters who represented the dark side of the press in the use of this dehumanising tag. The local Mount Isa press also broadcast the rumours which we felt were a veiled attempt to drive us out of town. It seemed like the honking of horns was getting louder on our corner, but then again it had always been a noisy area.

Lindy's quirky dress sense for Azaria, even if it was exquisite, now created a backlash. Lindy had a dress design diploma gained over three years from the Launceston Technical College and had created some fine quality and innovative designed clothing. Her design of a black dress, laced in dramatic red ribbon and boots, originally designed for Reagan, and worn by Azaria, created more grist for the rumour mill. It was not exactly my choice, but Lindy loved it. Our family was a bit arty and Lindy liked to make a fashion statement. The dress, however, added more fuel to the rumours swirling about us, fanned by the media. 'Oh yes,' people said 'Seventh-day Adventists are a cult and they believe in sacrifice in the wilderness. They read bizarre passages from the Old Testament, keep coffins in their garage and dress their kids in black dresses with red ribbons.'

On 24 August, 1980 the Brisbane *Sunday Mail* gave columnist Sylvia

Da Costa Roque opportunity to vent how she was hoping that we, the parents, would have cried all this week: 'I want to know that they were filled with anguish that they screamed in torment because such a dreadful thing happened'. Sylvia sharpened her sword of condemnation upon us. 'How marvellous to have such a faith in God' she pontificated in her all-knowing role of *Sunday Mail* columnist. To the *Sunday Mail*'s credit, Ms Da Costa did not entirely triumph. The following week's Sunday column prevailed with overwhelming letters of support for us by a ratio of 11:1. But the troubled waters for us were deepening.

It was beginning to get harder for us to grieve. The media and police actually seemed to be always somehow getting it wrong.

Next came the visit by Detective Sergeant Graeme Charlwood to invite us and our two boys to be interviewed at the Mount Isa Police station on 1 October, 1980. I was a bit perplexed about the need for further 'Records of Interview', but we were happy enough to do it. I saw it as a release to be able to talk and learn anything new if possible, but I was wrong. We were involved in the formal interview, which lasted the whole afternoon. The boys were also interviewed which was in one way therapeutic because it might have helped to relieve the sadness and loss in their hearts.

Aidan gave the following account. 'Me and Reagan were watching Daddy cooking tea and Mummy was holding bubby in her arms. I think Reagan had some tea and he went to bed in the tent. I think Mummy took him to bed. After I finished my tea I said that I wanted to go to bed and Mummy said she would take me and bubby up to bed. I went up to the tent with Mummy and bubby and I said: 'Is that all the tea I get?' Mummy said that I could have some more tea. While we were in the tent Mummy put bubby down in the cot and then I went to the car with Mummy and she got some baked beans and then I followed her down to the barbecue area. When we got to the barbecue area Mummy opened the tin of baked beans and Daddy said that bubby was crying and Mummy said 'I don't think so'. Mummy went back to the tent and said 'the dingo has got my baby.'

After Lindy's interview, having sat in the police anteroom for several hours, I was called in. Lindy was a very detailed person when it came to her descriptions of things and it seemed the police had been delayed by her ability to describe things at length. I was ushered in to a very plain-looking interview room at around 6pm.

At the desk were Sergeant Doolan and Detective Sergeant Charlwood.

One of Charlwood's first questions was, 'Before we start, did you bring your car?'

'Yes,' I said affably. 'I parked it just outside.'

'Do you mind if I get someone here to take a look at it?'

'Not at all,' I replied searching for my keys in my pocket. 'All the camping gear is out. There isn't much to see.'

'It shouldn't take long then,' Charlwood replied with a slight smile.

Detective Charlwood commenced the interview slowly with some protocols as if I were involved in something very serious, which of course I was, but not in the way he seemed to be treating the inquiry.

Charlwood was a lean and hungry-looking man with a personality that seemed to match it. His eyes were those of someone who did not trust anyone but himself. He gave me no indication that he either liked us or believed our story.

Sergeant Barry Graham, meanwhile, commenced a three-hour inspection on my Torana's interior. I had no idea what they wanted it for, but later I learned they were looking for evidence of blood. The intense search turned up nothing.

The interview lasted for an hour and a half. All the normal questions, nothing that was outstanding to my mind, but I had become unusually tired by 7.30pm. As much as I wanted to answer to the best of my memory, the emotional strain was telling. We had a five-minute break but Charlwood chose not to record any of this.

Charlwood then asked me: 'Did you know that Azaria's clothes were found folded?'

It was a question that took me by complete surprise.

'No,' I said cautiously.

'And wedged between rocks?'

I thought carefully. This did not sound either right or good.

He watched me intently.

'There were no dingo hairs on any of the clothing and none on the camping gear.'

'When do dingoes moult?' I asked, becoming really curious as to where Charlwood was heading.

'In August and September; they were moulting when Azaria disappeared. There was no saliva on the jumpsuit either,' he added.

'I would have thought desert creatures would not salivate much at all?' I reflected.

'They are just dogs,' replied Charlwood, as if he knew everything about them.

After a series of other questions related to the lighter colour of Azaria's hair in my photographs due to the skylight pale pink filter I used, and the time I last saw Azaria alive, he then hit me with another question that matched his cool crystal blue eyes.

'Do you know what happened to Azaria?'

'No,' I pursed my lips and frowned as I had always done from my boyhood. 'Except on the evidence we have given you, I do not know.'

I had answered exactly as I understood the word 'know' to mean—the context of absolute fact, or that I saw it all as a witness with my own eyes, which I didn't.

Charlwood then smiled again as if he was in supreme control, knowing much more than I did. 'Is there anything you want to tell me in relation to the disappearance of your child?'

I hesitated, searching for anything constructive to add to the interview, but was left with the bleak answer.

'No. Except for my continuing observation, and strong feeling that she was killed by a dingo or wild animal. What other alternatives? God only knows.'

Shortly after this the interview ended, but it was not without one final question, which I suspect was designed again to unnerve me.

'When the clothing was found, the booties were still inside the feet of the jumpsuit. Is there any comment you would care to make about that?' Charlwood seemed to think he had something in this question.

'No,' I replied. 'It does seem strange. But then again, it seems that we are dealing with a number of intangibles. But not enough is known perhaps about the wild. And only time will tell the answer.'

Charlwood gave me a 14-page transcript of my 'Record of Interview' and I made a few amendments after a careful reading which took longer than they thought. I stood up and said resignedly, 'Well that's it.'

Charlwood smiled again. 'I'm not sure about that. There is scientific work to be done.' (Record of Interview, between Michael Chamberlain and Detective Graeme Charlwood, 1 October 1980, Mt Isa Police Station.)

Charlwood appeared to disbelieve my story entirely. For the first time I wondered what sort of policemen I was dealing with here. If they couldn't perceive by my attitude and my answers that I was telling them straight from my heart and conscience, perhaps they had another agenda? Police, if they are really on the ball, should be able to discern honesty. That was the simplistic view I took and I was not about to change my mind about him.

The time was 8.30pm. Darkness had overcome the city and it seemed I had just awoken from a dream. What day is it? I had to shake myself back into reality.

'Your car is back in the carpark and here are your keys,' a policeman said. No other comment was made. I was as much in the dark about it as I was about the disappearance of Azaria when Constable Morris came to the motel on the morning after Azaria died when he said there was 'no news'.

Lindy and I did our best to carry on our daily lives as normal. Church friends came and went and offered their sympathies. None were negative or caused us any despair, but plainly the Church administration needed to remove my defenceless family out of the public glare and constant access to the media. We needed a buffer. This came in early December 1980, when I was called to Avondale College, the Church's South Pacific University campus, at Cooranbong, on the New South Wales Central Coast. It was here that I was invited to engage in a Masters degree on pastoral and biblical subjects. This might lead to the chance I had been waiting for: to travel to Loma Linda University and graduate in a Doctorate in Health Science. We were quite amazed at the reaction of the local Mount Isa

Church–many of those I had baptised or ministered to, decided to come to the College with me and contemplated embarking on a study program, or a new life. Our life had to go on.

Our big ordeal was to attend the inquest into Azaria's death held at Alice Springs in December 1980. I was told I should have a lawyer handy, so had requested a lawyer of integrity, someone who would be honest and upright from Alice Springs, Peter Dean, an honest man who, I was told, would not let any nonsense through. I remembered, while visiting my old parish haunts at Innisfail, I had dropped in to see 'Vince' a lawyer and a genuine man of Roman Catholic persuasion. His advice was very casual: 'If you are innocent, which you are, what have you to fear? Go to the Alice Springs court, as lambs to the slaughter! God, as your judge, will be your protector.'

Denis Barritt would preside as the Northern Territory Coroner. He was a stout, crusty, former Detective Sergeant of police who had graduated from law to obtain his new post. I was beginning to be extremely concerned about the policemen I was dealing with and whether they would be able to execute justice. I could understand how people became paranoid. I supposed that most of their paranoia was reasonable, if something really bad had happened to them in the past. To every action there is an equal and opposite reaction, sometime in the future. Barritt seemed to come with a reputation for honesty.

Somehow we got word that the Northern Territory Police Forensic Science Unit department had employed a trainee, with three months experience, to look at the case. It would be revealed later that, not knowing what an animal hair looked like, let alone a dingo hair, she plucked out one of her own hairs as a guide for her analysis, which was to find dingo hairs on Azaria's jumpsuit. She searched for dingo hairs and found a total of six, not many for dingo-ravaged clothing. Unbeknown to her, the jumpsuit had already been vacuumed for hair. A cardboard box containing the clothing also seemed to have been neglected.

The South Australian police, using a triumvirate of 'forensic scientists' who were reportedly experts in their field, aided her. We were warned that this group might now have a nasty surprise in store for us. Their research, reported in the *Adelaide News* by Geoff de Luca, had suggested that the 'confidential' evidence of this professional team sent to Inspector Gilroy 'had failed to find any evidence that baby Azaria Chamberlain was taken by a dingo, or by any other animal, at Ayers Rock' (*Adelaide News*, 2/10/1980). The inquiry was now turning an open-and-shut case about a dingo into a deepening 'mystery'. The home-grown forensic team was now positioned for the downfall of the 'lying Chamberlains' and a sensational breakthrough that would create a setback for Seventh-day Adventist credibility.

In the meantime, reports continued to trickle in about a dingo that might have killed Azaria. Not the least was the traditional Aboriginal elder of Ayers Rock, Nipper Winmatti. He related how there was (and still is) a killer dingo, responsible for Azaria's death, which roams Ayers Rock ('Killer Dog Roams Ayers Rock', *Townsville Daily Bulletin*, 13/10/1980).

Some members of the media put to me the suggestion, 'What if a human was involved, including an Aboriginal witch-doctor?' My reply: 'Extremely unlikely and if there was any human involvement, the person responsible would have to be out of their mind.' Nevertheless, I remained of the firm view that the evidence could only support a dingo attack.

Already, the publicity given to our private experience was starting to remove our 'ownership' of Azaria. From the moment Azaria died, she became public property.

4. *First Inquest, First Shocks*

In November 1980 I took my car to a Mount Isa car radio installer. There, Rohan Tew did part of the work to install a Jensen speaker system and cassette recorder. He informed the police that he had seen blood in my car, but failed to make any comment to me at the time, nor to his boss, Floyd Hart, who completed the installation work. Both he and his boss gave statements to the police, but Hart contradicted Tew, telling the police he saw nothing. All this would come out later, but we had new developments to contend with: various politicians were now becoming curious about the case. The gloves were off, but I didn't see it coming.

Senator James Mulvihill, during 'Questions without Notice' in the Australian Federal Parliament (Senate) 5 December, 1980, stated that I was afflicted with 'religious amnesia'. It was suggested that we should be subjected to lie-detector tests. This story was run by *The Northern Territory News* headline 'Dingo Baby's Parents Hit by Amnesia' (December 8, 1980). Mulvihill was the patron of the Australian Native Dog (Dingo) Training Society in New South Wales. As someone in high office who was vitally interested in the preservation of dingoes, it was not surprising that he would wish to protect the interests of wild animals in killing my daughter.

The inquest into Azaria's death was set down for Monday, 15 December 1980. As we entered Alice Springs airport we found the summer heat was merciless and the press overwhelming. Lindy and I moved with difficulty through the barrage of cameras and crazed reporters to get to some desperately needed rest at our first motel. A Church representative, Pastor Walter Taylor, accompanied us as a counsellor, and an observer for the Church was also there to keep us in check and advise us on our behaviour, to such an extent that he felt it his duty to rebuke us for leaving the motel room untidy and not making our bed.

The first inquest started strongly with cogent evidence presented for the dingo's involvement by a host of witnesses who searched that night. Many witnesses testified that dingo tracks had been discovered going to and from our tent. Derek Roff, the Chief Ranger at the park was quite sure that dingoes had entered the tent. The Aboriginal trackers observed that there was an extra weight being carried by the animal. The dingo had stopped several times to put a small body down to rest before continuing up the sand dunes and along the sand ridge. That dingo drag marks and tracks were found near the tent, was reported in numerous papers. Witnesses also testified reports of dingo attacks on tourists.

But unbeknown to us, a case was brewing for the dingo attack to be overthrown. It had not dawned on us, how or why the theory of 'human intervention' or a 'human link', that someone had somehow intercepted the dingo and had later buried the body of Azaria, was being advanced. I had expected some serious investigative research on how dingoes could have killed Azaria. After the primary evidence of witnesses who all virtually indicated that it was a dingo with Azaria's body they were searching for, there emerged a procession of evidence, as directed by the Northern Territory Attorney-General, from police forensic detectives and police scientists seeking another cause for Azaria's death. The theory was advanced in court by the Adelaide team of forensics, Sergeant Cox and odontologist Dr Kenneth Aylesbury Brown, that a dingo did not take or kill Azaria. It was a human act, according to them. The police forensic scientists from Adelaide were proposing that a screwdriver-like instrument had penetrated Azaria's jumpsuit, not dingo teeth, and that some type of scissors or knife had also cut it.

This did not impress the increasingly frustrated dingo expert, Les Harris, who had previously testified that the whole scenario around Azaria's death had left an unmistakable dingo footprint. As the Dingo Foundation President of Australia, Harris had communicated a view that for some of the media was too dogmatic, even though authoritative and compelling. It seemed that public opinion had a fair way to go before they could digest the shocking behaviour of Australia's wild dog during this given set of circumstances. Clearly there was too little in the public domain on the truth about Seventh-day Adventists beliefs, or the behaviour of dingoes.

By Wednesday, 17 December, threats to our lives were being discussed at court. The Northern Territory Government purported to be very concerned about our 'safety' and informed us that they had appointed a 'police bodyguard' to protect us from the growing threats to stab us or to blow us up, or in some macabre way get rid of us. But we received no threats or phonecalls. The policeman assigned to us was Senior Constable Frank Gibson. Within three days of 'watching out' for us, he confessed that this was in fact a lie. He wasn't protecting us at all but had been assigned to spy on us, something that clearly became harder and harder for him to enact. (That this was illegal was a moot point.) He had reported to his minders that he could find no evidence either 'in our conduct, conversation or demeanour that we were anything but totally innocent' of any blame in Azaria's death. Not to blow his cover we said nothing to anyone for a while.

Detective Sergeant John Lincoln, however, who considered that this case was being driven the wrong way by the Northern Territory police administration, had a different view about dingoes and had also become quite unpopular as a result. He considered that dingoes were far more dexterous than the Northern Territory Conservation Commission was letting on. But Lincoln never communicated his views to us and did not go public at that time. Nor did he testify at the first inquest.

The death threats delayed the inquest, as time had to be taken to discuss the implications. One man had threatened to 'blow her (Lindy) out'. The police guard was increased, but Frank Gibson remained with us, now on a very different level of relationship.

I well remember a moment with Senior Constable Gibson when there was a bomb threat against the Telford Hotel where we were staying. The media were sent pegging downstairs with the knowledge that at any moment a bomb might blow the hotel sky high, but the truth was that the media was more interested in shooting photos of us, the so-called cause of this pandemonium, rather than any explosion. A theory was bandied about, suggesting that the media themselves concocted the hoax. Frank said that his first duty was now in fact to genuinely protect us. I asked him, 'Which do you think has the most likelihood of going off, a bomb or the media outside?' We took one look at the crowd down below and decided we would be safer inside, and would rather live with the bomb. So we sat around the swimming pool, making small talk and discussing the state of the nation. Somewhat shell-shocked by the turn of events created by courtroom revelations, our trip home to uneventful Cooranbong was a relief. On the whole, almost everyone we met were sympathetic but that came largely from the Christian community. Our Christmas felt impersonal and disconnected. We had to turn our minds to a new harrowing experience at Ayers Rock and seeing for the first time where Azaria's clothing was found.

In the meantime, lawyers, Peter Dean and Philip Rice QC from Adelaide, had worked tirelessly to answer the bewildering interpretation now placed on the way Azaria died. Dean reminded me of a South African farmer with his quaint pith helmet and softly spoken, polite English gentleman's accent. Rice, on the other hand, was an enigma. He was a dour man, with a raspy voice, less polite and called a spade a spade. He had come to the Alice wearing a creased shirt and trousers, looking slightly frazzled under a balding head tufted by long windblown strands of greying hair. Rice also exuded an air of strange command, despite clutching an old dilapidated brown leather case tied together with baling twine. His credentials were strong and his extensive knowledge of Territory antics went before him. He could blend in with the Territory psyche and be affable, all the while playing his cards very close to his chest.

The first inquest reopened on Monday, 9 February, 1981 at Ayers Rock and it was traumatic. Both of us shed more than a few tears as we witnessed Azaria's resting place and contemplated touching the area where she may well have passed. The press were watching our reactions very closely also, and reported on my emotional state as we arrived. Headlines appeared: 'Azaria's father in tears', 'Rock view brings tears', 'Dad weeps for Azaria', (*Daily Telegraph*, 9/2/1981).

We heard evidence from forensic botanist Rex Kuchell, the third man in the Adelaide forensic triumvirate. He contradicted tourist witness evidence and Aboriginal evidence that the dingo had dragged Azaria part of the way. His theory was that dingoes drag things over bushes not around them and that on that basis there was insufficient evidence of leaf and ground matter on the jacket to implicate a dingo. None of this forensic trio held postgraduate or research degrees in botany or any other relevant discipline. Brown had never worked on dingo teeth marks before. Police botanist Kuchell operated from an absence of knowledge about dingoes. I felt that these men had been outwitted and outclassed by the cunning and skill of the dingo. In a rather bizarre Adelaide Zoo experiment with a leg of lamb, the dingo had unfastened two of the studs of the Azaria look-alike jumpsuit in exactly the same manner as had occurred on the real Azaria suit. But the forensic team remained virtually silent on this piece of 'insignificant' information. From the perspective of having gained one humble unit of chemistry towards a BSc gained at the University of Canterbury in 1963, I sat aghast, listening to their incompetent rationalisations.

The inquest heard how a considerable amount of blood had been found in the tent on a mattress, possibly enough to cover a small saucer. Coming from Azaria, this could have marked the place of a fatal wound to Azaria. The Northern Territory forensic representatives were focused on more conjectural matters and attempted to paint a picture of the blood formation on Azaria's clothing as sinister. Aidan, my seven-year-old son was quite unequivocal when testifying on the matter. He heard me ask Lindy, 'Is that bubby crying?' He clearly remembered his mother crying out 'A dingo has got my baby'. Aidan remembered her blankets strewn about the tent and her blood on Reagan's parka sleeve and on his own parka's wristband.

By now, Lindy and I found this extremely upsetting. We had seen Azaria's clothing a week after her disappearance, but now we had for the first time come very close to it. The press observed that any vestige of our attempting to look on the bright side had left us. Bill Hitchings, writing for *The Melbourne Herald*, reported that after having been politely chatty to court officials and even some of the press we now only spoke to close friends and our lawyers. We were presented as people who were 'under 24 hour police guard' to protect us, but for a growing number of Australians it must have looked as if we were now the culprits to be investigated rather than any dingo.

The non-detection of saliva on Azaria's clothing after a week in the bush and the interpretation by the forensic triumvirate of holes in her clothing not consistent with canine teeth marks were perplexing matters for us. Dr Alan Newsome, a dingo expert from the CSIRO, told the court that dingoes could smell food eight kilometres away and that a dingo could kill a kangaroo with one bite. This was sobering information. Evidence that dingoes had killed a number of Aboriginal children over the past 100 years and that the Ayers Rock dingoes were atypical. Human interference at close quarters and the fact that, now that tourists were told not to feed the dingoes, food sources were now limited for dingo mothers with pups, meant that in their growing hunger they were even more likely to attack children. The Court then heard that dingoes had recently grabbed at children in cars at Ayers Rock.

To try and remain calm after the court ordeal I would occasionally sneak out for a run around the perimeter of the town. One of the reporters, Malcolm Brown for the *Sydney Morning Herald* had insisted that I go for a five-kilometre run with him before court. This six-foot-one spectacled journalist wanted a story, but insisted he didn't. I should take him on board as good company, and in a strange way, security. I agreed, so wore a pair of trim, cool running shorts and a singlet. He wore a suit, tie and leather shoes. He proved to be no slouch, running with me nearly all the way. I rated him a true martyr to the cause of jogging. This article did appear in print the next day, on the Sabbath, Brown hoping I would not see it.

Brown was a 'straight' journalist not given to using emotive or provocative adjectives. He reported the truth in plain simple words and what you got was as reliable as anything could be in the media world. For some, he might have been a caricature of Clark Kent but in my book he was the journalist's Superman. He could write shorthand and take down accurately every word said, a rare thing these days. He had written or edited numerous books on crime, disasters and other matters that bring people to want to read newspapers. He seemed to eat, sleep and play the role of the reporter. Apart from keeping fit jogging, sometimes on the job in his brown or grey suit, I never discovered any other hobby of his, apart from being devoted to his German wife Inge and his children. Malcolm was blunt and to the point, not given to levity or telling jokes. One was aware that he had a vast store of knowledge at his fingertips, yet it wasn't easy to have a conversation with him until he had relaxed with a couple of beers. He eventually got the thumbs up from me.

There was now an attempt to present my more human face in *The Sun.* In Friday's edition 20/2/1981, writer Bill Hitchings commented on my 'love of tennis'... 'one of my great loves'. I had gone from one court to another to obtain some relaxation. In his article: 'It's nearly all over,' the following story was reported:

'Though still under constant armed police guard, he borrowed a racquet and played a few sets with a friend in the sweltering Alice Springs sun yesterday afternoon.

'Pastor Chamberlain, who has managed a few night jogging sessions, still under police guard, is a self-confessed fitness fanatic.

'A vegetarian and teetotaller, the blond and handsome young minister studies health and fitness as part of his course at the Seventh-day Adventist Avondale College in NSW.

'Pastor Chamberlain, 37, agreed that playing in Alice Springs' heat was tougher than he expected. 'But I have been a little too busy lately to play as much as I would like', he said.'

The accompanying photo was also fair to me, a small mercy for which I was thankful in an otherwise rugged two weeks of dreadful headlines.

Most of the press behaved like a gaggle of geese honking at the moon, desperate to get their shot at the end of every session. Their only opportunity was during our brisk walk from the court to the waiting car and chauffeured driver. On one occasion the press did get an insight to Lindy's persuasive powers while in conversation with Peter Dean. With hands planted on her hips and a brown leather handbag swung over her shoulder, Lindy was not going to let him off the hook on a point of order. John Bryson also noticed her determination, describing her as 'attractive but bossy, three quarter face with upturned nose and pert mouth, a young woman who was well used to calling the shots to her lawyer.' Editors had a field day. They ran it around the country.

A bombshell hit the court on day 13 of the inquiry, with the introduction of a Northern Territory forensic witness, Constable Moira Beryl Fogarty. The Coroner Denis Barritt revealed to the Court a forensic witness. Fogarty, possibly through no fault of her own due to inadequate training, had failed to find the all-important bloodstains in our tent where Azaria had died. Her failure to look for and to find a significant amount of blood had painted us as the culprits and not the victims. But when asked if this failure was deliberate, she denied it. The report on blood and hair seemed to imply that we had been liars. She told the court that there was no evidence of dingo hair or Azaria's blood in her report written for her superior. But it 'was not supposed to have ended up in court.' I sat there, dumbfounded.

Before the Coroner, Constable Fogarty conceded that she had missed vital evidence on the side of the tent, a fine blood spray, in fact. She agreed that her techniques in testing the tent had been flawed and inappropriate. Fogarty's shock appearance, reported in *The Adelaide News* (18/2/1981), had only made the inquiry more bizarre for me and my family.

Coroner Barritt was clearly annoyed. My mind also turned to the fine spray of blood on the wall of our tent. The forensic scientists had dismissed it as unable to be diagnosed.

The question about the absence of dingo hair had started to unravel also, but not enough to stop a biased Northern Territory-driven fraternity pushing in another direction. Dr Harding was now called as an expert on hair. His report exposed a serious flaw in the forensic investigation. He had found dingo hair on Azaria's jumpsuit, but on the tent blankets he had found no dingo hair except embedded hair, which had probably been there for many years.

If Barritt was surprised, the forensic investigators and Northern Territory police must have been more surprised and even annoyed that all the eyewitness tourists had so strongly endorsed our testimony as right. The forensic scientists on the other hand stood sharply in contrast, 'an outpost of disbelief'. Harding now wanted to change his testimony about the blankets when he learned that the forensic unit in Darwin had vacuumed these, with the information not having been passed on. The hairs that were vacuumed up were mostly white hairs likely to have come from an animal's face or mouth, it was reported later.

Barritt had other information about dingoes that strongly influenced his finding. For whatever reason, Ashleigh Macknay, counsel assisting the Coroner, had not called for, or obtained the presence of dingo expert Dr Laurie Corbett, an obvious key witness in this case. Only a transcript of his interview appeared. Corbett's description of the way a dingo would have killed our daughter was compelling. But it was too gruesome apparently for either the media or us to read. We demanded to read it and our wish was duly granted, but we were not allowed to keep a copy. The language of the Northern Territory's Sergeant Sandry interview with Dr Corbett was quite coarse in places. The description of how the dingo would have killed and choked her to death around the throat was so gruesome I did not need to read it a second time to get the message.

In his 23-page record of interview with Sandry marked, 'Conversation between Sergeant Sandry and Lawrence Corbett re activities of Dingoes', Dr Corbett was clearly being led by Sandry's theory that Lindy had killed Azaria sometime later in the afternoon. Sandry made out that it was her dead body that had attracted a dingo into the tent and to take its prey. Corbett described how dingoes don't salivate significantly unless they are around a female on heat or chewing up a tough bone. Dingoes, he said, will kill a lot of calves when no native or feral game is available. Dingoes are also particularly attracted to faeces that have the smell and flavour of breast milk, which explains their attraction to the nappies in the barbecue fire and also later near the lair. The (dingo) 'must have been pretty nervous in the tent' when it 'took the whole lot away'. Corbett then went on to describe catching a dingo in Sherbrook Forest, Victoria with 'quite an amount of human in it. It was from Jasper Gorge'.

When Corbett was asked about the blood on Azaria's jumpsuit, he admitted that the dingo would have gone for the throat, as it would go for a calf or a rabbit, 'They would bite them anywhere, the neck being first.' When Corbett was told that the baby was in the five to ten-pound range he replied. 'Well, if they're eating rabbit or an extremely young newborn calf, a border calf or something then they, an adult dog will, er, eat the whole lot, start at one end and eat the whole bloody lot. Just chomp, chomp, chomp down there...' Corbett then proceeded to show how a dingo would skin a rabbit. It would then depend on how the dingo pulled off Azaria's jumpsuit. At this point I stopped reading. I tried to walk away and forget about it, but I couldn't. I had already read too much from Corbett. It cemented in my mind the telltale behaviour of a dingo before and during Azaria's demise.

The Coroner requested a national broadcast on television of the finding. The Northern Territory police opposed this ('Police Bid to Stop Telecast', *Daily Mirror*, 20/2/1981). Their appeal was rejected. The nation was destined to stop work and hear the finding on national television two days later. Shane Maguire, described as the *Daily Mirror*'s 'man on the spot', waxed satirical. It is so tense here in Alice Springs 'you could cut the air with a knife,' he quipped.

Coroner Barritt had indicated that he was not looking at a murder case. Lindy had readily agreed that it was only ever going to be one of two things in a black and white case; either a dingo or a human killed Azaria.

On Friday, 20 February at 2.30pm, in halting solemn tones, Coroner Denis Barritt read from a manuscript that declared that a dingo had snatched and killed Azaria in the way that we had described.

The real surprise came when he introduced the notion that someone afterwards had intervened and had probably buried her body. It was believed, secretly, by some that the Ayers Rock rangers and police had apparently found Azaria's body underneath a ranger's house after losing the tracks of the guilty dingo. It was upon this knowledge that Barritt proposed 'human intervention'.

Barritt's final words were couched in an apology to us, as Azaria's parents, for the vicious gossip, rumour and innuendo we had experienced and endured. He said we were exonerated from any complicity or suspicion in any way regarding her death. It was a bitter-sweet experience for us, but the case was over and the book was closed on what had become one of the most polarising cases in recent Australian legal history. Near the end of that nation-wide broadcast, Mr Barritt spoke critically of the Northern Territory's police forensic-science division. He thought it an unskilled body. Barritt was so dissatisfied that he recommended the re-establishment of the entire division with other personnel. Barritt's moral backbone would not be rewarded however.

At the time of the finding, I found myself in a state of shock, still coming to terms with the second part of Barritt's conclusion, that after Azaria died someone had intercepted the dingo and removed her body for burial. 'Who would have done that and for what reason?' I asked myself over and over again. 'Why had they not come forward and what was being covered up?' Then, to answer the critics about the abundant health and wellbeing of Azaria I unfurled a colour poster print I had taken of Lindy with Azaria at six weeks of age. The act was designed to show what a magnificent little babe Azaria was, as well as to rebuke those who had spread malicious rumours that Azaria was a sickly and deformed child. Again, the press thought I had over-reacted, but I was unrepentant. It was my way of demonstrating my grief and loss.

The Christian Century, an authoritative American ecumenical weekly with an international readership, picked up on and affirmed the way I demonstrated my gratitude for the Coroner's findings. In front of a nation's TV cameras and journalists, before a captive audience, I fearlessly illustrated where my strength resided. It had its foundation in the New Testament teachings of Jesus Christ—in adverse situations, to remember that all Christians are Christ's ambassadors: 'On my account you will be brought to governors and kings as witnesses to them and the rest of the world' (Matthew 10:18). I told the press that the bottom line for me: was that 'Jesus Christ was our very dear Friend and Saviour' and I thanked Him for giving us the strength to go through this ordeal without stumbling. The response from the cynical press and its audience was to recoil, finding my faith 'too direct and simple'. (*The Christian Century*, 7/12/1988).

There were many in the Church who were questioning the facts of the case. In particular I was disappointed about the involvement of Dr Kenneth Brown, a Seventh-day Adventist from Adelaide. It was all very frightening, but I thought that God's will would prevail and I must trust in His strength to overcome.

In his finding, Barritt foreshadowed our new dilemma. 'Dingoes or tourism...that is the choice' he said in his finding. Human life must be preserved over that of dingoes (*The* (Melbourne) *Herald*, 20/2/1981). The behaviour of dangerous creatures must be exposed to arm tourists with information on how to remain safe. In the cause of conservation, the death of a baby was too high a price to pay, Barritt observed. But if we ever thought things were going heavenly well, we had no whiff of the hell that was in store.

Senator Peter Baume suggested at the end of the first inquest finding, on 24 February 1981, that parents at Conservation Commission campsites should be afforded more protection from dingoes than those just venturing into nature reserves and generally 'bivouacking in the wilds'. During the course of this reply another Senator (Cavenagh) decided to demonstrate the level of his sensitivity for our plight, by interjecting: 'But we have run out of kids to feed them.' This was typical of the distasteful jokes at the time. Stout defence of our innocence also occurred in parliament at this time but negative opinion always lingers longer. It is easy to muddy water, much harder to purify it.

In response to the Coroner's report, the Northern Territory Conservation Commission erected a dingo-proof fence around the Ayers Rock tourist park.

Steve Brien was one of the journalists present at the first inquest. 'Don't let the truth get in the way of a good story,' was Brien's slogan. On the first night of the inquest being held out at the Rock, Lindy was engulfed by fits of hysterical laughter. I remember it well because I was sitting next to her, feeling both shame and amusement, watching Lindy's reaction to the object of her hysterics. One of the members of the media, caught in the glare of other cameras all focused inward on each other, and blinded by their own light, tripped on a TV cord while trying to film her. The unfortunate man lurched out of control from one person to another, bounced off a log rail, then another journalist, before coming to rest in a heap of Ayers Rock dust. Brien and his photographer associate, Russell McPhedran wrote up this photo of Lindy's uncontrollable mirth, hands across her face, as an illustration of her strain and anguish. This photo was splashed across the front page of their Sydney tabloid, boldly captioned 'Azaria Anguish' (*Sydney and Newcastle Sun*, 11 February 1981). It was a lesson we had to learn over and over again. The press could manipulate any emotional reaction and use it to suit their storyline, to position an audience to respond in any way they desired.

For Brien, on the outside, we were 'The finest people that he had ever met. What had happened to us was the most shocking thing he could imagine happening to good people', he told us. He was preparing a book on us based on a concoction of misinformation laced with clairvoyant interpretations. He published his book two years later. Brien eventually left the *Sydney Sun* and the newspaper ceased to exist shortly after, allegedly in part because royalty stories were becoming boring and the Chamberlain case was over.

5. *Into a Darker Valley*

Our arrival back at Avondale College following the dramatic Coroner's finding, televised nationally by Channel 7, set a new benchmark in College operations, especially in their security system. Our new home was inside the College campus at 17 College Drive, Cooranbong (later to be called Central Road, its original name when designed in the 1890s). It afforded some privacy and I could walk to class in 10 minutes. This was a great improvement for our peace of mind and security. Another change was the new College president, Dr James Cox, a Harvard PhD graduate. He was an excellent replacement for the former double PhD scientist, Dr Eric Magnusson, who now lectured at Canberra's Australian National University.

Aidan and Reagan went to Avondale Primary School, an Adventist teaching school, near the College. After months of anxiety and grief, everything seemed to be working out for us at long last. Postgraduate study was not the easiest thing to slot into, but I was not alone in the class of nine or so other pastors invited to do the same course—others had similar adjustments to make. It was a gracious act by the Church to invite me and I was determined not to squander the opportunity.

We moved seamlessly into the second semester of 1981. Lindy had started an undergraduate course, a BA in Education and Art. She had come to College with some study experience, having completed a diploma in Dressmaking and Design at the Launceston TAFE in 1974. The media had almost left us alone, but were still fishing for stories about us even if claiming to be recording follow-up human-interest stuff. Life, finally, was getting back to normal, although the past was never far away.

Unexpectedly, while engaging in my postgraduate course, a stressful moment occurred. I was involved in the pastoral counselling subject at the Sydney Adventist Hospital (SAH) in Wahroonga, a hospital celebrated for its professional approach in surgery, and palliative care. Dr Tom Ludowici ran the classes and was a man of high esteem and skill at the hospital. Earlier in the day of Wednesday, 26 June, 1981, I was able to interview a prominent specialist on aerobic fitness in New South Wales, Dr Garry Eggars, as part of my 180-page Master's thesis (euphemistically named a 'project') on 'Aerobic Exercise and Wellbeing'. Following Dr Eggars' visit, I was required to return to the Sydney Adventist Hospital and continue my pastoral visits to the infirm. The main problem seemed to be visiting women over 30 who would recognise me and start talking about my tragedy. I could feel myself slowly descending into a state of depression and was beginning to feel sicker than many of the patients. I was becoming the comforted and not the comforter.

Men, on the other hand, although sympathetic, said little about my saga. I remember expressing the desire to some of my colleagues to get even, particularly with people who wanted to continue to question us on our version of events at the Rock. I was wallowing in a state of smouldering anger about the ongoing controversy. This was becoming scary. Azaria's death was consuming me, especially the exact moment when she died, as described by Dr Corbett. I thought of another ministerial colleague, Pastor Raymond Sills, who had lost two of his four children in a terrible motor accident in New Guinea and had to drive his dead children to a hospital. It must have seemed like an eternity in time. I had at least been spared from seeing Azaria dead, but not knowing the whereabouts of her body was traumatic.

On Thursday morning 27 June, I delivered a short homily to members of the physiotherapy staff and ate breakfast at the hospital cafeteria. From then on, the day went pear-shaped. Routine visitation on the general wards caused me to feel weirdly dizzy. I decided to scurry back to the lift hoping that none of the nursing sisters had seen me. Dr Tom Ludowici's wife, Pam, got to me and in a short counselling exchange encouraged me to go back to the wards and take courage with me. I agreed to return. There was no doubt that I was in trouble with myself, but it seemed nobody could unpack my anger.

The first discussion back was with a 23-year-old personnel manager. He showed an unusually strong interest in the beliefs and lifestyles of the Church and felt attracted to possibly joining it one day. This came as a surprise to me, as on my first visit he had been offhand, considering me as an intrusion. I had withdrawn discreetly. I discovered that he owned two prized V8 Holden Torana hatchbacks. Suddenly my ownership of a similar machine seemed to fire up our relationship. I was no longer just a stuffed shirt clergyman, but a person with something exciting to trade.

The counselling session for ministers resumed and I was invited to give my perspectives on life. Not a good move. I really needed to escape to get some time out. So I fled. Down the several flights of stairs I ran and jumped into my car. The car roared into life, assuming the familiar resonant beat of a well-tuned V8. I was in my other home. Out on the road I travelled to Hornsby on the Pacific Highway where I intended to make a right-hand turn into the main shopping centre. I wasn't thinking. I was still dreaming, trying to escape my depression, my mind far away. I took my eyes of the road and paid the price. I rammed the back of a Morris Mini Minor which then catapulted into a much larger Ford Falcon. The Falcon was only slightly damaged; the Mini was a write-off.

My car sustained moderate damage but was able to limp into a service station and to be towed home. From there, it was taken to a private panel-beater's residence at Sunshine, on Lake Macquarie. It needed a new radiator, fan, front and side mudguard panel but nothing else. At the time, I hadn't realised that my insurance was valid to 7/04/81 and I was now two and a half months out. The insurance renewal had gone to my old Mount Isa, Sunset address. I pleaded with the RACQ Queensland administration for some consideration but got nowhere, of course. I was up for $5,400 before starting on my own car, a considerable sum in 1981.

I rang the Sydney Adventist Hospital for transport support, feeling a failure and very stupid. It was almost as if they were on their way before I rang. I remember the friendly caring faces of my colleagues coming to greet me and to take me back to the hospital. That was just after I had threatened God that I had almost finished with fighting for His cause. I don't really care anymore, I thought. I'm almost over asking for help. Another colleague, Pastor Ray Newman offered to ring for a doctor to give me any assistance required. I had never been anything more than his acquaintance but I appreciated his insight and caring attitude. My greatest fear at that moment was telling Lindy that we were not insured and we had a bill of $5,400 to face.

When I arrived back at College Dr Jim Cox's wife, Alice, threw her arms around me and I felt like it was my own mother. It was instant therapy and I felt free to accept it.

'You poor dear,' she said. 'How horrible!' My sentiments exactly. My stupidity had been swallowed up in acceptance. But the feeling of security and acceptance was quickly over.

Without our knowledge, pieces of our tent, our clothing and Azaria's clothing were being re-examined in laboratories in Darwin, Adelaide, Sydney and London. They were photographed through microscopes and under ultra-violet light. Botanists and soil analysts were flown to Ayers Rock to collect samples of vegetation and bags of sand. In Sydney, textile scientists dug holes in baby clothes with knives, scissors and teeth from the jaws of dried dingo skulls. At the south face of Ayers Rock, an entomologist watched for hours the behaviour of desert flies as they crawled over a cloth he had moistened with blood.

John Bryson described the result of all this new activity. 'On 17 September 1981, Northern Territory police left Darwin by plane for Sydney. There they were granted a New South Wales search warrant. On 19 September, police parked two cars outside a house in College Drive, Cooranbong, and went to the door. This was a house owned, like others nearby, by the Seventh Day (sic) Adventist Church. The Chamberlain family had moved here, since their house in Mount Isa had become a tourist attraction.' ('The inquisition faced by the Chamberlains', *The Age* 10/9/1983).

Lindy and I had woken at around 8am on a crisp spring day and were lying in bed for a few minutes oblivious to what would happen next. I was thinking that I had to get up and attend a 9am elder's prayer study but was dragging the chain somewhat. I was not a particularly punctilious sort of bloke except on my Sabbath. I didn't realise that I was now a suspected murderer.

At 8.10am, there was a knock at our front door. Aidan answered. He was seven years old. Two Northern Territory detectives blocked the doorway. I was mildly curious why they should be here at this time of the day. One was Detective Sergeant Charlwood. He had a cheek, I thought, coming on our day of rest. It was as if the Arabs had come to Israel on Yom Kippur to destroy it. In an increasing state of shock, I dressed hurriedly. Charlwood's burly partner flashed his Northern Territory badge imperiously at us and I was issued with a search warrant for our house. When asked what they wanted, they informed us of a list of about 60 items. Okay, I thought, that shouldn't be hard. A whole band of police then traipsed in after them. 'This is preposterous,' I muttered under my breath.

The police knew we had always cooperated with them. We had bent over backwards to provide anything they wanted. That was probably what made them feel rather odd being in our house. Had they rung us in advance the result would not have been any different. We would have been happy for them to search for whatever it was they were looking for. But now, Charlwood and his thickset associate, poker faced, were deliberately making us feel like criminals about to get sprung. It felt like a bull terrier had entered our sanctuary looking for human flesh to sink its teeth into. Charlwood did apologise for interrupting our day of worship but he need not have bothered: what was to come later in the morning would indicate the hollowness of his apology.

Lindy was still in bed. She almost seemed nonchalant about their visit. I offered the visitors a seat in the lounge room, now numbed and shaken as it sank in that we were being targeted as criminals and maybe murderers. Several more police entered. What were they all here for? Ours was a close-knit private community. What would the neighbours be thinking?

Charlwood then warned us that his Chief Minister had called a press conference to announce the reopening of police investigations. That explained the presence of a Channel Seven helicopter circling over our roof and others joining soon after.

The police commenced their search at 9am at the back of the house, at the covered-in porch and laundry. They felt under ledges. They searched every nook and cranny, every dark spider-infested spot, each of them with poker face. None talked. Lindy now arose not feeling charitable at all. She was waiting for one of the police to find a red back spider latch itself to their finger. The burly constable with Charlwood took each bag and wrote officious-looking notes about each item, the date, a detailed description of its contents, and of course, his signature. His copious notes looked ludicrous and I tried not to laugh. They were only doing a job, I tried to tell myself. By the time the Northern Territory detective constable had found the 60th item he was carelessly stuffing it into the bag with hardly a note about its contents. No date, no signature, just a number. It seemed like a charade. They had deemed it inappropriate to talk and the air was so serious. They refused any drink or food. It was all part of the Northern Territory's image that their police were professional and efficient.

However, some did start talking by lunchtime and I was able to get some real answers about the camera equipment being used to photograph some items. At one stage, a detective grabbed hold of one of the three camera bags I used and was about to triumphantly walk off with it when I informed him that it was another one that I had taken to Ayers Rock. He looked a little embarrassed and, taking my word, replaced it with the relevant item.

Chief Minister and Attorney-General, Paul Everingham, had acted on advice he had reportedly received from the Territory's Solicitor-General, Ian Barker. Everingham notified the world through the media that his police force was raiding our home and that there would be a fresh inquiry. He also accused the media of behaving like 'a bunch of vampires', with their speculation being 'ghoulish' (*Sydney Morning Herald*, 24 December, 1981). All major TV outlets whether in cars, on foot, or by air descended upon out humble white weatherboard home. By late morning I counted at least three media helicopters, hovering, darkening our sky overhead.

The police had also asked to take my car. Not having any clue as to its whereabouts, I led them to its restoration place in Sunshine, Lake Macquarie. It was 15 kilometres away from home, where a private car restorer was working on it. Journalist Shane Maguire, reporting in *The Daily Mirror*, (16/10/1981) reported that New South Wales police had seized it 'from a Hornsby wrecker's yard'. That yard was approximately 100 kilometres away. My Torana had never been near a wrecker.

On the following Sabbath Lindy and I decided to brave College Church. We travelled in an old car lent to us by some Mount Isa friends. There was a very different feeling now in Church. I felt estranged. Only a handful talked to us this time to politely enquire if we were okay. The next day, Sunday 27 September 1981, I awoke at 7.30am to blustery but fine weather. It had rained during the night. The garden looked refreshed, as I prepared to do some weeding and pull some radishes, my favourite veggie, for lunch. At about 9.15am my eye caught a young, pleasant-looking gentleman from around the corner of our house.

'Hello. I'm from the *Sydney Sun*. You know my colleague Steve Brien?' He was nervous.

'Uh uh', I replied, already feeling my hair bristle.

'Could you give me a minute of your time?' He sounded as harmless as a dove.

It was an introduction I had grown used to. If I said 'Boo' it would be on page one in two-inch high headlines in the *Sydney Sun* or the *Daily Mirror*.

I was really angered by this intrusion. It was a week since the shock announcement about the inquest reopening. I had failed in my security and had relied too heavily on Paul Everingham's proclamations to instruct the media to end their speculation.

'How are you coping with the new inquiry,' the journalist asked smoothly.

'No comment,' I replied. I pointed in the direction where he might get the answer. It was the gate.

'There is a time and place for everything and I have absolutely no comment to make.' But I had said too much.

It was imperative that I keep quiet, regardless of my desire to protest my innocence. The media would make me appear to say anything they liked if I opened my mouth. The journalist left graciously but what he served up in the following afternoon's paper was a misinterpretation. The headline translated my comment into the notion that I was about to break my silence. The report stated that the strain on our faces was starting to show. It quoted me as saying, 'There is a lot I want to say.' It was a lie.

At about 12.15pm a young gangly looking youth ran from a house across the road to tell me that Stuart Tipple, a solicitor, had rung me. The message was astounding. According to a Christchurch radio station, I had been arrested and was now in jail. The dingo media were on the hunt. I rang Stuart back.

'Hi Stuart, guess what? I'm out of jail.' There was a roar of laughter as we reminisced over the last two days of weird experiences. But one thing was sure. I scanned the horizon and was beginning to question a police force and government who seemed to be hell-bent on our social and legal demise, along with their media.

By 2.30pm that Sunday afternoon the blowies had gone berserk, trapped in the corners of the kitchen window ledges. Outside, there was another buzzing noise. It was the idling motors of stalking journalists sitting in white cars with the telltale thick black CB type aerials. I sneaked around the corner of the house and jumped on the back of a friend's motorcycle. We sneaked in behind an unattended vehicle and watched the two white media cars from a healthy distance. This went on for about 20 minutes. One of the vehicles was a 1981 Commodore L, the other a 1978 Ford Falcon. The Commodore contained an overweight driver who smoked as though he was trying to commit suicide. His passengers, a shorthaired youth caressing a telephoto lens attached to a Nikon camera, and a hard-faced woman of about 30, presumably the journalist trying to find one of those elusive 'friends of the Chamberlains' to quote. But they would never be found. Just after 4pm, the youth raised his camera in his attempt to capture me on celluloid. He did so illegally on College private property and actually driving past me and my close friend and confidant, Colin Lees at the gates of my home. We then watched them creep back towards my house after parking their car out of sight, about 100 metres away. Lindy watched them approach also. Colin, now back with me, answered the door. He made some gestures and they left, disappointed.

Colin was a short but fit and powerfully built young man, a classic Greek stereotype from ancient Sparta or Athens. That was until he opened his mouth. Bedecked with a moustache and a head full of jet-black hair, a delightful Scottish accent now wickedly described our antagonists. Colin was my eyes and ears, and I was extremely grateful. I had the pleasure of baptising him, while at Innisfail, several years before.

The media were fearless and presumptuous. Reporters and paparazzi roamed the College corridors and classrooms with the familiarity of their own homes. Several journalists ran amok in search of Lindy and me; one armed with a bag of cameras managed a shot of Lindy's backside while climbing a flight of stairs to a lecture room. It was deemed worthy of the front page of a Sydney afternoon tabloid newspaper.

Our many friends were disbelievingly shocked and angry. We had assisted the police unreservedly but someone was feeding propaganda to the press. There was no giving up by the Northern Territory. Once told that charges might proceed by the College if they trespassed on private property further, as many as ten reporters would lie in wait on the short mown grass outside the College gates. After an hour they would fall asleep, before disappearing during the mid-afternoon as mysteriously as they had come.

On Wednesday 30 September 1981, there was tension from the moment I walked into the College administration building. A fair amount of animosity was being generated among students and staff by the press, by now. I was growing more worried about the safety of my two boys. There was no need to be re-identified by the press over and over again. Silence, we had learned, was golden and it gave us security, but it made the journalists as angry as hornets. They only ever wanted a 'harmless, innocent' photograph, they bleated. This would give me immunity from further harassment, they lied. So I rang Stuart Tipple, and told him what was going on in the College grounds during my lectures, during my private time, during a time that I needed to finish my second degree.

It was 'Robert' this time, the youthful journalist from the *Sydney Sun*. Once again he had been waiting for two days to talk to me. He wrote me a letter pleading for 'a break'. Shane Maguire, from the *Daily Mirror*, added his name to the letter. I was on to Shane and his biased reporting, tinged with more than a modicum of sensation. My reply: 'Sorry Robert and Shane. I am not playing your stupid game.'

The Alice Springs inquest had been punctuated with death threats of stabbing, shooting and threatened bombings of the hotel we stayed in; media reporting had caused all this. Stuart Tipple rang the editor of the two offending Sydney tabloids. Stop making a nuisance and confine yourselves to outside the private property of the College. Go beyond the gates and the police will be called. The journos now lay on the grass outside the gates of the College on Freemans Drive, day after day, week after week. They continued to sprawl out onto the small grass nature strip, faces to the sun or to the earth until around 2pm almost every day, waiting, waiting, and then sleeping out of exhaustion from boredom and inertia.

As a family we had to leave the College incognito. It was annoying and inconvenient. But it provided for students and staff a fascinating insight into the internal workings and machinations of the sensational media arm of the press, the *Adelaide News*, *The Northern Territory News*, the *Sydney Sun* to name a few.

Everyone, from the College president to the farm hand, became our eyes and ears. If Avondale students ever revered the cloak and dagger ethics of the media, or their work as honourable or glamorous, they know saw it was a double-edged sword. 'New Leads', 'New Clues', 'Azaria's Father Tells'. The theme was always the same. The news was that someone was about to break his or her silence. Get ready for the next serial instalment. Now a 'decapitation' theory emerged, or a mysterious interview on the Alice Springs road, followed by a search. It was all part of an elaborate ploy to force the alleged 'killers' of Azaria into submission. Cold and calculating, if not sinister intent, permeated these staged reports. The words of one AAP reporter from Alice Springs echoed in my mind. 'News is a luxury'. It is not a necessity. When there is none, newspapers create it, if the facts don't suit. In the case of the Sydney and Newcastle afternoon tabloids during 1981, I needed no convincing of that. 'But they won't win,' I consoled myself, 'because they, the media, are embellishing a lie.

It was turning into a 'show' trial. There was the 'show' of digging up the Uluru campsite to find Azaria, where police overturned many tonnes of soil with shovels in the hot September sun. It sent an insatiable media into another wild goose chase of intrigue. On 18 October 1981, Shane Maguire reported in *The Daily Mirror* that my car was in Alice Springs and was being cut up. It had been taken, wrapped in black plastic, via a RAAF Caribou from Richmond Air Base NSW, on a Wednesday afternoon. Its home in Alice Springs was reportedly to be huge wire cage, lit 24 hours, built especially for the police, to protect it from us! What was being searched for? I racked my brains about what could possibly be in there that was exciting them so much. Whatever it was, it seemed that, without even looking, they had already found it.

Several press vehicles had been hovering around the College grounds again trying to find out where we were. The papers now started making up stories about the mystery of our seclusion. But we were still managing to have a relatively free rein. Our eyes were peeled for strangers walking suspiciously around the grounds trying to blend in, when in fact they would stick out like sore thumbs. Looking official in their suits, collar and ties could not disguise them. Legal advice remained: 'Stay out of sight of their cameras.' Plans began to evolve for a sentry box in the College to filter the undesirables out.

Four weeks had passed since the police raid on our home. As usual, we were told nothing and any scraps of information we did glean came long after the rest of Australia found out. We tried to keep our lives and routines as normal as possible. Lindy was attempting to study for some upcoming undergraduate exams and was having problems trying to focus. My scheduled graduation for November 1981 had gone down the gurgler. I hadn't been able to start my thesis and I had attracted a couple of B minuses in my Masters grades. To graduate, one needed a B or a 3-point average and I wanted to get a 3.5-average, to be eligible for a place in a Doctorate in Health Science at Loma Linda University, California. I decided to take another 12 months to finish my thesis, to give myself the best chance of improving my grades.

Lindy and I were becoming frayed around the edges, to say the least. She was getting annoyed with me because I couldn't express my feelings about Azaria's death. I simply could not talk about it, without becoming a blubbering mess. The waters ran too deep for me and if I opened my mouth I would have just broken down. I burried myself in work on my thesis.

In a painful exchange, I retaliated by challenging Lindy to explain to me what she had done in the tent, the ten or so minutes she was away from the barbecue and why she did not zip up the tent after she left it. It was a question I did not need answering, but it got a highly emotional response, a response that indicated she would not forgive me easily for asking that question. I had been out of order to ask, but I needed reassurance because of the ridiculous and confusing direction this investigation was going. I was too angry and disillusioned about the police invasion to talk sympathetically. While I didn't regret asking that question, because I wanted to know exactly what she saw, I also knew that she alone saw it, and I could not speak for her, only for me on this moment in time.

Aidan and Reagan were distressed and were fighting like Kilkenny cats for no apparent reason, but I knew they were agitated that their parents were under attack. My family was being torn apart from the outside, and it was becoming increasingly difficult to hold it together.

Avis and Cliff Murchison, Lindy's parents, had been patient stalwarts in Nowra and had done their best to encourage us all. Now in their mid-sixties it wasn't much of a retirement bonus to be trying to pick up the pieces of our crumbling lives. My parents, Ivan and Greta across the Tasman, felt helpless. They felt like they were stripping their gears through revving from anxiety and floor pacing, not knowing what to do, except fire the odd angry shot, courtesy of the media, across the NT bows. From 2500 kilometres away in cool Christchurch, it didn't seem to be having much effect in hot and humid Darwin. But the New Zealand Seventh-day Adventist Church was backing my parents 110 per cent. And it cheered our souls too, when they fired broadsides in the media, defending us.

Lindy complained that the stress was causing her father to go grey prematurely. My father had developed high blood pressure and was warned he could have a heart attack. For my parents to be prescribed tranquillisers was unheard of. Both were strong people emotionally, although my father could become very heated in a conflict situation. Extremely conscientious and hard working, they were also deeply respected in their local farming community. Was this the legacy they would face? Seeing their offspring go to the wall for something they were falsely accused of?

During a Sabbath meal in the North New South Wales Conference president's home, I was asked if I felt capable of ministry. In other words, was I up to preaching sermons, conducting house calls and giving biblical instruction to people who showed an interest in Seventh-day Adventist beliefs and lifestyle? It wasn't an easy question for him to ask. I was a big headache for the Church now. He decided that it would be a good idea for me to write a letter to the Church executives and invite them to have my immediate future discussed. I knew I was in trouble performing my pastoral tasks as I could no longer focus on my ministerial work without facing many questions, however positively inspired.

My blood pressure, like my that of my father, had also taken a hike. I didn't think I was old enough to have to worry about that yet. A doctor friend quietly checked me out: 160/100. 'Hmmm,' he mused. 'Not bad, especially for what you're going through'.

I just couldn't believe it. I was normally 125/80, not this scary measurement. Since my chosen theme for Master's research was about the relationship of jogging to wellbeing, I began to think I had better take that to heart. My anger for my daughter's death was surfacing. Inadequate signposting and warnings had made our baby vulnerable. I felt that the Northern Territory Police and some politicians were not content with seeing Azaria dead. Did they want to destroy our family?

Everything I held dear seemed to be stripped away. Not only had I lost my daughter, my marriage and family was crumbling, my parents' health was suffering, my work was under a question mark, I couldn't complete my theses, my health was also suffering. Save the animals, but inflict insufferable pain on the humans.

The anonymous mail now became incessant. A typical example with the original spelling and grammar read:

'Chamberlains

You cannot hide behind the shadow of the cross

Your greedy for money

Have to pay

You will be arrested soon or later

SOON!

Where is your child Michael?

What hast thou done?'

The letter felt surreal–fake–as if from someone who was not quite the full quid. Another letter read:

'AND THE LORD SAID UNTO YOU, WHOSOEVER SLAYETH THE CHILD VENGEANCE WILL BE TAKEN ON HIM (YOU) SEVENFOLD!!!

YOU BLUDY TV STAR (sic)

WE TRUST IN JUSTICE

THE DINGO'S ARE NOT GUILTY

YOU MR AND MRS CHAMBERLAIN' (sic)

Colin Lees now took charge as my unofficial spokesperson, telling the media that I had 'come close to the end of being 'a nice guy...He had lost four kilograms in the past four weeks', (*Melbourne Herald*, 20/10/1981).

When I awoke on the 29 October 1981, I mused about how the press had left us alone for a total of eight days now. But they would be back. A *Sydney Morning Herald* journalist had said that there were only two things keeping *The Sun* and *The Daily Mirror* alive now and that was Royalty and the Chamberlains. The ratings and advertising money kept luring them back. Different cars would come and go. They would either park absurdly close to our doorstep, perhaps to demonstrate how ethical they were, or three houses down the road with their backs to us, squinting through their rear-vision mirrors. Their faces often looked tortured or painfully bored. The old hacks kept coming back for a sniff. Younger ones came and then vanished into the ether, like the early morning mists of sleepy Cooranbong. One could almost feel sorry for their predatory-styled life. The short, hand-written notes in the mail did not abate. Just a brief interview or a photo and we will all go away, they promised. We won't harass you anymore.

In the meantime, the Northern Territory public relations machine was winding up the public. The message was one of 'validating' the Northern Territory-directed forensic investigation led by Dr Kenneth Brown. His apparent 'chance meeting' with Professor James Malcolm Cameron in the London Metropolitan Police Club, where, according to Dr Brown, he happened to have my daughter's jumpsuit handy. ('Chance meeting led to Azaria Evidence' *The Sun Herald* 13/12/1981), This caused Cameron, 'London's dingo expert', to find 'startling new evidence'. Azaria's head, he alleged, 'had been removed from her torso' (*Sunday Observer* (Melbourne) 25/10/1981).

As a result of this purported 'evidence', Everingham and Desmond Sturgess, a newly appointed lawyer driving the investigation, along with Northern Territory Police Commissioner Peter McAulay and Professor Cameron, visited the Rock.

On the same day, 25 October, the Church came out with its own message for the Northern Territory and the public. Pastor Russell Kranz, the South Pacific Church's public relations director stated that the Church backed us and would support us. The Chamberlains 'have been condemned without a trial', another Church official was reported to say (*The Sunday Telegraph* 25/10/1981). More information was leaked by the police to New Zealand's Christchurch *Press* at the end of October, suggesting that it was now a pair of scissors that killed Azaria. Cameron assumed that he was in possession of all the facts provided by Dr Kenneth Brown, but he seemed not to have been told everything about the investigation, as we would find out later (Transcript of the First Inquest pp653-679)

Lindy's closest friend, Julie, who called Lindy 'big sister Joybells', now decided she had seen enough of the trauma for her erstwhile childhood friend. Speaking from her home in Ringwood, Victoria, she described Lindy as a fun-loving woman who had a passion for picking up babies and cuddling them. Lindy and Julie, as teenagers, had loved to dress up as men in trousers, suits, top hats and moustaches. On one occasion Julie dressed as a horse and Lindy rode her, Julie told the paper ('The

Lindy I Know', *Melbourne Herald*, (31/10/1981). But the relationship soon fell apart. A close friend of hers had sent private photos of Lindy in a one-piece bathing suit to the newspaper. This morsel of history could hardly be passed up. The publication, at a very sensitive time, brought pandemonium and loathing to our home. Lindy was hostile. She was paranoid that any new information about her would attract a negative interpretation. The bond of trust between the two women was irrevocably destroyed.

I too had become paranoid. Colin Lees was alarmed that my personality was almost unrecogniseable and observed: 'When I first met Michael in 1978 he was the Pastor of the Innisfail Seventh-day Adventish Church. The Church believed and still advocated many years later a healthy lifestyle, incorporating both healthy eating and daily exercise, largely thanks to Michael. He was leading a health and fitness group, running every Sunday and it was suggested that I join this group in an endeavour to combat my high blood pressure.

'Michael was a highly competent and confident young man. He had a way with people and was a good public speaker and leader on a number of topics, including discussions in areas that were not church related.

'Five years later in 1982, Michael enrolled in Avondale College as a post-graduate student. The media frenzy around the Chamberlains had escalated. As part of his post-graduate studies Michael was required to present seminar workshops at local churches. I was astounded at the change in Michael. No longer was he the vibrant, confident man I had known. He was scared of meeting people. The idea of talking in public filled him with dread. He was paranoid, expecting people to treat him with anger and negative comments, I hardly recognised him. I was shocked and wondered if he could ever survive.'

On 2 November 1981, we published a press release to inform the public where we were at. In essence we said: 'Six weeks have now elapsed since the opening of a new inquiry into Azaria's disappearance. So far the reasons for the investigation have baffled us. We have been left in the dark and have no more knowledge than what we read in the newspapers. My graduation from a MA had to be delayed until next year. Lindy also had to drop some subjects in her BA Education degree. We wish to remind certain members of the media and the police that the loss of Azaria had caused great pain and sadness and we take exception to the manipulation and senseless inhumane efforts with speculative reporting by an irresponsible section of the press. Our two boys have had to be sent away for 10 days because of this situation, despite the fact they desperately need their parents.'

John Bryson saw it this way: 'His (Brian Martin, the New Solicitor General's) department would be in charge of any moves to re-open proceedings. Surrounded by TV cameras, he commented no further than to agree he was in Alice Springs. Denis Barritt had been called already to Darwin. Newspaper reports of evidence that Azaria was decapitated were denied. On radio the Chief Minister admitted flying to Ayers Rock on 24 October but refused to say why. Rumours were strong of a Crown application for a fresh inquest, but the Supreme Court notices did not list it.'

Sometime, at a secret location and time, probably mid-November, 1981, Mr Justice Toohey at the Supreme Court of the Northern Territory, heard that application. The Crown's new evidence was produced. It was taken in closed chambers and without notification to our lawyers or us.

Paul Everingham revealed the quashing of the first inquest to the press on 19 November 1981. We found out press on Friday 20 November when two TV channels descended on our home on the same day. The cameras had been rolling even as they approached the house. One was at the front door, the other at the back. They left with nothing to report.

Paul Everingham saw nothing improper about this action to quash the first inquest and reopen the second inquest. Much later, 14 years later in fact, he told *The Northern Territory News*:

'I always acted in an objective fashion, I do not recall being required to take any action in the Chamberlain matter as Chief Minister, although I was involved at one stage as Attorney-General.

'In the circumstances of this matter the Attorney-General properly acted alone without consulting the rest of the Executive because he was acting in his character as Principal Law Officer.

'Other than appearing as the public face of the Government in the matter, my major contact with the Chamberlain case was when I was approached by then Police Commissioner, Mr Peter McAulay with a request that as he was in possession of certain new evidence I should consider applying to the Supreme Court to reopen the inquest.

'As a consequence of that I sought advice from the Solicitor-General, Ian Barker, who referred me to an outside consultant, Des Sturgess.

'After Mr Sturgess had given the matter due consideration he advised me that I should apply to the court to re-open the inquest and that was done.

'Mr Justice John Toohey, then of the Northern Territory Supreme Court, took the decision and the inquest was re-opened.

'I consider that I acted properly as Attorney General in all the circumstances and it is quite clear that a jury and two Appeal Court Benches thought likewise.

'As the first holder of those offices I did everything possible to establish benchmarks of propriety and respect for the law.

'I therefore take exception to the bald statement that 'The Executive Chief Minister and his Cabinet were against the Chamberlains—of that there is no doubt'' (*Northern Territory News*, 23/12/1995).

Erwin Chlanda, an Alice Springs reporter, rang us. He expressed his dismay at our lawyers not being able to be represented at the secret quashing. The *Daily Telegraph* announced the first inquest as 'The inquest that failed', while a Channel 3 helicopter from Newcastle buzzed our home. This seemed to be an increasingly deadly game played by the Northern Territory authorities, designed to outwit and exhaust us, our lawyers, and anyone who might defend our innocence.

Ironically, at the end of October, *The Melbourne Herald* (27/10/1981) devoted a full page to a dog attack on a two-year-old girl named Regan. These canines, described as 'terror dogs...almost ate her alive', according to the baby girl's mother.

6. The Second Inquest: Trial by Ambush

'The forensic criminologists made their memorable comeback, proving beyond doubt that the Australian public had faith in the unseen if it is packaged as science rather than religion.'
Lowell Tarling, *Rolling Stone*, 1984.

The Northern Territory Government and senior police either did not or could not openly admit that a dingo could take a child from an open tent at Ayers Rock. This was despite evidence that in 1977 there had been a report that a dingo did in fact kill a child in the Territory. The police preferred to run with a much more bizarre and unrealistic horror genre theme, influenced no doubt by films in vogue at the time, including *The Exorcist*, *Rosemary's Baby* and *Omen*, where religious-type symbols were associated with supernatural powers. In the raid on our home on 19 September 1981, the police had seized a very old family Bible in our home that had become a collector's edition. The book was taken because one of many wood-cut diagrams was interpreted as significant to the way Lindy might have taken Azaria's life: it illustrated the death of an Old Testament unfortunate, by means of a tent peg to his head.

When two Darwin detectives arrived on the doorstep of Max Whittacker, one of the key eyewitnesses at Ayers Rock on the fateful night, for a second time in late 1981, they began their questioning in a very different and selective manner from their first inquest interview. Mr Whittacker had recounted to Kevin Hitchcock, a Channel 10 investigative reporter, that the detectives had 'mentioned to us that they had been instructed when they left Darwin that they were to dismiss from their minds anything to do with a dingo having taken the child.'('Dingo Case Confession Pressure', *Daily Sun*, 23/07/1981). Quite astonishingly they told Whittacker: 'They mentioned to me that they thought that it would not come to trial, and that they expected an early confession from the Chamberlains.'

I recognised that police and government people working as strategists, think that innocent people might confess to something that did not happen just to get release from the constant harassment. At one stage during the first inquest, a Northern Territory official was alleged to have said: 'If we pour enough pressure on them (the Chamberlains) they will break'. ('Dingo Case Confession Pressure', *Daily Sun*, 23/07/1981).

Following the first inquest, the area and method of investigation was shrouded in secrecy. The result was that the reopened investigation, code-named 'Operation Ochre', made it impossible for us to access any legal information. In a situation involving such heavy government interference and parochialism in a frontier territory, smaller in population than my own City of Lake Macquarie, only a non-adversarial-style inquiry through a Royal Commission could get to the truth. The truth would be that in the heart of their National Park, dingoes are allowed to kill children. There have been many examples of such methods before and since this case, some having made the screen, such as Erin Brockovich, where corporations and governments have been exposed for covering up the truth through fear and greed for the industry dollar.

The glare of the spotlight on us was now spilling onto the Seventh-day Adventist church, and it was starting to feel the heat, me in particular as one of the ministers and so-called 'princes' of the Church. Sociologist Dr Robert Wolfgramm suggested in 1981 that the Chamberlain saga acted as a catalyst to polarise the Australian public by encouraging the highly prejudicial belief that we belonged to a 'crackpot religion'. Our tragedy inadvertently highlighted the mistaken belief that Adventists were 'sectarian 'deviants'' in hiding, or having 'something to hide'. This caused some Church leaders to later describe the year as one of *annus horribilis*. Indeed, the decade would be regarded by many in the Church, especially in Australia, as the most difficult in living memory.

In November 1981, a respected friend and growing confidant, Gordon Hammond and his wife Sally, moved back from Western Australia to live in Sydney. He told me how relieved he had been (like so many other Seventh-day Adventists and Christians, not to mention other people in Australia and New Zealand) when Coroner Barritt verified our account of Azaria's death. Gordon also expressed deep concern that we had not had time to grieve over her death alone and without public interference. He was upset when I told him later that what had happened to me was that my actual memory of Azaria had been almost submerged by the events surrounding the defence of our story in court and elsewhere. I had told him, 'Gordon, I cannot even remember Azaria. I have forgotten what she was like'.

Gordon, like so many others interested in the real nature and behaviour of dingoes, recounted a conversation about how Aboriginals fared with these canines he had with Sergeant Ed Lawtie and his wife Margaret, while stationed at Laverton, West Australia. The Lawties' duties included assisting tribal and traditional Aborigines who lived deep in the interior of that state. Margaret's private conversation with women of one of the tribes about the impact of dingoes on their children revealed that it was a known fact that dingoes had taken their children. Their cultural mores, however, made it a forbidden topic to discuss.

Following the new inquest announcement, a lone voice in the media, Ken Blanch, writing in 'Viewpoint' (*The Sunday Sun* 1/11/1981), criticised Paul Everingham for reopening the case. In doing so, Everingham must now 'bring it to a proper conclusion in the shortest proper time', Blanch wrote. But Everingham wasn't listening. For us, it looked bad and we didn't have a clue how to deal with it.

The second inquest started on Monday 14 December 1981. It was shaping up as a hostile affair. The Northern Territory police and forensic department had received a drubbing from Barritt. Everingham instructed his newly appointed Solicitor-General, Brian Martin, who had replaced

Ian Barker, to re-open the case. The plan was to have all first inquest evidence before this Court in writing only, thus attracting no further media attention to it, and making the new forensic findings and hypotheses the centre stage for the new 'facts'.

Gerry Galvin was appointed. He gave every opportunity for the press to photograph and publicise my car instead of tracking or photographing the dingos of Ayers Rock.

The decision was made to break with convention and allow the press gallery in a crowded court to sit in the jury box. In a further display of unorthodox court procedure, he intended to call Lindy and me as the first witnesses, which was highly unusual if we were defendants later likely to be charged.

More than 50 reporters and photographers, described as 'a barrage of television and still cameras', crowded the jury box and other prime seats. Bill Hitchings, journalist for *The Sun,* was among those who fought for a position; he described Lindy, who was dressed in white as 'my attractive wife'. He wondered whether she or I was ready for a fight. Our potentially expensive, sharper legal team consisted of two new members, Christchurch born and Canterbury University criminology law-trained solicitor, Stuart Tipple and the determined and intuitive Andrew Kirkham from Melbourne to assist Philip Rice QC, our coronial counsel.

The Alice Springs public seemed hostile, and the court felt unfriendly. Desmond Sturgess, the hawk-eyed and hunched Coroner's assistant to Gerry Galvin, presented a foreboding presence in court, to the extent that *The Newcastle Sun* and other papers accorded him the title 'QC' which he did not have.

I overheard Philip Rice say at various times during the first days of this inquest: 'This isn't an inquest... It's a trial and a trial by ambush... We haven't even received a list of witnesses to be called... These people are not playing the game...We're wasting our time here... Let's prepare for trial and get a fair hearing.' Lindy and I dug in, determined not to give another inch, which included being asked to provide her handprints as requested by Professor Cameron in an attempt to compare her hand against dust prints in Azaria's jumpsuit. If they wanted this they would get it, but at the proper time and place.

Rice accused Sturgess of presenting a 'very strong, very dexterous, inquisitorial examination'. I wondered if the second inquest was just a formality? We were given no warning about what was coming and documents were not given to our lawyers until the forensic witnesses appeared at the inquest.

The first inquest coroner, Denis Barritt, was not happy. He wrote a letter of protest to the inquiry, highly critical of how the new inquest came about. A perfectly valid first inquest was quashed, our presence or our lawyer's presence to speak to their perceived Star Chamber action was denied, and as a result, any rights we had to defend ourselves were trampled on. Barritt had been 'ambushed' too: He was given two hours notice to get to the quashing, 1500 kilometres away in Darwin. His understanding was that we as Azaria's parents had a right to attend as well but we had been excluded. ('Azaria; Ex-Coroner Protests. Letter on Hearing', *The Melbourne Herald*, 16/12/1981).

Barritt was aware of the unprecedented amount of hate mail flowing in. Because we were Seventh-day Adventists, and I was an ordained pastor, there was reason enough according to some press reports, to link Azaria's death with sacrificial ritual and witchcraft. Letters threatening our lives were sent to our home, to the police, and to the courthouse 'in such volumes that police later used wheel-barrows to move them about,' Bryson reported ('The inquisition faced by the Chamberlains', *The Age*, 10/9/1983). The levels of notoriety, rumour and misreporting so concerned the first Coroner that he had agreed to telecast his findings, on condition that they not be edited or rearranged.

John Bryson commented: 'There was no other case in which two coroners used such dissimilar and unusual procedures when inquiring into the same death' ('The inquisition faced by the Chamberlains' *The Age*, 10/9/1983). Galvin took a back seat and allowed Sturgess to control the inquest and to come into frequent clashes with Rice and Kirkham. Bryson again astutely observed:

'Mr Sturgess was a senior barrister from Brisbane, whose courtroom stance often resulted in the lectern supporting much of his weight. It was a mistake to confuse that posture with nonchalance. There was interest in the courtroom; in the way Sturgess would handle Sally Lowe because her evidence was so unfavourable to the Crown and critical to our case. Four minutes into her evidence, Rice stood to make his first objection. As he hitched his trousers the copious folds in those trousers seemed to attract the cartoonist, Horner, who was then sketching them from the back of the court. Rice was a man of wit and charm also. His first protest was made obliquely. 'I will make an observation that might help the general conduct of proceedings before your Worship,' he said. 'The usual procedures are not being followed.''

The problem was that Lindy and I had not yet received an outline of the evidence, or a list of the witnesses.

'We are shadow-sparring,' Rice complained. 'Mr Sturgess is proposing, for reasons best known to the authorities who instruct him, to simply call witnesses without giving a summary, even to your Worship at this stage, of the nature or extent or of their purpose in being called.'

'Mr Sturgess?' the Coroner said. 'I will bear that in mind, and see what I can do.'

Bryson observed: 'In the normal course of the inquest, those who may be in jeopardy of trial are first shown proofs of the evidence against them. After all that evidence is heard, they may be asked to testify themselves. If Mr Rice and Mr Kirkham were wondering how much information they might be given before each new witness entered the box, the answer was not long coming.' ('The inquisition faced by the Chamberlains' *The Age*, 10/9/1983).

Sturgess turned to summon his next witness. 'Call Michael Leigh Chamberlain,' he said. Kirkham was on his feet, 'We object to the calling of Mr Chamberlain at this point. Mr and Mrs Chamberlain, in certain circumstances, have rights in these proceedings as to whether or not to give evidence. It can only be a real choice if it is known what evidence is going to be called.' Kirkham stated his recollection of a Supreme Court judgment, which had recently confirmed that principle. A copy was on its way from Melbourne. He had sent for it at 9.30am the day before. Bryson found this interesting.

'Andrew Kirkham's face was capable of wonderful innocence, but he had been a barrister a long time and had, evidently, some early suspicion this might happen. Mr Kirkham's documents had not yet arrived.' ('The inquisition faced by the Chamberlains,' *The Age*, 10/9/1983).

Sturgess leaned further over the lectern. 'This is a totally unparalleled application,' he said. He intended to call us forthwith. Scientific evidence would then follow. If we wished to claim privilege against self-incrimination, we must announce our choice now. Of course this would further play into the media's hands and increase our chances of being further negatively portrayed by them. Sturgess continued: 'I am subject to your Worship's direction, but apart from that, I control who shall be called and when they shall be called, and the order in which the evidence is presented.' By lunchtime, some radio stations had already got this exchange wrong. They were reporting that I had claimed privilege, refusing to give evidence at all, on grounds of self-incrimination.

Philip Rice QC, alarmed at where the Court was heading, continued his interjections. He warned Sturgess and Galvin that putting us on the stand was against natural justice unless we were to be charged, in which event, the case should proceed to trial. This would have subverted the Northern Territory's planned showcase of forensic evidence used to quash the first inquest. The drip-feed to the press of the new coronial evidence, in the attempt to make the public de facto judge and jury, now had to have an authoritative voice and authentic ring, through this inquest. The media build-up of the purported new evidence had caused the Australian public to at best look at us now as poor misguided fools or at worst as heinous baby killers, full of deceit and guile. Probably 90 per cent of Australians might have thought: 'Why have an inquest? Remand them in custody and send them to trial immediately.' Phil Rice shook his head in despair and anger at the Coroner's assistant's approach to the inquest proceedings. ('Azaria: Lawyers clash', *Melbourne Herald*, 15/12/1981).

I gave evidence despite the improper order of witnesses and the examining continued for four hours, while Rice and Kirkham continued to protest the unfair style of questioning. 'This is cross-examination,' Mr Rice complained. It was a point with which Justice Muirhead at the trial would later agree. But Galvin would not retreat.

'I see no reason to change the ruling,' Mr Galvin said, 'or the nature of the question. I do not feel I am doing anything wrong.'

I had no problem allowing Sturgess to examine my actions at the Rock and the reasons for our eventually leaving. Sturgess focused on people who may have bled in my car and I gave him a very complete answer with one exception: I could not remember the name of the young man who had rolled his car and injured his head on the Cairns Highway in 1979. This seemed to be the vital explanation for any concerns of possible blood residue left in the vehicle and it vexed me not to recall the man's name. After more questions about my movements between Sunday evening and Tuesday, when the police, after telling us nothing, had suggested we go home on the basis that there was nothing more constructive we could do in staying there. Sturgess then turned to my car-cleaning habits. Although he was in a deadly serious mode, I was laughing inside. Sturgess tried to portray me as someone who cleaned the car and its carpet so fastidiously that I had something to hide. The reality was that vacuuming and using a little soap and Armoral, a vinyl sheen product, was about the extent of my interior cleaning. I was a bit embarrassed about this, if only because I had been shown up as a lazy cleaner.

The document Kirkham had summoned from Melbourne finally arrived and, though late, was handed up to the bench. It was Alexander's Case. Referring to an inquest in Victoria, Mr Justice Gray had said this: 'I am somewhat surprised at the course of events in this case because, to my knowledge, there has been a long-standing practice in the Coroner's Court not to call a witness who is likely to be implicated in a serious crime...It is in my opinion a wise practice.' Here was revealed a serious implication for the administration of justice in coronial courts. 'Those who were very much under suspicion of a grave crime,' as Mr Justice Muirhead later described us, should be called last, when the allegations against them were known. 'Otherwise, the privilege against self-incrimination favours only the guilty, for they know better than others what evidence they may have to face. As things presently stand, a witness who stays silent, whether innocent or not, seems to be guilty. We should be trying to achieve precisely the opposite.'

Gerry Galvin understood the dilemma posed by this mode of inquiry. He referred to it often. His duties were conflicting. He must hear relevant evidence, but he should not allow public prejudice to influence the minds of future jurors. And he must do this while the nation hangs on every word. It was a problem no one was able to solve. Galvin took the course offered by Des Sturgess. It is the right of the Coroner to be guided by the counsel assisting, since there are no rules that must be strictly followed. Was this an example of how it worked in the Northern Territory?

On the lead up to the second inquest, Bryson's analysis was incisive. 'After the first inquest into the death of Azaria, the Chamberlains were suddenly refused any further knowledge purported to have been discovered about her death. Of the secret quashing of the first inquest their lawyers were refused any information or representation. Likewise, the first inquest Coroner was refused any information or representation. The Chamberlains and their lawyers were refused any information on the London pathologist's spurious evidence that quashed that inquest by suggesting that there was evidence of a bloodied handprint on the back of Azaria's jumpsuit, or that in his opinion Azaria had been decapitated. The Chief Minister forbade this pathologist to speak to the Chamberlain's lawyers.' ('Police investigation and management of potential evidence. Natural Injustice: The manipulation of evidence in the Azaria Chamberlain case').

Jim Oram, writing for *The Daily Mirror* and *The Australian* (16/12/1981), believed I had 'shown astonishing strength in coping...in a coldly precise atmosphere of the Alice Springs Courtroom...with one of the most bizarre, tragic and public mysteries in Australian history.' I was facing stifling cynicism in an atmosphere of persistent disbelief so, even with right on my side, I had to deal with it in the way I knew best. It certainly did not stop my tears when I saw my daughter's jumpsuit with the pooling of an estimated 75–80 ml of blood around her neck area and on her singlet. Although overwhelmed by the new evidence, a few stalwart friends had helped us to process the maze of incongruous evidence from the new forensic scientists. My brother, Peter, could not handle it and fled the scene. My best friend Colin Lees was stoic.

The headlines kept coming and looked dreadful: 'Blood in the car'; 'Handprint' on the jumpsuit; 'Foetal blood' on the carpet; a 'spray under the dashboard'; 'a throat cut by a scissors'; 'blood stains on a knife' and on the camera bag. All this 'evidence' came within a day or two from the prestigious London authority, Professor Cameron and the eloquent Joy Kul from the NSW Health Department. This was what the Northern Territory Government had been gloating over. My 'screaming yellow' car, as described by James Oram (*The Australian* 18/12/1981) was now rolled out as some slain evil monster in the Alice Springs police compound. I saw the smugness on the faces of some of the Territory's officials. According to the police, our destruction was nigh. The night of the cry from Lindy: 'That dingo's got my baby' was sublimated by our new darkest hour of being called liars and murderers of our own daughter. I knew it was all a tissue of incredible forensic lies.

A newspaper clip (from an anonymous source, as usual) had arrived in our mail. It read: 'Dingo Puzzle: Who disposed of the body?' Overprinted on Lindy's face were the words, 'It was no dingo, only a two-legged one! You look what you are!'

Perhaps this was the greatest moment for the Northern Territory Chief Minister in the case, with it now accelerating to fever pitch. Retired Brisbane barrister, Dan Casey, 'generally regarded as the finest criminal lawyer to practise in Queensland' suggested that this headline alone would have set the stage for significant prejudice. 'The abhorrence that enters your mind would force some kind of prejudice,' he said in the *Sunday Mail.*

We knew that the second part of this inquest, commencing in Alice Springs, February 1982, was going to be gruelling. My legal team was sick of the continuing adverse publicity. So, as we got off the plane at Alice Springs, Peter Dean, my original first inquest solicitor, and his old friend Paul Brann, the manager of Ansett Industries, devised a strategy. It might have been foolhardy but it was going to be exciting. Because the media had always seemed to be one step ahead of us, Brann organised a car to lift us directly from the tarmac departure gate, adjacent to the plane. In front of our vehicle, a rather underpowered luxury Japanese station wagon, was an airport security van that he had arranged to pull up beside the plane. We took our lumbering vehicles up the tarmac airstrip and slid out the aero-club gates. The press raced for their cars, trying to block off the exit. Unbeknown to the media hounds behind us, we had obtained permission to go through the restricted Australian Air Force gates, conveniently banned to the media.

Just as we were congratulating ourselves on leading our pursuers astray, the press cars raced into view again. They were faster than us and caught up like Red Indians about to scalp a stagecoach full of defenceless women—and there were ten of them!

Heading for our motel no longer seemed to be a good idea. Stuart Tipple was having an anxiety attack about more bad press, so we dropped him off at the Alice Springs Casino. Peter and Paul looked at each other, and then looked at us. A phone call was made and Peter began to smirk.

'Well, are you up for it?'

Lindy and I grinned, 'Why not!'

We now drove down the back lane of Peter's office, very slowly. We were stalling for time. Like lambs, the press followed us, all ten of them. There was a second phone call, 'We're ready,' a woman replied calmly.

Peter jumped out of the vehicle and raced to the back of his office and out of sight. Paul drove off at a leisurely pace and gave us a sightseeing tour of some of the most boring streets in Alice Springs. The paparazzi followed and the trap was set.

Paul and his wife Barbara were the co-conspirators. Suddenly, we were at our destination.

'Are they still behind us?' Paul asked.

I turned to examine the glistening white Fords and Holdens behind me, now coated in a thin film of Alice dust. I counted ten cars. 'I think they're all in,' I replied. The lane we had entered was very narrow; much of it lined with high corrugated iron fences, providing a prison-like effect. The air was still and the heat stifling. We were about to trap the unsuspecting paparazzi. Suddenly, a large four-wheel drive vehicle slipped mysteriously out of nowhere like a giant green conger eel, and blocked the end of the lane in front of us. We stopped in front of a narrow gate neatly camouflaged in a corrugated-iron fence. Before the press could jump out of their vehicles we had escaped the predators, locking them in to the lane way. The press emerged from their 40 degree heated chariots like killer bees just as another vehicle moved in behind them to close off their escape route. We slipped through an air-conditioned house, lingering a moment to lower our own temperatures, and then out to a waiting car in the next street. We could hear the paparazzi freely practising their expletives and threatening blue murder.

We drove directly to the motel. The press were left in limbo and knew not where we had gone, this time. There were none of the headlines that Stuart had dreaded. A later report suggested that the media wanted to lay complaints about their right to 'freedom of the press'. But the incident would be the last happy memory of having freedom from the press for a very long time.

With our car supposedly 'awash with foetal blood', according to Joy Kuhl, 2HD radio Newcastle proclaimed: 'When the trial goes to court, the world might find out just why Lindy Chamberlain cut the throat of her tiny daughter'. It was because of the feeling of the general population, that Lindy had killed Azaria, that this radio station felt immune from the defamatory consequences of broadcasting it.

Malcolm Brown offered a concise comparison between the two inquests. 'The first inquest was about dingoes,' Brown said, 'this one is about blood.' Joy Kuhl's 22 examples of foetal blood evidence she had tested and discovered all over the front of the car had persuaded Galvin single handedly. No new dingo evidence was allowed.

Joy Kuhl said that she had once visited Avondale College to see where we lived at 17 College Drive. She had never called in to say hello or anything as personal as this. Joy Kuhl had only visited to get some objective context to see what we lived like. At the second inquest where she made a sensational debut with her unbelievable findings in my car, she demonstrated her skills with an audience. She could clip across concrete floors on high heels in a pink dress and stark white handbag with the aplomb of a princess. She looked excited and confident. She would be the perfect witness before a jury.

The juggernaut of Crown forensic investigators and their desired outcomes were now clearly seen by all. *Australasian Spartacist* concluded that Sturgess 'had earned his laurels' in successfully 'setting up the murder charges against Lindy'. We knew that the Crown's light at the end of the tunnel was a freight train packed full of scientific lies. We had spoken but had not been heard. It was once again a time to remain silent. We now had to wait for our day in another court. Desmond Sturgess, renowned as a defence legal counsel, would for the first time turn prosecutor.

At the time we didn't know that our case was the last one in the Northern Territory where a Coroner could charge witnesses in an Inquest, without referring it first to the public prosecutor. And so what proceeded next was eerie. We were neither arrested or handcuffed, nor fingerprinted. We were not remanded in custody. We were simply bailed for the inconsequential sum of $5,000 each.

We did not have to report to the police at any time. We simply had to front up to the Alice Springs Supreme Court in April, later that year. Did they hope we were about to abscond? They wished! We could not bear to think about what would come next.

7. The Trial of the Century

Returning home after the second inquest was not as dreadful as it could have been. Word had got around that the Northern Territory had shafted us. Forensic science had been enthroned as primary evidence and the sole arbiter of truth. None of the evidence from Ayers Rock first inquest witnesses next to us at the campsite, or the evidence of the Aboriginal trackers of finding dingo tracks carrying a load away from our tent, was given any consideration at the second inquest.

Several key witnesses, including a senior detective sergeant who was the first police officer at Ayers Rock along with Michael Gilroy, were also not called by either side.

Everingham told the media 'in the interests of justice and fair play' that there should now be no further comment on the Chamberlain case until the trial. (*The West Australian*, 4/2/1982). But my mother, Greta Chamberlain, was not about to stay quiet. In answer to a Christchurch journalist she replied. 'Our defence will now have the right to bring all the witnesses to identify that a dingo took the baby as the first Coroner found.' (*Christchurch Star*, 3/2/1982). Such family defence was encouraging. If your parents don't support you and believe in you, then you have just received the most telling indictment. On that basis, not one relation of either the Chamberlain or Murchison families, whether represented in Australia, New Zealand, the United Kingdom or the United States, would have said anything other than: 'We believe these people to be innocent,

Your Honour, so help me God.'

The Master of Arts degree graduation in which I should have been a participant had come and gone. The macabre events leading up to the second inquest had squashed any hope of that. Now I had the task, if I wanted to grapple with it, to go on and finish the degree with a merciful six months extension to complete a thesis of some 80,000 words.

What became my biggest challenge now was to sideline my furious feelings and trial dread. I spent much of my time in the eucalypt forest behind our large rambling old white house where I could walk, on the Avondale College estate, unseen and unhindered and also run every day. I had to try to clear my mind of paranoia and pre-trial jitters and wipe away anything that would wreck my coherence in thesis writing.

There were growing concerns that we would not get a fair trial. Justice must now 'be seen to be done' was the theme of *The Australian*, (4/2/1982). As the result of a trial by media exposure, selecting a jury would be an 'extremely difficult' proposition. The editor defended the media's involvement with the curious argument that the first inquest media TV coverage had been the catalyst for the second inquest that exposed the first inquest's 'incongruities', according to the Northern Territory Chief Minister. It was now a chance for 'the police to have a go' but the editorial recognised that even if we were cleared, we 'would bear a stigma'. Even the normally non-political and ultra-conservative Adventist Church magazine, *The Australasian Church Record* in an editorial headlined, 'Trial by Media' (8/2/1982) revealed sceptism about Paul Everingham's very public involvement in the case, as if by a politician.

Everingham, on the back foot, accused us of seeking media attention and even going out of our way to get it (*The Adelaide Advertiser*, 2/2/1982). My response to Everingham would have been: 'Place yourself in our situation. If you had lost your daughter and were now treated as the villain rather than the innocent victim and bystander, would you have run and hid when an imperative message had to be sounded? Well, we're back and we won't shut up any more than the Australian Journalist Association on the 'Balibo Five' journalists' murders in East Timor. Just as for them, we have the right to protest until the justice wheel has turned full circle.'

Another blow for the Church was struck when the South Pacific Adventist's Public Relations Director, Russell Kranz, appeared in the *Perth Independent* (14/2/1982) using an article abridged from 'The Chamberlain's Church'. *The Sun Herald* claimed that Adventism gave us courage to continue on. Our case provided an opportunity to air the views of minority religious beliefs and to fire a shot across the bows of those who dismissed the Church as just another cult. Immense annoyance had been created inside Adventism with it being confused with the no blood transfusion organisation of Jehovah's Witnesses. To counter this confused thinking, it was made known that the Church operated hundreds of hospitals and medical clinics worldwide and not one of them would refuse to give blood to a patient in need. Despite the terrible position we were in, the Church administration saw it as a free advertisement for communicating the proud lifestyle and beliefs of Adventists.

On the other less savoury front 'Benelong' (*The Sunday Telegraph*, 14/3/1982) revealed that a 'Paddington Guitar Flogger' was collecting jokes for his book on Azaria's death. The media was not only dehumanising Azaria, in calling her 'the dingo baby', but now Lindy was 'the dingo mother'.

Lindy and I plucked ourselves out of Cooranbong for a week's break, courtesy of Dr and Mrs Brian Hammond, Gordon's parents, at a secret location. We had the large house to ourselves and occasionally ducked out to do some local grocery shopping while maximising our time swimming at the beach. It was a holiday overdue before I hit the research for the MA thesis. The boys spent alot of time with Lindy's parents at Cooranbong. We were relaxed enough to get our fervent wish about adding another daughter to our family around November. Because the trial would be in April, Lindy would be able to disguise the impending birth of our new child. We knew it was a tricky situation. The media would take it any way they wanted, but we were determined to keep it a secret.

The plans changed however. The Northern Territory, through the prosecution's request, switched the trial from 19 April to 13 September, at Darwin. Their reason was that an Alice Springs jury might be too parochial and come with preconceived and biased opinions.

Philip Rice was not available for this trial, so we looked further afield. The Good Weekend, *Sydney Morning Herald*, (20/3/1982) reported that we had retained 'gentleman lawyer' John Harbor Phillips, aged 46, a Melbourne QC who had conducted 150 murder trials as a criminal defence lawyer. Billed as 'the big one', our trial was originally considered to be run by Des Sturgess, described as 'a very strong, sharp and determined' cross-examiner for the prosecution. John Phillips, on the other hand, did not engage in 'terror-like, bully tactics', it was claimed. Saturday Magazine, (Brisbane) *Courier-Mail*, (27/3/1982).

On 8 April 1982, I slipped away from Cooranbong at dawn en route to Cairns. I was on a secret mission and had to be alone The purpose was to try and explain the huge question mark over my car's detainment in Alice Springs and the mysterious appearance of 'foetal blood'.

It reached back to a balmy Cairns' afternoon in 1979 when Lindy and I, with the boys, were returning from a beach trip north of the city. About 70 kilometres from Cairns as we rounded a bend of national Pacific Highway we came across a strange sight. Before us was a smashed-up purple Holden HQ panel van and a bloodied male staggering over the rocks to the ocean, apparently to wash the coursing blood from his head. A gathering crowd watched, spellbound as to what the driver, Keyth Lenehan, would do next. Lindy and I took one look at the dazed man, and both armed with first aid certificate knowledge, jumped out of our car to assist. We had to quickly organise a one-lane road closure and then go to the rescue of the victim to prevent him from falling off the rocks into the sea and drowning, then cautiously carry him back to our vehicle

The crowd stood motionless as they watched us do our work to stabilise him, and bandage his wounds with an emergency first aid kit. I hastily photographed his damaged vehicle for the record and sped off with the injured man lying down in the back of our yellow Torana. Lindy nursed his head, which was still oozing blood through his bandages. To prevent any mess, we used several blankets to stem any blood flow onto the seats or carpets. We saw no transference at the time, but we could not be sure. One thing we had not calculated was that in our context, no good deed in this world goes unpunished.

The journey was swift with hazard lights flashing and we reached speeds up to 160kph. We hoped to intercept the police but there was no sign of them. The hospital received Lenehan and his parents were notified. I recorded this event in a *Cairns Post* column, 'The Good Life' (20/6/1979). The general ignorance and rubber necking displayed at that accident site led me to write about the need for more first aid certificated persons. In a medical emergency your intervention might help save a life, I wrote.

It was with considerable difficulty that, on 13 April 1982, I tracked down Keyth Lenehan. I had spent three days trying to find him, but I had no leads until an hour before I was forced to leave, due to a cyclone advancing on the city. Lenehan had been expecting us, he said, after he heard about our problems with the police over the Torana. I obtained an affidavit concerning his rescue and on the possibility that blood had seeped down the seat or on to our carpet.

By 7 June, 1982, the media had somehow got news of Lindy's pregnancy. It came, they said, from 'the family', which meant it was her parents. True, we had prayed for, and knew that we had, a girl. We had gone to an ultra-sound clinic in Newcastle to have it confirmed that indeed our greatest wish had been granted. Lindy was carrying a healthy little girl! Those who loved us were ecstatic; those who thought evil of us were horrified. Steve Brien reported that we were planning to call her 'Azalea' or 'Athalia'. But those seeking to be judge and jury had missed the point. It would have been a very brave and foolish man who would seek to have another child with a woman he thought had killed his first cherished daughter. As *Rolling Stone* writer and Adventist Church critic Lowell Tarling observed:

'It's almost unthinkable that a normal, clean-living clergyman and Justice of the Peace could not only cover up for a wife but then give her more to carve up...This was his strongest testimony and something that could not register even one point in the judicial system of a nation.' (*Spectrum*, Vol. 15, No. 3).

About this time a 'purebred dingo' made headlines in a West Australian newspaper, when it mauled Toni Plumb, a four-year-old girl at Barcaldine,

Western Queensland. It was described as 'almost a horrible reenactment of the tragic Azaria Chamberlain case', where, according to her mother Louise Plumb, 'a placid pet (had) turned devil.' The dingo, Mrs Plumb said, 'was all mouth' and 'big enough to grasp a baby by its head'.

Mail kept pouring in, much of it very supportive, some of it with small donations. There was little we could do to acknowledge it all, even some of it, so overwhelmed had we become with pre-trial preparation. Some of the mail could not have been answered even if that was our inclination. It came from thrill-seekers and the obscene element of the community, 20 letters were coarse and full of unrepeatable material, while others were simply illiterate scribblings.

At 5am on Sunday, 5 September, Lindy and I left Aidan and Reagan in a sleepy state in their beds, to be cared for by Lindy's parents. It was a painful goodbye. We would not see them for nine weeks and not knowing the trial outcome, it might be years. We had made no plans. We simply did not believe we could lose the trial.

We flew to Darwin via Brisbane and Alice Springs on an Ansett jet. Lindy was feeling sick for most of the journey. We were informed that Des Sturgess and NT Registrar, Phillip le Fevre, were on board but at the other end, in first class. We sat at the back of the plane, all in a class of our own. Our lawyer, Stuart Tipple, described the various witness statements to be presented at the upcoming trial. The air hostess, feeling generous, gave us more chocolates than we could eat. The plane was peppered with media, some we recognised from the second inquest. The suspense was awful and I tried to imagine myself on a journey somewhere else for the day.

Our lawyers had planned our arrival early so that we could be thoroughly briefed and be installed in our new quarters at the Seventh-day Adventist residence, less than a kilometre from the Supreme Court. There were no jostling reporters, no TV cameras restricting our physical movement, not to mention our facial expressions. The minister, Pastor Graeme Olsen, was an ex-police detective who knew the Adelaide forensic triumvirate, especially Sergeant Cox for whom he had worked and had an uncomfortably high regard. Darwin Church members, Darryl Kum Yuen and Gordon Feitz were also at the airport and made us feel very welcome in an otherwise surreal situation. We were whisked away in a matter of seconds before bewildered airport onlookers. I recorded our new home was 'quiet and humble'. It was originally the minister's fowl house and had been painted a disgusting lime green, with little air and no air-conditioning.

Graeme Olsen seemed to be 'our man in Darwin' by the way he fielded telephone calls from *The Daily Mirror*, AAP, and many others. Reporters wanted to know where we were penned up. Graeme apparently told them nothing. But a couple of days in and we were feeling so cooped up in our cramped conditions that it felt very much like our prelude to prison. Gone was the Travel Lodge Motel with bodyguards. We ate in the house but most of our time eked out an existence in the hen house. No running anywhere, walking or shopping. Even getting to church would be a problem. It seemed to be the wish of the local minister.

Sturgess announced that the trial would be extended from four to seven weeks. Our legal team had nothing to do with the extension and viewed it with scepticism. The new QC for the prosecution, Ian Barker, offered a cherry—a private bodyguard. We rejected this for two reasons. It would look bad, and remembering the previous bodyguard Frank Gibson, the senior constable who admitted he was a plant and had defected to our side, we didn't want to take any other risks like this, so we chose to go it alone and take what came. One request that our attorneys did advise us was to allow a studio photo for TV and newspaper groups of which only Channel 7 and the Murdoch press (*Northern Territory News*) attended. We also got word that Charlwood's verballing of Lindy in an unofficial 'secret interview' with a hidden tape recorder strapped to his leg, during a car trip from Cooranbong to Toronto police station on 19 September 1981 was inadmissible, as was the *Woman's Day* article for September 1980. Since 1980, we believed that the police had monitored and taped every phone call we had ever made. The phone was impossible to speak on and sometimes cut out after 15 seconds, especially when we were making long distance calls.

I asked Graeme Olsen to take me out to Berrimah Prison just in case one of us might be wrongfully convicted, because the thought was keeping me awake at night. 'It's just like a motel,' Olsen chirped. 'Never mind, you don't have to be so negative.' He seemed to assume we were already going there. Unforgettable was the Berrimah Abattoirs 200 metres upwind from the jail. The blood-curdling screams of pigs as they met their end in the slaughterhouse, the disgusting smell of putrefied blood, entrails and death as it wafted across the female prison section was an added incentive to stay away from this place of foreboding.

The week before the trial started, while talking to Stuart Tipple, I began to realise that I wasn't coping at all well. When analysing a police witness testimony I swore. That may not been a big deal for the average Aussie, but Seventh-day Adventist ministers don't do that. Seventh-day Adventist churches and schools abhor it. I knew I should have apologised to Stuart for this intemperance, but decided against it. Besides I really meant it and I might find other expletives to use, so an apology might sound hypercritical. The room suddenly felt cold. I thought Stuart appeared reflective but perhaps I had driven his own mind to take cover under the blanket of my despair.

Being separated from my two boys didn't help my frustration, despite being away only three days. Avis Murchison, Lindy's mother, would take care of them, but as a very strict vegetarian she was zealous about what the children could and could not eat. I wasn't sure how Aidan and Reagan would go on a diet of predominantly raw vegetables. Our attitude to Adventist belief and lifestyle was a little more moderate. Lindy's dress sense, which, while stylish on many occasions, was always bound to get church members talking. 'Dear God,' I cried inside: 'How will I go being away from them for up to ten weeks?'

The Sabbath arrived and I went to Church, as was my custom. The media were visible now. They had either followed us or had staked us out and at least one camera was visible through bamboo bushes across the other side of the road. I walked through the Church's plain glass doors, escorted by Darryl Kum Yuen, Gordon Feitz and another friend. They felt they were on a mission and a bit of an adventure, I guess. They kept me informed of all the media activity during the service and the lurking paparazzi, of which I recognised nearly half. On the way, we foiled at least two long telephoto lenses from snapping us. I suspected they would paint me as a hypocrite going to Church. Now these pests were obviously setting up a stake out and would probably pass a note to me pleading for just one photograph to keep their editors happy. On the way out we went quietly. The price we had to pay was to endure the staccato-like clicking of many Nikon motor drives. I pretended to be oblivious to them.

On Sunday morning, 12 September, I awoke at 4.45am. In just a few days the ordeal would begin. Not feeling particularly well, I jogged a nine-kilometre lap around the city. It felt surreal, like a scene from the futuristic sci-fi classic *BladeRunner*. I saw a few people staggering home from a big night out at the disco, club or whatever. Graeme Olsen drove behind me, which was his custom every time I left for some exercise. I did feel a little more secure, but I was also wondering if he thought I would do a real runner, a result of our third world living conditions, the two small rooms with their sickly pale green paint and dull flickering fluoro lights. I thought of Lindy now seven months pregnant and showing. She was uncomfortable and more cranky than usual and it was not hard to get into an argument with her. I tried to remain calm by reminding myself that despite being the most challenging seven weeks of our lives, we stood before God and had nothing to fear. We would overcome and go home as free people.

Over and over again my subconscious was casting up the words: 'There is nothing to fear if truth be allowed to be seen.' I was not with Lindy when she saw the dingo and while I had no doubts about her recounting the truth, I just wasn't there at that moment and had to accept that I could not say I saw it also. A dingo had taken Azaria from us and she is no more. No one can return her here except by some impossible event. I was over asking why we had been dealt this fatal hand. But being tired of asking did not mean I was giving up on the search for meaning. Could I remain resolute and strong in waiting for the answers? I felt I was on the front line, bearing an unrelenting attack on our credibility and the Church, but for what: as pawns of politics and the mighty tourism dollar?

8. Collateral Damage

The fact is, as we said at the beginning of our discussion, that the aspiring speaker needs no knowledge of truth about what is right or good...In courts of justice no attention is paid whatever to the truth about such topics; all that matters is plausibility...Never mind the truth—pursue probability through thick and thin in every kind of speech; the whole secret of the art of speaking lies in consistent adherence to this principle. Plato, Phaedrus 272.

Early on the morning of 13 September, 1982, Avis and Cliff Murchison sent us some Old Testament words of admonition from Exodus: 'Now therefore go and I will be thy mouth and teach thee what thou shalt say.' It was complemented by the Psalmist's counsel: 'For the Lord will help me; therefore I will not be confounded: Therefore have I set my face like flint, and I know I shall not be ashamed.' I felt somewhat fortified by this knowledge but being more conversant with the New Testament would have liked my strength to be drawn from there. I was grateful nevertheless. Second inquest coroner Gerry Galvin had made the unprecedented decision to allow the media in the jury's seats to closely scrutiny of us; now the trial would become another arena for Everingham, with a special media room set up with four closed circuit TV sets, costing $20,000 and another first for Australia (*Time*, 1/11/1982).

Under challenge by the Territory's Crown Law Department, we, the defendants, faced a major problem: legal aid. We had fewer resources and less money to fight our case. Much less. We had to pay for our own preparation and defence. The Northern Territory would not and had no intention to pay for any of our preparation for the Darwin trial.

Greg Cavenagh, our Darwin connection solicitor, drove us to the destination in a solemn but assuring mood. 'Look straight ahead and hold your head high,' he said. I could see a crowd of people ahead. It looked as though many police were present and another barricade had been set up outside the Darwin Supreme Court. At 9.38am we arrived for the 10am commencement. We walked up its steps in a daze, not knowing what to expect. The barrage of media were all demanding attention, none of them wanting to give us passage through the imposing gaping doorway. There was a flurry of TV cameras; cameramen raced with comical haste up the stairs in their moment of power and control. The physical energy expended would have done credit to an Olympian. It felt like a nasty dream; so unnecessary and stupid. But that feeling was immediately replaced by the solemnity of the Court at 9.45am, when we sat down heard the words 'Regina vs. the Chamberlains'. THE QUEEN VS MICHAEL AND LINDY CHAMBERLAIN!

Selecting a jury was fraught with danger. Our grave disadvantage was that Ian Barker and his prosecution team were hometown boys. They would know the who's who of the community and be tuned into the mindset of many of the potential jurors. Darwin, while not Alice Springs, was still a small parochial city capable of being whipped up by spin from people in power around the town, or with an agenda. The Territory population of just 160,000 had most of them, 100,000, clustered around Darwin. Twelve jurors, nine men and three women, were chosen. Every one either had personal contacts or were the friends of politicians, police or government officials. We were able to weed out a few worrying persons from the jury, using our legal connections and other friends in the community, but our team was far behind the eight ball when it came to a comprehensive knowledge of the jury names. I think we were able to profile about half of them. The real question would hang on their parochialism and reverence for the Northern Territory's protected underdog tourist icon—the dingo.

Acting Chief Justice James (Jim) Muirhead, draped in a crimson robe, arrived at exactly 10.03am. The packed Number One Court of 120 people rose as Justice Muirhead entered. The sombre moment matched the austere wood-panelled surroundings. It would allow unprecedented publicity, the TV monitors directly relaying the proceedings to an adjacent building filled with media.

Muirhead was the son of a South Australian Police Magistrate, and a former infantryman and Judge in Papua New Guinea. Appointed the First Director of the Australian Institute of Criminology in Canberra in 1972, Muirhead joined the Northern Territory bench in 1974 and became a Federal Court Judge of Australia.

The Crown suffered its first blow when it was told it could not use the evidence taken from us at the second inquest driven by Des Sturgess. Mr Justice Muirhead ruled that it was unfairly taken. While our evidence was given voluntarily, and according to law, Justice Muirhead thought two things had interfered unfairly with our ability to choose whether or not we should give it at all. The first was the unusual secrecy with which the Crown treated the evidence to be heard against us. The second was the likelihood of irremediable public prejudice should they choose to remain silent. Bryson put the nagging question in retrospect: 'What were the prospects of (the Chamberlains) receiving a fair trial by an unprejudiced jury in the Northern Territory according to law?' ('The inquisition faced by the Chamberlains' *The Age* 10/9/1983).

Our expectations of justice in this trial was short-lived. I had to bite my tongue as the former Northern Territory Solicitor-General, Ian Barker QC, launched into brutal questioning. He stunned the hushed Court with the accusation that Lindy was a 'fanciful liar', who had violently murdered her baby. None of the children could have possibly done it or anyone else for that matter, according to Barker. He argued it was Lindy and Lindy only. As for me, I was purported to be a clever cover-up agent, following the discovery of her 'crime' and that was equally difficult for me to stomach. Was I missing something here?

But our own lead QC, John Phillips, was on cloud nine when he saw the battle lines drawn up. I tried to fortify myself with the words of

W.K. Clifford, the British mathematician, scientist and philosopher: 'It is wrong always, everywhere and for everyone to believe anything upon insufficient evidence.'

'Now I don't contend ladies and gentlemen, that dingoes are gentle creatures, nor do I contend they are never dangerous, but what we do know as Australians... is that they are not notorious man-eaters...you are entitled to take account of your general knowledge and common sense in a case like this, and if your general knowledge tells you that dingoes are not known as a species for killing and eating human beings, then you can take all that into account in deciding the likelihood of the truth of the dingo theory.'

It was a very, very cruel day for Lindy, emotionally and physically. Her seat was not designed for pregnant women and people who saw this were either extremely sympathetic or horrible with their gossiping tongues. At least the guards who flanked us were courteous and helpful. Lindy would eventually obtain two pillows to ease her discomfort, but the assistance came from Correctional Services.

There were no prizes for guessing what we felt when we arrived back at our 'fowl house'. Yes, we were given cool drinks and it was suggested that it was only 'early days', but I was in a state of shock. The media were impressed with Ian Barker. I overheard one journalist describe him as 'as cunning as a rat'. There was no prima-facie evidence in this case to prove guilt. Barker said himself that his case would be circumstantial, built like a 'bundle of sticks'.

'You see it is the totality of the evidence which gives this case its strength. I don't like using metaphors, but it's not a chain where the loss of one link is going to destroy the chain. It's rather the proverbial bundle of sticks which derives its strength from the totality of the bundle rather than from each of its component sticks. And it all adds up if you consider it as a whole.' (Supreme Court, Transcript p3038).

He would construct the evidence and convince a jury with no body, no motive, no weapon, and no basis for an opportunity to have committed the crime. It was simply not his job to prove anything on these fronts. Barker was now using Tom Pauling as the prosecution assistant. In the first inquest Peter Dean had employed him for a briefing for our team. It all seemed very strange, but then, as people kept telling me, 'it could only happen in the Territory'.

The Northern Territory Conservation Commission duties were to deal with, maintain and monitor the protection of the native animal and reptile population and the plant environment generally. The question that rang in my ears was: 'Who had been involved in the decision to deny Ranger Roff bullets to cull the pest dingoes? Was one of those animals that were earmarked to be shot the one that killed Azaria? How far would this government extend itself to get its own way?' It was left for the Psalmist to again quieten my angry spirit: 'Thou shalt seek them, and shalt not find them, even them that contend with thee: they that war with thee shall be as nothing and as a thing of naught.'

The prosecution now called for the testimony of the witnesses Sally and Greg Lowe from Tasmania and Judith and Bill West from Esperance, West Australia who, on the night of Azaria's disappearance, recalled the harrowing events just as we had told it. It was not without deep anxiety for the prosecution. I silently wept, reliving those events. Azaria had left so much blood in the tent and so much blackness in the night. The prison officers, followed by Andrew Kirkham, then Stuart, tried to give me solace outside the green-painted vertical bars of the jail quarters, downstairs in the Supreme Court. Those witnesses would have to be discredited for us to be convicted, I thought. These were awkward moments for the prosecution, for they had to get them in and out of the witness box without their testimony having any real impact on the jurors; hence they were up first and best forgotten. If you want the truth trampled, I had learned, bring it on first so that the confusion that comes after it, grubbies it, finally burying it.

Parochialism reared its head early on the second day of the trial, with the sight of two 'well upholstered' females in their thirties, drooling outside the courthouse with messages of sympathy for the dingo. 'The dingo is innocent' was emblazoned over their T-shirt. Barker, in the meantime, had walked around inside the court holding a dingo skull before him, clacking its teeth in front of the jurors, while we had to endure passively his satirical behaviour. Barker then took my daughter's jumpsuit, held it up high in the court dangling it before the jury. *Bulletin* journalist Geoffrey Wright's, impressions fitted my feelings exactly: 'The jumpsuit—a poor pathetic brown-stained little garment, savaged by age and scientists, the little legs dangling and dancing with the movement of the crown prosecutor's hand; the singlet, likewise stained and aged, scarcely enough to cover a kitten's back' was the most insensitive and depersonalising thing I had ever witnessed.

After court was finished for the day, I traced a path to the shop that had sold the offending T-shirt. The last thing the owners would have expected was a visit from me. They were red-faced, denying any responsibility, but I was satisfied that they had lied. Justice Muirhead called them 'fools'. I could have found a more choice word. It would be hard to forgive them.

The rest of this first week went by with many moments of trauma and heartbreak. Inspector Michael Shamus Gilroy and then Chief Ranger Roff both testified to bolder dingo activity at Ayers Rock. Roff testified that he had warned the Conservation Commission and had written a letter to the head of the Commission, seeking permission to cull the dangerous dingoes with his .22 Hornet rifle. This happened several weeks before we arrived. On the fateful night, paw prints were seen around the tent. Several searchers up on the sand hill where the dingo had dropped Azaria's body for a rest, had described the imprint of the crepe material of her clothing. Evidence of the dingo being tracked by Aboriginals was presented at the first inquest. Neither side called the Aboriginal witnesses.

The police presented evidence of Lindy crying in deep distress. Box Hill School teacher Murray Haby, another visitor to Ayers Rock on 17 August 1980, said he followed the dingo tracks with inch-deep drag marks of Azaria's body in the desert sand between the paw prints after Azaria was taken. Evidence was given that there was little doubt that these animals could carry weights of 9½ lbs for a considerable distance.

So far, the witnesses were unequivocal in their assertion that a dingo had been responsible for Azaria's disappearance. Mrs West had seen moist blood in our tent. A nurse, Amy Whittacker, described Lindy as numb after the loss of her baby. I was described as looking strange, as if I were trying rigidly to control my emotions. The week later, when Wally Goodwin had found Azaria's clothing, so graphic was the positioning of them that his daughter, on seeing them, ran off crying in distress. The shock was too great for his wife who also turned away. This now forever dispelled the completely false rumours that circulated in the Northern Territory of 'folded clothing stuffed in a rock crevice'. Wally Goodwin described the clothing this way:

'The jumpsuit lay on its back the feet in the air with the neck of the garment facing a large rock and the feet pointing towards the road from where (his) family had walked down a worn animal track.

'The singlet was inside the jumpsuit, and the nappy lay to the right with torn pieces of nappy lining scattered about.' (*Daily Sun*, Sydney, 17/9/1982).

This was the first time I had a clear understanding of how the clothes had been left. There are no words adequate that could describe my feelings at that moment. I just couldn't bear to think about it.

Goodwin had considered photographing the clothing as the first record of seeing it, but decided not to for two reasons. The police would do it and if he placed it with his family record of the Rock visit, the police would subpoena it for a coronial inquiry. Unbeknown to him, his decision not to photograph the clothing's position created serious problems for us, because 99 per cent of the time, a policeman's evidence will carry more weight over a layman's. Goodwin would find his testimony largely sidelined.

No cogent evidence of blood on either Lindy's or my clothing was ever presented. Witnesses and police did testify to my anger and despair over Azaria's disappearance and my description of her empty crib as 'a horrible lonely whiteness'. A surprise witness, Keyth Lenehan, who I had visited in April was called by the prosecution. He testified that our treatment of him after his serious car accident in Cairns in 1979 had been nothing less than that of 'good Samaritans'.

But these testimonies were not from scientists; they were not from 'expert' witnesses and the information they gave was accorded as 'secondary' in strength. Eyewitnesses were prone to getting things wrong. In contrast, forensic experts got it right because they were objective and accurate measuring scientists. They were a breed apart from the common humble eyewitness. This information would be structured and disseminated early in the trial so that when forensic 'evidence' was presented, it would appear much more important because it had been measured in a laboratory. The Crown appeared supremely confident that their new 'infallible' forensic science triumvirate of Professor James Malcolm Cameron, Joy Kuhl and Professor Malcolm Chaikin would carry the day. Their evidence had invalidated the first inquest finding and it was their evidence that was designed to be the knockout punch, overruling all the Ayers Rock witnesses, a blow from which we could never recover.

The second week opened with the police forensic interpretations of Azaria's death. The clothes Lindy wore and the determined look on my face were being reported, as the days began to wear us into the ground, in what was being touted as 'Australia's most celebrated, most expensive and most bizarre murder trial.' (*Weekend News*, West Australia 18/9/1982). Enduring the persistent denials of any dingo involvement from the forensic boffins was highly exasperating and most of the media reported it with relish. Dr Kenneth Brown again fronted the stand, but only briefly, before more qualified forensic scientists testified to the probable inability of a canine to create such phenomena.

One mechanic who had assisted in the installation of a speaker system and cassette recorder in my Torana hatchback testified that he thought he saw blood in my car. His boss, who also worked on the car, strongly contradicted him later (but did not give evidence at this time).

Malcolm Brown exhibited his eye for detail. He noted our attention to clothing and grooming, despite the ordeal. He noted Lindy's pregnant discomfort in her squirming and wriggling to find the magic position for relief, which was never found. An occasional jerking limb was a sure sign that the baby, at seven and a half months, was preparing for exit. (*Sun Herald* 26/9/82). The jury experienced, momentarily, a lighter side with a photo showing 'a dingo blown up,' described unwittingly by a prosecution lawyer. It raised a laugh from the normally tense jury, but not from us. One of the prosecution lawyers was tattooed, another was observed with shabby, unpolished brown shoes, and a female court orderly wore a high split dress, according to the hawk-eyed Malcolm. (*Sun Herald* 19/9/1982).

The prestigious *Bulletin* news magazine (28/9/1982) described the Darwin trial as one of 'Drama and Pathos'. The trial, the magazine claimed, was the biggest event since Cyclone Tracy in 1974. The writer, Geoffrey Wright, observed how the lawyers huddled at the bar table, evoking the image of a 'rugby scrum... all looking unbearably hot in their black gowns and wigs, alien creatures in a land of eternal summer.' Another curious phenomenon was the Chief Minister, Paul Everingham, and his office, monitoring our courtroom and the media in his own building. Journalists were intrigued by our transport vehicle carrying the number plate beginning with AZ—a curious coincidence, I would have thought. At the end of each day, the 60-odd journalists described by one journalist, 'like meat ants aroused from their nests', rushed out to write some new trivia about our presence. Prince Charles and Princess Diana had an Australian rival, when it came to breaking news. We chose to walk in and out of court as if these news-gatherers did not exist, looking straight ahead, and taking our time in our normally 15-second journey. Yes, we were 'media royalty' but at the bottom of the pack, at the other end of the spectrum. Again Geoffrey Wright observed that we had adopted 'a dignified entry and exit without a Frank Sinatra-like frown, scowl or tantrum.'

On the 14th day of the prosecution's witnesses, we heard about the so-called 'hard evidence' and the bloodstains in my yellow Torana hatchback. Blood that was 'sticky to touch', according to Constable James Metcalf in a spray-like formation under the dashboard. (This was 13 months after Azaria's alleged killing.)

Now it was Joy Kuhl's turn to take the box, with her sensational discovery of 22 different findings of baby (foetal) blood in eight areas of my car. Her presence had an expectation about it; polished, almost suave; a neatly groomed and eloquent performer in court.

But it did not go perfectly for Mrs Kuhl. Under rigorous cross-examination from John Phillips QC, she blurted out that she had destroyed every last piece of the original 'hard evidence' of her original blood tests. There could be no repeats to demonstrate 'baby blood'. Neither could she verify what she had said was in fact the truth of her experiment, because she had not photographed her original results. Here was the first of what I term as the major three 'lies'—alleged facts which we knew were simply not true and which were relied upon in the application to quash the findings of the first inquest: that Lindy had killed Azaria in the car, that Lindy and myself had disposed of the body, and that we had placed the clothing in a strategic place.

So sensational was this revelation that a full transcript of the cross-examination by John Phillips of Joy Kuhl's confession was published in many newspapers, including The *Weekend Australian* (23/10/1982); *Border Morning Mail* (2/10/1982); *Illawarra Daily Mercury* (2/10/1982) to name but a few. It had to be the turning point of the trial. But would a parochial Darwin jury accept its relevance? Would they have even noticed? At least one female juror did notice and spoke up later, even in the face of reprisal or legal action by the Northern Territory Government.

Joy Kuhl stood down on 16 October and it was apparent that the evidence being given by Professor Cameron was also showing cracks. His theory, that Azaria's throat had been cut through a human act, was soundly rebuffed by the director of Geelong's Public Hospital, pathologist, Dr Vernon Douglas Plueckhahn. Neither was there any evidence of a bloodied human handprint on the back of Azaria's jumpsuit, Plueckhahn argued. 'From my experience and my study of this clothing I would consider Professor Cameron's statement completely unfounded,' he said. (*Launceston Examiner*, (22/10/1982). It was an observation not lost on Malcolm Brown and other savvy media reporters. Here was the Northern Territory Government's second pillar of key evidence; evidence now being mauled after having been secretly used to quash the Barritt first inquest.

If the sensational bits from Cameron got all the headlines, continuing to irrevocably damage our reputation, some daylight was also appearing through the cracks of Cameron's assumptions, based on the incomplete information from Dr Kenneth Brown (Transcript of the First Inquest, pp653-679). To offset the scepticism of Brown, Dr Hector Orams, a reader in dental science at Melbourne University, said that it was likely that dingo's teeth marks could have been responsible for the alleged cut marks on Azaria's clothing. But no experimentation was presented to prove that dingoes can cut clothing material. Somehow we needed scientists to front up with clothing like Azaria's and demonstrate that dingo's teeth were capable of a shearing action. In this we stood flat-footed.

The Crown then launched an attack on the credibility of Monash University lecturer, Professor Richard Nairn, arguing he was part of an 'ivory towered scientist set' from Melbourne. Nairn, Ian Barker claimed, never got 'forensic dirt' on his hands and therefore could not possibly understand what a forensic scientist knew. Nairn had described Joy Kuhl's analysis as 'very crude analytical work.' The sensational 'foetal blood spray' under the dashboard was quite inconsistent with the real thing, rather more like a Coca Cola-based substance. Constable Metcalf's description of it as 'sticky to touch', made no sense as 13-month-old blood.

Nairn backed Newcastle University scientist, Professor Barry Boettcher's four main reasons why Kuhl could not possibly have found baby blood in the car. Boettcher was a tall, balding, physically powerful man and a top blood specialist in his field in Australia. He was well qualified to allege that Kuhl had used a faulty reagent to get a foetal blood result. As it turned out, he was supported by all the defence experts, declaring that in fact there was no good reason to think any blood in the car was present, let alone foetal blood.

Joy Kuhl, Boettcher said, had misunderstood her criteria for finding it and had messed up her use of the reagent. Those who subscribed to Kuhl's thinking were demonstrating more faith in a forensic scientist than all the Christians who went to church believing in God. On that basis, the shrines of forensic science would be filled to overflowing; such was the blind faith in this form of scientific method. But as I scanned the jury, the gaze on some of their faces told me that they could either not understand the evidence, or had already made their minds up. It was quite worrying that this jury was mingling with the police during breaks, and their interpretations, where offered, would be given credence.

Craggy-faced, chain-smoking Les Harris, was an experienced dingo handler and witness for the defence. He was a no-frills, no-nonsense, hard-nosed man. He had no sympathy for our religious belief or lifestyles, but he felt strongly enough to stick his neck out and present the abilities of dingoes in context at Ayers Rock. Importantly, as the president of the Dingo Foundation, he was in no doubt that a dingo was responsible for Azaria's death.

In summary, Harris' original letter (to the first inquest Coroner, Denis Barritt), stated some gruesome views. A mammal weighing 10 pounds could be consumed in 20 minutes. A mated pair could probably consume it in 10 minutes. If a dingo took a baby, it was possible that there may be no evidence left after 30 minutes. Such animals can excrete their meal within 24 hours. A female dingo has been observed to carry a wallaby of 20lb for half a mile without stopping. A male dingo has been observed to carry a large hare (approximately 8–10lb) up a 30-degree slope for 600 feet without stopping. With regard to eating, dingoes are fastidious and are able to manipulate inedible foreign matter without difficulty.

Answering the three vital questions, Les Harris concluded with the following answers: 'Could a dingo have taken the baby? Yes, with ease. Could a dingo or dingoes have removed its clothing? Probably, yes. Could a dingo or dingoes have totally consumed the baby? Yes, without any doubt.'

We deeply appreciated Harris's input but there was something lacking in his presentation that did not convince the jury: he did not have a PhD to his name. His manner in describing how a dingo would go about killing Azaria was frightening and authoritative but some might have mistaken his knowledge as based on arrogance rather than experience. There were numerous witnesses who were called to say how dangerous dingoes were and how they had been attacked, chased or stalked by them, but none of them could tell us that dingoes had killed a Caucasian child.

By Thursday 20 October 1982, both Lindy and I had endured nearly six weeks of courtroom drama and tedious forensic analysis. My time was coming to give evidence and I was becoming as nervous as a caged animal. On Thursday night 21 October, Lindy had some advice for me before I testified. 'Stay calm, listen carefully,' she said. It was good advice. I was not a particularly coherent witness when it came to discussing my daughter's death under adversarial conditions. It almost seemed our place had been bugged. Lindy's advice was somehow telegraphed to the prosecution, for in an extraordinary series of questions he discovered what Lindy had said to me. I felt awkward and debated if I should just reply, 'I don't recall'. But that wasn't my way. The headline, I could have guessed. Very big and bold, across the front page of the broadsheet of *The* (Melbourne) *Herald* (22/10/1982) next day, it screamed: 'Pastor: Lindy said to 'stay calm''.

In my cross-examination by Barker, the jury appeared to have thought that the seemingly resigned and almost pedantic way in which I answered questions about Lindy was not convincing enough to absolve her from guilt. It ultimately came down to my use of the words 'know' and 'knowledge'. As a minister of religion in the Seventh-day Adventist Church, my training was that all knowledge was ultimately only known by God as an omniscient, omnipresent and omnipotent being. For humans, most things in life were not a matter of fact, but of faith, because you were not there to evidence them, and anyway, what you see may not always be the reality. Only God can know, ultimately. So in my cross-examination by the prosecutor, there was an element of annoyance on my part, running throughout. I was always thinking: 'I have to go through this ridiculous interrogation because you have got me here on false pretences!' I am going to make sure that my answers are as safe and unassailable as possible. The defence were annoyed by my performance. They must have groaned inwardly at the apparent lack of fight in my answers.

Concerning my part on the night of 17 August, I could answer confidently and definitely 'yes' or 'no' because (of course) I was there. It was my actions, in point of time, that were in question. I could not answer 'yes' or 'no' about what Lindy was doing outside of my vision, hence outside of my knowledge. Thus I stated what I thought about it. I could state as fact, that there had been no confession by Lindy about any involvement in Azaria's death. There had been no cover up, no burial, no cutting of clothing and no sorties out into the bush in the middle of the night to bury her.

Ian Barker zeroed in on the fact that Lindy was the last to see Azaria alive. Here my resignation began to overwhelm me again as I tried to recall the extreme pain of the night. I was asked about my alleged comments to Constable Frank Morris about Azaria and the will of God, of which I was not aware, but to protect myself from appearing a liar, I simply had no recourse but to say, 'I can't deny I might have made a comment about it.' My problem was that the general public, including the police, are liable to misunderstand or look at theological comments too simplistically. I had a tendency to adopt a literal approach to Barker's questions. While this was influenced by my post-graduate training, it was now exacerbated by the instruction that my lawyers had planted in me as well, 'just stick to what you saw and heard' and this I did faithfully—too faithfully, it seemed.

To Barker's crucial questions, 'Did your wife cut the (Azaria's) sleeve; did she cut the collar?' I replied, 'I don't think so'. I meant by this answer that I had no knowledge of this. I could not say, 'no' to the question 'Did she kill Azaria?' because I knew the next question would have been, 'How do you know?' And not being there all the time, or omniscient, I would have opened myself to having to backtrack. I adopted the path of caution. Hence, when asked 'Did you bury the jumpsuit with the child in it?' I could unequivocally state as a fact, a definite 'no'. When asked if Lindy did, I answered 'I don't think she did.' I had no knowledge of her ever having done this. Had she been in my presence every minute of the night I could have said 'definitely not', which I always thought but could not say in all honesty. In other words, I took the question literally in the sense of truthfulness and my belief that only God can know because I wasn't physically there. I answered the question theologically myself, in faith.

Although it was acknowledged by other lawyers that my answers were 'technically correct', in fact 'models of precision', what was lacking before a jury was an indignant response of outrage, which in hindsight I should have demonstrated. My answers had, however, shown none of the deviousness or any elaborate charade that the Crown was accusing me of.

Next it was Lindy's turn on the stand. Barker's angle was that if Lindy had seen the dingo leave the tent and if Les Harris's claim that dingoes hold their heads up high when carrying prey, why did she not see what was in its mouth? It seemed a fair question. Lindy maintained that all she had seen was a dingo with its head low shaking something. She admitted seeing nothing in its mouth. If Lindy could meticulously describe its head and ears to a jury why could she not say anything about its mouth? The answer may lie in the fact that the tent had a triangular entrance with the narrowest point at the top. For a dingo to negotiate a load, the lower it held it, considering that the flap was wider at the base, the easier the animal could have executed its departure with its head down at the lowest point.

Lindy's response was that there had been a low railing in front of the tent that had created a shadow from a 100-watt lamp 20 metres away at the barbecue area. That answer was verifiable, as I remember the railing and the light myself. Speculation was rife after this point, as no one had ever witnessed a dingo move through tent flaps with a live baby in its jaws in similar conditions. If there had been two dingoes, a view that both Derek Roff and Dr Newsome considered a possibility, then Lindy had seen the wrong animal.

But to make too much of this was to attempt to stereotype human behaviour when plainly every individual has potentially a different way of reacting. 'To know something is true and to accept it, are two different things,' she reflected, under inquiry examination. To add weight to her thinking, three other witnesses at Ayers Rock, shortly after Azaria's disappearance, did exactly the same thing. Derek Roff, Frank Morris and

I, all disbelievingly checked the tent to see if Lindy had been mistaken about Azaria's absence.

Before the jury and summing up, John Phillips pounded the desk with the response that ten 'salt of the earth' witnesses from north, south, east and west had declared Lindy's 'love and affection' for Azaria. Because motive, according to Bond University's Professor Paul Wilson (one of Australia's top criminologists) was a vital component to proving guilt, the prosecution's response had no credibility. In the face of a cacophony of accusers, bereft of a motive or reason for this crazy accusation, Phillips was enraged sufficiently to accuse the Crown of being 'stone motherless broke'. Not presenting a motive was like plucking the centrepiece jewel of evidence from the Crown.

The third member of the Adelaide forensics, Rex Kuchell, laid the groundwork for the accusations and I hadn't seen it. His testimony about the dirt and alleged lack of leaf matter on Azaria's jumpsuit was supposed to link me with some bizarre burial. Barker said I did not do enough searching on the night of Azaria's disappearance and did not go to the Rock the next day to search. He was trying to find out where it was that I was alleged to have 'helped Lindy' and do her alleged 'dirty work' to bury Azaria in some place unknown.

It was, in fact, the police who had told us to stay put at the motel and not travel to the Rock the next day, in case they had any new information for us. We had done what we were told to do.

We were about to see how, when the accused gives any answer at all, regardless of how truthful or innocent that answer is, it can be reconstructed to convey an entirely different meaning for the jury and can be used by the public to condemn you. Here was the classic example: Barker, bereft of any information leading to my alleged involvement as 'an accessory after the fact', got the headlines he desired: 'Father denies baby burial'; 'Father: Why no search?' *Perth Evening News* (22/10/1982).

The fact that I had gone out looking five or six times, in different directions for up to 200 metres away, in dense spinifex and desert bush, was not regarded as meaningful searching! When asked why I took a number of photographs at the Rock after Azaria's death, I stumbled in my reply to Barker and broke down in the witness stand, covering my eyes with my hands. In fact, apart from being a keen photographer, I had taken the photos in order to show and warn others about the dangers of camping with children in that area around Ayers Rock. This wasn't music to a Conservation executive member's ears. As the *West Australian* (22/10/1982) accurately represented it: the time in the witness box had been, 'A torrid day for Michael Chamberlain.'

I was exhausted but relieved. It was up to the judge to present his final address in this bizarre case and we were confident that the prosecution attack was so fraught with holes and lack of direction in all its non-prima facie evidence that Lindy and I now could truly bank on going home and staying there. I had seen the good, the bad and the ugly—the best and worst of human nature. If truth was on our side in an Australian Supreme Court, right would prevail.

My defence team had conducted themselves as warriors, showing ethical restraint and moral courage. The prosecution had appeared to have won, but only technically. I asked myself, how could they prevail when it was so wrong? How could they win with such unethical behaviour? It was the duty of the Crown to lead evidence favourable and unfavourable to its case, this trial had been full of telling omissions by the prosecution of evidences of our innocence.

9. Guilty as Charged?

Ian Barker QC now commenced his summing up. His main attack on me was that I 'wasn't curious about the fate of Azaria because I knew of my wife's guilt'! He had positioned me as someone who was guilty of protecting a woman who had allegedly committed a heinous crime. This could be easily observed and deduced, he alleged, from my behaviour which was 'inconsistent' with 'what would be expected of parents if they believed their child had been carried off into the night by a wild animal.' At that moment I seem to have simultaneously scratched my head, already covered with stress pimples.

What was the accepted mode of behaviour, I wondered, of parents whose child had been 'carried off into the night by a wild animal?' How did Mr Barker think parents should behave in that situation? Did he know? How dare he tell me how to behave in such a traumatic event.

He then delivered another incredible circumstantial premise. In addressing the forensic evidence, he told the jury:

'Could I now refer to the subject of blood generally? I see your eyes glazing. Like Mr Phillips, I lament those innocent days when I thought a haptoglobin was something that dwelt at the bottom of my garden. But I'm not going to waste a lot of time about it because you heard it all.

'Joy Kuhl, we say, is a competent, honest, experienced, forensic biologist.

'Dr Baxter (her superior) is a competent, honest, even more

experienced, forensic biologist...

'We put Brian Culliford forward as a competent, honest experienced forensic biologist. He happens to be in charge of the world's leading forensic science laboratory.

'I'm sorry ladies and gentlemen; I can do no more than give you the world's leading forensic biologists.'

Barker then continued 'I simply put it to you that it is surprising that they (the Chamberlains) did not make more active inquiries about the search before they left the National Park.' I think that the majority of the jury accepted this submission.

It was now evening on 2 November, 1982. Waiting for the verdict while the jury was out did not seem real. I could get as much as three years in prison. I felt socially filthy and spiritually forsaken. That night I felt compelled to ask Lindy two questions:

'If you get jail for life tomorrow and no parole, as suggested, what do you want me to do with your belongings?' Her answer was 'Whatever'. On reflection, my question was really quite stupid and hopeless, but at the time I could not see past the permanency of incarceration.

The second question was asked in the context that it now felt that there was nothing I could do right in her eyes.

'If I promised to do my best for you while you are in prison and make a mistake in trying to do it, would you start a recriminatory process towards me?'

Her reply was disappointing:

'Well, I wouldn't be around to do anything about it, would I?'

I reacted angrily: 'That's not a good way to answer a sincere question when we are trying to recommit our lives to each other, not knowing if or when you will ever be let out of jail.'

In our current lives, with every moment monitored by the media and our every phone call listened in to by the police, we were under overwhelming pressure. Acting graciously and affectionately in normal married life had become a thing of the past. Lindy, having suffered a tragic loss and under growing suspicion, had been perceived as tough and hard, through her public performance and comments. Her anger catalysed a campaign of vitriol against her.

Acting Chief Justice Muirhead, in his summing up of the case, warned the jury not to let mere suspicion or conjecture cloud their minds. Justice Muirhead's summing up was complex and long, consisting of 227 pages. The defence team seemed satisfied that he had directed them not to use conjecture and to rely only on the facts. If the jury stuck to that, in the light that there was no motive, no body, no confession and that all the evidence was circumstantial, with a strong alternative eyewitness explanation for Azaria's death, commonsense would prevail.

Andrew Kirkham was now so sure of our win in court that he told us we could 'build our house' on being home for Christmas and perhaps considerably sooner. I had a graduation to attend for my Master of Arts degree. But this matter was far, far away from my mind at the moment. Even more important was the eagerly awaited birth of our new daughter.

In another city in another state Muirhead would have probably moved the jury enough to acquit. But this was Darwin. The satire and sarcasm of the ultimate dingo's insults, published in a book of jokes about Azaria's death, was obscene and unforgivable. T-shirts were produced to portray disgusting and dehumanising images declaring the dingo's innocence. These were symptoms of the underlying psyche of the mob. The belief that Lindy appeared not to cry over the loss of Azaria, but could clinically discuss the way a dingo would have peeled her clothes off, led her to being judged as callous and cold. Such ingredients in the cauldron of public ferment changed her from the victim to being victimised in a medieval-like witch hunt. The fact was, Lindy could and did cry many times behind the scenes, but her religious culture and environment did not encourage such a public display.

Similarly, perceptions about my religious beliefs, as a minister of a relatively minor and media-shy church, were entirely misjudged. Although not by any means cultish, Amish or Quaker-like in shunning the world, the Church was strongly focused on a sectarian standards-based belief system and culture. My calmness and stoicism in tragedy were condemned as coolness or fanatical religious belief. Perceptions predominated over fact; fantasy was preferred to reality; and truth was condemned as stranger than fiction. Consequently, the reality of what happened at the Rock was transformed from a mystery, dumped for a more politically and financially expedient outcome. The jury continued to stay out hour after hour into the second day. This was not a good sign.

At last, after some seven hours, the jury filed back into the courtroom to deliver their decision. They were the ones who looked guilty. There was no eye contact with us. As they faced the gallery they stared straight ahead or looked down. 'Do you find the accused Alice Lynne Chamberlain guilty or not guilty of murder?' asked Justice James Muirhead. The verdict came in a solemn death rattle-like tone. 'Guilty, Your Honour'. There was only one sentence for this conviction in the Northern Territory: Life imprisonment with hard labour. There was no parole. It was all or nothing. I was pronounced guilty of being an accessory after the fact and was bailed for a ridiculous sum of $500, with my sentence to be handed down the next day.

Bryson reported that Justice Muirhead was aghast. It had been the hardest trial he had faced. There were a few seconds of disbelief then terrible rage in the courtroom. The prosecution could not believe they had won. The defence could not believe they had lost. Reporters had to rewrite their copy that they had prepared for an acquittal.

I shook my head several times. I looked at Lindy. She sat motionless, expressionless. I looked across at the judge. His face appeared to be ashen grey then a scarlet purple. At least one of the jurors appeared to be sobbing. A number of the public were crying openly. My defence lawyers were in a state of deep shock. This 'kittenish, attractive' 34-year-old wife of mine, described as 'a perfect little mother' and 'a good Samaritan' was actually an alleged child-killer? A woman of good, even 'unblemished character'? As the jury filed out, *Sydney Morning Herald* journalist, Malcolm Brown was unable to hide his disbelief and shock. In half-breathed, half-spoken tones, he was overheard to exclaim: 'You pack of bastards.'

Lindy was led away half an hour later to the Correctional Services car to be taken to jail for the term of her natural life, never to be released. As she passed by, tears welled up in her eyes and trickled down her shell-shocked face. She waved to me, but it was no ordinary wave. It has haunted me for the rest of my life. It was as if she was leaving this world, never to return. 'This was it,' she was saying to me.

She had told me that I should consider ending my relationship with her and try to find another life, but that was intolerable for me to consider. I told her that in no way would this happen and that I would fight for her vindication no matter what it took. After Lindy was taken away, I was driven home to Elizabeth (Liz) and John Parry's home to face a terrible night. I think I awoke a dozen times that night. Any meaning in life had gone out the window.

Being given a suspended sentence by Justice Muirhead was a great relief as I was potentially facing a three-year prison term with no parole. With it came a three-year $500 good behaviour bond. I was free to go home. The judge gave his reasons for the minimum punishment. It was in part based on my previous good character and partly for my need to care for my children. The children's grandparents had explained the basics situation, but we kept the details to ourselves. What I said to them was to never stop believing that their mother would one day be out and we would somehow find some way of getting justice. The question was when?

'The children need their father and their father needs them. He will never be a private person again,' said the judge. He was right.

The prosecution did not contest the lightness of this sentence. They agreed that I 'did not have any forewarning of the child's death and that I did not play any part in it.' As gracious as it sounded, it was cold comfort. The jury had nothing to go on to convict me, except the impressions of certain people. As in Lindy's verdict, based purely on circumstantial evidence, I had to ask myself over and over again, 'On what circumstantial evidence was I found guilty?' There was no body, no weapon, no confession, no motive and no hostile evidence from first-hand civilian witnesses that night at the Rock. Indeed, all affirmed our testimony. There was no evidence of post-natal depression or any history of deviance in our lives on either side; no convictions for anything. I was a Justice of the Peace for Queensland. I was now an unfit character who could not maintain any of the normal privileges entitled to an Australian citizen.

In the judge's reference to my sentence, he said something else that

I did not agree with. 'It is in the very nature of a man that he should stand by his wife.' If I had known at any time or place that my wife had committed such a serious felony, I could never have tolerated being silent for any length of time. A confession of such a magnitude would have resulted in a revelation to the appropriate authorities. For me there is no moral worth or value in shutting up.

The writing was on the wall. I was judged a condemned man and as a minister of religion, I may as well be dead in the water. Certainly I was a sitting duck for anyone who wanted an excuse to make a prejudicial decision against me. There could never be any future for me to serve the Church as a minister again. There might never be an opportunity to work outside of the Church either. Mud stinks and mud sticks. I was extreme public property and my acquired notoriety would never allow me to serve as an unblemished servant of God. The Church would sooner or later ask for my credentials and I would have to resign. This in itself would be a crushing blow that I believed I would never recover from.

I was beyond tiredness, pale and physically sick. As I tried to walk out of the court I stumbled and blacked out. Fortunately, Stuart Tipple was close by. He managed to catch me before I crashed to the stone floor. In an instant I was conscious again, but shaky. I was helped to a waiting car that sped away from the back of the Supreme Court.

It cannot be denied that Barker had put his best efforts into his brief, including theatrics, wit, humour and bursts of rhetoric. I realised the frightening side of a courtroom is the overwhelming motivation on the part of the lawyers to win the argument.

Barker had worked his way up from a small town practice, to attain the rank of Territory Solicitor-General. With his 'devastating irony', according to journalist Ken White, Barker had 'torn the defence team's arguments to shreds', and had carved for himself 'an indisputable niche in the annals of Australian criminal history'. (*The Northern Territory News*, 2/11/1982). Turning something that was relatively simple to solve, into something that was a complicated maze of mystery and a labyrinth of forensic descriptions, brought a great promotional platform for forensic science. Its supporters could push for more funding in Australian training and reduce the need for overseas experts. And, added White, about the Northern Territory Attorney General: 'Paul Everingham had got his pound of flesh' (*The Northern Territory News*, 2/11/1982).

The media had also done the Northern Territory's bidding and had prepared its audience for the popular decision to protect the dingo. Such was the euphoria that when the news of our convictions was delivered over the loudspeakers at Claremont Raceway, Perth, Western Australia at 8.30pm on the Friday of our verdict, anyone would have thought people were responding to the latest great rock star. Professor Paul Wilson, writing in his book *Murder of the Innocents*, which was dedicated to us, said he had observed a worrying new form of macabre humour. One obscene example, 'How do you bring up a baby?' Answer: 'Stick your fingers down its throat.' Journalist, James Oram summarised Territory opinion in his headline: 'The dingo didn't do it,' that: 'It was as though people had had their sport, their excitement during the trial, but were appalled at the verdict. It wasn't a sexual pervert, a mass murderer or a mutilator who had been sent to Berrimah Prison on the outskirts of Darwin, but an attractive dark-haired woman with far-away eyes, a 34-year-old with two living children'.

The prosecution team celebrated long into the night, partying around the Darwin Hotel swimming pool. French champagne at $40 a bottle flowed freely between gulps of red wine and beer (*The Sunday Telegraph* 3/11/1982). It was not entirely without incident, however. I was told of a skirmish between a writer and an Adelaide broadcaster in which the latter landed in the pool, fully clothed. Such was the obsession of the Northern Territory; one member of the Government team was reported to say later, 'I don't care if Azaria walked into the courtroom right now. I would still say the bitch is guilty.'

Picceen Masters was the proprietor of the Golden Wattle Florist Shop in the Darwin Mall. She signed and dated a document to say that: 'At the end of the trial, a woman entered the shop and ordered flowers on behalf of the prosecution team for people involved in the trial of the Chamberlains—such as the bailiff of the court, two secretaries and the typists in the pool—thanking them for all their work. The woman remarked that she had

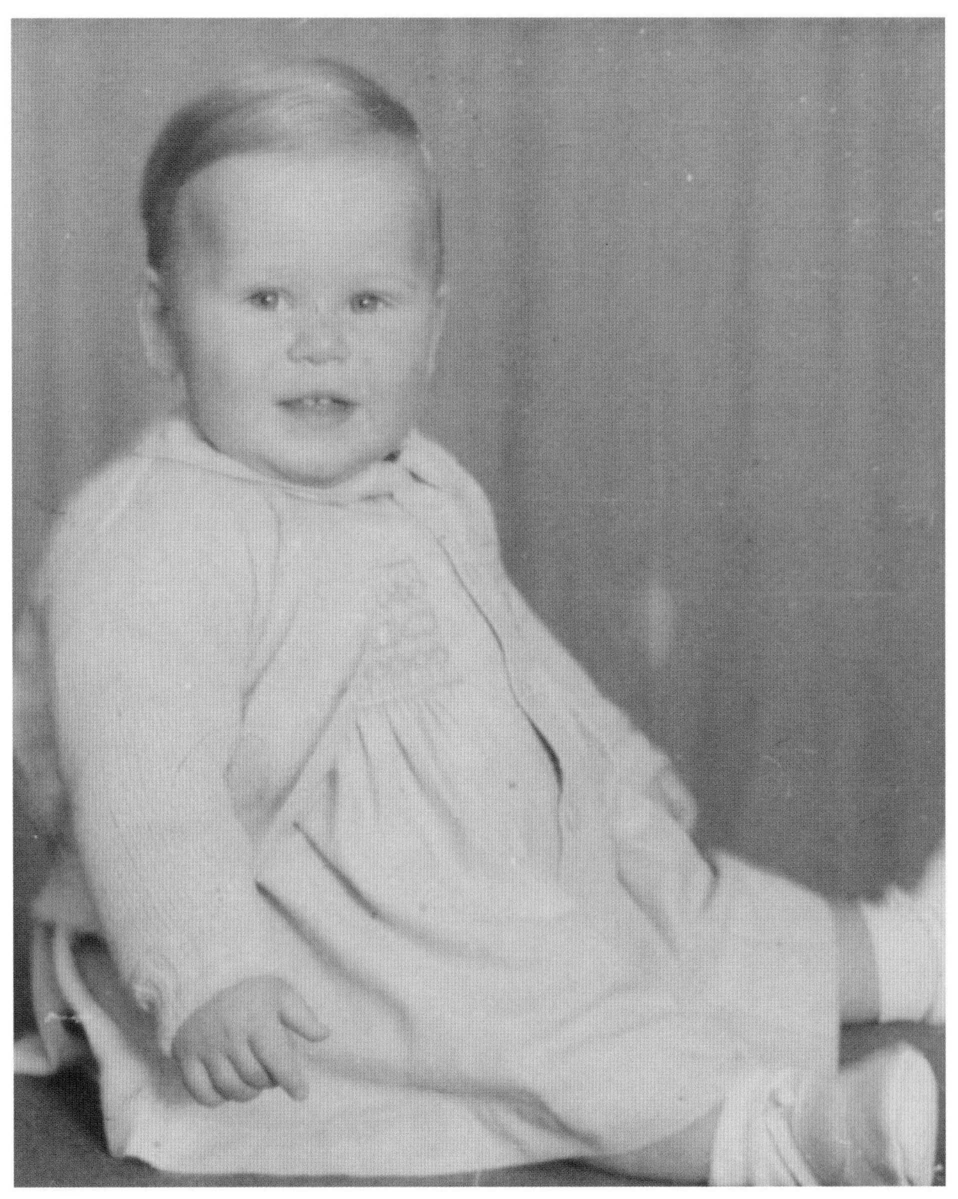

Here I am, Michael Leigh Chamberlain aged 6 months, born in Christchurch, New Zealand, in February 1944.

Above: My season as Captain (centre) of the First XI for Lincoln High School in 1961.

Below: My engagement to Lindy in 1968. *Broken Hill Newspaper.*

Above: My first graduation for BA (Theology major) from Avondale College with (from left) my parents Ivan and Greta Chamberlain, Lindy, me, Avis and Pastor Cliff Murchison.

Below: Lindy with me at my first graduation, 16 November, 1969.

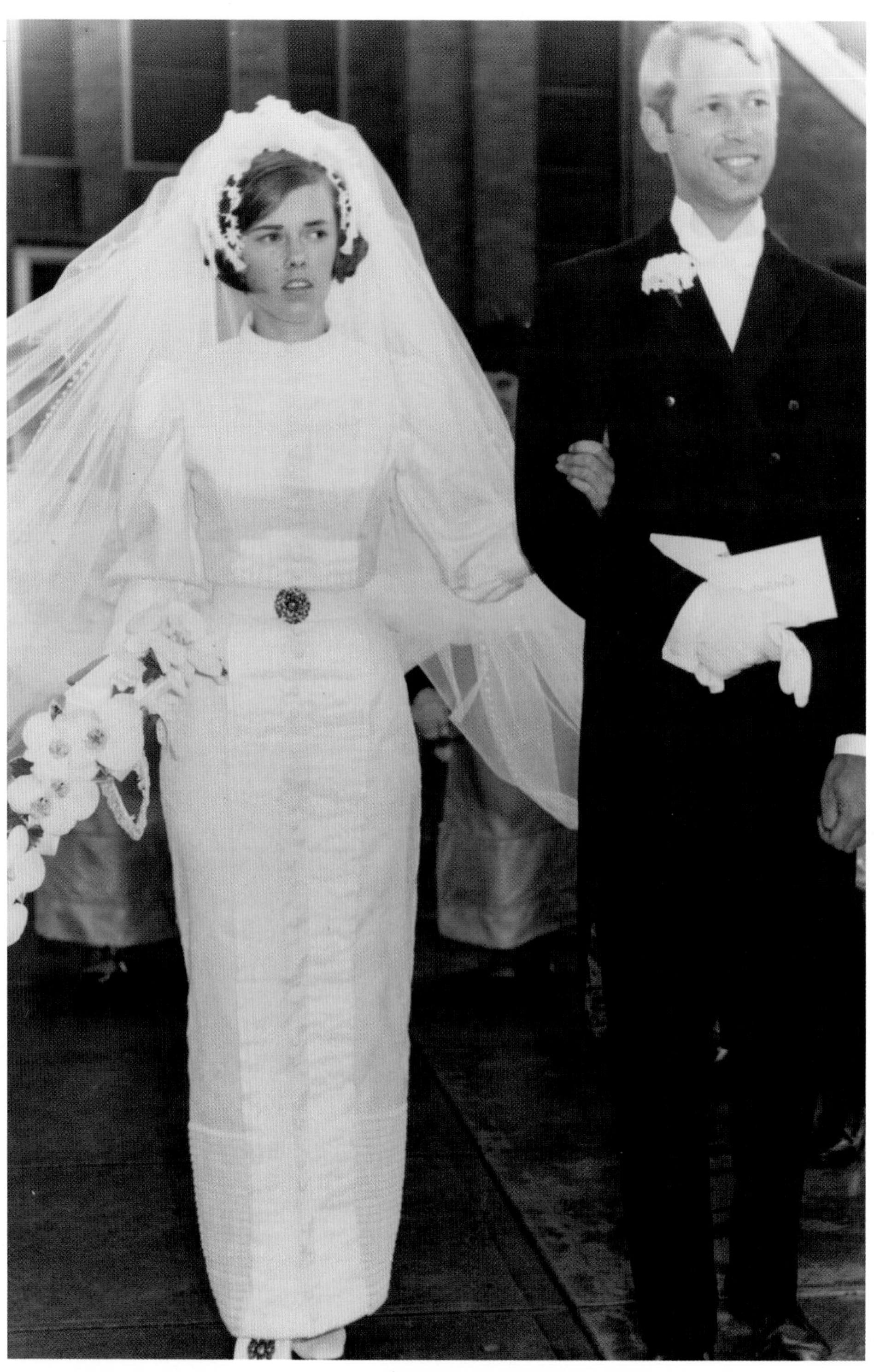

Lindy and my wedding in Wahronga Seventh-day Adventist Church on 18 November, 1969.

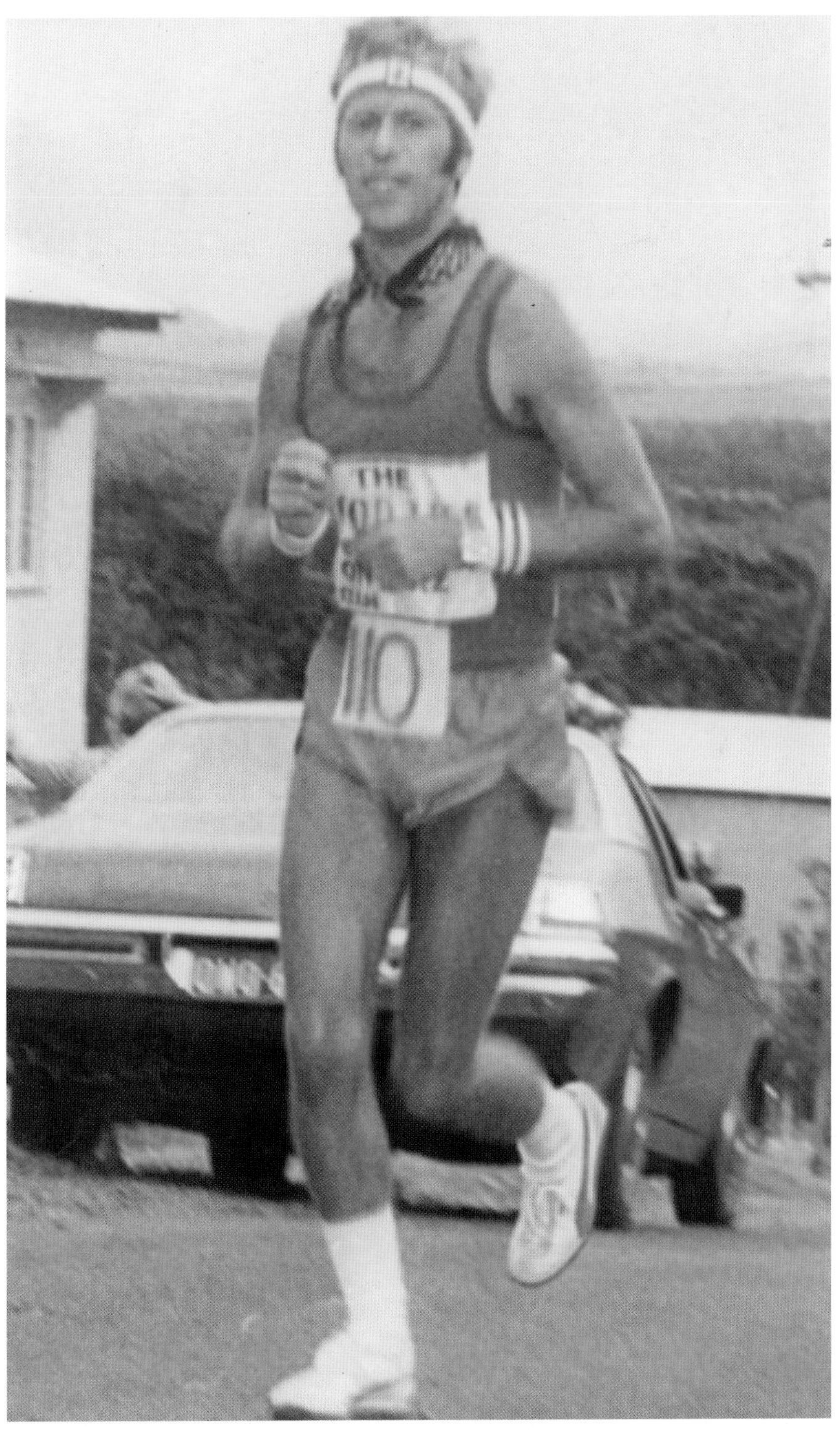

Running in the 1978 Innisfail 12 kilometre run, North Queensland.

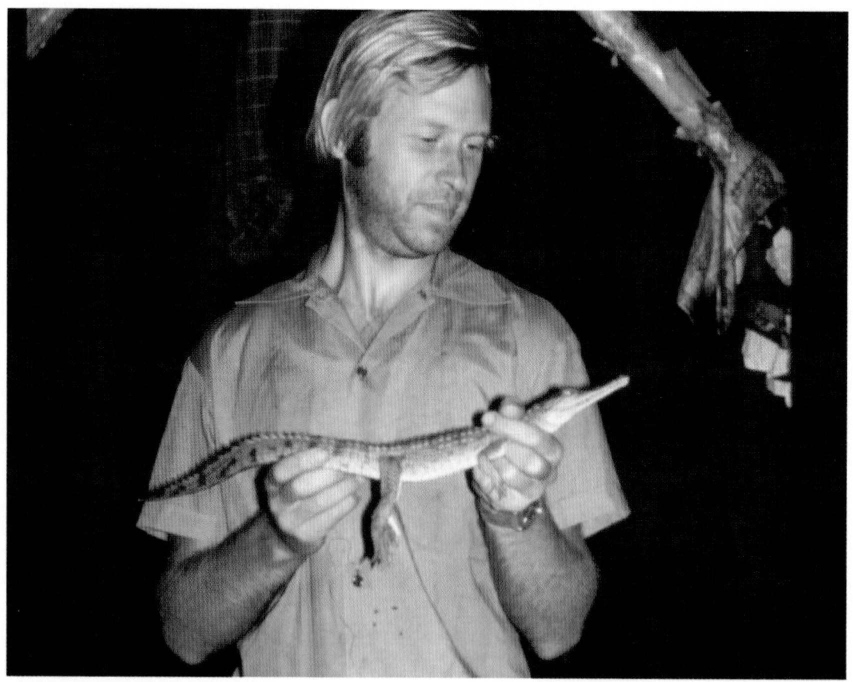

Above: 'This one is big enough, now where is mama?' Catching a baby freshwater crocodile at Strathgordon Station, Cape York, 1977.

Opposite: "But where is my Barramundi?" - with a Saratoga.

Below: Lindy and I on our Cape York Adventure Safari, Strathgordon 1977.

Above: Lindy having a smoko break, Cape York Safari Expedition, 1977.

Opposite Page: Lindy impersonating my photography stance with my camera on Kerry Packer's estate, March 1986.

Below: We encountered several obstacles on the Cape York Safari, 1977.

Above: Photography on the wing, during the trial. Corroboree Lagoon, NT.

Opposite page: Azaria at home, Mount Isa, 16 June, 1980.

Below: Lindy with Dr Irene Milne (holding Azaria) at Mount Isa hosptial, 11 June, 1980.

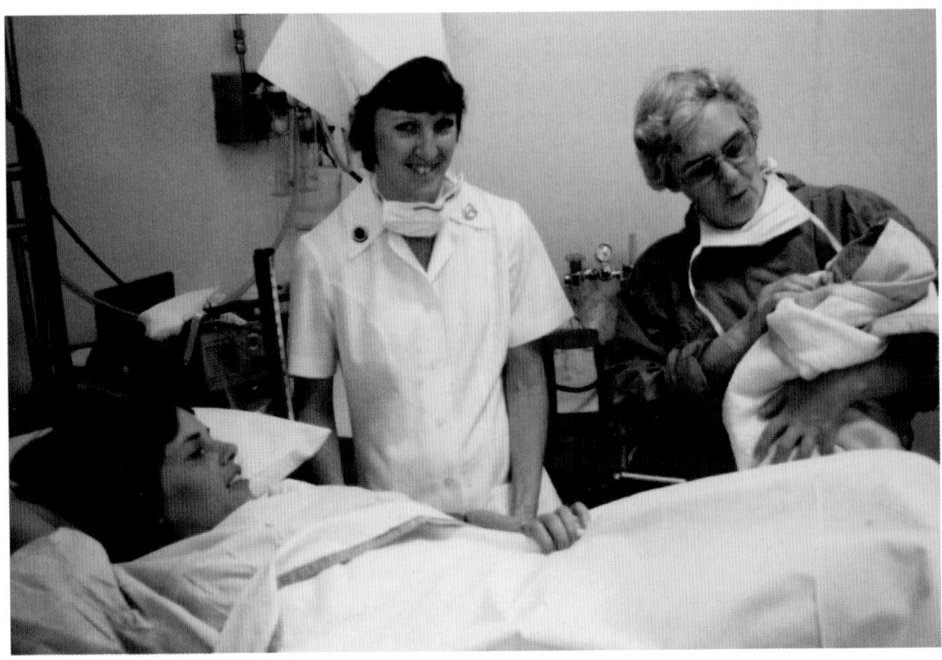

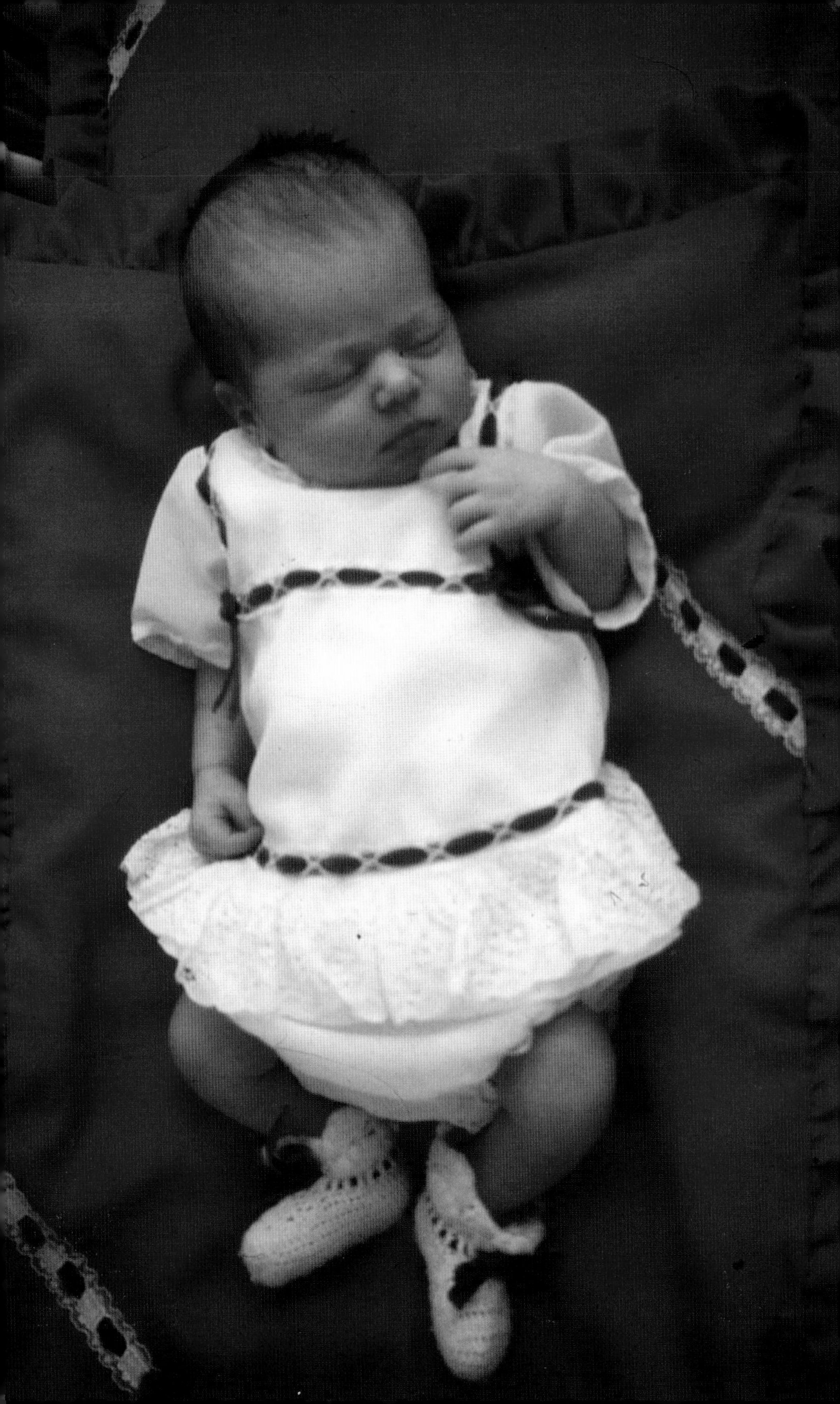

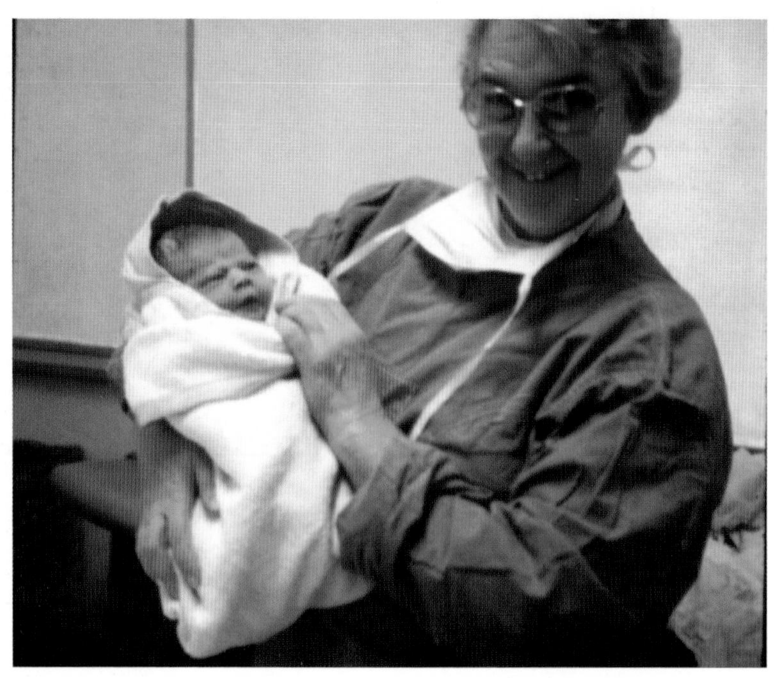

Above: Dr Irene Milne holding Azaria minutes after her birth. 11 June, 1980.

Below: Azaria two days after her birth in Mount Isa hospital, 13 June, 1980.

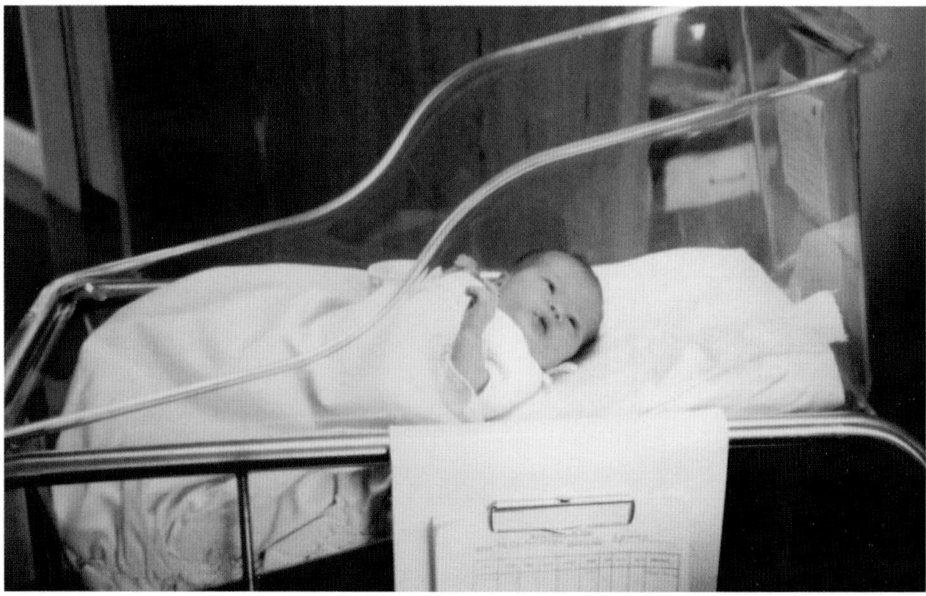

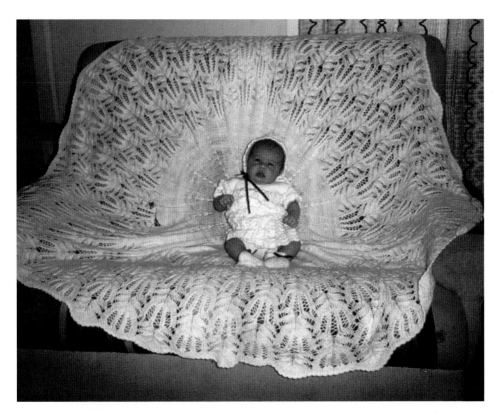

Above: Lindy made a crochet rug for Azaria.

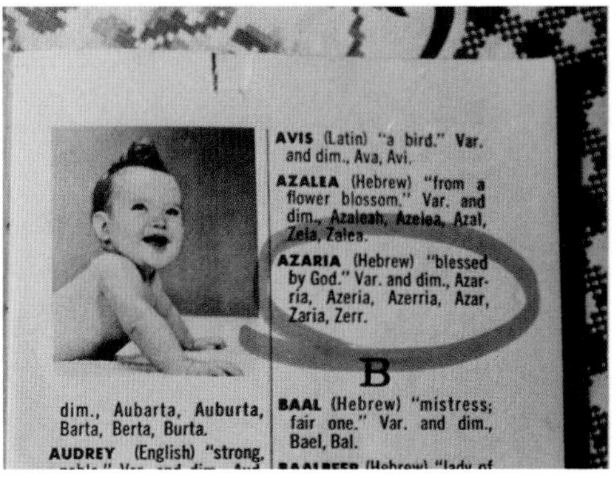

dim., Aubarta, Auburta, Barta, Berta, Burta.

AUDREY (English) "strong,

AVIS (Latin) "a bird." Var. and dim., Ava, Avi.

AZALEA (Hebrew) "from a flower blossom." Var. and dim., Azaleah, Azelea, Azal, Zela, Zalea.

AZARIA (Hebrew) "blessed by God." Var. and dim., Azarria, Azeria, Azerria, Azar, Zaria, Zerr.

B

BAAL (Hebrew) "mistress; fair one." Var. and dim., Bael, Bal.

Above: The book from which Azaria's name was selected showing the meaning of her name as 'blessed by God'.

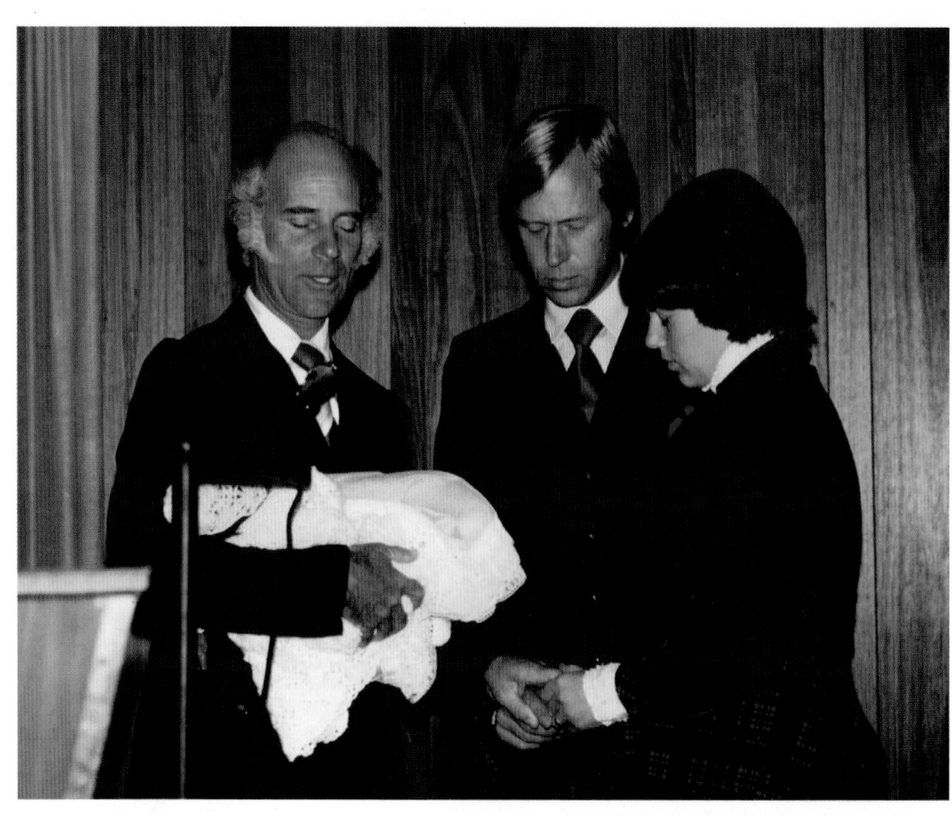

Azaria's dedication six weeks after her birth, at Mount Isa Seventh-day Adventist church.

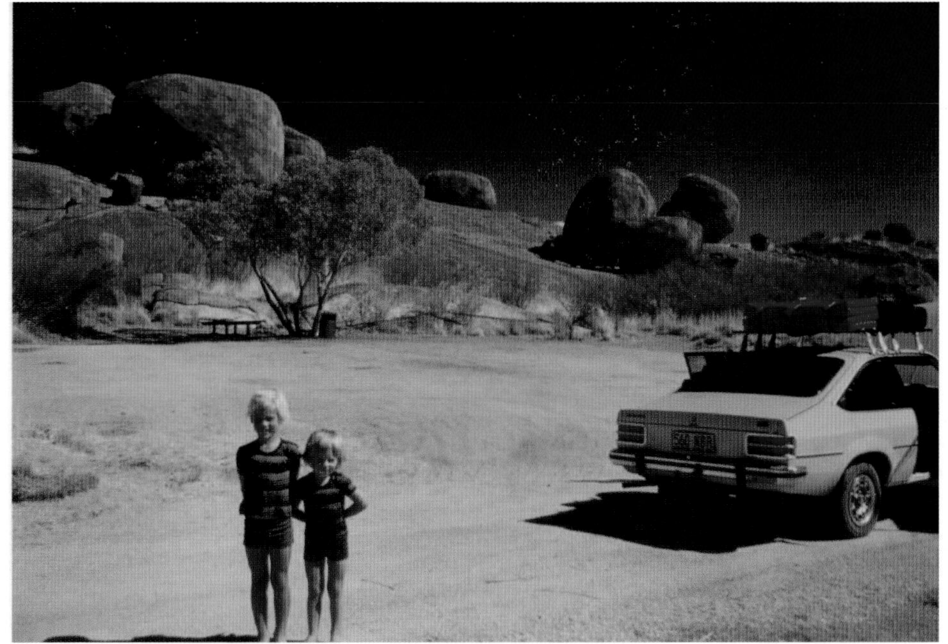

Above: Heading up for Ayers Rock, passing the 'Devil's Marbles'. Aidan and Reagan beside the V8 Torana hatchback, 15 August, 1980.

Below: The family and the hatchback at the turnoff to Ayers Rock, midday on 16 August, 1980.

Above: Holding Azaria 20 metres up from the base of Ayers Rock at about 2pm, 17 August, 1980.

another $1000 to buy champagne. The bouquets for the secretaries were to the order of $100 each. The following morning Tom Pauling's secretary came into the shop and ordered flowers for him with the message 'Sorry'. The secretary intimated that these were for Mrs Pauling because the party had gone on all night and he had not come home.'

Not long after Lindy went to jail another woman entered Picceen's shop and said,

'It's alright for Lindy Chamberlain. What about the poor jury?'

'Why the jury?' Picceen asked.

The lady pointed to the flowers and said: 'These flowers are for my friend who was on the jury. And he's got to live with the guilt for the rest of his life.'

Undeterred by the whole draconian saga, Malcolm Brown made it his business to embark on a visit to Berrimah Prison, where Lindy had spent her first few nights. He told me later of his rueful embarrassment at being locked up while on his self-conducted excursion to find her. 'I was appalled at what I saw,' he said. 'Here was this beautiful, innocent woman torn from her family and thrown into a virtual cage on the marshy flatlands of the Darwin hinterland for a crime I knew she had not committed, keeping company with the female flotsam of that part of the world. Even though Lindy was cheery, I was devastated.' (Letter to Michael Chamberlain 2/12/2008).

The prospects of a Federal Court Appeal and the chances of winning were gloomy. But now the *Melbourne Age* released a provocative Nicholson cartoon of a jury verdict hijacked by television. The heads of the 12 jurors were festooned by 12 TV screens. A donation was received by Stuart to help pay for the legal expenses, which would be huge. It was signed, 'Pagan pensioner'. 'God bless pagan pensioners', I thought. When I arrived home there were around 250 letters for me to mull over. These were dominated by feelings of anger and rage about our injustice. I decided to answer all of them, even if it had to be a circular letter.

Stuart Tipple asked me on 3 November 1982 who would look after our daughter when she was born. The custody issue looked bleak. Other women had been able to retain their babies in jail, but we felt that the

Northern Territory Government would not be sympathetic to Lindy. It was of great comfort, however, that one shining light in a dark place, Dr Douglas Mounsey, bravely granted his approval for my presence at our daughter's birth. Of further relief was that Mounsey was also happy for Lindy to keep her baby with her. The only problem would be, for how long? It was one thing for a child to suffer birth in jail hospital conditions but quite another thing for her to remain in prison. The prospect sickened me. Prisons are not places for children to grow up.

I wasn't in any hurry to divulge our daughter's name to anyone. We had thoroughly researched the name and while there might be meanings that came close, there was no exact meaning for this spelling because of its originality. We had neither seen in print or ever heard of any child called by her name. Anyhow 'Kahlia' was a feminine derivative of 'Charles', and that would be a safe enough meaning if it were linked to the kings and princes of England! We had been advised to call this girl 'Jane' or 'Jill' to silence the tongue-waggers but Lindy would not hear of it. I then tried to persuade Lindy to have her own name planted somewhere around the middle, but for some unknown reason Lindy would not buy that idea either.

The *Sun Herald* was the next paper to voice alarm on 3 November, also with another broadside into the jury verdict. The Sydney paper challenged the jury verdict on whether it had been 'a fair deal' for us after 'so much damaging evidence' at the second inquest. Another provocative cartoon under the signature of Zanetti, adorned the article. We were standing before the judge, and the jurors were represented as 12 rather eager, hungry-looking baying dingoes. My eye caught a second cartoon and the judge was reading from a petition stating Lindy was guilty. The sheet was loaded with paw prints. This media dissent caused in me a premature sense of triumph. (Lindsay Murdoch, who had covered the trial rang me for a comment on the evening of the 30th anniversary of Azaria's death, 17 August 2010. He told me that he knew of no journalist covering the case by the end of the Darwin trial in 1982 who thought we should be found guilty.)

And now Joy Kuhl felt the urge to speak to the media. In her press interview, Kuhl claimed she felt it was actually her on trial. 'The following day was my 40th birthday. I badly wanted to be home with my husband and three daughters... I sat alone in my room going over my notes and crying...My integrity and professionalism were under challenge...I felt I was on trial...I was under tremendous pressure but I have great confidence in my work and that saw me through.'

However, she admitted the trial 'had its lighter moments. The press all sang Happy Birthday as I walked into court and the Sheriff handed me a card...My daughters became 'celebrities' at school—Laraine even signed autographs for the other kids,' Kuhl beamed.

The Second Wave: Towards a Royal Commission

10. Unto Us Another Daughter is Given

The guilty verdict greatly affected the standing of the Seventh-day Adventist Church in the community. In a state of shock and tribulation, the Church itself felt that it was on trial. Church members, whether in the workplace or at non-church social occasions were often forced to defend themselves as reasonable law-abiding citizens, who were not cultish or did not countenance 'Jonestown'-style activities. Even Australian Christians generally, regardless of their denomination, felt they were on trial.

My first visit to the jail, Lindy's new 'home', 10 kilometres out from the Darwin CBD, on Saturday 30 October, was intimidating. The unsubtle array of surveillance devices, and large imposing airborne cameras over-arching the razor-wired drab grey brick security enclosure looked starkly odd against the mildly hazed blue sky. The prevailing barbaric sounds and stench from the squealing pigs across the road, meeting their fate at the Darwin Abattoir again added to the feeling of being in a science fiction horror film. We were carrying a number of suitcases and personal effects to Lindy as she began her life sentence with hard labour in 34 degrees of unbearable humidity.

We said very little. How could we not? We both felt mortally wounded, dazed. It was as if we were submerged in muddy water, with no idea where we were, and the air supply was short.

Pastor Olsen, now acting as the Darwin Church media spokesperson, chirped annoyingly: 'She is a strong little thing making the best of it.'

On Sunday 31 October, I flew home to see my children in Cooranbong, at long last. We had been apart for eight weeks. It would be a tough moment amidst the joy of seeing the boys. As I stepped off the plane at Sydney Airport, I saw a host of reporters waiting at the gates. I was in no mood to talk to them. I left that to Stuart, the last off the plane, loaded up to the armpits with legal documents. He told the waiting media that the anticipated first Appeal would be presented within 28 days. Meanwhile in Ellesmere, New Zealand, my very anxious father, Ivan Chamberlain, told the Christchurch *Press*: 'My son and his wife are innocent. I never thought any offspring of mine would be treated in such a way by a sister nation' (Christchurch *Press*, 1/11/1982). These words came from a deeply disillusioned man who had served the RNZAF as a pilot instructor and Warrant Officer in World War II and had an abiding respect for the New Zealand police and legal system.

With a conviction that sentences you to more than 12 months jail, whether suspended, or detained at Her Majesty's discretion, your status as a citizen is entirely changed. I was now officially a person of unsavoury character. To travel to another country was illegal. Fortunately, as a New Zealander, I could 'hop across the ditch' for a merciful weekend or enjoy a month with my relations. I later enquired into my status to re-enter Australia. It took seven consecutive calls to learn that the Federal Inspector at Sydney Airport might be able to provide an answer if I was on the prohibited list to re-enter Australia. To get the right information I was asked to ring the New Zealand Consulate followed by the Immigration Department, the Permanent Resident section, the re-entry visa section and the Federal Police section. When at last I spoke to someone who might help me, a senior sergeant and told him my name, he replied: 'Oh yes. I had better check to see if someone as notorious as you could re-enter.' Yet, thankfully, I did not have to report to any police station and I could move anywhere I wished—in Australia.

Meanwhile, Northern Territory Police Commissioner, Peter McAulay, told the world that the case had become all 'too emotional'. After all, it was 'just another mystery that was solved', he said. He did not fear any criticism about his police force because he 'was pleased with the police operation... When did we hear of any allegations from the Chamberlains of police malpractice?' he asked. When questioned if he had learned any lessons from the Azaria Chamberlain case, his answer was: 'No we have learned more lessons from other major investigations'. (*Sydney Morning Herald*, 3/11/1982). He told another Northern Territory 'confidant' that I had tried to be the hero and protect Lindy, but that I was now on the verge of telling all about her crime.

The Northern Territory police and government had gone a long way to deny natural justice to us, said the *Bulletin* (30/8/2005). At least one professional witness, at the campsite on the night of 17 August 1980, took a view that a dingo had taken Azaria and that we were point blank innocent. Aboriginal trackers who had been so effectively used by police forces in Australia and who had tracked the dingo that had killed Azaria on the night, were not called by either side to give their compelling testimony.

The Supreme Court verdict, claimed one newspaper, made Australian cops 'sick and bloody tired' of breaking up brawls because of the Lindy Chamberlain guilty verdict. The police wished they had never heard about Azaria Chamberlain. 'Every second blue is over this case,' a Melbourne Sergeant complained. The two camps, those who believed it was a dingo or that it was at least not proven beyond reasonable doubt, and those who believed she was definitely guilty because of her behaviour, her looks or some other intangible, were now constantly at loggerheads. (*New Zealand Truth,* 10/11/1982).

'Letters to the Editor' abounded. Newspapers and magazines were so inundated that they had to close correspondence on the subject. One Northern Territory Aboriginal girl living in Wandoan, Queensland, said she had seen so many dingoes 'hanging around Aboriginal camps 'as pets'' she could put all comers straight about their real nature. 'My people do not regard these lovely animals, so called, by a misguided few, as 'sensitive loving pets' but as ruthless hunting dogs...that lived only to hunt and kill.' Her authority came from her experience with her father who was a professional dingo trapper and well known in the Northern Territory, and corroborated by her 'full-blood grandfather'. If dingoes were harmless creatures, why did 'her father receive good money for trapping them on grazier's properties?' she argued (*Australasian Post*, 8/9/1983).

The media put to me privately that I should change my name and leave the country after the trial. My legal status as persona non grata had placed me at the mercy of people and exposed me to crackpots like the 'dreamer' clairvoyant from Burleigh Heads. He came forward to claim an 'impressive record of correctly predicting events in Australia and on the world stage' and could reveal the truth about us. This proclamation convinced one local editor to amuse his readers with his story. The dreamer had 'implicit faith in the gruesome story about us' and could verify that Azaria's parts 'were buried in three boxes'. The locations were 'so vivid in his mind' he knew where to find them. Azaria had told him these things and in her final appearance the month before she had revealed how Lindy 'had stabbed her in a large yellow box'. This was true because 'the baby Azaria told me that her mother would escape from jail and will leave the country soon with Mr Chamberlain.' Lindy and I were powerless to deal with this vicious nonsense. We were at the mercy of any innuendo that the media chose to print portraying Lindy as a murderer. A vicious element was emerging in Brisbane: people wanted to lynch or hang Lindy. Placards were seen in the street: 'Dingoes have suffered a great injustice. Why shouldn't Lindy suffer justice?' Signs appeared with a hangman's noose. But despite all this, as an innocent person, I remained proud of my name and believed deep down that somehow, some way, justice would not always be denied and that it would rise up one day to restore our good names.

The questions confronting us now were: How quickly could we lodge an appeal? Would Lindy remain in jail until the end of the appeal?' One thing was certain however: we were in no mood for trade-offs or compromises. Lindy and I had gone from being unknown people to infamous victims, pilloried, convicted and sentenced, but we would never lie down and give up. In a letter to the Orange newspaper, Phillipa Bennett, suggested just that, claiming: 'The Chamberlains have been crucified by the public, press and our legal system.' On top of this, came news that 'dingo pathologist' Professor Cameron was 'a bungler', a message too late for the jurors to hear. Judge Gerald Butler described Cameron and his fellow pathologist,

Graeme Snodgrass, as persons whose 'evidence was tainted by blunders', and filled with 'rubbish' *Brisbane Sunday Sun* (7/11/1982).

Dr Western Allen and Robert Brinsmead were among the first to campaign publicly in Australia to reverse the decision. They organised the first pro-Chamberlain rally in Brisbane with a modest but orderly crowd of 500 in attendance. (*The Sunday Times*, Perth 7/11/1982). It was a small beginning of a rear-guard action, a tiny ray of hope, probably a bit premature, but well intentioned.

University of New South Wales Law Faculty's Professor Julius Stone entered the debate, warning of the 'notorious danger' of circumstantial evidence alone, especially where no motive is produced. He advised a change in the law to allow warnings to be given to juries in such circumstances, or for controversial circumstantial evidence to be withdrawn. Next came one of Australia's most distinguished judges, Sir Reginald Sholl, who informed the media in a talkback radio session, that he had 'grave doubts' about the Darwin trial verdicts and had felt most uneasy. Sir Reginald, who had been a trial judge for 16 years and an Australian Consul-General in New York for three years, did not discount the claim that a dingo took Azaria. There was 'a genuine probability' that we were innocent. This trial had provided him with greater doubts than any trial he could remember. 'I would never have jailed Lindy,' he said. For that reason he was prepared to put his judgment on the line and seek an inquiry into the way we were convicted (*Brisbane Sunday Mail* 7/8/1983). Sholl was now 80 years old and had never met Lindy or me.

The immediate pressing question for us was: What would happen at the Federal Court Appeal? 'Not much,' replied our legal team. The reason was that Justice Muirhead had provided such a fair and balanced summary to the jury, expecting them to acquit, that there was little to complain about his handling of the case. Another difficulty lay in the fact that our scientists were continuing to analyse the reasons why the case went so wrong.

On 10 November 1982, Gordon Hammond drove me to Sydney airport to return to Darwin for our daughter's birth. The Church Aide, Pastor Ron Craig, quizzed me about my conviction and asked searching questions;

as well he might as the Church controller of the legal purse strings. He appeared to be relieved at my vehement affirmation of my innocence and reiterated that the Church was not going to desert us now that we were formally criminals. The Australian and New Zealand Seventh-day Adventist Churches seemed now to lock themselves in for the long haul in proving our innocence.

Recognising me on the Darwin TAA flight 480 from Sydney, a young flight attendant asked me about the case. I lamented, 'If only I could prove what really happened—I saw nothing. I heard a cry that I thought was Azaria and that was the last I knew of her existence.' I felt as though I was fighting the whole of Australia, but of course I wasn't. It was only 95 per cent of Australia and this flight attendant was now one less.

But the news just days before, at 12.30pm Saturday 6 November, that Lindy would not be able to keep our baby with her in prison, had caused new hostility and depression in the Chamberlain camp. Lindy was devastated. I felt no better and could not hide it, causing people to remark on my poor demeanour. It had been a bad day all round, but a constant flow of sympathisers and flowers came by our little home. The press were also constant in their demands for a response. They got nothing.

Lindy's mother, Avis Murchison, asked Lindy if she could care for the baby and Lindy said yes. But I wanted Kahlia come home and live with me and the boys. Avis was an elderly person with a sick husband, for days confined to his bed. Trying to look after a very young child, and all the rest of the family was too much. My vision was to have Kahlia to be brought up in a rich learning and loving environment and her grandparents could not do that anymore. Furthermore, it was not for Lindy alone to make such a decision, ignoring my wishes.

It was a bad time for people to ask how I felt about the whole deal. I had to be careful and in doing so I must have seemed evasive. But to be frank, I was so confused I didn't know what I thought. It was like trying to sort out fresh eggs in my hand while having rotten eggs forcibly crushed around them.

By the time of my next scheduled visit to Lindy on Thursday, 11 November, I was in Darwin preparing for our baby to arrive. Lindy rang and broke the news to me, that 'I would be able to see our baby for just one hour after the birth and that was it'. She couldn't talk any more. She choked and sobbed uncontrollably. A little later in the conversation I asked her, 'How soon did they say they would take the baby off you?' She replied, still sobbing. 'I will not be able to see her at all'. I reflected: 'How much more psychological cruelty could she endure? If this despicable act occurs I am going to need a lot of support to get this little mite down to Sydney by plane and then what?'

Part of the temporary solution arrived on 15 November. Lindy's parents with Aidan and Reagan arrived in Darwin from Sydney. I was also told by a Northern Territory official that after the birth, Lindy should be heavily sedated and that she should refuse any milk suppressant on account of a possibility of contracting breast cancer. She should fight for the right to express her breast milk and to be able to pass it on to our baby. While the blow for Lindy was another in a series of unforgivable outcomes, our little girl's future was paramount. The local news bulletins, both TV and print media, announced through the Director of Corrective Services, Bob Donnelly, that according to the *Northern Territory Prisons Act*, he would decide whether or not Lindy could breastfeed the baby after birth. It beggars belief that something as natural as breast-feeding a child should be decided on by the Corrective Services.

Early on 17 November 1982, the jail phoned Liz Parry, our friend and main Darwin contact, to inform us that Lindy was installed in the Casuarina Hospital in Darwin and that she was having contractions at two to three-minute intervals. Lindy had been secretly rushed to hospital at 5am from the jail. I dressed in haste and was driven at high speed to the maternity wing. As I approached, there seemed to be a huge delegation of media. Every TV reporter and media station appeared to be there. But the press would have to be content being outwitted by local knowledge once again. A Sydney newspaper offered me $20,000 for a peek photo of the little girl. That amount of money could do a lot, but I refused. She must be kept out of the public glare for as long as possible.

When I reached the obstetrics ward on the sixth floor, several plain-clothed police and a hospital security guard, brandishing a two-way radio, intercepted me.

'You will not be allowed in to see your wife or your daughter being born until it is all over, Mr Chamberlain,' a balding Special Services official told me, wearing an insipid smile.

It was like trying to stop me from breathing.

'That is quite unacceptable,' I replied, 'You should realise, sir, that I have prior authority from the doctor supervising her birth, Dr Douglas Mounsey.'

The man with the shiny balding head stood silently, smiling, waiting for my next move. This was now a game of chess and it was my move after feeling like it was checkmate. I knew that the Northern Territory authorities would deny us taking any photographs at her birth. There would be no memory of what she was like...nothing.

'Well then, I demand to speak to Dr Mounsey.' I replied. There was a long pause waiting for a response, but they would have been recording my every word and move.

'Ok, if you continue to obstruct my entry to see Lindy and my newborn daughter I may consider calling my own press conference. Pick your headline. Whichever it is, it won't be pretty with those baying journalists out there grinding on the story they have all been stalking me for.'

Another interminable 15 minutes went by. The Special Services men had stopped smiling and had retreated behind locked doors in earnest conversation. Under heavy armed prison escort, the number one threat to the Territory was let in.

'We apologise for the delay Mr Chamberlain,' a contrite guard replied. 'Your authority to enter was delayed by mistake.'

The reunion was a wonderful but tense affair. Lindy was under huge psychological pressure. But to see my newborn child was magic and like me, Lindy was ecstatic and relieved. In a modern and ultra-clean looking environment, our new daughter, Kahlia Shonell Nikari Chamberlain, came into the world on the morning of 17 November 1982 at approximately 10am. No one would be told of her name until many days later, however. The threat of the removal of Kahlia was like the sword of Damocles over Lindy's head. She did not know how long she would have Kahlia before she would be taken off her. But at least Kahlia was born safe and well, thank God! The attending nurses and female prison guards were warm and accepting and remarkably, gave us space. (I was so grateful that I grabbed the most empathetic and friendly prison guard, Mrs Yardley, picked her up off her feet and swung her around the hospital ward.) They left Lindy and me with our one-hour-old daughter to enjoy a brief moment of bliss. I was told that I had exactly one hour, but we got closer to four. I shall forever be grateful to those legendary nurses.

Unbeknown to me, the Northern Territory Community Development department was anxious to show the world that humane decisions were being made about the arrival of our new baby. It had also been suggested that Kahlia might become 'a ward of the state' (*The Sun* 2/11/1982). The press inevitably tried to get to me later that day to report. But I declined again, instructing a spokesperson to tell the waiting hordes: 'Lindy had a girl. Mother and baby are doing well. It was a safe delivery.'

Everingham was not aware at the time that his decree to keep Lindy from Kahlia was about to be overruled. Our lawyers approached the Sydney-based Federal Appeals Court on 18 November. Two of the three judges, Justices Fox, Northrop and Lockhart, accepted that Kahlia's best interests were for Lindy to be freed under bail of $300 in order to look after her. Ian Barker opposed the bail, but to no avail. The successful bail application now allowed Lindy to fly home with us. This was totally unexpected but the joy was restrained in the knowledge that jail loomed large if the Federal Court appeal failed.

On 21 November 1982, at 4.30am, unseen by and unbeknown to any media, Lindy was spirited out of Casuarina Hospital by helpful nurses with our four-day-old Kahlia. It was already a hot and humid morning and sweat was pouring off us, despite the sunrise being an hour away. Our car, driven by our Darwin solicitor Greg Cavenagh, sped through the deserted Darwin streets under police escort to the airport. Lindy got RAAF, VIP treatment at the airport. I was supremely grateful to whoever had arranged this and said a prayer for God to bless them. The RAAF, with the assistance of Darwin Seventh-day Adventist Church members, supported Lindy until the TAA Boeing 727 flew out of Darwin. Privacy from the media and security from any insane and crazed Darwinians trying to hurt or kill her was of paramount importance. We were escorted to the rear of the aircraft where no one was allowed to sit within 10 rows of us. I sat beside Lindy in one of the rear passenger seats.

There was one moment of terror when a hoaxer called from a Darwin phone box threatening to blow up the plane we were on. The plane was delayed for 30 minutes while police and bomb disposal experts searched for the bomb. One might have been forgiven for saying: 'It all goes with the territory.' Every passenger on this flight was security checked. A large catering truck obscured the boarding entrance of the plane. Two journalists faked busting to go to the toilet at the rear of the plane. As they passed they looked furtively in our direction to try to capture a description of Lindy and the baby. One of them approached me but Greg Cavenagh intervened and sent the man on his way.

Meanwhile, back at Avondale College, preparations were being made for our arrival and personal security. The Church had acted strategically, politely inviting all media to leave the grounds and not to return. A new sentry box armed with guard dogs was erected for our security. I was overwhelmed: the floodlights, the official-looking barriers and the uniformed security men at the gate. Nothing had ever been seen before like it at Avondale and the whole town was agog. Part of the security arrangements, that we transferred behind the security gates to 5 College Drive, the inner sanctum of the College, did not meet with Lindy's approval. She seemed put-out by this 'unnecessary' decision.

It was a security arrangement, I tried to tell her, and she needed to accept this while she was under bail conditions waiting for the Federal Court Appeal in April 1983. The other house we had stayed in for eight months was larger and had given us more latitude but we were not paying for this and had to put the best spin on the move and be grateful. In the eyes of the law we were convicted persons and must accept the restrictions.

It did not take long for the security to be tested by the media. Steve Brien, for the *Sydney Sun* newspaper was ready to draw any blood out of the Ayers Rock saga he could, reporting: 'TV Man: Scuffle over Lindy' in a front-page headline. The 'man' was Mike Munro working for Channel

10, who pushed his way into the College with his camera crew after being told by a College security guard to leave. His pretext was that he wished to speak to the College President, Dr James Cox. The College administration was in no mood for any media ruses, stating that the College was adamant there should be no access to us for any reason except through our attorneys. 'I have orders not to allow members of the media inside,' the guard told Munro. 'Please leave immediately.' The intruders had acted as if it had been their divine right to walk anywhere in the College for any reason. Munro did not get it. We would have been in jeopardy with Lindy's bail if the media had have interviewed us. Lindy would have been arrested by the police and taken straight back to jail for contempt of court.

Yet Munro was not willing to take no for an answer and moved forward. He seemed keen to wrestle the guard at the boom gate to gain entry. With no police in sight, the guard had little option but to physically restrain Monroe and escort him to his taxi. Monroe, by no means a small man, alleged he had been grabbed by the neck and pushed back towards the car. He also claimed that the guard tried to grab the camera.

The politically astute Dr Cox responded to Channel 10's complaint. 'No one bothered to call me,' he said, 'but if the media were seeking a comment I would be happy to provide them with one.' He apologised to Channel 10 for any perception of misconduct by the guard but added that the Channel 10 reporter must also accept some of the blame. Dr Cox remarked that 'the reporter should have respected the need for us to co-operate with police and law officials and take all necessary security precautions in order to live within the requirements of the Federal Court' (*Hobart Mercury*, 23/11/1982).

Moves were afoot in the town to start their own action committee for an inquiry into the case. Dr Gena Levitch, a former Seventh-day Adventist, told the press: 'Many people are very upset. They feel they have been betrayed by the judicial system. We believe the conviction puts all Australians at risk.' His action, supported by other intellectuals, artists and professionals in Martinsville, west of Cooranbong, helped buoy my spirits. This was not a Seventh-day Adventist-inspired operation but a group of secular dissenters. 'Hey,' I thought, 'perhaps there are more people who have seen through this injustice than I gave credit for.' Gena Levitch saw a terrible imbalance from past media reporting. The media had portrayed Lindy to shape her as a woman with no feeling. But Levitch observed, 'If you understand their religious background, you'd understand her behaviour' (*Sun* 4/11/1982).

The following month, the *Sun Herald* (26/12/1982) had stories and photos of the joy and gladness of the rich and famous, Prince Charles and Princess Diana with Prince William cradled in their arms, adjacent to Azaria and Lindy 'tried and convicted of the murder of her baby daughter'. The paper remarked that having been discussed in 'every living-room in Australia was details of the story that remain a nagging mystery'. The *Daily Telegraph* (26/12/1982) called 1982 'The Year of Joy and Tragedy' and 'The year of the baby'. Our picture was juxtaposed with Princess Diana's baby. There had been 'Many battles of heart and home', another headline read. The text began: 'In review, 1982 was a year of war and tragedy...' with the Falklands War cited along with our convictions and Lindy's release pending the Appeal. Also listed were the deaths of my favourite, Princess Grace of Monaco, and of Ingrid Bergman. The *Daily Telegraph*'s headline on 31 December headlined: 'That was the year that was: Azaria, politics and jobs dominate headlines.' This time also regrettably marked the end of a professional relationship with John Phillips QC, who was appointed as the public prosecutor of Victoria. His duties would include preparation for matters of the Australian High Court, Supreme Court and County Court.

Also during the month of December my mother, Greta Chamberlain wrote a memorable letter from the farm home at 'Thongsleigh' on the banks of the Selwyn River at Ellesmere, directing it to the New Zealand Prime Minister, The Right Honourable R.D. Muldoon.

'I write to you as the mother of Michael Chamberlain. You may regard this letter as one of bias but nevertheless I seek your attention to the following remarks. Let me commence by saying that I have absolutely no doubts as to the innocence of my son over this whole utterly bizarre and incomprehensible affair. A mother knows her children and their ways better than any other person on earth. While nobody is perfect, and that includes my son as much as I love him and am proud of his calling and achievements, in all honesty it would be gravely remiss if in any way I was to misrepresent the truth as I know it in this impassioned letter.

'Sir, I wish to say categorically, that at no time in the past or present since before during or after the loss of Azaria have I had any reason whatsoever to doubt my son's truthfulness over this whole affair. Although I do not know my daughter-in-law as well as my own flesh and blood, I still must say the remarks I made about my son must be said about her also. My son is the type of person who, if guilty of a misdemeanour, cannot hide his distress for long. His depression and fears are too easily transparent, and his conscience too strong for him to hide the truth of any wrongdoing. He was called to be a minister of the Gospel. He remains a minister of the Gospel. He continues to be as resolute about his knowledge about the loss of Azaria as he was in the beginning...

'Both my head and my heart inform me that this has been one of the most shocking miscarriages of justice in modern Australian legal history... My son and his wife are both New Zealand born citizens, and as such, I wish to register my protest that this sort of thing can happen to New Zealand citizens without my Government being aware of the situation. I therefore seek your objective influence to do all that is within your power to press for the thorough investigation into the affair, should the impending appeal not be upheld and the verdict be quashed.

'Should you wish to check on my own integrity as a person in the community you are welcome to do so. I have just completed a term of six consecutive years on the Seventh-day Adventist Church executive body governing the South New Zealand, and was the first woman to be selected to such office. For the last eight years I have worked for the prestigious J. Ballantyne and Co. Ltd. and am an authorized person on the staff.

Yours Faithfully, Mrs Greta Chamberlain.'

Meanwhile I received my Master of Arts degree at Avondale College from Michigan, Andrews University. Avondale's Academic Dean, Dr Alex Currie, speaking on Sunday, 28 November to a *Sydney Morning Herald* reporter, said: 'We've all been amazed how Michael was able to come back and complete his degree this year.' Anger had propelled me to some extent but I am certain that the motivation given to me by God was also responsible for my success. Part of me wanted to demonstrate to the Northern Territory that although they could destroy reputations they would have a problem destroying my will or character. I am an emotional person who can sometimes be overwhelmed and appear to be too meek, an unpopular trait in the postmodern world of self-assertiveness. But this was only one side of me. The other side was to be deeply grateful to my class colleagues when they practised what they preached, mediating for me to delay a crucial exam for 24 hours when under particular duress. The German lecturer in Old Testament Biblical Studies, brilliant in his field, seemed to have adopted an Old Testament, 'the letter of the law' attitude and despite my problems with court preparation, was going to fail me by refusing to give me an extension of time to prepare.

The applause of the 2000-odd people in the College auditorium was tumultuous and sustained. The standing ovation and constant clapping overwhelmed me to the extent I became very embarrassed. I had never seen this at a College graduation. I was momentarily stunned. As my name was called, the cheering and applause went on and on. As I touched my cap, shook the hand of the dignitary, took my degree, shook another hand, left the podium, forgot to sign the registry, walked to my seat, sat down, wept in gratitude and the applause still went on. It was a red-letter day, a signal that I seemed to be on the way back. Also Kahlia's name had been made official and the community was in a state of unfettered euphoria.

Surely nothing worse could happen for a while, but I was wrong. The erudite members of the press had by now scoured the world's languages and came up with their meaning of the name 'Kahlia'. It came, they said from an Aboriginal term meaning 'male dog' (*The Sunday Telegraph* 26/11/1982). (Dr Norman Young later wrote in 'Prejudicial factors in the Chamberlain convictions', 10/7/1986, that the false interpretation was based on a 'precarious phonic link with a single place name in one Aboriginal dialect'.) To refute this type of linguistic madness in a rational argument with the media, would have been futile.

11. The End of the Line?

Those who seek the sunrise must live through the night.

Michael McHugh QC, appealing on our behalf at the Federal Court, had some fresh evidence of our innocence and stated that Lindy's tears were one indication of a not-guilty person. She was 'No Lady Macbeth' he had said in his introduction on 28 February 1983. Furthermore, the QC had queried the impossibly short time Lindy would have had to take Azaria's life. In casting doubt on the prosecution experts, McHugh was disadvantaged by not having yet received the new blood evidence from Behringwerke, Germany, likely to refute all Joy Kuhl's findings because she had used the wrong reagent to test for foetal blood in my car. Being in possession of that information would have kept Lindy out of jail.

At 10.04am on 27 April, 1983, Stuart Tipple rang with the awful news that the Full Bench of the Federal Court required us to be present at the Federal Court buildings in Sydney in two days time. I broke the news to Lindy and she became very emotional. Her worst fears came to the fore, and mine weren't far behind. It was unthinkable that Lindy and I would again face a lifetime of say 20 years apart. For me it was the beginning of the fight for justice.

To continue with her day classes in first year BA Education at College became mission impossible. Lindy had no choice but to begin packing in earnest, anticipating the worst. Two large suitcases were opened and as I lamely offered to help, I tried to forget what I saw. It was like preparing for death. A parole officer's words kept repeating in my brain, giving me stomach cramp: 'You don't win court appeals easily.'

Lindy could not settle, even for a minute. Always on edge, face strained beneath a shallow smile, the imminent fateful day to hear the judgment coming relentlessly closer. The boys and Kahlia were effectively distracted. They, at least, had friends coming to mind them while we were out during the day and were always in caring, loving hands. Our close friends were wonderfully unselfish and understanding. It was a time when unconditional love seemed all around us, but in our personal lives it felt as if we were sponges with an infinite capacity to receive but nothing to give.

It was a very stressful time made worse by the publication of public opinion poll in the March edition of *The Bulletin* on Lindy. Forty-two per cent of people thought Lindy should be locked away for life. Only 40 per cent thought she should be shown any mercy with a remitted sentence. The other 18 per cent were undecided. Her main sympathisers were women over 50 years old, with only 35 per cent locking her away for life. Her main antagonists were teenagers, of whom 48 per cent believed that the key should be thrown away. (*The Bulletin,* 10/4/1983).

Despite all else around me, I knew I had to continue in my exercise regime, three times a week running up to 30 kilometres. It re-energised my will to keep fighting. I always ran with friends, ministers and scientists from the adjoining Sanitarium Health food factory to the College. I trained gently for Fun Runs around Lake Macquarie, Newcastle and the Central Coast. My sons were now nine and seven and I encouraged them to jog a few kilometres as well. They did not complain too much. They were robust and energetic for their age and quite competitive, especially Aidan.

My obsession at this time remained with reading and scanning every piece of news I could lay my hands on relating to our case. Had there been any intrinsic guilty feelings I would never have started this archival activity. But deep inside I felt compelled to keep all documents and become a shrew that compiled material which now filled many four-drawer filing cabinets. It was my preparation for research and the potential war on injustice.

I was grateful to be gainfully employed on a part-time basis in assisting President Jim Cox with research on secondary students and their reasons for selecting Avondale College. I also became a key photographer for the Church's related publications, College magazines, and other sundry productions, many of them ending up as full page or double page spreads.

We lived to some extent off people's donations and charity. But the Church also supplemented my income with the three-quarter salary of a retiree. Many Church members invited us to lunch or evening meals. We owned little, but financially we were relatively happy. I don't remember lacking any major necessity. We purchased a two-year-old white Ford Falcon XD GL through an auction. The car had been a detective's vehicle and I remember, when detailing it for the first time, finding a silver .38 special calibre revolver bullet case and projectile in the car boot.

The dreaded day, Black Friday, 29 April 1983 started early. Lindy and I arose at 4.30am, and quickly dressed, trying not to think what the day might hold for us. It was Lindy in particular that I was deeply upset about. She might never come home again. One of the carers had arrived early and was watching over the sleeping boys who would be attending school as usual. She tried hard to be brave about the day, but was clearly upset like us all. Kahlia had gone to the capable and loving hands of Wayne and Jenny Miller only 10 kilometres away in Morisset. This was Lindy and my choice for the time being.

Lindy now performed one of her hardest acts ever. She went into the boys' room and reminded them of the possible consequences of this day's proceedings. I saw the tears in the boy's eyes and the droplets slowly curling down their cheeks. As our car crossed the Sydney Harbour Bridge two hours later, Lindy squeezed my hand. Was she thinking this could be her last look? We arrived at the Court around 8.40am. The traffic was light. I would have given anything for this day to be just a dream. We again tried to outwit the media, but three photoflashes were enough to get us on any front news page in the nation and the world. If I felt numb and nervous as I stumbled from the car, what must Lindy be feeling? At exactly 9.45am we were ushered into a packed courtroom. It was deja-vu.

As was my custom now, following legal instruction, I looked neither left nor right. Just straight ahead, expressionless.

At 10am three judges entered the court. 'All stand,' intoned the court officer. We sat down and within 60 seconds it was all over. It was swift and cruel. Lindy was again pronounced incarcerated for the term of her natural life. She would be delivered into the custody of Mr Fred Mercer, Superintendent at Berrimah Prison, Darwin. It had occurred in the second highest court in the land. Would we ever dare to go to the highest authority for justice, the High Court?

Meanwhile, in Darwin a carnival atmosphere prevailed on the hot and steamy night of the decision. People were eating, drinking and laughing. James Oram, the *Daily Mirror* journalist (29/4/1983) wrote of the supreme faith that the Darwin crowd had placed in their own, a faith that the Federal Court now endorsed. Oram, 13 years later, described Lindy's face 'as of stone and it remained unmovable'. In his hotel bar it was announced over the intercom, 'The dingo is acquitted...the dingo didn't do it... The bitch has been found guilty.' *Herald Sun* (17/12/1985). Oram recorded how 'the patrons cheered and whooped' as if they had heard the winning result of their favourite football team.

Lindy and I had lost our Federal Court appeal. Two women took her to a room on Floor 22 where she was held in custody. Plain-clothes Federal police at first observed the rest of us in silence, but after the first hour they relaxed and chatted, freely holding Kahlia and eating food with us in the cafeteria. It was a very traumatic experience for the four who came and supported us. Ross Sorbello, a new friend on the scene, had been an objective and intelligent graduate of the College Theology faculty. I liked him because his counsel brought reflectiveness, devoid of emotional baggage. Ten years my junior, he was logical, perceptive and objective. He had sort of attached himself to me, seeing the almost impossible mission I was on and, like a brother, escorted me as a guide and counsellor. The three ladies who came to support us, Jenny Miller, Ann Degan and Denise Roy wept openly with us on several occasions. The press would never see these tears of extreme anguish.

When my brother, Peter, learned of the decision he was visibly shaken and angry. He exclaimed, 'Oh God no! I feel so sick for Lindy and Mike. Over the last month she seems to have lost all courage and hope. She was simply living from day to day. Now it has happened I just feel sick. I have never been more sure in my life that Lindy is innocent. Even if she had killed the child, there is no way Michael could have covered it up.' Peter, an exceptionally strong and fit man, said that the entire episode of the three-year saga had affected the family's health (*The Daily Mirror* 29/4/1983).

At about 2.45pm we all left the tight security of the Federal Court building. Kahlia, wrapped in a white crochet rug, was kept from the prying eyes of the media but again several photographers tried to score. Their cars followed us into the middle of the city where at one set of red lights, a very agile press photographer jumped from his car and sprinted up to our vehicle. His flash got Kahlia almost squarely between the eyes at 20 centimetres away. He left rubbing his hands with glee as he escaped back to his car. Had Kahlia not been between him and myself I think I would have jumped out of my car and ripped the film from his camera.

Such was the tenacity of the press. We were trailed for the full distance to Mulawa, the woman's detention centre at Silverwater prison. There, before our eyes, were a whole battery of cameras and journalists. We did not stop, but instead drove straight ahead and around the prison complex to find the women's quarters. As we entered the bleak stalag-like prison, with its imposing four-metre-high silver razor-wire fences, the cold dull thunk of the padlock keys gave the impression of icy, soulless permanence. We went through several checkpoints like this, deep into the bowels of the jail.

The next day we were granted permission to have Kahlia fed by Lindy four times for the day and were excused from having to run the gauntlet on foot from the media's telephoto lenses. We were also permitted to see Lindy five consecutive days before her transfer to Darwin. Such was the build-up of public tension, the press became highly frustrated as a result of lack of personal comment and would have tried almost anything to get near her. One female *Sydney Morning Herald* journalist considered an ambitious plan. She wanted to ring the police and confess to all of her unpaid fines in the hope she might be locked up in the same section as Lindy and get the scoop of the year.

On Monday at midday I sought permission to see the Superintendent and Deputy to clarify procedure on entering the prison by car (as I approached the prison and had the car stop, press cameras jammed hard against my window) but only the Minister for Corrective Services could give us special rights to escape the cameras. Lindy, I was dismayed to hear later, was receiving fewer privileges than the regular prisoners. On Wednesday 4 May, the fifth and final day at Mulawa, Lindy would fly out for Darwin. I had little sleep, waking often in fear of not catching any glimpses of her this morning. Our little group of vigilant ladies tossed up how to say goodbye—whether to use 10 buckets of white chrysanthemums, a simple posey or nothing. I need not have bothered: the prison guards slipped her out very early. By 6.30am we were figuring out how much longer we would stay, when Channel 10 informed us that Lindy was at Sydney Airport. I lapsed into heavy depression for the rest of the day. I spoke to no one and walked around in a dull stupor.

Kahlia would now only be a precious memory for Lindy. Kahlia was a beautiful little thing who was being fed well. She was on breast milk from her foster mum Jenny who had a little girl, Tiana Jade, a few months older than Kahlia. I was grateful that at least I had Kahlia and I had my boys, Aidan and Reagan who would really need me now, quite desperately. But I would no longer be able to express my love for Lindy either physically, or by letter, or face to face, or even by phone and I did not know how long this would last. It was as if she were away at war, missing in action, with all the uncertainty that it brought with it.

Everything was now monitored. A police informant was put on my tail to monitor every movement. My phone was tapped. At least Kahlia did not know what had happened; although one day she would find out. She was oblivious to this malignant act.

Within the first two weeks of Lindy's return to jail, around 11 May 1983, I was asking myself about Kahlia's future. Would it be best for her to be with Lindy in the 34 degree Celsius humid heat of the Berrimah Prison? Would Kahlia's security and character development be assured in an environment of persons with undesirable character traits ranging from murder or violence or ultra-selfish agendas? (Lindy already knew the type of people she was forced to mix with and not all of the dangerous ones were just fellow inmates.) If anything untoward happened to Kahlia in prison what rights would Lindy have, or me for that matter, to get a proper resolution?

On consulting Stuart Tipple, the advice came back to make an application for Kahlia to be with Lindy, then seek a transfer for her to Mulawa after six months. I contacted a child psychiatrist, Bob Adler, concerning the welfare of children under two in challenging situations. The messages I received were that children up to the age of 18 months could be fed by an affectionate bonding person other than the mother, without serious consequences. If at least one parent was the permanent bonding contact, with supplementary support from a nanny-type person, Kahlia's well-being would be assured. A child's security and bonding comes from the familiarity and trust in 'gaze, hugging and kissing, and continuous attachment'. Behavioural psychologists considered breast-feeding optional, but they weren't nutritionists and I had a view that breast milk was created for a reason and that its nutritional value was second to none.

The information I received favoured the view that for Lindy to care for our daughter in the insecure and nefarious environment of a prison would not be in the best interests of Kahlia or the rest of the family. However, if a restricted environment did not dramatically affect a child's development I was quite willing to consent to Kahlia being with Lindy until 18 months of age. Whichever way it went, the choice was not easy, that was for sure. Greg Cavenagh was adamant that Lindy should apply for Kahlia now, and this she did. I guess a little selfishness was creeping in here, for my boys and I would be heartbroken if Kahlia left us, the identity and bonding we so desired would evaporate, not to mention the deep concern in the College community. Given Lindy's frame of mind, I was becoming concerned that any letters she wrote for publication might contain words and sentiments that would undermine the efforts or morale of our growing band of supporters who wanted an inquiry into the evidence, especially forensic evidence that had convicted us. Stuart thought I was being somewhat paranoid about this. But I chose to be discrete, if not more understated.

On 20 May 1983, I received a longed-for letter from Lindy. Not usually an enthusiastic letter writer myself, I was fired up to reply. The big problem was what to write and what to leave out. I dared not be too personal, since every communication was scrutinised. This was also the question of my friends and relatives. 'What can I say?' Gordon Hammond and Ross Sorbello came to check on my well-being. Ross, thinking strategically, provided me with three options for the future: Either I accept the guilty verdict as charged and have Lindy leave prison without a fight within say two years, or seek an inquiry into a miscarriage of justice which does not criticise the Northern Territory, or thirdly, seek an inquiry into claims of a cover up and a deliberate conspiracy to cause miscarriage of justice. The first proposition was unpalatable and the third seemed impossible to achieve, but the second was appealing, at least for the Northern Territory! Before he left, Ross advised me to take out a life insurance policy. I signed for a modest $150,000.

The next day I was made aware of the work of John Bryson. I was told that he was a writer and lawyer who lived on a yacht. He was rich and was hard to contact. I was told that if he contacted me I should consider carefully before I denied any request. He had courteously sought permission to print an article with the title 'Azaria, a trial for everyone', and I gave it. Bryson possessed that curious blend of incisive analysis, wrapping it in a creative blend of insight and imagery that could not fail to ignite a time bomb under an act of serious government indiscretion. On his own admission he 'did not care for us' and he 'did not warm to us personally' (*Newcastle Herald* 28/11/1995). His offhandedness towards me did not faze me. A legally contexted 'documentary novel' seemed the most appropriate way to go, given such a sensitive case. Bryson never contacted me, other than the hour he spent clarifying a few simple points leading to fact.

The dreaded Federal Court judgment needed to be copied in triplicate, and, courtesy of the College and with the assistance of a supporter, the task was done quickly. It remained gratifying that the Church still wanted to pour money into our exoneration and to support us with unconditional love. I felt overwhelmed by their unwavering support. It was confirmed that they would back us in yet another Appeal, this time to the High Court of Australia. If that appeal failed, it was the end of the legal line for us. Forever we would remain criminals and the butt of every foul and pestilent slur.

12. One Last Chance?

My voyage to see my wife imprisoned in Darwin's Berrimah Prison was on 19 June, 1983. I had miscalculated the busy Sydney traffic, however and I arrived terribly late at 7.54am in the Sydney Airport Ansett terminal. All was not well. The Ansett official stared at me in my forlorn state.

'The plane has gone. The plane has gone! Can't you see? The plane has gone! You had to be here 15 minutes ago to have any chance.' I was devastated by his response. I could see the aircraft was still on the tarmac.

An hour later I was on another plane but it went the opposite way for a 1000 kilometres to Adelaide before heading towards Darwin. There was a mood shift on the Adelaide to Darwin route. My mood was morose and I saw the passengers, mainly Territorians, as the enemy.

I was given some good news just before I left home, however. On 14 June, Stuart informed me that Behringwerke, the German manufacturers who made the blood reagent, now officially corroborated Professor Boettcher's testimony in the trial, that Joy Kuhl had used the wrong test for foetal blood in my car.

This revelation was particularly important for the spray pattern under my car's dashboard. In the second inquest, Crown pathologist, Dr Tony Jones had made the most sensational and terrifying claim of the whole court case. He had testified that, 'On close inspection, in my opinion, the blood spurt was travelling from the front of the vehicle toward the rear of the vehicle. It's a fine spray and I would say it has come from a small artery.'

'The heart was beating when the blood was spurting?' Sturgess had asked him.

'Yes, it was from—that's right, from a living animal or human and from a small artery.'

The front page of every newspaper in the country heralded the ghastly news.

This 'blood' description had been the most critical and sensational piece of evidence nailing us to a guilty verdict in the Darwin jury trial. When it was again presented as flawed forensic science in our appeal to the Federal Court, two of the three Federal Judges had not recognised its significance. Joy Kuhl's supervisor, Dr Simon Baxter, swore on oath that Kuhl was telling the truth, and Brian Culliford, from the London Metropolitan Police Laboratory, approved of her methods. This corroboration appeared to have won the day with this Court.

In the trial, Barker made light of the spray pattern. 'I don't know that you're asked to find that all Toranas are sprayed under the dash with the blood of an infant as some sort of benediction or ceremonial rite when the cars are sold...We know that on the real (Chamberlain) plate there is blood. We know that the blood is part of the pattern...all we say is that (second) plate is irrelevant.' Second inquest Coroner Galvin found that four of the six reasons for committing us to trial depended on traces of blood in the car and that if the dashboard spray was the most sensationally damning one, it was absolutely vital to find the truth about this. The facts were that there was more than one other Torana plate with similar spray patterns, but Holden did not wish to comment.

Then there was the fine blood spray on the side of our humble text, mistaken for a mosquito blood smear, or something else equally ridiculous. If ever there was evidence of Azaria being attacked by a dingo in our tent, this was it. But from the moment the forensic examination began, the dingo attack seemed to be an unpalatable option for the Northern Territory authorities.

My first visit to Lindy forced me to meet the jail superintendent,

Frederick Mercer, who struck me as a power freak. His steely grey eyes bored into you as he scanned your whole being from behind his large office desk, upstairs in the prison tower. He seemed to relish the idea of removing stray media who ventured onto his prison turf. Any filming had to take place more than 100 metres away, at the end of the prison driveway. Even the mere presence of a camera this far away would send the security guards into apoplexy, flying down the driveway to apprehend the evil ones. I heard him tell one guard: 'Cast your beautiful blue eyes towards the prison entrance and behold what I think is a television camera. Go and check it out will you?'

Mercer gave me a lecture on how to behave in the prison. I was to be given 'exactly one hour with Lindy and that will be all for the week,' he said imperiously.

When I saw Lindy, 55 minutes later, she looked as if she had been crying. Her eyes and lips were heavy with make-up. When she nervously set eyes on Kahlia, now seven months old, in her stroller, Lindy asked me to pick her up and hand her across. Kahlia was uncomfortable and wriggled. 'You take her, she doesn't know me anymore', Lindy said in a flat weary voice. Alas, it seemed to be true but towards the end of my first visit, Kahlia began to focus on her and allowed Lindy to pick her up. Mercer begrudgingly gave me three one-hour visits from Monday to Wednesday.

On the second visiting day, Mercer again put me through the ritual of adopting proper decorum in the prison. He rang the control box and told the guard to 'Cast your eyeballs toward the gate and see if any media are there. Take their number plates down.' He continued to not allow us the privilege of going outside to talk on the pretext that 'snoopy media cameras might be lurking'. Lindy was again upset, this time with what she described as 'nosy prison warders' discussing her mail between them. Postmarks on the envelopes indicated that someone seemed to be withholding her mail.

The prison chief made no call on me for the final visit. I broached the subject of Lindy's parents' attitudes towards me and my growing irritation. They had charged me to write every day, in their letter to Lindy, underlining this admonition three times. Lindy's eyes went watery and she squeezed my hand. 'My feelings have not changed for you. I still love you,' she cried. Clearly she was struggling and appeared unwell. She complained about pain in her stomach and another personal physical matter. The prison doctor said that her unwellness may have resulted either from her breast milk drying up or acute stress from being in jail. I think the latter was the more likely. We now talked freely. I think we both tried not to focus on the 10 weeks we would have to wait until the next round of visits. Kahlia, on this occasion, went to sleep in Lindy's arms after she had been fed. At last Lindy had felt the real Kahlia and could hold a memory of smiles. Lindy, who had lost her first daughter under cruel circumstances, had now seemingly lost her second daughter under equally cruel circumstances. I wondered many times just how much of this she could take. I said my goodbyes with a hug and then an extended embrace and a kiss. At any second I would be told to disengage, by Lindy, for fear of punishment by the prison. We waved from the car as we drove slowly away from the prison car park. Through the prison bars we saw Lindy wave back. 'Oh Dear God, is that my wife in there?' I thought.

Aidan and Reagan must have wondered many times what was going on in their lives to have parents that attracted so much turmoil. No other parents within cooee, whether in the local district or anywhere in Australia, were under such an extraordinary siege. At school they met regular challenges about their mother and were often required to defend themselves, sometimes physically, which I heard was met with appropriate force. I tried to offer basic details about the what and why of the most recent happenings, but it was as difficult for me as a parent to discuss it, as it was painful for them to hear it.

Difficult also was for them to tell me about their tribulations. They knew I was now gazetted as a criminal and anything I might do to defend them could place me in double jeopardy and put me back in court. I had an 18-month suspended sentence to defend and was on a good behaviour bond. I was lucky I didn't have to report to the police station every week.

We had one common pursuit however, which was the joy and discipline of physical exercise. I was still jogging eight to fifteen kilometres and my two boys now took up their own running. They were now nine and seven years old and Aidan, particularly, was running five to eight kilometres at a time. It sounds excessive, but you have to realise that this boy, at the age of six, once rode his shiny new bike in Mount Isa for 50 kilometres along the highway with older children and under adult supervision. The running sure beat the humbug of scrapping with each other. I believed that boys needed to have physical challenges and pursuits if they were to become real men and acquire identity and self worth.

A little later on in life, Aidan took up dirt bike riding, with one of his early bikes coming from the former Channel 10 second in charge news director, Kevin Hitchcock. This was to stand him in good stead as from his early 20s, he began performing competitively around Australia and New Zealand on his two very fast 250cc KTMs, until injury ruled him out.

As we stopped in town for several minutes for a bite to eat, a young teenage girl pulled herself away from her mother and ran up to me.

'Are you Michael Chamberlain?'

'Yes', I said.

'My mother and I are praying for you.' She vanished as quickly as she came. That was two unknown supporters I had in Darwin. What I didn't realise then was that there were many more who would put their hand up.

Sandra Smith was the wife of Adrian Smith, who had roomed next door to me as a College student while at Avondale in the late 1960s. She was a vivacious bold spirit who now taught at Pine Creek Adventist School. The Darwin Church ladies were denied visiting rights with Lindy, so Sandra rang Superintendent Mercer.

'Hello, my name is Sandra Smith and I am wondering how I could arrange a visit with Lindy Chamberlain?'

'Who are you? What are you to Lindy Chamberlain?' Mercer asked abruptly.

Sandra, stunned, answered, 'Oh, well we are friends of Lindy and Michael. They stayed with us one night before the first inquest. Michael was an assistant minister in my husband's family parish.'

Mercer was sceptical. 'Yes, well, we are getting a lot of enquiries to visit from people who are just on an ego trip.'

Sandra countered. 'Well it concerns me that she has been here two weeks and no female friends have been permitted to visit her. I am concerned that she may feel abandoned.'

Mercer replied: 'Well, you are going to have to write to the Director of Prison Services stating who you are, what connection you have with Lindy and how often you can visit.'

One of the senior Darwin Church Deacons, Bernice Pannekoek, responded immediately to Mercer's edict, endorsing Sandra as a bona fide Adventist member. Sandra had permission within five days to visit one hour per month on the Sabbath.

The first visit came as a shock for Sandra. Lindy, on meeting her, spent the majority of the period on 'small talk'. She was unable to discuss prison routines but said in whispers that she was lacking in protein (Lindy was a vegetarian). When it got too hot, Sandra put her legs up on the bench in the shade of the umbrella to get away from the afternoon heat. This brought an immediate response from the tower guards. 'You are being watched. Put your legs down!' Although Sandra had been promised an hour, the prison moved on them after 30 minutes and asked her to leave. Sandra told me later: 'I found it extremely exhausting and intimidating. One feels so helpless. The warders hold all the aces. If you don't shape up, there are a hundred ways they can get you.'

My last visit to Lindy was one of despair and profound sadness. I felt gutted and terribly alone, so alone that I didn't care to think more than an hour ahead. It was not until I was flying over Mount Isa for Sydney that it fully hit me that I was on my way 'home'. But, where was home now? Was it Darwin or Cooranbong? I was finding my memory was much worse than normal and my ability to concentrate spasmodic. Even the simplest things I did were hard to recall. I had resorted to a diet of Wrigley's chewing gum; Juicy Fruit and PK were the favourites, but a perpetually moving jaw was not the prettiest sight.

Back home, I was introduced to a serious defender of our cause, Betty Hocking, a member of the Canberra ACT Legislative Council. She had been in contact with the Seventh-day Adventist Minister of the Canberra National Church, Pastor Graeme Brown. I had known Graeme back in the late 1960s during College dorm days when he was an Assistant Dean. Betty represented the Independent Family Team party. She was in no doubt that her push for an inquiry would do her no good in the eyes of many of her parliamentary colleagues. 'It's a political hot potato. The story of the Good Samaritan comes to mind and somebody has to do it,' she said. But this did not deter her from following her conscience and sticking her neck out for us, come hell or high water. A more dedicated down-to-earth Christian in politics I have never met.

Betty Hocking was not a lone voice in raising public awareness about our injustice. In Brisbane, Dr Western Allen and Robert Brinsmead, former Adventists who had already fired the first public salvo in holding a public rally for us, were pushing for an Inquiry. Celebrated Churchill Fellowship winner, Melbourne sculptor and social activist, Guy Boyd, and schoolteacher, Robert Sutcliffe, were developing awareness and support for our cause in Victoria. A West Australian group had been formed and a North New Zealand cell was inaugurated under the leadership of a friend from Christchurch Boys High School days, Dr Bill Peddie. A cash appeal had been launched by the head of the Chamberlain Support Group in Christchurch, Joy Chandler, to build up funds to assist us in our High Court appeal in Canberra.

We were now cut off from any further legal aid as it was thought that the prospects of winning any High Court appeal were very limited. *The New Zealand Sunday News* (3/7/1983) reported that Lindy's 'Father-in-law, Christchurch farmer Ivan Chamberlain, (had) attacked the decision as a deliberate bid to 'stack the cards' against the attempt to clear her name...There was absolutely no reason for Lindy to commit this crime. My wife and I will go to our deaths defending Lindy.'

On Bastille Day, 14 July 1983, I tried to take stock of the hopeless situation we were in. For centuries the Crown had always had a head start on accused and convicted persons. For the defence, the problem always came down to if there was enough money in the kitty for a responsible fight. In our case, Legal Aid was a funding source for our defence work, but the Crown had a ready supply of taxpayer funding. Up until now, we owed the Church around $143,000 and it was rising. (*Sunday News,*

3/7/1983). We had no foreseeable prospect of repaying the money. Another problem was the access to Crown forensic tests. Where was the fairness and independence in the Crown's methods of presenting evidence? I came to the conclusion that full scientific reports should be made to the defence counsel well before any courtroom testing of the evidence. Defence counsels should have available to them, privately, forensic scientists for testing to disprove allegations made by the police.

I had left Sydney heartened by a private investigation arranged by Adventist businessmen in Sydney, Phil Ward and Don McNicol. It was their contention that following Barritt's first inquest findings, the 'persons who disposed of Azaria's body', at Ayers Rock, should be exposed. But it became apparent that the fledgling pair of private investigators were creating an unhealthy stir when making inquiries in Darwin.

The Northern Territory papers were awash with their investigation and it was apparent they were walking into a hornet's nest, with the police none too pleased. I became relieved that I had nothing to do with it, as there was little evidence of their professionalism despite their big-hearted intention. The Northern Territory Police set out to thwart their efforts. McNicol went to Channel 10 complaining about police harassment.

Lindy did not like what Ward and McNicol were doing. The general consensus was that this publicity could send our inquiry backwards. Phil Ward, as the financier of this investigation, lacked knowledge of the well-oiled Northern Territory public relations machine. Phil Ward rang me, and after applauding him for his intentions, I engaged in a heated argument about his investigation methods. His theory was that two Ayers Rock rangers, other than Derek Roff, were the real 'accessories after the fact' and that they had knowledge of a pet dingo named 'Ding' and its activities concerning Azaria's death. Phil wrote me a stinging letter about my supposed lack of passion to solve the mystery.

It was now around mid-July 1983 when I once again turned my mind to my Torana and, with a photograph in hand of the mysterious spray pattern under the dashboard, looked for other cars that might have similar markings in the same place. The first person I spoke to was a ministerial colleague, Webber Roberts, who owned a metallic green Torana V8 hatchback, similar to mine. It was an easy find because I often watched him drive off from College through security gates and down College Drive. Webber was only too willing to let me take a peek under his front passenger seat. With a spotlight in hand I had discovered a pattern of some kind of spray that seemed a bit familiar. On the basis of the prosecution case, a small child might have been done a mischief in this car, as well, I mused sarcastically.

During the Darwin trial, Dr Jones was prepared to admit that the markings on the plate from Webber Roberts' car looked similar to those in my car. It may have appeared a misdirection to the jury when Justice Muirhead in his summing up, told them not to make too much of the second plate's similar markings. It was not an error at law. It was, however, a grave error in scientific management. Although several defence experts in the trial had challenged the concept that 'a spray of Azaria's blood' was under the dashboard of my car, they were never armed with any significant and potentially explosive knowledge to break the prosecution's case. The next question was obvious. What was it and in how many other V8 Hatchback Toranas could this pattern be found?

The analysis of blood was a very specific discipline. It produces very specific reactions. If this substance wasn't blood what was it?

Les Smith believed he could make a contribution in solving the forensic conundrum. Though he held no forensic PhD, just a Diploma in Applied Science, he had solved the logistical problems on the cutting edge of applied technology for a large and successful organisation, the Sanitarium Health Food Company. His frustration was that in any research it would have to be verified by a man with 'letters', despite his disciplined research on careful, methodical and exhaustive scrutiny. He decided to visit various car yards for clues.

The Newcastle's car yards unearthed four more Toranas like mine with remarkably similar patterns. Les Smith's unexpected find became more gratifying when all of the car yard owners demonstrated an extraordinary generosity when he asked to cut the four plates out of the 'crime scene' Toranas. The car yard dealers willingly parted with them. The only proviso was that Les replaced the plates, which he did by riveting on new metal strips. It seemed to signal a positive message about the 'crime', punishment and innocence questions concerning us, plaguing the Newcastle public. Stuart Tipple took possession of the dashboard plates and had the substances and markings exhaustively tested.

An event on 17 July brought fresh trauma. Reagan was playing several doors up from our College home when, allegedly, another boy about his age foolishly threw a sealed glass bottle into a fire. The bottle exploded and a piece of flying glass ripped into Reagan's eye. Blood began to dribble from near his pupil and everyone was thrown into panic. An ambulance was called and Reagan was taken to the Royal Newcastle Hospital. We had no idea about the extent of the damage but it looked bad enough for him to lose his eye.

Dr Brian Hammond advised rest for Reagan while serious surgery was considered. A Newcastle eye surgeon, Dr RK Pountney, advised me that an exploratory operation on Reagan was needed, to see if there was any glass in his eye and to check if the retina had been detached by the accident.

On Wednesday 20 July, Reagan had the operation. Reagan's retina had not detached; there was a slim chance that he would keep his eye, but he would probably have no vision. It was a matter of being thankful for small mercies as Reagan's eye was turning out better than could be expected. Dr Playfair from the Sydney Eye Hospital would now make the next decision Mr Donnelly from the Darwin Correctional Services expressed his sympathy for Reagan's condition and apologised for the heavy-handedness directed at Lindy when she was cut off in an urgent phone call about Reagan's future operation.

My family doctor, Richard Drew, was concerned that I was going under. 'You need a lot more rest otherwise you could suffer a major illness,' he said. That was all very well but how do you escape stress when you are Michael Chamberlain? What can you do when you are on the way to being an insomniac? Go running? Instead of taking a gentle sleeping tablet I was advised to take a glass of wine before retiring to bed at night. Well, that was radical for the tee-totalling Adventist who had taken the baptismal oath never to let strong drink pass his lips.

Reagan's next operation at the Sydney Eye Hospital, in the hands of Dr Playfair, could not have been more successful. It lasted three hours between 1.30 and 4.30pm on 1 August 1983. Playfair removed a cataract, with new stitches inserted across the front of the eye. There was now a fighting chance that Reagan might have some peripheral vision, perhaps 10 per cent, in his damaged eye but he would now be legally blind in that eye. It was a terrible result to have to come to terms with, and, as Denise Roy remarked, a mother's love for the empathy she can give in such a traumatic situation just can't be replaced. Reagan, despite his bravery, must have bled inside not to have had that comfort and assurance. This event was made the crueller by the Northern Territory refusing an application for Lindy to be at his side in his hour of need. Even one day in his presence would have been a concession for compassion and human decency. But it did not happen.

On hearing of Reagan's accident, Guy Boyd wrote to me on behalf of his family, advising me that he would be sending a petition around Melbourne in early 1984 to have Lindy freed, and that he expected to obtain 100,000 signatures. It would be the largest on record for a public inquiry.

He also sent a letter of sympathy from their home in Sandringham, noting that, 'some of the media have become more sympathetic since the trial verdict. We have seven children and eight grandchildren too, so you are getting plenty of support from the Boyd family.' He said. It was great encouragement from such a respected Melbourne family.

After Reagan's operation Denise Roy thought he might like to write a letter to his mum.

'Yes, how will we start?' he replied.

'With the place and date,' Denise answered.

'Room 105, Sydney Eye Hospital, Sydney.
Dear Mummy,
I hope you can get out of jail and come to see me. I miss you. I have for a long time...'
And how many kisses will we put on the bottom of the letter?'
Reagan answered, 'Ten thousand.'

13. The High Court Decides

I left Sydney with the boys on Monday 5 September, 1983, for Darwin to find Lindy better than on the previous visit. But she was still stressed and was suffering sleep deprivation. Headaches plagued her, together with anxiety caused by fellow prisoners, she nicknamed 'Zeta' and 'Carrot Eater', who constantly tried to intimidate her. Food caused her problems, especially the hot curries. When she went to the toilet her urine caused a burning sensation. The following morning, Lindy learned that I had sent an enlarged portrait of her to the Melbourne group, headed by Guy Boyd, which drew an angry response from her. I realised there was always going to be a liability in making decisions of personal interest and sometimes these had to be made without Lindy being consulted. The boys, however, did have some happy moments during this dreary time when visiting their mother in jail. On Friday morning Aidan and Reagan experienced great excitement when off the Darwin Jetty they caught five queen fish weighing around one kilogram each.

Lindy was able to make some high-quality craft work for the Prison's entry into the Darwin Show. The Corrective Services Department won several prizes, thanks to her, but they could not name her. She was also making a clipper ship out of copper, standing about one metre high, which was intended for Aidan's room. Lindy was in quite good spirits and was sure that 'God was in control', and that it was only a matter of time before she would be let out.

My next visit to see Lindy happened just one month later with Stuart Tipple, Denise Roy and the children accompanying me. We left Cooranbong for Darwin at 5.10am. Stuart was much more relaxed than usual. His visit to Alice Springs was to assess Cawood's and Morris' knowledge about the night we lost Azaria, and the finding given by Barritt that at some time after Azaria died there had been some form of human intervention. There had been persistent rumours that the Territory Government employees at the Rock knew more than they were prepared to divulge. Stuart noted that Constable Morris in particular, was tight-lipped.

Some optimism was building in anticipation of the High Court Appeal in Canberra, set down for 29 November 2003. More messages were trickling through about Professor Cameron's efficiency.

The Dingo Foundation of Victoria's Val Roach, herself an owner of dingoes, had made contact to inform us that Bernard Sims, for the prosecution, was out of his depth when attempting to deny a dingo attack on Azaria. But this information could not be used at any High Court as only evidence heard by a jury or the admission of fresh evidence was relevant, which could clearly change a jury's decision if it was available.

In the meantime, Lindy was looking remarkably good and was pleased to see me. She seemed ecstatic over her physical condition, now boasting that she had lost 14 kilograms since she was confined back to the cells. She claimed this had caused a loss of 22 centimetres around the hips, an impressive statistic for a woman a fraction over 5 feet tall. We talked as if we were long-lost mates, quite a change from the rather disastrous angry visit on my last trip. Lindy had now been in jail for six months. We had been allowed just one and a half hours to talk personally. Lindy expressed gratitude for the special album I had prepared for her with the 30 photos she was allowed. My visit lasted for just half an hour, but it felt like five minutes.

The next major milestone was our appeal to the High Court. With six friends I made an appearance on 28 November 1983 for the opening of the Court, led again by Mr Michael McHugh QC, before a full bench of five High Court Judges. I was described by the media as 'looking tense but still athletic', but maintained my silence before them. The High Court building was imposing. Its appearance had the solidity of a medieval glass castle encasing all the wisdom of the best Australian legal minds. But this Court signalled for me that we were dead in the water. There wasn't a great deal new we could add to this appeal but were conscious that crucial questions we could answer now could not be relayed to the Court because of the type of evidence it was allowed to receive. This included Aidan's testimony, and the nature of the blood in the car. Because this information couldn't be heard at the Federal Court, it wasn't admissible in the High Court. We would have to await its decision for three months, but the strictures had for us turned it into a formality of failure.

Michael McHugh led the proposition that the spirit of the trial could be summed up as not a case of the prosecution having to prove guilt but the Chamberlains being forced to prove their innocence. Lindy, in other words, 'had to prove her innocence'. But it was also about demonstrating the stupidity of the blood spray evidence under the dashboard in my car, a factor most critical to the appeal. The major problem about this was that we had now had proof that the tests had produced false findings, but the forum for presenting that evidence had passed at the Federal Court Level. A High Court could only hear the problems faced at the Darwin Supreme Court trial and deliberate on whether a jury acted reasonably on the information given to it.

Ian Barker, on the other hand, while now accepting that Azaria was alive at 8pm on Sunday 17 August as many witnesses had testified to her activity, argued that the High Court should accept the jury verdict. This approach evoked a negative response from the High Court Chief Justice, Sir Harry Gibbs. 'That, in effect is inviting us to wash our hands of it and say that it was all a jury matter. That would seem to give inadequate protection to the accused,' Gibbs was reported as saying in the *Sydney Morning Herald* (1/12/1983). Because we had decided to spare Aidan the trauma as an eight-year-old of having to enter the witness box in Darwin, we obviously had one less important witness to counter Barker's claim that Lindy never went to the tent with Aidan but in fact had gone to the car with Azaria to cut her throat in the front seat with her scissors.

McHugh argued that it was virtually impossible for Lindy (or me) at some stage, later in the evening, to have taken Azaria out of the car and bury her somewhere in the dunes, undressing her and then taking her clothes somewhere around the base of the Rock. There was absolutely no witness evidence to suggest that whatsoever.

Following our High Court appearance we awaited the Appeal decision, due late in February 1984. By 5 February, Stuart Tipple was suggesting that he would be interested in examining any new evidence that Phil Ward and McNicol might have to offer from their investigations around the Rock. The difficulty lay with a witness, who claimed that he saw the dog named 'Ding' after it had been alleged to have been shot six weeks before Azaria's death. This witness was unsure about how accurate his memory was. But Ward and McNicol must have thought Stuart's test for cogent and compelling evidence was too high and they looked further afield to solicitor Trevor Nyman and barrister John Lloyd-Jones.

Stuart also suggested that I might like to accept an invitation by John Bryson to be interviewed up to three hours before he went to press with his book following all the legal appeals. Apparently Bryson had a short list of all the media personnel who had a modicum of integrity and was willing to help us not be tricked in giving information to journalists who would abuse it.

Former Seventh-day Adventist and Avondale College student, Lowell Tarling, wrote to me in December 1983 outlining a strategy that I should take up with the media. Tarling was a maverick who excelled in the creative arts and literature field having become an author and critic of Seventh-day Adventist culture. He was now a feature writer for *Rolling Stone Magazine*. Tarling suggested that: 'The best way of getting my own back when an injustice had been done is by applying social pressure back on the doers of that injustice. By that I mean, using the media in such a way as one's enemies appear to be the bad guys. The simplest way of doing this is by pointing out specific injustices that may seem small but they are immediately provable.

'You should nail various reporters while the camera was rolling about their innuendo in headlines and general word choices. You are in the position to attack journalists on minor inconsistencies of which there must be hundreds of damming mistakes. Face to face confrontation is good when they are shown to have slandered you.

'Contrary to your lawyer's advice I recommend that you do make yourself available to the media...in one to one interviews on your turf. Don't do it on their turf at any price. Avoid press conferences...make them come alone...no friends for (their) moral support. However you may like to have a friend along. Always run your own tape recorder.'

Lowell Tarling's view was that in any new interviews to argue for a public inquiry, I should permit tape recorders, but that I must be in control of them. 'Don't avoid the Geoff de Luca journalist types of this world. But once the tapes are running turn the interview back on them. Ask them why they said this about you. Didn't they know at the time that this 'fact' was inaccurate? Why didn't they check that point? Why didn't they ask you? Tell them you are always more than willing to cooperate. As a writer, I promise you, it's awful being on the receiving end of such questions. You will be able to transcribe their responses, cull them and use them when you do your own book.'

Of Jim Oram, Tarling claimed, 'I am sure he will believe you if you give him reason to believe'. I wasn't so sure about this advice. I valued his detailed input but I could not disclose to him my reasons for continuing to adopt a low-key, conservative response to the media: the more economical you are in using the media, the more the media can be manipulated. It was good advice, I thought, but when could I use it I wondered? Not yet.

The verdict of the High Court came down on 22 February, 1984. In a word, we had lost, but not by much. The finding of Sir Harry Gibbs and Sir Anthony Mason was against us but appeared at times to be conciliatory in their deliberation. We would not concern ourselves with Sir Gerard Brennan, the fifth High Court judge who found against us. He was an avid conservative Roman Catholic, who seemed to take a hard line in favour of what the jury saw and heard, and for him the original jury verdict, in principle, needed to be protected. The other two High Court judges, Lionel Murphy and Sir William Deane (later the Governor General of Australia) upheld our appeal and would have quashed the verdicts if the 3–2 verdict had not have been against us.

We had reached the end of the line legally. We had negotiated every hoop and hurdle in the recognised course of legal appeal and appeared to have nowhere else to go. I was by now pretty scared. Terror was taking hold of me. Only I must never show it. This wasn't one person who I was fighting. It was a government, I took a deep breath. And I knew. I had to make a decision. Could I go on? Was there really a choice?

I should go on. I made the decision, I must go on.

On the steps of the High Court on that fateful day, feeling very much like Gough Whitlam on the steps of Parliament House after being deposed from his prime-ministership in 1974, I declared to the baying press: 'Lindy and I are innocent people. We will not stop fighting to clear our names and the names of our family. This case is not over yet.'

If *A lea iacta est* were the words that Caesar exclaimed while crossing the Rubicon River on his way to become Rome's Emperor, then its translation, 'the dye is cast', had to somehow, in this moment of dreadful despair, be turned around. But how?

Ian Barker had argued in the trial that his model of evidence was based on 'a bundle of sticks'—that you could build your house of evidence on its foundations. But as the big bad wolf in the 'Three Little Pigs' proved, the bundle of sticks was vulnerable as anyone testing it for a secure foundation based on the facts would find out. My foundation had to be built on a rock.

Stuart suggested to Lindy and me that we should develop a new plan. This was not the end of the line he said. The priorities were to assess the next legal avenue to reopening the case, the New Criminal Code set down in the Northern Territory that could still deal with the receipt of fresh evidence. But to do this we had to gain sufficient public support to create an entering wedge. The next step was to obtain Lindy's release on license. Some said that this trial was discriminatory in that had Lindy been black she would have been released immediately on a bond. It seemed that racial prejudice worked both ways depending on the context. Our third task was to reassess the Northern Territory administration's attitude to the case. Should we go in 'softly, softly' so that it did not drive them into a siege mentality and prevent a public inquiry? The fourth matter surrounded the re-examination and promotion of Sally Lowe's evidence, which had been a thorn in Ian Barker's side, because she could not be moved to change her testimony: that she heard Azaria cry just before Lindy raised the alarm.

I had gone to Canberra with a prepared statement in my pocket but it was not about a High Court victory. The *Sydney Morning Herald*'s report, following my speech, headlined it: 'A case that will not die', and from this I took courage. Trial witnesses were incensed. They now wanted to speak their mind at rallies to support us. Our only hope was to obtain a Royal Commission into the case, but in Stuart Tipple's mind this was a long way off.

Around the Rock at this time, according to Dr Dianne Johnson, tourists were being entertained by guides quipping: 'What's wrong? Have you lost your baby?' Or I would come into the frame as having remarkable physical fitness and the one who had climbed the Rock in equal record time.

'The two major changes were that the camping grounds were no more and that a massive pink, red and orange Yulara Resort had risen from the inhospitable sands. The area where Azaria's clothes were found had been fenced off.

'At the mention of the Chamberlain case an otherwise garrulous, verbose and friendly Uluru Park Ranger froze and became mute. The silence which followed was huge and unforgiving, and there was a clear feeling of trespass.' (Dianne Johnson, *From Fairy to Witch: Imagery and Myth in the Azaria Case*).

Following the High Court Appeal, Steve Brien defended the charge that the Northern Territory police had a vendetta against us. We did not know that Brien was about to publish a book called *Azaria: The Trial of the Century*, that would disclose what he called 'bizarre details'. This was to shore up his headline: the 'Police had a duty: to get the killer of a baby girl' (*Sun Herald* 11/3/1984). His information about the supposed significance of the Fertility Cave and a black and red dress that was originally made for Reagan, was totally discredited.

The coffin that I used in my quit smoking programs was particularly salivated over by the hungry media. In fact it was not the first time this device had been used. The Sydney Adventist Hospital in Wahroonga had used it in their quit smoking program. The coffin was neither particularly small nor was it white as reported. It was approximately a one-metre long pauper's coffin purchased for about $17 in 1977 from an Innisfail undertaker.

Of course, not all Adventist ministers used these in their promotion of the dangers of cigarettes for public quit smoking programs. In the words of Dr Norman Young: 'Those more interested in Archeological programs might have a replica of Tutankhamen's death mask, or slides of carved pagan fertility idols, Inca or Nabataean sacrificial altars, Egyptian mummies and ancient tombs etc.' This was all part of the practical side of community work to determine our origins, how we arrived at our lifestyle today and what the future might hold. The coffin, however, was a very handy shock tactic to encourage cigarette smokers who had paid their $20 to throw their cigarettes away in this 'flip-top box' for good. I would tell my audience after a motivational film: 'Throw your cigarettes in. If you don't, they'll throw you in.' Packets of Ruby and Drum tobacco, Marlboro cigarettes, pipes and all manner of smoking paraphernalia would tumble into the box and everyone would be smiling. It was if they had all been exorcised and, now clean, were ready to face the good life.

Generally, the Five Day Plan was very effective and we had a lot of success and it was well documented in the media. The *Reader's Digest* published an article on the Seventh-day Adventist Health initiative 'How to Stop Smoking in Five Days' back in January 1975. At this time the Church was at the forefront of not only making people aware of the dangers, but also doing something constructive about it. Cigarette addiction was as hard to kick as heroin addiction, it had been claimed. In my own zeal, I had taken on the tobacco companies in 'The Good Life' *Cairns Post* column, during the late 1970s in an effort to promote the Five Day Plan. So, Steve Brien's claim about 'Lindy's baby coffin', and a 'small white coffin in the house' was all part of his pathetic research.

Despite Azaria clearly meaning 'Blessed of God' throughout Hebrew antiquity, Brien continued the innuendo about her with the line, 'Wasn't it (the name) a little odd?'

Constable Metcalf was also driven to search for other meanings for my daughter's name. Dr Norman Young describes Metcalf's search in his book *Innocence Regained* (p16). 'Constable James Metcalf was still assiduously ransacking name books in the Mitchell Library (Sydney), searching for a meaning for Azaria. At this time (December 1981) Metcalf admitted to the (later) inquiry, he still thought Azaria might mean sacrifice in the wilderness and that there had "been some sort of cult or religious cult or killing". Any Rabbi or Hebraist could have corrected this linguistic nonsense, but the story was too good to be bothered about checking its accuracy,' Young observed.

Azaria was the feminine of the masculine 'Azariah' which is translated 'The Lord has helped'. The popular meaning for Azaria, 'Blessed of God', may be found in the *3000 Uncommon Names for Baby* book that could be purchased in 1980 for 75 cents. The book was 'for special girls and boys, special names with their origins and meanings'. The name 'Azalea' was just above the name 'Azaria'. The name 'Azazel', was an offensive word and its meaning was associated with the devil. To have accused us of this preposterous notion would be akin to accusing an Anglican clergyman of calling his daughter 'Satan'.

'The allegation that the Chamberlains had a biblical murder marked,' in the Bible was another invention of the dingo media in the Northern Territory. The Bible, owned by Lindy and alleged to be underlined in a sinister place, merely had a transfer of an ink irregularity from an etching on the opposite page. Chester Porter later stated that the allegation was 'without any foundation whatsoever'. But Brien painted Lindy as religiously unbalanced and that she had offered Azaria as atonement (Steve Brien, *Azaria: The Trial of the Century*, p126).

Anthropologist, Dr Dianne Johnson wrote a highly critical review of Brien's book in the *National Times* edition 23-29 March 1984. It was timely, for Brien's book had seriously depressed me and it was cheering to read the headline: 'Most tawdry account of the Azaria Chamberlain saga.' Brien, she stated, had taken 'much license with the facts' but 'with little evidence of artistry or insight to justify his doing so.' He had 'blended opinion, myth and fact' with 'almost no respect for our dignity or our right to privacy'. Yet this was his rationalisation that he was 'only doing his job'

(*National Times* 23–29/3/1984).

On 9 May, 1985, Dr Dianne Johnson requested my permission to assist her in an ABC Australian Women's Co-operative venture. I told her in my letter of 23 May that the areas I did not wish to discuss were media interference with justice (requested of me by the Australian Law Reform Commission) and evidence given in the inquests and trial. What was on the table was the effect of Lindy's imprisonment on her and the children in the context of huge public interest and wrongful conviction; the role of fatherhood in such a situation; the effects of convictions on high-profile persons including ministers; psychosocial changes that occur in people who are either pro or anti Lindy. My final comment came in the form of an angry broadside. If Lindy Chamberlain is innocent (and I know she is) what is the price that Australia owes to this woman? Many people might gladly exchange her last five years with that of a martyr.

A new docudrama emerged that exploited our condemned status and further sensationalised our 'crime'. Lowell Tarling suggested that playwright Frank Moorhouse, the writer of the defamatory and 'darkly numinous' docudrama, *The Death of Azaria Chamberlain*, and I should get together for a chat. But Moorhouse had declined, as the film was virtually complete and talking to me wouldn't have changed anything. Moorhouse must have been very confident that the High Court would find against us. Had it quashed the verdicts, Moorhouse would have found his film in contempt of court.

This screenplay writer concocted a dramatic re-enactment of Lindy's initial revelation to me, on the terrible night. In it he had been totally ignorant of Adventist belief and lifestyle, when he tried to re-construct a scene at Ayers Rock in August 1980. Here Lindy, 'in thrall of demonic obligation', acted by Elaine Hudson, was seen feeding Azaria in my car with Ayers Rock glowing in the background. Following the 'unconscionable representation' of the event there is a debauched dialogue between Lindy and me which I only reproduce here to show its complete fabrication:

'Michael, listen to me, bubby's dead, I have sent her to God.'

'You said there was a dingo.'

'Michael...'

'Oh my God!'

'You must stand by me, we must stick to the dingo story for the boys, for us and for the Church. We must place ourselves under God's law and mercy.'

'My God! I do not believe this!'

'Before God's eternal law human law is nothing. Azaria has gone to God, you must grant me forgiveness.'

'I can't forgive you, only God can forgive you.'

'No, I have God's forgiveness, it is your forgiveness I need. Azaria will live forever. She will be forever an innocent of God. God is here, God is in the Rocks and in the wilderness. Azaria is with God!'

The words ascribed to Lindy are impossible for any Seventh-day Adventist to actually say or believe. Moorhouse's presentation of her beliefs was grossly inaccurate and an insult to the Seventh-day Adventist Church. The Seventh-day Adventist Church, in fact does not hold to the notion that on death everyone automatically goes to God, paradise or the pearly gates. This takes a little longer. The judgment and the Second Coming of Christ precede this event, while the 'spirits' of the dead are in God's trust until the resurrection of the dead, whether 'good' or 'evil'.

Dr Norman Young explains this further: 'Before breakfast Moorhouse has Lindy believing six utterly false views. His dialogue has her dismiss human law as insignificant, affirm a pantheistic reverence for 'The Rock', praise God's eternal law while blatantly breaching the Sixth Commandment, accept divine forgiveness without repentance, and maintain concern for her Church while flouting its standards. The pantheist and animistic belief emitted by Lindy that 'God is in the Rocks' is alien to the Christian beliefs, let alone Seventh-day Adventists. It demonstrated Moorhouse's serious lack of understanding of Christian and Adventist doctrine'.

Elaine Hudson, acting a dreadful imitation of Lindy, and the ABC Play School's John Hamlyn, in an equally inept portrayal of me, were hired by Frank Moorhouse to create a mystery that never was! It was an open and shut case where the only 'crime' that was committed was by the Northern Territory Conservation Commission to deny Derek Roff the opportunity to cull troublesome dingoes.

Moorhouse was fortunate that, in the criminal context we had been placed, we could not take the matter to court. But I did take the first step with an injunction in the Federal Court of Australia against United Telecasters Limited on 28 February 1984. Through the office of Brennan Blair and Tipple and on behalf of the Church, I swore: 'I have never had any such conversation with my wife and the religious beliefs and references expressed in that conversation do not reflect and indeed are contrary to the religious beliefs of myself, my wife and the Seventh-day Adventist Church.' The injunction failed and Moorhouse's damaging production was shown on numerous pay to air and cable networks for many years later.

Moorhouse rationalised his production in the following remarks reprinted from Dr Belinda Middleweek's thesis: 'Dingo Media? R v Chamberlain as a model for an Australian media event.'

'In my lifetime as an author...no other case has excited the public imagination more than the disappearance of Azaria Chamberlain. Even before it came to a coroner's court, the public imagination, or if you like, folk imagination had been inflamed by it and was weaving its own tales. The disappearance of Azaria Chamberlain was one I would call a psychic drama. It had all the elements: strange behaviour in the animal kingdom, strange names 'Azaria', the 'Devil's Marbles', 'Fertility Cave', a little known religion and powerful mythologies. At the centre of all this was the elemental bond between a mother and her child and our dread of infanticide. The story I will tell you rests on all that is safely known of the case.'

This was never an explicit scenario invented by the Crown, nor anyone else until Moorhouse came along. In promoting himself to the role of social scientist and anthropologist, he attempted to inject into his unsuspecting audience strands of 'deep communal memories' derived from 'European folk law' with a sprinkling of 'Aboriginal mythology'. His attempt to weave gothic-like notions of infanticide and child sacrifice into his film damaged the core truths of our belief system.

In viewing the film, I was astounded how such a revered documentary maker like Frank Moorhouse had ignored the fact that Aidan was with Lindy during the attack on Azaria. He ignored that Greg and Sally Lowe heard Azaria cry; the background of dingoes preying on Aborigine children. He completely departed from what we said on the Alice Springs first inquest courthouse steps. Moorhouse was offensive in his attack on our family planning with the advent of Kahlia; the inappropriate and graphically sensationalised account that never took place of Lindy killing Azaria, used as the 'bait' to draw viewers in; and the provision of the missing motive.

Lowell Tarling suggested that if I did not like the film, my response could 'kill the influence of the film if I did it right'. Apart from revealing the inaccuracies of the film—especially stupid mistakes on Moorhouse's part—the other thing I could do was to say on record 'Why didn't he talk to me?' 'You could virtually accuse Moorhouse of declining to meet with you, given the opportunity.' Plainly, Tarling wanted to set me up to do an interview with him sometime down the track, but that was a very long way off. His choice of magazine; either *Rolling Stone* or *Playboy* would have virtually excluded the more mainstream audiences. However, I had to recognise that every heart and mind had to be reached in order to change them. Tarling had just submitted to *Rolling Stone* in 1984 a recent article on the saga and it was a skilfully written and heartening read.

Seventh-day Adventist belief was now scrutinised more closely than ever before and, driven by our controversy, many people sought to condemn the Church. Tarling, in a clever turn of phrase, determined that 'One of the reasons why the public tended to favour the dingo (innocence) above Lindy was because the dingo wasn't a Seventh-day Adventist'. Despite assurances from Seventh-day Adventist clergy, the laity can plainly see that people do not respect them for their faith. He cited a 1977 sociological study that indicated, apart from cult religions which demonstrated absurd paranoia towards the world, Seventh-day Adventists generally had the highest fear and loathing quotient with 27 per cent of their converts, indicating the most hostile feelings to the outside world. For me, this knowledge came as a severe shock and disappointment. I was not born into Adventism and was glad that despite all my other contexts, this was not one of them, which could lead to anti-social views.

In *Beyond Azaria*, Lowell Tarling wrote, 'As surely as Azaria was taken by a real dingo, the Chamberlains were taken down by a pack of baying journalistic dingoes and their publishers.' Ethical considerations and concepts lost ground to strange tales about us, often with gothic or spiritualistic overtones. In many cases, the higher a person's status in media exposure, the more likely he or she will be the target of satirisation. They will have to experience being the targets of potential misrepresentation and ongoing speculation. Lindy and I seemed to have risen to that status.

Tarling suggested that many people in the church had unfounded views about non-Adventists being evil or bad people. (*Rolling Stone*, March 1984). Too many (Adventist) people would not go to places because they feared that some mystical 'force' might over-power them. Tarling pointed out that this had the effect of turning full circle on the Church. Because Adventism considered that it must protect itself and its culture by not venturing outside the prescribed domains it was seen as unnecessarily secretive. Certain Church administrators and evangelists, who warned against going to the cinema, opera and other entertainment events, drove this unfortunate misunderstanding of Adventists. What was missing was the advice, that it was not people per se, who were wholesale evil characters but their deeds that determined their character and influence. (*Beyond Ellen White: Seventh-day Adventism in Transition*, Michael Leigh Chamberlain, PhD. Post Pressed, 2008). Malcolm Brown concluded that had Lindy and I 'been part of a mainstream denomination in 1980, so much of the public hysteria might not have been provoked.' (Everlasting nightmare, Weekend Feature Article, *Sydney Morning Herald*, 13–14/9/2008).

In an investigation by The *Newcastle Herald* in 1995, the media proclaimed that Seventh-day Adventism was, in fact, not a weird cultish belief system, but very much a practical Christian Church with several variations. 'The Seventh-day Adventist Church holds the same basic beliefs as do most Christian denominations. The only essential differences are that Adventists observe Saturday rather than Sunday as the Sabbath. They observe vegetarian dietary laws in the belief that 'the body is the temple of the Holy Spirit'. They pay tithes to their church, that being 10 per cent of their income and believe that the second coming of Christ is imminent' (*The Newcastle Herald*, 18/11/1995).

Dr Belinda Middleweek, writing in her thesis ('Dingo Media? R v Chamberlain as a model for an Australian event', PhD thesis, University of Sydney, 2007) provided a model and analysis of how the media initially dealt with us and our case. She advocated five stages in the media's processing of a truth in conflict. These included the first stage described as Metaphorisation, and the following stages: Dissemination, Commodification, Mythologisation and Simulation.

Dr Middleweek described how the media and the purveyors of drama, out of the literal events that befell us between 1980–1982, created the symbolism. The loss of Azaria first portrayed us as victims of loss and tragedy. This evoked national sympathy. But it was short-lived. A new low was struck when we were paraded as pariahs by gathering forces attempting to destroy us just three days after Azaria's death. Our characters' personalities and the truth about Azaria were pored over and dissected repeatedly.

The Brisbane *Courier-Mail* indulged in some hyperbole in its first paragraph about the case: 'Everyone's agreed. It's just not like the dingo', implying already that our story was 'suspicious'. This was juxtaposed with the opposite renditions of dingoes at Ayers Rock symbolised as behaving 'like wolves' despite being wary of man. The animal that took Azaria was rightly represented as having made 'no sound' within our earshot. Later media began to personify this thief as a being of more value and credibility than us. The focus of attention was no longer the loss of Azaria but on us as the culprits.

In western Christian males, stoicism is a likely first base for processing the shocking propositions. As the alleged 'guardian' of my wife's secret, I was isolated in a 'cloak of mystery' to ponder my lot and reflect in silence my feelings, words and actions. As a 'shadowy background figure' my actions were more implicit than my wife's. My 'uncompromising religious beliefs and stoic faith', according to Dr Middleweek, were severely judged and condemned. Never mind the ultimate physical and emotional shock when the verdict of 'pariah' and not 'victim' was declared. My physical collapse after the sentence, the 'wincing' and 'turning away', looking 'quite ashen' demonstrated the ultimate pain of a 'self-effacing' and 'overly emotional' man being falsely accused after two years of tribulation. A new poll on readers, following the failure of the High Court Appeal in 1984, revealed that while 53 per cent thought Lindy guilty, only 16 per cent considered her innocent, with 31 per cent undecided.

Gay Alcorn, writing in the *Newcastle Herald* (28/11/1995), described Lindy as 'tough, difficult... If Lindy was strong Michael was vulnerable.' But Gay Alcorn was misguided when she quoted me as saying 'the loss of our baby was the will of God'. If I ever said this, it was in the context that God allows things to occur even that which He does not approve of. He sees into infinity what will ultimately be for the greater good. As terrible and unjust as so many things are in this world we live in—'enemy occupied territory', to quote Oxford English Professor C.S Lewis, author of the Narnia series of books. The language I used was the repetition of a traditional Christian answer when confronted by an inexplicable horror. As the Adventist theologian Dr Young stated (Michael Chamberlain's) 'words are the learned response of a man trying to retain, despite everything else, his theistic universe where no sparrow falls without God's knowledge and His will.'

John Bryson interpreted my demeanour at the first inquest as 'appearing to suffer a religious and personal crisis in front of a nation'. He viewed my evidence at the trial as if I appeared 'to understand little: not the questions: not the answers, not the dangers to come, not the ways of the world around him' (*Newcastle Herald,* 28/11/1995). He was right in most of his assessment, but I don't think I ever lost sight of the big picture: Who I was; where I was going; what I had to do and my end game. Nor did I ever lose sight of the existence of a Christian God in my life. I doubted many times the purpose for all this seemingly unnecessary loss of life, resources and time, fighting for legal and social survival, but I kept coming back to the fundamental cause for my existence; that I had been bought with a price that Jesus had died for me and that God's grace was sufficient in time of need.

What Bryson did see was my way of expressing anger through a 'forceful religious calm' which after a while appeared to some to crack. I may have appeared to have had my moments of self-doubt, but my belief in Jesus Christ never faltered. Realising after the trial that it was now mortal legal warfare, jungle style, I had to find armour for the deadly combat to come. Combat against a confused population, a prejudiced police force, a reactive Chief Minister and government legal system and a press that measured my every breath. I told the *Australian Woman's Weekly* in 1994 that I was actually 'an extremely determined and resourceful person, but I never wore it on my sleeve. That's one reason why I am still alive today. And I know by the grace of God I have done my best.'

The Newcastle Herald in 1995 published the comments of one juror among the nine men and three women who had observed us for seven weeks first hand. He said he did not believe that, based on the evidence they heard at the trial, he made the wrong decision. 'I came away from it thinking that our justice system was the best in the world. We have a fair system. Everyone has the opportunity to prove their innocence.'

When asked how he thought Lindy came across in the witness box he said, 'I prefer not to comment.'

'What about Michael Chamberlain?' Buckland was asked.

'I believe Michael Chamberlain is a man of extreme courage and loyalty. I think he should be commended and remembered as a man who stuck by his wife, thick and thin. I have a lot of respect for the man' (*Newcastle Herald,* 'Life After Azaria' 28/11/1995).

Seventh-day Adventist Dr Kenneth Brown had reported our High Court failure to a captive audience of Adventists in London. The supposed 'proven' cutting of the jumpsuit by a pair of scissors in Professor James Malcolm Cameron and Professor Malcolm Chaikin's eyes was absolutely the final word according to him. The dingo could not have possibly been involved. Their teeth can't cut cloth. This had also convinced the jurors and the Federal Court judges. As a result of this testimony, I do not recall hearing from any Adventist in England again.

But countering this now was Les Smith, Sanitarium Health Foods scientist, on the trail of this terrible evidence. He was deeply shocked and angered when at last he could view Azaria's jumpsuit, now public property and available for interpretive gaze. He first saw it at the High Court in September 1984. His attention was drawn to the many ragged edges in the clothing that no scissors were capable of making.

Ayers Rock is a physical location and icon, a mecca for tourism but also (as Uluru) a cultural and sanctified indigenous dwelling place of deep spiritual and mystical symbolism. It was variously known as the 'red centre', the 'dead centre' even 'a huge beast at rest'. Set up against Adventism were powerful sociological, political and financial forces. In contrast, some misguided members of the Northern Territory Police offensively interpreted Adventism as a weird cultic and dangerous fringe system. The police servility to a parochial and protective frontier defence system and the powerful juggernaut-like grip of tourism and Territory identity, driven by a lack of resources and expertise, drove them to conduct a subjective search.

By 1982, we were already household names, and the views about us were well on their way to creating a national myth. The media, satisfied that Lindy was, as convicted, a criminal and liar, was now at the mercy of any interpretation of her criminal behaviour. For the time being, she and I could do absolutely nothing legally to protect ourselves against slur and slander. She was locked up, denied a voice. I was at least free, if not in a jail of my own, a glasshouse full of its own speculation and ongoing vilification. But our cause was not lost. Some at least believed that their faith in us was not in vain.

Religion writer Alan Gill, writing in the *Sydney Morning Herald* (16/9/1988), was also fascinated by the adversarial stand taken by other Churches towards Adventism. He related how the 'Letters to the Editor' mailbag received as many as 100 Azaria letters a day during the trial. He dispelled the idea that other Churches thought Lindy innocent. This, he said, suggested that the Seventh-day Adventist Church retained an image problem because other church groups saw it as 'a small cultic group and worthy of suspicion'. Gill recounts how at one stage he overheard two bishops in the Anglican Church indicate that Lindy 'did it' because she felt that to sacrifice her child would be pleasing to God. Other heads of denominations 'pondered the precedent set by the SDA Church in agreeing to underwrite the costs of the Chamberlain's defence'. The question was asked of me: 'how could I, as a Seventh-day Adventist Pastor, lie to protect my wife under oath. Did I resign after the final avenue at the High Court because it became too much for my conscience?'

Seventh-day Adventism, Gill opined, was an ecclesiastical shorthand for a flood of exotic movements, formed in the 18th and 19th centuries, which had as a common denominator, a concern about the Second Coming of Christ. The roots of modern Seventh-day Adventism lay in two larger-than-life 19th-century figures. The first was an American Baptist preacher, William Miller, who believed that in Scriptural prophecy, a day stood for a year. He calculated that Christ would return on 21 March, 1844 and being proved wrong, adjusted it to 22 October, 1844. The second was Ellen Gould White, the Church's revered commentator on its beliefs and lifestyle.

Gill linked me to the 'excommunicated' Dr Desmond Ford, 'formerly this country's leading Adventist theologian'. I was unsure what this was meant to prove. Was I supposed to be an aberrant Adventist because of it? True, Ford had taught me and, then ten years later, challenged, Gill said, '(Ellen) White's theories...which led to the establishment of the Seventh-day Adventist Church in 1860'. That I had been a student of Ford, who held a double doctorate, was of some interest but Gill never asked me what, if any, 'aberrant' views I had picked up from Dr Ford. I happened to deeply respect this man for his integrity and Christian ethos, although I had not been able to be as certain of Ellen White's 'scholarship' problems as he had been. Ford had been one of the most influential in bringing the Church out of the trough of legalistic and sectarian thinking, I believed, and was a true New Testament-orientated scholar. What Ellen White wrote as an acculturated Evangelical American woman of her time, a moral icon and one of the most influential and prolific writers, did not warrant any serious Church member to discard her work. Gill concluded his discourse with the remark: 'Apart from the Miller connection and their preference for a Saturday Sabbath, the beliefs of modern Seventh-day Adventists are broadly on a par with Evangelical Protestantism...' Then came the Chamberlain affair, which renewed—with a vengeance—the church's image problem.

Dave Hansen subverted this in a major way with cartoonist Mark Trounce, using their literate and visual skills, in the production of *Dingo Lingo*, concocted as a kind of 'instruction' book on a hundred ways a dingo could kill a baby: you can toast it, mince it, turn it into hamburgers or shish kebab. This was one of many joke books, passed off as in the tradition of irreverent Aussie humour, which profiteered from our tragedy.

14. The Reconnaissance Mission

By mid-1984 I believed that a jury verdict could be reversed. Not only did it have to be possible, it now had to be available, appellate courts non-endorsement notwithstanding. But it could be light years away. 'Cheer up,' I thought to myself. 'Things may now be getting worse at a slower rate.'

I knew that I could not carry on my formal work as an ambassador for my faith in a formal sense any longer. It was quite apparent from the sentence brought down on me at Darwin on 29 October, 1982, that I could never be the same person again or ever expect to turn back the clock. My resignation from the ministry was, for me, inevitable. The press noted this to have been caused by family pressures and health concerns. But there was more to this than met the eye.

Lowell Tarling asked me three months before my decision whether I would continue with my work. My answer was simply 'Who will let me? The last four years have certainly changed my approach to life. As a minister looking back, I see myself as having been a bit naïve on certain aspects of life. Realism in the horror of our situation caused me to become a great deal more pragmatic, and at times even cynical, but not quite totally disbelieving in man's integrity. However, I remained a spiritual person in the Christian sense. I was perfectly willing to be judged and criticised, but ultimately God and history would make the final authentic call. I now had to keep ever before me the motto: Hope is a good thing and no good thing ever dies; get busy living or get busy dying'. In early April 1984 I resigned.

The reaction to the High Court's refusal to overthrow our guilty verdict began to draw widespread discontent and anxiety that all was not well with the legal system. Dialogue between the media and the concerned public was growing. Through a process of 'communal dissatisfaction' our 'pariah' status was changing and it was being precipitated by supporters' rallies, highlighting glaring flaws, demanding the retracing of the evidence and a fresh diagnosis.

Mushrooming support groups around Australia and New Zealand, spurred by new scientific data countering the prosecution's 'bundle of sticks' theory, turned the finger back to the Australian wolf.

The power of the support groups through Dr Bill Peddie was an example of the amazing dedication of my New Zealand friends and supporters. He had a Doctorate of Philosophy in Science and as a teacher of science had written a number of textbooks. Although I had lost contact with him, when he heard of our travail he rang me in 1983 with a barrage of questions. Bill was a pragmatist with a quirky sense of humour. Utterly reliable, he acted in a measured way, with every word carefully chosen. I knew that what he said he meant. He was a good friend to have, and a tenacious enemy of medical wrongdoing.

Bill was deeply concerned about all the implications of our case. He felt uneasy about the trial transcripts after he had made it his business to read them. His concern drove him to write *Azaria: One Kind of Justice*, a 46-page treatise on the pros and cons—mainly cons—of the guilty verdict in 1984. In his book, he described me from his boyhood days as having five main interests: my Triumph 500 Speed Twin motorbike, sport, Christianity, music and girls. Of Lindy, he said that she was rather forthright, but otherwise a friendly, normal home-loving girl. In the matter of naming Azaria he made an interesting observation. Azaria's other names, he said wryly, appear to have escaped public speculation: 'Chantel' a Gypsy word meaning lead singer and 'Loren', Teutonic for branch of laurel. Bill concluded in a remarkable interview in 1984 with the *New Zealand Woman's Weekly* that: 'There is evidence which shows not only that a dingo took the baby but which dingo did it and why it was covered up.'

Guy Boyd was emerging as one of the most powerful public players, taking a considerable amount of time to research the case, and putting pen and paper where his head and heart was, wrote a timely treatise on the Ayers Rock witnesses evidence titled *Justice in Jeopardy*, published in 1984. In his book, Guy had taken some very complex and specialised evidence and had skilfully provided a simple, but not simplistic explanation. The Northern Territory was afraid of the truth that his book contained. *Justice in Jeopardy* was banned from the Darwin City Council's Library as a Darwin resident and Chamberlain support member, Jacqueline Bowhey, found out when she offered to donate it. The book was returned to her on the pretext that it was on a too controversial subject.

Guy was keen for me to be interviewed by Bert Newton in a 10–15 minute TV interview. Newton was a comedian, and I doubted his ability to maintain the seriousness of the theme that this case carried, regardless of how sympathetic he might be. It may have been a nationally broadcast show but it was important to get everything right. I was also asked to give Mike Willesee consideration and it seemed he was keen to lure me into his interview studio. But he wanted money to interview me! As I sat in his office discussing the pros and cons I began to feel very strange in his presence. I left, glad to be away from a conversation that seemed to be heading into a war of words on air.

Another powerful player was legal heavyweight, Sir Reginald Sholl. I discovered that he was incensed by the guilty verdict and called for new laws to prevent people from being convicted on circumstantial evidence alone. 'I think that the Crown theory of murder by scissors is almost absurd and I am amazed that the jury accepted it,' he told the *Sunday Sun* (4/3/1984).

A month after the High Court Appeal, a headline backing the Northern Territory line, appeared in the *Sunday Sun* (25/3/1984): 'Lindy had time to slay her baby.' The scientist alleging this was a Dr Douglas Wilson, a Queensland government medical officer who had worked with Professor Cameron, and claimed to have worked on our case. I had never heard of him and was bemused that he had surfaced to put his two-penny–

worth in. He said that Lindy 'had ample time to kill her baby' and that he 'had no doubt that the evidence collected in the case was correct...I was completely satisfied with the conclusion Professor Cameron reached'. Wilson had studied under Cameron and was convinced that on the three occasions they worked together in Australia on the Azaria case, Cameron was the right man. This was the last of the press articles that I saw trying to shore up the prosecution's case for the trial verdict.

Law Reform Commissioner, Justice Michael Kirby, weighed into the growing disquiet. In a comprehensive and critical report on the trial, a *Sydney Morning Herald* journalist summarised Kirby's concerns in these words. 'Would it have been possible to have found a jury in Darwin that had not been affected by the massive publicity before the trial?'

Justice Frank Gallagher, a retired former Deputy of the Conciliation and Arbitration Commission, also felt considerable disquiet. He told the press: 'I think it was a very, very, unusual jury to convict the woman on that evidence...But the jury did not have to give its reasons, which is one of the weaknesses of the jury system...it might have been that some people based their decision on factors entirely unrelated to the forensic evidence, such as personal objections to the clothing Mrs Chamberlain had worn or the fact that she had become pregnant.'

Dr Max Whitten, Chief of the Division of Entomology CSIRO, Canberra, and the President of the Australian Genetics Society, said he had 'severe misgivings about the capacity of a lay jury to make a proper judgment on the forensic evidence of the case. There is no way the jury could make a proper evaluation of the evidence whether the blood was foetal or not foetal when it was presented to them over several days and they were unable to take notes.'

On the matter of Joy Kuhl's evidence, Paul Ward, Deputy Director of the Institute of Criminology and a chemical engineer, said he was 'very concerned' about the verdict (*Sydney Morning Herald* 4/4/1984).

The Northern Territory News put a different spin on the new evidence that was coming to light on the probability of dingo involvement. It saw it as 'an assault against the Australian legal system.' (*Northern Territory News*, 4/4/1984). The following week, the *Territory News* spat out another edict from its editorial pulpit. 'The continuing extraordinary public speculation about the fate of Lindy Chamberlain must be stopped. If Mr Robertson (the new Attorney General) is unable to do the job, then the Chief Minister, Mr Paul Everingham (the former Attorney General), should return immediately to Darwin from wherever he is at the moment, to do the job for him.' The editor then claimed that his newspaper was under attack from 'a conspiracy...to cajole and bully it into joining the hysterical call for the unjustified release of a convicted murderess'. (*Northern Territory News*, 11/4/1984). Had the tide turned?

Again, on 13 June 1984 *The Northern Territory News* put forward the need for an early election. 'How the Territory's case is advanced worrying about some addle-brained Democrat's (Senator Colin Mason) motion on the Chamberlain case is a mystery... At the risk of their appearing like Tasmania's Michael ('The Mouth') Hodgman (he was an ally for the release of Lindy) we must have representatives who will fearlessly put our point of view regardless of party political allegiance.'

The Darwin support group worked within a small, insular and highly volatile community. Whatever happens in Darwin especially can become highly emotive and personal for sections of the community. To be a member of this support group was not for the faint-hearted. Everyone in Darwin read one newspaper, knew at least one policeman, politician, lawyer, ranger and juror. The group slowly and painfully came to the conclusion that the quest for any truth or justice in Darwin for us was virtually impossible. They levelled their condemnation squarely at four sectors: the Murdoch-owned *The Northern Territory News* (highly prejudicial against the Chamberlains); local political bias, police bias, incompetence and selective gathering of evidence; rumour–mongering and horrible T-shirt displays. Of deep concern to the support group activists was the manner in which *The Northern Territory News* preconditioned the jurors with its often prejudicial reporting, especially up until the High Court Appeal and after.

In early May 2004, Northern Territory Solicitor-General, Brian Martin, met with Stuart Tipple in Sydney. This surprised Stuart somewhat as it was usually he who was trying to contact Martin for direction. But the

Northern Territory Government wanted their own psychiatrist to examine Lindy. Unhappy with their intentions, I laid down some guidelines.

1: Any psychiatrist visiting Lindy should be authorised by us.

2: A lawyer, with our consent, must be present.

3: If rule 1 could not be fulfilled then we would insist that an independent psychiatrist be present.

In our view Lindy must remain in the Northern Territory jail to maximise the exposure of the Government's injustice.

The media attention and the vigorous action by the growing throng of Australian and New Zealander activists were building towards some kind of legal storm. Talk of pardon was mooted in the media. The *Sun Herald* was one paper dedicated, it seemed, to try to make amends and I should have known that Malcolm Brown was in there with full battle dress on. But what we did not want was a pardon, as the *Sun Herald* (6/5/1984) promoted in Lynch's cartoon or even a release, if this meant that the case just faded away. We did not want it to go away. We wanted a full dismissal of the charges and exhoneration. 'Bring it on,' I screamed inside.

The screening of a new and somewhat controversial documentary from Channel 10, presented by investigative reporter Kevin Hitchcock, was viewed by a number of the 300 activists in Darwin. The uncut version of the documentary stirred more ferment in the frontier city. It contended that there were government employees out at Ayers Rock who knew the dog that killed Azaria and had not told the whole truth about what had happened after she died. Further alarm for the Northern Territory came from 31 scientists, including distinguished researchers from the Australian National University, who had put their names forward to protest against the Crown forensic evidence presented in the trial.

The following day, Stuart informed me that the High Court might intervene to make a judgment on our having access to the forensic exhibits if the Northern Territory police refused to check their evidence. Mick O'Loughlin, now the Alice Springs Crown prosecutor, told us he would have to go to Darwin to pick them up. Privately he thought we should be entitled to obtain them without having a tug of war with the Attorney General's Department—after all the property was ours anyway.

More evidence on dingoes was also coming to our attention. Malcolm Brown (*Sydney Morning Herald*) reported that a retired engineer, Keith Perron, said that in 1960 he and a party of surveyors had camped by a waterhole at the edge of the Western Desert, Western Australia, when they saw Aborigines trying to spear a dingo. 'So we wondered why they were doing it. The head man said 'Bad dog, It has been eating piccannini!'' Perron, now retired and living in North Sydney remarked: 'We had a fair bit of experience with the natives. This sort of thing was going on all the time. Dingoes have been a treacherous type of animal. We have had them on the stations. We used to breed cattle dogs from them. But you would never turn your back on a dingo.'

Paddy Barlow was a supervisor of the New South Wales Border Fence in the 1970s and 1980s. His thoughts on the 'longest man-made fence in the world' as stated by *Time* (12/07/1988) were made public on the dingo for which this fence had been largely created. 'There is a sheep industry inside the fence', he said, 'outside there is none...The dingo is a smart sneaky fellow...its only use has been in crossbreeding to produce a type of cattle dog.' Described generally as 'a medium-sized dog, the male dingo has an average height of somewhere around 55 centimetres and can often weigh 20 kilograms. In comparison to most domestic dogs the dingo has a stronger chest and broader head, larger teeth, especially the canines, dense hair and it cannot bark. It is iconic for its eerie wolf-like howl'. *The Living World of Animals* (1970) claimed that it was 'probably the only pure-bred dog in the world, directly descended from a single race of wolf.' Barlow left a parting shot on Azaria. 'Let me put it this way. The wild dogs I know would not have done it. They wouldn't have gone near the tent. But a half-domesticated dog (dingo) would...don't you worry about that.'

Phillip Holden, an ex-professional hunter and well-known author on hunting, described the dingo in *Along the Dingo Fence* (1991) as 'a top hunter, a flexible opportunist. His motto may well be 'If it moves eat it.'' Dingoes do not object to eating lizards, hares, rodents, grubs, and birds if necessary, including emu. The well-known diet includes kangaroo, wallaby, pigs, especially young ones, calves and sheep. Holden suggested that a little known fact is that north of Charters Towers in Queensland, dingoes even dine on Chittal deer! Soft fruit has also been on their diet. They are supreme hunters and scavengers, whether for fish on beaches or almost anything in the Australian outback. In reality the dingo is Australia's top mammalian predator. It may be very wary but it need not be afraid of any other Australian mammal,' said Holden.

In the Melbourne suburban local newspaper, *Knox/Sherbrook News*, Mr Fritz Maaten reported that he was prepared to testify that a dingo could have taken Azaria at Ayers Rock. He wished to attend the Wantirna Chamberlain Support Group meeting with a dingo and provide living proof of the dingo's capabilities. Describing himself as 'non-religious' he said he was 'outraged' at the guilty verdict. Now, as the Director of Melbourne's Reptile and Fauna Reserve, and a lecturer on wildlife, his expertise arose from working with an oil company on stations in the Northern Territory. Maaten stated that the 'media had done its bit', painting a 'grossly inaccurate picture of the whole situation.' His next remark was succinct and chilling for all dingo lovers. 'My comment is quite frankly this, that if a dingo entered a tent at Ayers Rock at that time of the year and found an unattended baby at ground level, it would be acting abnormally if it did not take, kill, carry off and consume that baby.'

The potential danger of a dingo taking a child was increased even more in August (when Azaria disappeared) because this was when dingoes had their cubs and there was more competition for food. When asked why no remains were ever found of Azaria, Maaten replied: 'Mammals are usually consumed entirely, nothing is left. A solitary dingo would consume a mammal weighing five kilograms in 20 minutes. A mated pair would probably consume the same in less than 10 minutes.'

It was Maaten's observation that a dingo could excrete the waste of an animal, or a child, in under 24 hours, sometimes as quickly as 10 hours. He added: 'It could therefore be said that at 8pm on the night after Azaria disappeared nothing could be learned by the examination of the stomach contents of a dingo (on the next day). As far as the removal of the jumpsuit goes, the manipulation skill and ability of dingoes is very high—far higher than dogs—and probably as high as that of a young primate. The absence of saliva traces is not at all surprising considering the fact that dingoes do not salivate over their food as dogs do' (*Knox/Sherbrook News,* 2/11/1983).

This last piece of information was pertinent, even from the standpoint of forensic scientists, regarding the absence of dingo saliva as evidence of Lindy's alleged cover-up. Ian Barker had dismissed Lindy's statement that Azaria was dressed in a knitted woollen matinee jacket over her jumpsuit when she was taken from the tent. The jacket that Lindy had described in a very detailed manner, as was her custom about almost anything you asked her to comment on, was a pivotal point in which the prosecution accused her of being a 'fanciful liar'. This was just one more part of Barker's 'bundle of (circumstantial) sticks' notion, and the jury chose to believe him, rather than Lindy Chamberlain.

An increasing number of people in high places were also ready to defend our innocence. Senator Colin Mason, a Federal Democrat, introduced a bill to the Senate on 14 June 1984 seeking a public inquiry, one that would have 'all the relevant powers of a Royal Commission'. The Northern Territory Attorney General Jim Robertson immediately had a nightmare about revisiting his game of injustice and damned the idea as 'an extremely dangerous course'. He urged all senators to 'reject this outrageous proposal' (*Northern Territory News* 7/6/1984). Doug Anthony, former leader of the National Party and Deputy Prime Minister (*Courier-Mail* 3/8/1983) indicated his anxiety, and the Premier of Queensland, Joh Bjelke-Petersen said he believed that a dingo had killed Azaria (*Sunday Sun* 8/4/1984). Two major eyewitnesses, Tasmanians, Greg and Sally Lowe, spoke to Liberal Shadow Member of the House of Review, Michael Hodgman, about their anger over the injustice. Hodgman approached the Northern Territory Attorney-General, suggesting that there was indeed a prima facie case for an inquiry and that there were allegations of cover up and that 'the course of justice had been perverted!'

By the beginning of June 1984 I was facing a dilemma with the emerging new legal team. It revolved around trying to appease certain support groups who now wanted a different instructing solicitor. Some support groups were promoting the idea that Stuart Tipple had lost his way in the case. Lindy was hotly opposed to their interference, but I wanted to hear them out. This greatly annoyed Lindy and she seemed to lose faith in my judgment and wanted to exclude me from her future decisions. I sensed a very significant deterioration in our relationship and it wasn't good. The proposed new legal team, consisting of solicitor Trevor Nyman and barrister Lloyd-Jones, neither authorised by Lindy or me, wanted Stuart to hand over his forensic evidence to strengthen their case. I suggested a compromise that perhaps the Nyman team would specialise in the eyewitness testimony and Stuart on the forensic science. When I broached this notion of twin instructing solicitors, Stuart, to his credit, did not bat an eyelid. But he was worried about the ultimate team for the new legal venture. I now began having misgivings about the Nyman/Lloyd-Jones direction, because of the manner in which only two support groups were driving them, the question of who would pay for this second team, and the egos that were involved. The two groups wanted us to hand over the controls.

By 18 June, 1984, I had all but given up trying to think only like a lawyer. It now seemed pragmatic to think like a political guerrilla fighter on account of the dirt that I was copping. There was new evidence on the supposed blood tests in the car and the source of the damage to Azaria's jumpsuit but we had a problem in showing it to Territory Solicitor-General, Brian Martin. While Martin was eager to get the evidence in his hands we had serious doubts about his objectivity.

August was a month to dread. On the first day I found myself at an all-time low. I remember sitting at the kitchen table alone on a rainy day considering my position. The two boys were at school.

I had virtually nothing, except the clothes and furniture in the College rented house. I could not go anywhere without being followed. I could not talk to anyone on the phone without strange things happening. The phone exhibited unusual noises or would just drop out after a short time. I could not express any intimate feelings to Lindy by letter for fear they would be exploited at the Darwin end. I was barred from talking to her by phone, and even if I could, there was a minder at the other end.

I had no permanent job, although I was grateful that the Church was sustaining me on 70 per cent of my original salary. While I dearly loved and cherished looking after my 20-month-old Kahlia, shared with foster parents, I was learning what it was to be a mum and a dad wrapped into one and it was the fourth anniversary of Azaria's death.

I also felt that despite the numerous offers to help me in various chores some probably well-intentioned women were looking for something more from me: if I showed any emotion or inability to cope, women would try to counsel me or mother me depending on their age, a response that I did not know how to say no to without offence. I was consumed by confusion and despair. I was committed to my wife, who I prayed to be reunited with.

There was a bright moment for me on 13 September when I was visited by a revered Aboriginal man, Burnham Burnham. His long white beard and flowing hair contrasting with his dark skin felt like he was a personage out of Dreamtime. He had come to my home to tell me that the traditional people around Uluru (Ayers Rock) would not talk about what happened to Azaria. 'The Aboriginal people all around there know the truth and remain silent observers of the catastrophe,' he said. Burnham also informed me that Noel Fullerton Smith, 'The Camel Man', witnessed the taking of two Aboriginal babies 60 miles south of Alice Springs. 'I am totally convinced that there has been a grave miscarriage of justice. I plan to produce and present a half hour documentary 'Dingo Trackers and Azaria.'' Sadly, Burnham Burnham died before he accomplished his goal.

My trip to Darwin on 15 September, 1984, and subsequent encounters with Fred Mercer, began with me seeing him at his desk in a stony mood. I was motioned to sit down. I came armed with the knowledge that interstate visits could command an hour or more per visit, but this was at the discretion of the superintendent. Mercer would allow only half the time, half an hour per visit. It seemed he wanted to penalise Lindy in some way for something I was not privy to.

'What you're offering is unsatisfactory, Mr Mercer,' I said. Mercer dropped his glasses and peered over the rims. I don't think he could believe his ears. Without warning he called for a warder to come into the room.

'Mr... will you come in here please?'

'Oh dear,' I thought, 'is he going to have me escorted out for contradicting him, or perhaps lock me up?'

'Get me the records of Chamberlain,' he barked at his servant.

I prayed that the records weren't doctored.

'Yes, er hmm,' Mercer reflected as his steely blue eyes surveyed the documents.

'What time do you want to see your wife, Mr Chamberlain?'

'Two o'clock each afternoon,' I answered.

'Alright, you can have one hour each visit,' he said.

While the boys were anxious to see their mum again, Kahlia was not. She did not recognise Lindy and clearly wanted no part of her, while her two brothers sought and received kisses and hugs. Lindy was stoic. She seemed to understand that it would take time and was prepared to wait. But for me, it was an embarassing and awkward moment as I felt for Lindy in her abandoned state.

The following day I visited Bob Donally, the Correctional Services boss. I sought permission to get a photo of Lindy and place it in Kahlia's bedroom.

'If I do that, Mr Chamberlain the security of the prison will be jeopardised,' Donally retorted.

'Ok', I replied. 'If this is an issue and you think it fair, would you put your reasons in writing, please?'

'Oh, I don't think we need to do that, Mr Chamberlain.'

'Well, my reasons for this are that Lindy has changed so much that Kahlia finds her unrecognisable when she comes here. And besides Kahlia would have a record of how her mother was like during her first few years.'

Donally was unmoved. Kahlia would have to go without. Lindy would remain bereft.

Prison is a punishment, but the Berrimah Prison added to the punishment. Lindy had to endure other prisoners eating succulent peaches, a fruit that she adored, in order to taunt her. Warders would also eat gourmet foods in front of her, smirking as the food slid down their gullets. When it was known that Lindy had a favourite TV program at 8pm on a Wednesday night, she would be locked up before it came on, when on every other night she was subjected to others' TV programs.

Meanwhile, Detective Sergeant Kevin John Lincoln had come out of the shadows, disquieted and angry. What he had to say did not correspond with the Northern Territory cop line. He had left the force to become a private investigator. Lincoln was on duty at Alice Springs police station on the night of 17 August 1980 when the senior constable from Ayers Rock, Constable Frank Morris, had radioed that a baby was missing from the camping area. The next day he had travelled with the top Alice Springs policeman, Inspector Michael Shamus Gilroy, to interview us.

When Malcolm Brown, now chief reporter for the *Sydney Morning Herald*, interviewed Lincoln, he discovered evidence that the Northern Territory Crown had not wanted to know and had brushed under the carpet. Only as a result of leaving the police force did Lincoln now feel free to talk. He told Malcolm Brown that, 'if he had been allowed to give evidence at the second Coroner's inquest and the trial he would have greatly strengthened the Chamberlains' case...His evidence, strongly supporting the dingo theory, was largely ignored'. He said that when he saw us the day after Azaria's disappearance 'the couple were breaking down and weeping. Brown wrote that this was contrary to what the prosecution had alleged at the Chamberlains' trial, that they had been unreasonably calm and even callous in the aftermath of Azaria's disappearance.'

Detective Sergeant Lincoln had taken photographs of 'huge paw marks a matter of centimetres from Azaria Chamberlain's cot and found what was probably blood on the ground outside the Chamberlains' tent'. He stated: 'I observed that at the rear of the tent there were several huge pug marks indicating the presence of a large dog. These pugmarks were on the right-hand side facing the tent and also, ones which I considered to be significant, were at the rear of the tent near the roadway...These sketches were produced at the first inquest and I have not seen them since. I also observed what appeared to be congealed droplet-type material on the earth in this area which was completely foreign to that area.'

The samples of this material, Lincoln said, were never tested. The photographs taken with Constable Morris' camera, he was told, did not come out. He told Malcolm Brown, 'What had appeared to be a fine blood spray on the wall of the tent and blood on the ground near the tent supported a case that a dingo had gone inside, got the baby and carried it out, he said.' (*Sydney Morning Herald* 22/9/1984). According to Erwin Chlanda, senior reporter with the *Centralian*, I was told that Lincoln was, by far, the Alice's top detective and should have been placed in charge from the night of Azaria's disappearance.

Three days later, *The Northern Territory News* (25/9/1984) published a report from Hillary Tabrett, an Ayers Rock ranger at the scene on 17 August 1980. She claimed that the 'baby's blanket' was observed by her at the Ayers Rock police station and it appeared that there were blood and puncture marks on it. Tabrett said that at the time, she was 'absolutely convinced' a dingo tooth had done the puncture.

With the growing public perplexity at the continuing unfolding of fresh evidence favourable to us, Dr Terry Annable wrote to the High Court's Justice Gerard Brennan. In his very detailed letter Annable took umbrage at Brennan's time-honoured but increasingly controversial stance that highly technical evidence was a question 'for the jury alone'. Annable observed: 'In my position as a lecturer in clinical sciences, I could see that Mrs Kuhl (among others) had little experience in the major areas under investigation. How on earth then could jurors agree on things that Professors of Science cannot agree on?' (Letter to Mr Justice Brennan from Terry Annable, 20/12/1984.)

Bill Wentworth, former Federal Minister for Aboriginal Affairs, called me on 16 October 1984. It was very late in the day and I was about to retire to bed. He had talked to Paul Everingham, hoping to convince him to reopen the case or at least showing some respite for Lindy. Several Chamberlain support groups were running roughshod over our wishes and Wentworth expressed concern that unless a united front was presented, the whole thrust for a good outcome would collapse in a heap. The push by Phil Ward to enter Territory politics and try and win support for an inquiry might well have a negative effect on Everingham, especially if he won the election into Federal Parliament. But I tried to explain to Mr Wentworth that the new forensic evidence, as good as it was, wasn't ready to be aired, and on past performance there was no guarantee that

Everingham would do anything with it. Wentworth admitted: 'You have every right to be sceptical about the Northern Territory Government acting impartially to the new evidence that you have.' The conversation spun me into a new bout of depression and by 18 October I was again at a terrible low and experiencing near-sleepless nights.

Lindy was requested to have discussions in jail with the alternate legal team headed by Lloyd-Jones and Nyman. Stuart was able to report back to me: 'Lindy was not rude to Lloyd-Jones on this occasion. The first time she was a bit tough on him but this time she appeared in very good spirits.' When Lindy asked Trevor Nyman, 'Can you keep confidence?' it was reported that Nyman was stunned by her audacity. Lindy had an abiding trust in Stuart and nobody was going to top that.

By early December 1984, Paul Everingham was elected a Federal Member of the House of Representatives. His Commonwealth Parliamentary debut for the Liberal Party was a much-heralded and speculated-upon event. It was claimed that he was the right man for the job because of 'the claims he had made so strongly that he, and only he, can fight the Territory's case effectively.' Mr Everingham was described as 'a street fighter' who would 'guarantee his voice would be heard' (*Northern Territory News*, 3/12/1984). He was also known as the 'father' of the high-profile Yulara Tourist Resort.

But the Australian Law Reform Commission had also become active, scratching its head over the power of hotly disputed forensic science dictating a jury to bring in a 'unanimous' verdict beyond reasonable doubt. I was approached by one of its Reform Members and invited to comment. This spurred me in the belief that somewhere, somehow, some credible authorised body would take another look at us and the administration of justice.

On 15 December 1984, I addressed a Chamberlain Support rally in the Wahroonga Seventh-day Adventist Church. The Church, through the Chamberlain Support group led by Mrs Ann Campbell, had become proactive about the value of justice and was prepared to make it a legitimate topic on the Sabbath day. I was extremely grateful, for here was a moment when I could vent some of my own anxieties. It would be one of many occasions. What I said was this:

'Four years and four months have transpired since the disappearance of our daughter Azaria Chamberlain. The process of obtaining full and complete natural justice in this matter has been for all of us here today, an incredibly eye-opening and gut-wrenching experience. You, like I, have probably lost a lot of sleep and shed a lot of tears. I am surprised it has not sent some of us to our graves or to the asylum by now. It has certainly taken its toll on human relationships.

'I need not tell you that the issues are as grave for my fellow Australians as they are for me. That is why you are here today. Few would have dared to think of the necessity for such a meeting today. Now, few would deny its necessity here in this place.

'In the New Testament there are some telling pointers concerning social injustice. If you would quote the law, then Jesus tells the Body of Christ, 'the weightier matters of the law are justice, mercy and faith' (Matthew 23:23). If you want to talk about prisons then Paul says: 'Remember those who are in prison, as if you are a fellow prisoner, and those who are ill-treated, since you are also liable to bodily sufferings.' (Hebrews 13:3).

'We are at war and it is a costly one. We will need to fight it inch by inch, sometimes going sideways. There are no rehearsals for this struggle. There are no paths to follow except the path of grace. Though we forge ahead into the unknown we still know two basic things. Lindy Chamberlain is an innocent woman needlessly incarcerated in a hot and steamy Darwin jail. Christ died for us and while we walk through the valley of the shadow of death, we will fear no evil, for our Redeemer lives and one day He shall stand up upon the Earth. Peace be with you all.'

At the Chamberlain Support group Newcastle rally on 3 October 1984, I told the audience through a spokesperson and Avondale College Senior Lecturer in History, Dr Don Hansen: 'The jury's atypical behaviour in bringing down a conviction contrary to a favourable summing up by the judge...I believe will be seen as one of the most perverse jury decisions ever seen in Australian legal history. It is now known that real evidence has been deflected or withheld from a court that could have acquitted us.

'The system must now be big enough to recognise that a very real miscarriage of justice has occurred and that an inquiry, above self-interest and without fear or favour, must be conducted into the events that really took place on the night of 17 August 1980 and the following months up until the trial.

'I believe that the evidence is now available to prove virtually beyond reasonable doubt that Mrs Chamberlain was the innocent victim of a wtich-hunt. The problem is, can we trust a very small group of people in a Territory with an ultra-light population, no bigger than a third of Newcastle, to be big enough to expose themselves to an honest inquiry?

'Well may we have grave doubts as to the intentions of the government, should they seek to reinvestigate this case, unless a judge or commissioned QC selected by an independent body, heads up that inquiry.

'Can this Territory Government be trusted? When it shows a harsh and unconscionable attitude to a letter, which included two specialists' recommendations, for a mother to be able to visit her seven-year-old son and comfort him through the trauma of losing his eye.

'Furthermore, what would you think if you had stayed away four and a half months, the longest time ever, to appease the Darwin Jail Superintendent, only to have your jail visits to your wife slashed by almost half, and to be further told that there would be no more phone calls to your wife, virtually for any reason, including matters of vital legal importance, such as choosing legal counsel for future representation in a court of law.

'And what would you think if an answer for licence application to have your wife released was being delayed, month after month after month. The Government already had access to two specialist reports on the mental health of Lindy Chamberlain, both of which show absolutely no evidence that she could hurt anyone and indeed would not hurt anyone. Now they want another psychiatrist's report to see if she is fit to be released!

'Apart from that, what would you think if your wife, or your mother, who by present-day standards had already served 18 months jail in a maximum security prison, for a crime that she never committed, for a crime that never happened, and for a crime that in all other states now almost always gets only a good behaviour bond. On these matters it would seem that the Northern Territory has some of the harshest and most archaic laws in the

Commonwealth, and has much to answer for.

'Well might one be excused for suspecting that justice is being obstructed. Peace be with you all.'

On the same day of October 1984, *The Northern Territory News* published a headline alleging that the 'Northern Territory (was) ignoring new evidence'. The Northern Territory Crown would not agree to give access to the vital forensic evidence used to convict us. Without this, no finalisation of the defence's call for an inquiry was possible.

Bryan Rodgers, a Newcastle resident in 1986, reported that he had actually been an eyewitness to the death of an Aboriginal child killed by a dingo while in the Northern Territory near Tennant Creek. He claimed he reported it to the police at the time.

By 2 November, I had recovered from my depressive mood and with new resolve prepared a submission to the Northern Territory Corrective Services. It would be on jail conditions for women. Through subterfuge, I had collected some useful evidence. I also received information on request about the jailing of women for infanticide. The results indicated that Lindy was the first ever to go to prison for the alleged death of a child under 12 months. Stuart had a 20-minute session with Brian Martin who flatly refused to further consider a licence application for Lindy. This Territory justice suggested that 20 years would be an appropriate sentence. 'Oh why go half way?' I screamed to myself. 'Just lynch her and be done with it. That's what you want isn't it?'

In January 1985, I took a four-week break with my children and flew to my parents in Christchurch, New Zealand. The four weeks seemed like four minutes. They still lived at 'Thongsleigh' Ellesmere, a rich-soiled farming district 30-odd kilometres south of the city, first settled by my Chamberlain ancestors in 1878. Thongsleigh was one of the second-generation homesteads, which was designed with a long wide hallway leading to five bedrooms, a loungeroom and a dining room. I was glad to be back, surrounded by my old original haunts, my mother's exquisite farm cooking with garden fresh vegetables and lamb. I was in heaven. Unfortunately, my commitment to vegetarianism suffered a hit travelling regularly from Alice Springs to Darwin, where the vegetarian selection wouldn't have kept a rabbit alive.

Utterly exhausted, I was also looking forward to spending time on the clean, shingle-bedded Selwyn River, fishing for elusive trout. Hunting these feisty, succulent creatures along a river stretch of five-kilometres had been my love for a long time. The pristine subterranean-fed river from the South Island's Southern Alps was well stocked in summer with fish from half a kilogram to 2.5 kilograms in weight. I had some wonderful memories from my late teenage years of catching up to eight of these beauties in one hour of fishing mid-morning, with dry fly, from the deep holes into the rapids.

My children put on weight from the fresh farm produce. My father was a fastidious vegetable grower and seemed to have almost every known vegetable in his garden. After a poor start with a distressed stomach and diarrhoea, Kahlia replaced the pounds that she had lost and was growing outwards almost too quickly. The creamy New Zealand butter was also a hit with her and the boys.

I went on a tramping and hunting trip with my brother Peter into the Southern Alps around the Mount Cook and Fiordland National Park but even there the media were in search of me, stalking me as their quarry, hoping to get an interview. It had been my custom to jump the 2000 kilometres-wide Tasman 'ditch' between Australia and New Zealand every 18 months and spend weeks in the mountains. There, with family and friends, I would occasionally bag a trout or take a chamois (French mountain antelope) for meat. At one stage a media chopper flew suspiciously low over us for about 20 minutes, springing some chamois out of their camouflaged cover, before we disappeared into the dark alpine flora with them.

Back home from New Zealand, we flew a few days later to Darwin via Adelaide. Jan Hughes, wife of Dr Owen Hughes, the chairperson of Avondale College Education, accompanied us. She was not used to flying, and this trip would take a fair amount of energy out of her. At Adelaide I lost my ticket. The solution, I was told, was to reapply at Darwin. Thankfully I was allowed back on the plane, one of the few benefits of a familiar name and face.

This flight always exhibited a change of culture and pace, as you moved towards the equator. Sydney to Melbourne was formal; dark-suited men, finely attired women with serious looks and quality food. From Brisbane, Mount Isa or Alice Springs to Darwin it was another world. Flying over the middle of Australia was like floating on a red sea of dust. The scenery was unchanging; the sky was so monotonously blue you would pray for a cloud or some relief on this never-ending journey. People smiled more, were relaxed and jocular, their faces brown and weather-beaten. Shoes gave way to thongs or wide brown, cracked bare feet; they sat slouched in their chairs, ate less appetising food and drank more alcohol. Ties were only worn by 'turkeys' who hadn't been initiated; government attire or 'Territory rig' was an open-neck short-sleeved shirt and shorts. But if a southern press paparazzi member appeared you might put your tie back on—if you could find one.

I was feeling anxious about how I would find Lindy. I had not heard from her for six weeks; you couldn't just pick up the phone to the Darwin jail and say, 'Hi, can I speak to Lindy Chamberlain?' There were no telephone privileges. I had received glowing reports about her condition in jail from other visitors, particularly the Darwin Support Group. Apparently she was becoming the fittest female there, losing weight and becoming her old physically vibrant and attractive self. But that was only half the story of course. It would be my ninth trip to see her.

On my first morning visit to the jail I got a fleeting glimpse of what I thought was an attractive young girl in a blue dress who was lifting the lid of a large rubbish skip. She was on tiptoes and her suntanned calf muscles were flexed in the morning sunlight. Her dark hair, dark glasses and tiny waist caused me to take a second look.

'Who could this be?' I wondered. I hadn't seen anyone answering that description in the jail before. 'What could she be in for?' Suddenly it dawned on me. 'What the heck! That's my wife!'

'My stomach has shrunk here,' Lindy said with a smile, 'so I don't think I'll have any real problem about not putting on weight when I get out. Eating better or richer food now doubles me up. The food in here gave me real pain at first. I had diarrhoea for the first six months.'

I thought about this as she was speaking. Her mind seemed almost in another world, removed from reality. The real reason for her toilet problems was more like the stress of coping with jail life, I thought.

'When I get out I would eventually like to clean myself out in Darwin, have a rest for 36-48 hours, with a really good sleep. Then I could go to a few shops, and buy some clothes and things. Then I would like to be escorted down to Sydney with someone like Rod (Jenkins—my New Zealand born cousin). He is big and intelligent, or the Ansett Airlines Manager in Alice Springs, Paul. Failing that, even Stuart could escort me home. I would then like to go home and spend a fortnight at some isolated beach then go to the Sydney Adventist Hospital for tests.'

It was a sobering time for both of us, as Lindy and I discussed our future together. We made some plans, albeit tenuously, about our children when she got out. It all seemed a bit fantasy-like. Her stay in prison was officially 'for life', yet here she was making plans, with her usual attention to every detail for her release.

Lindy had grown stronger by the day in asserting her rights to control her own legal destiny. There was decreasing input from me. In a letter to Nyman from her Darwin prison cell on 28 February 1985, Lindy wrote that in Nyman's correspondence to her, 'I can hardly say I was impressed'. She said she had asked for affidavits and instead had received 'opinions' and 'advice'. She said: 'It appears you did not understand so I will reiterate it to you...I require eyewitness affidavits immediately...I also require the opinion of 1800 pages odd, finished or not...I hope this letter will help eliminate further procrastination in the issue you were engaged for.' On 18 March 1985, Lindy cut loose from her second legal team, who were investigating any Ayers Rock police or ranger behaviour that might implicate them in a cover up of Azaria's disposal after her death. I was shocked. It was my view, rightly or wrongly, to reflect on their work and make a decision jointly.

The return trip to Sydney was another problem for me. I had forgotten my tickets, again, left behind at my Darwin residence. On my final visit, Lindy had said I looked very tired. The five visits to her had come and gone with frightening speed. Perhaps it was because they had been more pleasant than usual. No tough moments for once. Kahlia was now accepting Lindy, believing that this mysterious woman was actually nice. Perhaps it was because my mother, while I was visiting New Zealand, had put Kahlia straight and had told her 'The naughty people in Darwin put mummy in jail.' I felt Kahlia was too young to hear or understand the real traumatic truth about why Lindy had been jailed. Another passenger was with us; a kitten we had named 'Cougar Blue' a British Blue-grey shorthaired kitten given to Kahlia by one of our loyal Darwin supporters. To Kahlia's disappointment it was transported via TAA air cargo and we all had our fingers crossed that it would be all right after the epic voyage back to Cooranbong.

West Australian and Northern New South Wales interests were now driving the Chamberlain Support Group thrust. This arm of the movement was about to achieve public status from an interview by Richard Morecroft and Geraldine Doogue on ABC television on 15 April 1985 who described them as a 'dedicated group of people'. I waited for the evening interview with bated breath, but it wasn't happening. I rang the ABC with some interrogation of my own for the Chief-of-Staff for the ABC. He was apologetic but also evasive and I felt like I was a fox terrier after a rabbit. It was probably bad behaviour on my part, but I had to let my pent-up anger against the media out somehow. He did not know who I was and I didn't want to tell him. I was trying very hard to keep out of the media spotlight. My anonymity felt refreshing and as he eventually grudgingly admitted, the failure to show the segment was said to be due to 'electronic problems...human error...and confusion'. He then apologised for the failure of this item not appearing. The interview would be delayed to the following night. Fortunately, it ended up as a bit of a blip on the radar, with no damage to the integrity of my own attorneys resulting from it. It did, however, kick-start the view that we needed a professional public relations team to counter all the past bad publicity.

Eight days later I sat in barrister Maurice Neil's Sydney office where my legal team decided to invite the well-known Charlton Public Relations machine on board to design a strategy to focus on and publish four compelling facts that the Northern Territory Crown had screwed up.

These included the fact that the blood reagent to test for foetal blood was wrong; the alleged blood under the dashboard was not blood at all; Azaria's jumpsuit could be shown to have been damaged as a result of dingo teeth cuts; and the claim that no dingo hairs had been found on the jumpsuit was false. It was also decided to approach TV journalist Michael Willesee and his producer, Phil Davis, to get this message out on Willesee's high-exposure and high-ratings show. The show was duly aired and received prime time exposure a few days before we sent out our written submission.

On 25 June, 1985 we presented our case to the Northern Territory for an inquiry. One of the principal reasons for an investigation was the fact that a jury had convicted us with: no motive, no weapon, no body, no confession, a total lack of opportunity on our part, and that we were of good character. Lindy was of sound mind and there had been no evidence of post-natal depression. Our new evidence would show that dingoes could produce the various teeth marks to explain the cutting characteristics on part of the jumpsuit, that dingo hair was found on the jumpsuit, and in the tent. The blood allegedly found in the car might not have been blood, and if it was, it certainly wasn't foetal or Azaria's. Furthermore, the eyewitness evidence of the campers, all of them, supported the truth and reliability of our testimony about what took Azaria's life.

15. *Parliamentary 'Privilege' and the Case for an Inquiry*

The chorus of concern about a perceived injustice continued to grow louder. It was as if a political and legal backlash against the Northern Territory had engulfed us. Liberal Senator Peter Baume contacted the Northern Territory Government to warn them that a reinvestigation of the case was on its way. He had listened to Les Smith's presentation on the 'cuts' in the jumpsuit and Professor Barry Boettcher's presentation on the 'blood' in my car. After National Party Queensland Senator Ron Boswell attended a Chamberlain supporters' rally, he contacted the Northern Territory Attorney General to tell him that if he did not open an inquiry, the Senator would. His support was weak but it was growing. Next came National Senator, Bob Catter, my former Mount Isa Federal Government Member. He said that after having met me, he found it very difficult to see how the case had been proven against us. Senator Austin Lewis, a former solicitor, said that: 'From the outset I have been concerned about the case presented against these people and I believe that they were wrongly convicted.' Keith Wright, MHR Labour, declared: 'I am convinced that Lindy is innocent.' Other members of parliament were declaring that it looked like a miscarriage of justice. The Honorable Tim Fischer, later the National Party leader and Deputy Prime Minister, declared early in 1985: 'I will lend whatever influence I may have to the cause of justice.'

One of the best-known women in Australia, Ita Buttrose, also entered the fray. Ita was rapidly becoming a champion for our cause in seeking an inquiry. She was the editor of the *Australian Woman's Weekly* and former Editor-in-Chief of the *Daily Telegraph*. She wrote a sensitive and perceptive report on the personal aspects of our plight. I broadcast this welcome encouragement in the *Azaria Newsletter*, the official news reporting service that I had set up with the editor, Nonie Hodgson. Ita's entry reflected yet another turning point in the media's attitude and evaluations of our case. Like many other people in Australia, she told me that she had originally thought that Lindy Chamberlain probably murdered her daughter. Now, after talking to me, and having read the new evidence and opinions collected by the Chamberlain Innocence Committee, she believed there was sufficient doubt about the case to support the call for an inquiry (*Azaria Newsletter*, August 1985).

Democrat, Senator Colin Mason, a member of the Chamberlain Innocence Committee, declared in the Federal Parliament on 18 September 1985, that Lindy's imprisonment 'was an affront to all reasonable opinion and an affront to any rational view of what ought to constitute justice'. A letter from the Chamberlain Innocence Committee, led by heavyweight former justice, Sir Reginald Sholl, delivered a powerful message, outlining the new forensic evidence, with Northern Territory Labour Senator, and Federal Cabinet Minister, Bob Collins, firing the media cannon (*Northern Territory News*, 18/9/1985). Collins was conscience-stricken by the power of the evidence. For him, our case was 'an extraordinary miscarriage of justice'. He felt compelled to call 'as a matter of urgency' for a 'Judicial Commission of Inquiry'. It must be established 'with the widest terms of reference'. Such terms of reference, I hoped, would bring into play the undercover activities of the police, the role of the Northern Territory Law Department and the Northern Territory Government and the way the media leaks were orchestrated to steam-roll us to a second inquest and trial. I was also out to unmask Joy Kuhl's spurious blood evidence.

Bob Collins was now armed with explosive material that would create great discomfort, and ire, among his colleagues. An alarmed *Northern Territory News* editor responded to Collins' call for an inquiry. The editor stated that in Collins changing his 'previously impeccably silent stance...(it) did nothing to serve the interests of justice in the Northern Territory'. The editor claimed that, although Collins was 'one of the more accomplished politicians in the Territory', his highly public call was 'untimely and unwise'. The paper repeated its claim that Collins' call was an 'attack on the legal system'.

The Territory media machine now wound up the Northern Territory public with the information that three of the scientists who had cracked the jumpsuit mystery cuts were 'Seventh-day Adventist scientists' (*Sunday Territorian*, 22/9/1985). Dr Norman Young thought that the Northern Territory paper's front-page headlines would enrage me. But it had the opposite effect. I photocopied the article several times and posted it on every noticeboard I could find around the Avondale College precincts. Religious prejudice and bigotry will always be unmasked sooner or later, and the Adventist Church, having its fair share, was used to dealing with it. This battle was also about religious prejudice. The headline explicitly confirmed what the Church had always suspected, that the Church itself was on trial, but instead of driving it underground the news quietly galvanised the Church. The prejudicial leak by the Northern Territory Police and Government might work for a while, but truth was on the march, with its boots on. Bob Collins rang the author of the article, Frank Alcorta, and challenged him to ring the German blood reagent firm himself and check out how good Joy Kuhl's work had really been.

Apparently Alcorta did just that, and it had an almost immediate effect. According to Collins, Alcorta came back to him in a 'remorseful state' and told him that the editorial policy towards the Chamberlains would probably change after they had a meeting. It seemed to work. Articles about us seemed mellower–for three weeks.

Seven days later, on Sunday 29 September, Ita Buttrose phoned from Darwin.

'Hello, I'm Ita Buttrose. Can I speak to Michael Chamberlain please?'

'Good morning Ita, You are speaking to him.'

'I've just been visiting Lindy in jail. She's very different from what I expected.'

'She is very human isn't she?' I answered.

'She's a petal,' Ita replied. 'Lindy said some very angry things about the jurors and the Northern Territory administration of justice, but it won't help to print those things just now. I really hope you get an inquiry.'

Northern Territory new Chief Minister, Ian Tuxworth, telexed the Labor Prime Minister, Robert J. Hawke, on 1 October 1985, to bring the errant Collins into line. He feared the Northern Territory judicial and political systems could now be brought into disrepute. Our personal friends in the Territory, surgeon Dr Tony Noonan and his wife, Liz, the chairperson of the Darwin Chamberlain support group, were also bombarding Tuxworth. An exchange in a lift caused considerable discomfort for the Chief Minister, who had no answer to Dr Noonan's accusation that he was weak.

The time had come for me to make my own pilgrimage and protest to Canberra. I selected a local man to accompany me. He was long-time friend and scientist, Dr Geoffrey Madigan, who would be able to assist me in explaining to any Federal Member of Parliament the trickier parts of the evidence. Furthermore, he knew the local scientists Burnett, Smith and Chapman and had worked alongside them in former days. I journeyed to Australia's capital on 13 October 1985 in my old 1974 refurbished white Chrysler Valiant Wagon bought at a local government auction for the princely sum of $1500.

On the first day, 14 October 1985, I met with Senators Chris Publick, David Vigor, Ron Boswell, Baden Teague and Colin Mason, the last four of whom were convinced of an injustice. I also met with the Member for Dundas, Philip Ruddock, later Australia's Attorney-General. Ruddock was supportive but, like most astute politicians, gave little away. He did, however, promise to write to Northern Territory Attorney-General, Marshall Perron. Ruddock supported the view that an inquiry or new court case of some description was necessary. As this was all I sought, I was most grateful. On the other hand, Senator Vigor suggested the use of a Senate Select Committee to bring on an inquiry, and offered to talk to the Minister for Territories, Gordon Sholes.

Senator Publick, a Liberal, was sceptical but willing to listen. He appeared to be well informed but was worried that Parliament was setting an unhealthy precedent and opposed the idea of a jury system being replaced by a panel of experts. Another concern was that Lindy was adamant that it was a dingo and not a wild or stray dog. As an enthusiastic environmentalist he may have secretly wished to protect the dingo from adverse publicity. I made it plain that I wasn't there to prove my innocence; that would take too long. I was not there for popularity stakes but for the very explicit purpose of convincing politicians that enough doubt existed to hold an inquiry.

Other politicians who gave me an audience included Senators Barney Cooney, Alan Missen's researcher, John Hall, and Senator Sir John Carrick. Carrick took the view that whatever else occurred: the Northern Territory should have first bite of the new material. But if this was inadequate, an independent inquiry would need to be set up. Carrick then turned on me in a rather confronting manner.

'Do you realise the consequences of reopening this whole case up again? What if it turns out unfavourably for you? Mr Chamberlain, what do you really think of Lindy's story?'

'I believe her. It fits with everything I saw and observed,' I replied.

'I note that Aidan was never called to give evidence. Why? Would not that have been a good choice? He was interrogated by the police, was he not?' said Carrick.

'Yes he was,' I replied assertively, 'but my legal team considered they had done enough to convince a jury of our innocence. Aidan was eight at the time and we felt that to put him through more trauma was unnecessary.'

'Ok, I will speak to Senator Durack (Federal Attorney General) about this,' he replied. Carrick had put me through the most intense questioning of any parliamentarian so far. I felt I had passed his test.

Liberal Senator Warwick Parer had another take on the call for an inquiry: 'You should recognise, Mr Chamberlain, that you can do nothing without the support of the Territory. My hands are tied until they bring down their Report and this is in line with my Shadow Attorney-General's advice.'

'I understand,' I replied contritely.

'Well. I have every confidence in Paul Everingham. He is totally bipartisan and has no axe to grind whatsoever, let me assure you. He would not be interested in any interference as he sees it as an entirely judicial matter.'

Another MP, Keith Wright, informed me that he had spoken to the Attorney-General and suggested that a senior Crown law officer be appointed to oversee the new material. I queried this suggestion. 'What if the Crown law officer was biased?' Other members I spoke to included Michael Hodgman (Liberal, Tasmania) who was particularly supportive. 'I raised your matter in the party room last year in June after I received quite an offensive reply from Northern Attorney-General Jim Robertson in April. I asked that they consider a Commission of Inquiry. There were some misgivings in the party room. Members have expressed some sympathy but there is a strong feeling that they should not set a precedent to cross state boundaries. You know your Tasmanian witnesses, Greg and Sally Lowe, were very strong in their testimony. I have no doubts that they were telling the truth. That is strongly in your favour. I intend to say something in Parliament about this.'

'Thank you,' I replied, 'Sergeant Charlwood kept her as a pregnant mother sitting on an uncomfortable seat for hours.'

Hodgman looked thoughtful, 'Well now...let me tell you what your best bet is, and I say this having been a member of the Tasmanian Bar for a few years. Do not try to argue for any proof of innocence at this time. I should warn you not to get your hopes up about any objective approach from the Territory. You are also going to have to keep some of your support groups in check. They could wreck your early chances of obtaining justice. They must focus on Lindy and an inquiry and not go off on any hare-brained tangents and attack others.'

Although Hodgman did not mention anyone by name I knew he was referring to a certain antagonist in Western Australia who wanted Stuart Tipple removed and who had accused him unfairly of being too naïve.

Hodgman had picked up on Stuart Tipple having come under increasing fire from a maverick West Australian Support Group, controlled by an authoritarian female who appeared to want to scuttle his work. 'The boy in long socks' he was nicknamed and there was a naïve misunderstanding about his painstaking and reputable investigations with Professor Boettcher. The West Australian Support Group leader described Stuart as 'incompetent'. This was far from the truth. John Phillips QC, endorsed a letter from Andrew Kirkham, sent to the Avondale College president, which said: 'In my 17 years of practice at the Bar I have not had a better instructing solicitor or a solicitor who worked harder or contributed more by way of instruction, preparation or invaluable advice towards the present case. I do not consider any solicitor could do more than what Mr Tipple did in attempting to secure an acquittal for Mr and Mrs Chamberlain.' (College President, Dr James J.C. Cox letter, 12 April 1984).

Hodgman added: 'Rather, concentrate on probing the aspect of a miscarriage of justice through the strength of the new evidence and any other grounds that can be used. Any publicity that is constructive for you must be kept going.'

Gratified at his obvious concern, I left his chambers with a new spring in my step.

Regardless of our internal conflicts and their disconcerting effects, our agitation for an inquiry was shaking the foundations of the Northern Territory Solicitor-General's Department. At the same time, we were concerned that our agitatation may affect Lindy's time in prison.

My next interview was with Liberal Federal MP Ian Cameron who behaved coldly.

'Why have you come here?' he asked indignantly.

Senator Noel Creighton-Brown also gave me the cold shoulder, it appeared, but as he continued to ask questions on the new scientific evidence, I saw another side.

'So you think your wife is innocent, do you?' Creighton-Brown looked me in the eye.

'Yes.'

'Why?' After my answer, he started expounding on strategies to keep the justice ball rolling. 'You are going to have to work on more senators. Here is a list of names...I should tell you that I will support a Senate inquiry in due course. But a petition to the Governor-General to set up an inquiry is your best chance you know.' It had been a harrowing experience, which turned good.

Harry Edwards MP was my next call. 'Very nice to meet you, Michael.' He beamed. 'I have a close working relationship with Lionel Bowen and I sit next to Paul Everingham in the house.'

John Hodges, a Liberal MP, told me: 'I tried to contact the Ayers Rock Rangers but they were very tight lipped. It rather shocked me, because I know those guys quite well and I knew Ian Cawood kept a pet dingo.' His Rock experience with the Northern Territory Conservation and police employees was the same. The ranks were closed.

One of my final interviews during my visit to Canberra in 1985, was with Liberal MP, Neil Brown who questioned me vigorously. He reminded me that there could be a stumbling block, constitutionally–all was dependent on the Northern Territory's response. I think he was alluding to a conflict between Territory and State's rights. 'You will have to let this take its course,' he said, 'but if their reply is negative and enough time goes by, there will be Federal action. We have to be sure of our rights at Federal level, however. We need to be sure we have the power to conduct an inquiry. At any rate, I am certain you will find Ian Tuxworth would like to help you if he can.'

This last comment surprised me. Northern Territory Chief Minister Ian Tuxworth's previous appeal to the Prime Minister was designed to clip the wings of Bob Collins' support.

It was time to leave the Capital Territory of Australia. On my journey home from Canberra, my local Charlton Member of Parliament, Bob Brown MP, (not to be confused with the Leader of the Australian Greens party, Dr Bob Brown) released a statement to the national press on 17 October 1985. He said that a 'passive position' was untenable and urged the Northern Territory to open an inquiry. The doubts he now had were 'numerous, challenging and disquieting'. He issued a warning to all who might oppose him: 'Do something or I will be seeking the intervention of the Commonwealth'.

I decided that a second shot at Canberra was needed to press home the advantage. On 5 and 6 November, 1985, I returned to the capital, with more energy and resolve. This time I took Dr Owen Hughes, head of the

Avondale College Education Faculty. Owen had become an increasingly significant player and a sort of mentor to the family, while his wife Jan was passionate about my children's welfare. They had brought up their children to be very responsible, gracing the local private Avondale High School honour board with no less than four school captains.

My appointments were with Senators Margaret Reynolds, McKiernan, Bernard Kilgariff, Susan Knowles, Michael Baume and Human Rights Deputy, Peter Bailey on 7 November.

Queensland Labour Senator Margaret Reynolds was first on my list of interviews.

'I take the view that it is a Northern Territory matter but that does not mean I am not interested in your new evidence. A recent poll in the Northern Territory suggesting that Lindy should be released doesn't mean she is innocent. Our report will be going into the Attorney-General in the New Year,' Reynolds said.

I replied that I couldn't see how the Territory News was ever going to be objective in its reporting. 'Look at the way they mishandled the blood report from Behringwerke in Germany about how it shouldn't be used to detect foetal haemoglobin under certain circumstances. On this basis Bob Collins is prepared to support an inquiry,' I replied.

'Yes, that may be so,' she said, 'but will the Northern Territory Country Party Caucus, Mr Chamberlain? Look, the bottom line is this: I do support an inquiry in principle. That's the least we can do. The Feds should push for a date and a decision. And there is something else you might like to think about. Go and see Peter Bailey, the Human Rights Deputy in the AMP building here in Canberra.'

Senator Michael Baume, cousin of Peter Baume, said: 'I have appraised the new scientific evidence and I think you deserve a proper hearing on this.'

Former Minister for Defence in the Liberal Government, James Killen MP, warned me that I was on business that would have severe consequences for me if I were not strictly on the level and telling the whole truth. But I assured him that I was not some media-seeking larrikin, stirring the political cauldron for deeper notoriety.

Liberal, Western Australian Senator, Susan Knowles was keen to learn more from me about the case and questioned me at length. 'Do you feel that the Northern Territory had any 'interest' in convicting Lindy? Do you have any complaints about the Northern Territory administration?'

I was guarded in my answers, explaining that I was not in possession of all the answers but that I knew that something was wrong and it was raising alarm bells.

Knowles then questioned Lindy's behaviour at the inquests and trial. 'Your wife appeared very cool and calculating in her comments about Azaria's death and her knowledge about dingoes.'

'I don't think you understand how Lindy thinks and reacts to emotional issues in public,' I said. 'Her religious background has conditioned her not to reveal her true feelings and not to wear her heart on her sleeve. Furthermore, Lindy was keen to look neat at all times and she had an almost obsessive eye for detail. Her stoic looks and appearance at the first and second inquests were, after all, at least six months past the death of our daughter and to some extent she was recovering.'

'Well thank you for coming, Mr Chamberlain,' she concluded. 'I will be making a value judgment on the matter and will vote accordingly.'

Liberal Northern Territory Senator, Bernard Kilgariff, was one of the last on my list and perhaps the hardest to lobby for an inquiry. The conversation with Kilgariff was not happy; in fact, I felt somewhat ill at ease. We decided that to demonstrate the new scientific evidence, rebutting the foetal blood evidence at the trial and the incisor cuts to Azaria's jumpsuit, was the best way to break through his suspicion of us. Kilgariff stood up, continually glancing ahead for the next page of evidence. He appeared to be shaken by what he saw.

At the end of our session I asked Senator Kilgariff if he wanted to know the truth behind this evidence.

'Without delay, I can assure you,' he replied.

Owen Hughes and I agreed that this visit had unsettled Kilgariff and had placed him in a dilemma.

On the second day of my parliamentary visit Senator Colin Mason raised the question before the Senate about why a Royal Commission was urgently needed. Senator Evans jumped up, cutting short his speech. Mason was, however, able to make the point that the Northern Territory was taking an abysmally long time replying to the Chamberlain Innocence Committee and their submission which stated that 'every day Mrs Chamberlain spends in prison is an indictment of your legal system.'

My final moments in Canberra were spent visiting Commonwealth Human Rights representative, Peter Bailey. It was like talking to a statue, an anti-climax after the many quality responses from Members of Parliament. His answer after our presentation was: 'Our jurisdiction only covers Commonwealth law.'

I questioned his judgment as this being a Territory-driven matter, who else could I turn to? As a last resort I left the Human Rights Commissioner, Dr Norman Young's paper, *The Religion Factor*. I also left a summary of our new scientific findings, for good measure. I left the building with a similar feeling to Owen: 'Don't expect too much from Human Rights.' I kept asking myself, 'Did human rights cover the Chamberlains or was it just "forest" rights and they could ignore the "wood"?'

On balance, all was not lost, not by a long shot. Justice was on its way, surely. With Collins pulling hard in the Northern Territory, along with Mason, Boswell, Edwards, Michael Hodgman and Bob Brown, here was an escalating, bipartisan Federal thrust, and the Northern Territory Government was looking nervously over its shoulder.

16. *Darwin Under Siege*

The Northern Territory Attorney-General's Department had tried to control the tide of new information. Attorney-General Marshall Perron tabled a report by Solicitor-General, Brian Martin. Titled 'The Martin Report', it sidestepped the substantial new forensic evidence and found 'none of the nine matters covered in the submission either forcible or convincing'.

Ian Barker had resigned from his job and was now the Crown prosecutor. Brian Martin and Ian Barker went back a long way to 1963 when they became legal partners in their Alice Springs law firm Barker and Martin Solicitors.

According to Justice Mildren in his book *Big Boss Fella All the Same Judge*, in 1985 Ian Barker had been invited by Ian Tuxworth and his government to beome the new Chief Justice of the Northern Territory but he declined. Brian Martin later went on to become the Chief Justice of the Northern Territory.

While Martin had taken the key prosecution witness and supervisor of Joy Kuhl's work, Dr Simon Baxter, with him to Germany to check Behringweke's reagent, he concluded that there was no reason for a judicial inquiry. According to Paul Toohey ('Life at the Top End', *The Australian* 15/7/2000) he concluded there was nothing wrong with the reagent she had used to such 'a devastating effect against Lindy'.

My inner response was: 'You think I will never find out the truth.'

My mission was to get public acceptance for all the bad things I hadn't done and recognition of all the things the Northern Territory had done.

Unbeknownst to Perron, the Federal Labor Caucus was discussing the Northern Territory's resistance to the inquiry on the same day that the Martin report was released. Bob Brown signalled he would move for a conscience vote in Parliament, if Tipple's Innocence Committee submission was rejected. Brian Martin, who had run the prosecution case as the Solicitor-General in 1982 was in an obvious conflict of interest situation. He had invited himself to appraise his own case, a disease that appeared to be all too easily caught in the Territory.

An Ombudsman's 29-page report by George Masterman QC into the New South Wales Health Department's Glebe Forensic Laboratories on their allegation that foetal blood was found in my car, stated that: 'The failure of the Laboratory to either retain the test slides or to make photographs of them in the Chamberlain's case prejudiced the defence.' It was therefore 'wrong conduct' according to Ombudsman Masterman. New South Wales Minister for Health, Mr Mulock MP, rejected the report. But curiously, the Laboratory was instructed by Mulock to keep slides of all significant work for two years and even longer in serious criminal cases. (*Daily Telegraph*, 17/10/1985).

Dr Simon Baxter, supervisor of Joy Kuhl's work, resigned from the New South Wales Forensic Laboratories. Baxter told the *Canberra Times* that he had been fed up with pay and conditions and resignation had been on his mind for a while (*Canberra Times*, 25/9/1985). The Chamberlain case had also been partly responsible for his reason to resign. When interviewed by ABC television's presenter, Geraldine Doogue, Baxter denied that either he or Joy Kuhl had altered their views, but that he was glad to move on. His trip to Germany with Brian Martin to see the blood reagent company, Behringwerke, 'had not changed his mind' about foetal blood in the car, he told the ABC interviewer. But Baxter agreed in hindsight that it was obvious that the plates with the alleged foetal blood samples should have been kept. At the end of the interview, Dr Baxter admitted the Chamberlain case had become a nightmare. Baxter, an Englishman, reportedly returned to England to work with prosecution forensic blood expert Brian Culliford, but in an area away from forensic science.

The *Sydney Morning Herald* (13/11/1985) in an editorial: 'Lindy: the Senate's Turn,' reported on the pros and cons of a Federal Senate debating the case. The Brisbane *Daily Sun* editorial (15/11/1985) championed Lindy's release, but on the basis that three years incarceration was enough and now was the time for justice to release her. In response, Lennon's cartoon quipped: 'Well...er. Merry Christmas. No hard feelings on your release eh?' Meanwhile *The Australian* (14/11/1985) contained an editorial accompanied by an insensitive cartoon. 'Time for mercy in the Chamberlain case' it proclaimed. Such messages could only intensify my ire. Both papers had ignored our demand for a public inquiry. I muttered to myself: 'It's not mercy we need. It's justice, you clowns.'

Roman Catholic commentators and some Federal politicians had promoted Paul Everingham as a potential Liberal Prime Minister in the wings. He had the media's ear. But as the 'new boy in the long socks' his political ambitions were already under scrutiny by many other parliamentarians. He had risen quickly, becoming the Territory's first Chief Minister in 1978 and the Leader of the Country Liberal Party. In 1984 he was elected to the Federal Parliament.

Now, accompanied by two members of the Innocence Committee, attorney Stuart Tipple and Canberra MP Betty Hocking, I arrived early on a Wednesday morning in the middle of November, 1985, at Parliament House. It was again a covert operation, doing our best to avoid the paparazzi, while trying to find Senator Mason's office and the Senate gallery. The purpose was to listen to the proceedings, in particular Mason's headline address. Mason stood up and accused the Northern Territory of conducting 'a secret inquiry into the new evidence presented by the Chamberlain Innocence Committee' and called 'for a free vote in all divisions on the matter'. Both Senator Evans and Senator Durack, the Senate Liberal leader, refused to endorse Mason's request. Everingham had convinced them that his Liberal attorneys had acted speedily to answer the Innocence Committee's challenge. However, Evans had conceded that the Northern Territory had taken an 'inordinate amount of time' to respond. His speech concluded with a call to have Lindy released (on licence), regardless of guilt or innocence.

But Lindy and I had a pact. She knew and I knew that to be released before an inquiry was announced would reduce the pressure on the Northern Territory to reveal the truth. It was a tough decision on our part, very tough, especially for Lindy, as every day longer she was in jail meant a day longer before we could get to know each other again and try to pick up the pieces of our family life after almost three years of separation.

As I left the Senate gallery, the media throng I had come to have a love-hate relationship with, surrounded me. I hightailed it to the sanctuary of Mason's office. It was impossible to settle my thoughts under this kind of pressure, so after consultation with Stuart Tipple and Mason, I decided to make a brief statement to the newshounds. The Northern Territory Attorney-General, Marshall Perron, had sent word that he had not received a formal request from me through Tipple to request Lindy's release on licence. Senator Carrick, after a conversation with Stuart Tipple, sent a telex to Perron requesting her freedom. I expressed thanks to Durack and Evans for their efforts to obtain Lindy's conditional release, telling the media:

'I am obviously greatly heartened by the comments of Senator Gareth Evans and Senator Peter Durack, recommending my wife's immediate release on licence. Whether or not she is released, we will continue to fight for a just conclusion and for our names to be cleared. We have always ultimately sought an open Commonwealth judicial inquiry and this remains of supreme importance to my family and me.'

The press, surprisingly, was not hostile. They were well represented and the television and print media coverage was fair, with the exception of the Darwin press.

Everingham was not so calm, lashing Senator Mason for exploiting 'the plight of the unfortunate Mrs Chamberlain for his own ends'. Mason, he said, had used the 'grubbiest of reasons' to gain popularity for himself' and 'prop up a flagging political career'.

After The Martin Report was tabled in Darwin, Collins stood up and castigated the incumbent government, calling them 'drongos'. He was promptly expelled from the Northern Territory Parliament for seven days. When Labor Senator Button, a valued wit of the party, was asked about Collins' expulsion he reflected wryly: 'I think that the most important thing...is for systems of government to be...put on the stairway of life. I do not know how long it will take them to climb that stairway to a degree of enlightenment and sophistication such as we have attained in the Senate, but let me say, that I think that in the case of the Northern Territory it will be a very long time.'

On 19 November 1985, Brown lost the vote to obtain an inquiry into our case by 41 votes to 22. He was 'stunned and disappointed'. But he should not have been too surprised.

The drive for justice appeared to have ground to a standstill. *The Northern Territory News*, backed by its network of big brothers around Australia and anchored by Murdoch-owned *The Australian* (19/11/1985), reported everything it could to deny a dingo attack. A Mitchell cartoon in the flagship paper floated a satirical cartoon proposing freedom for Lindy, Normie (Gallagher) an extreme union activist and (Lionel) Murphy, then Attorney-General for the Hawke Federal Government. Two amiable and innocent-looking dingoes perched on top of Ayers Rock, on seeing the freedom placards approaching, muttered: 'Cripes—we must be getting the blame for everything'.

A very different perspective on the same day was published in the (Brisbane) *Courier-Mail* revealing a satirical picture of a soulless media. A Leahy cartoon pictured the Darwin jail being visited by an animal of dubious character with dark glasses and a press cap. The animal was unmistakably a dingo. Here was the press, in a rare and refreshing criticism of itself. It had come unexpectedly and was overwhelming.

A week later, the Liberal Shadow Attorney-General, Stephen Spender, smashed the hopes of every supporter for an inquiry. In solidarity with the incumbent Federal Labor government (26/11/1985), he declared that any intervention by Federal Parliament into the Northern Territory decisions on our case 'would be an unwarranted abrogation of the Northern Territory's powers and a usurpation of the authority of the

Courts'.

On this proclamation there was simply nowhere left for us to go. We had hit a brick wall.

The Northern Territory News appeared to do an about-face in the publication of a Tony Dean cartoon. From Perron's Attorney-General Office a key marked Berrimah Prison was thrown away. The final showdown had laid bare the Territory's judicial intransigence.

Meanwhile, Collins returned to the Territory Parliament after his seven days of exile on 21 November 1985. He had learnt nothing from his punishment. Instead, his expulsion had fuelled the fire in his belly for an inquiry. Collins delivered a three-and-a-half-hour forensic exposition, based on Stuart Tipple's submission, to embed it into the Northern Territory record books. The Murdoch-owned *Sunday Territorian* (24/11/1985) labelled the speech 'long and dull'. Collins reported two of the prosecution scientists, Dr Simon Baxter and Andrew Scott, were feeling uneasy about the new results, and were calling for an inquiry. He quoted Joy Kuhl's supervisor, Dr Baxter, stating that the investigation into our case had been a 'foul-up from the start'. Collins made an ominous prediction. 'I say in all seriousness that the Northern Territory's credibility is on the line in respect of this report. It has not yet hit the deck, but it will be hauled over the coals over the next six months by people a lot smarter than I.'

Sir Reginald Sholl wrote to the Federal Parliament on 3 December 1985, suggesting that if Federal Parliamentarians considered themselves 'decent and fair-minded' then they were now being hypocritical to their oath. His letter asked them if the following message was the one they wished to communicate to Lindy (and me).

'Well, we know we have the power to intervene, and at any rate to investigate the case again, but sorry young lady, we are afraid of offending the Northern Territory Government in its new found grandeur; we know there is quite a lot of new evidence which, if accepted, would be likely completely to exonerate you, but (without waiting to hear what your advisers say in answer to the Northern Territory Solicitor-General's attack on it), we, like Pontius Pilate, wash our hands of the whole affair.

'...If anyone could regard that attitude as anything but weak, heartless and thoroughly un-Australian, we feel sorry for them, and hope they have a happier Christmas than Mrs Chamberlain will have.'

Aiming at a wider target, the single most effective document that would change the minds of the majority of the public was now hitting the bookstores. *Evil Angels*, by John Bryson, would severely shake the Northern Territory Law Department. The title is based on warnings given to the Church by the 19th-century Seventh-day Adventist educator, Ellen White, who described how Christians would encounter more than their share of trouble, including the sneering triumphs of evil angels. Evil angels are people who demonstrate prejudice and self-interest at the expense of fair honest-minded citizens.

Bryson's book was an analysis and reflection on the Northern Territory legal system, media and politicians, and described the fascination of society with our downfall. It presented a powerful indictment of people without integrity. One of our Royal Commission lawyers, Dr Ken Crispin, who later became a Supreme Court judge and President of the Court of Appeal in Canberra, described Bryson's book as causing the press to 'clamour in an orgasm of expiation for the case to be reopened.' *The Australian* book reviewer stated; 'I defy any right minded person to read this book and conclude beyond reasonable doubt that Lindy Chamberlain killed her child.' Many profoundly underestimated the power and authority that Bryson's analysis would have nationally and internationally.

On Tuesday 3 December 1985, I caught a plane to Darwin. I was alone. I had been losing weight, was constantly tired and listless and was overwhelmed by fears of seeing the boys become teenagers and Kahlia growing to womanhood without her mother. The prospect of facing years alone without Lindy was abhorrent.

As usual for this time of the year, the grey Berrimah Prison was enveloped with odours of animals and stale body sweat, and shrouded in ominous storm clouds. Taking an umbrella was superfluous. As I approached the inner sanctum to see the prison chief, a warder asked in disdain.

'What's your name?'

'Michael Chamberlain,' I answered, thinking to myself, 'You've seen me before. Do you need five forms of identification before you lock me up also?'

'OK, Mr Mercer has asked you to wait,' replied the monotone voice through a shallow speaker in a dark stuffy room. It was 2.05pm, temperature 33 degrees, humidity over 95 per cent. I waited and waited. After 30 minutes I went to the red phone and rang the Deputy Director of Correctional Services, the ironically named Barry Barrier.

It did not take long to explain my concern and even less time for a reply.

'All right,' Mr Barrier replied. 'I'll see if I can get these blokes off their arses.'

In less than two minutes I was ushered into Mercer's office by a stone-faced man with a beard that looked like rats had been at it. Mercer came in and said nothing as I sat down.

'I'm over here, Mr Mercer in case you hadn't seen me come in', I said with a slight smile.

'Well, Mr Chamberlain,' he retorted. 'Visiting hours are on Friday, Saturday and Sunday.'

I remained silent. He knew I was in Darwin for just three days and it was now Wednesday.

Not getting a bite, he picked up the phone and rang the female prison section.

'What's the staffing situation like, Mrs Barham?'

'We have just two on,' she replied.

'When can Mr Chamberlain visit his wife?'

'In five minutes.'

Mercer deemed these 'special visits'. Whatever they were, I was grateful to get the full three hours in the three days I had booked in. Lindy was surprised and overjoyed to see me. She had been given two minutes notice and was embarrassed about her appearance, particularly her hair. She was looking as good as I had ever seen her. 'Oh, dear God,' I thought 'What a waste of a young attractive woman's life. This is the real crime.' We were able to kiss and hug in a manner we had not experienced for nearly three years. Despite the strain our marriage was under, there was still a strong physical attraction between us. She felt small, very wiry and taut. We talked about going back to New Zealand one day to tramp through the Southern Alps. We would tramp hundreds of kilometres.

Stuart Tipple accompanied me back to Sydney on Friday 6 December 1985. He had been doing his own reconnaissance and I wasn't as yet privy to what he had discovered.

At this time *The Age* (4/12/1985) published doubts about the worth and accuracy of Joy Kuhl's forensic blood tests from my car. Dr Ben Sellinger and Dr Eric Magnusson from the Australian National University also criticised the accuracy of the blood tests.

Two days later, former Federal Minister for Aboriginal Affairs, Bill Wentworth, after denouncing The Martin Report for its treatment of the new blood evidence, rang me and suggested that I travel to Melbourne to see Greg and Sally Lowe, Murray Haby and John Bryson. But I could see danger signs in mingling with these witnesses if I was about to get a Royal Commission. I did not want to compromise their raw, honest views, nor be asked in court if I had influenced them. Sadly, I declined to see them but I sent a message to John Bryson telling him I could see him in Sydney.

Unbeknown to us, my next early-morning trip would be my last to the Darwin prison to see Lindy. It was now 2 January 1986. The weather was already stinking hot, humid and driving my three children crazy. But I felt that an all-out showdown with the Territory was imminent. I had purchased the most recent model XF Ford Fairmont Ghia from Christies Local Government Auctions in preparation for any decision to release Lindy. I wanted the best for her. The dark-tinted glass contrasted against the metallic silver paint with every available luxury inside. It gave my children a rare feeling of security and protection from the outside world. The vehicle was ghostly quiet and my children felt it should be named 'The Grey Ghost'.

My mother was also up early that day. She had just heard the Northern

Territory Chief Minister, Ian Tuxworth, give his Christmas and New Year blessing to the citizens of Australia and New Zealand. She immediately penned a scathing letter of rebuke to the Territory Chief. My mother was known as a peacemaker in her country district, very tenacious on the table tennis table, as her myriad finals silver cups would show, but away from her sport she was a peaceable and fun-loving human being.

We stayed with our friends, John and Liz Parry, for two weeks in order to see Lindy. The early dip in our friends' pool each morning before visiting Lindy had been totally refreshing, even if within five minutes of getting out you were again in a lather of sweat. Unthinkingly, I greeted Lindy with the announcement that I had been for a refreshing swim, although the first for several months.

'Oh, I am so sorry,' I just remembered. 'You haven't been for a swim for nearly three years.'

'Five', she said.

We pulled out some photos of Kahlia's third birthday, thinking that Lindy would enjoy seeing them. Apart from her birth, Lindy had missed all of Kahlia's birthdays.

'Look,' Lindy said, summoning the head 'screw', as she insisted calling them. 'This is what vegetarian food is about', pointing to the fine and colourful array of dishes in the photograph.

We had hired a car to travel the 40-odd kilometres back and forth to the jail but on this day the fuel pump failed. We endured 34 degrees of heat in near 100 per cent humidity for two hours before being able to climb into a replacement, a fiery red new Alpha Romeo. The new car was courtesy of Sue Priori, another great friend who with her husband owned a dealership in the city.

Our last visit with Lindy was traumatic as she was by now showing the signs of having been in jail for too long. Lots of tears, mingled with sorrow and anger. After that harrowing ordeal it was time to give my children a treat, a visit to one of Darwin's celebrated tourist shows, the fish farm. When we arrived with Liz Noonan, the kids were busting to use a toilet. The sight of the magnificent fish suddenly took their minds of their urgency for a while, but eventually, I had to find a place for my children to relieve themselves. There appeared to be no formal area for them to go. We went searching on the premises, and came across a sight I will never forget.

Standing in the midst of a very large shed I saw a man. I asked him for directions to a toilet. As he turned to face me, the shock of recognition overwhelmed me.

'I am sorry about the condition of them but they are ...' and pointed.

'Excuse me,' I enquired politely, 'are you Marshall Perron?'

This man, the most powerful legal man in the Territory, was holding my wife in jail, I said to myself under my breath.

'Yes,' he replied calmly, 'and you are Mr Chamberlain.'

'I guess there isn't much I can say,' I said, trying desperately to remain polite.

'No, it would not be appropriate to talk about your case,' he responded in a legal tone.

Trying to think quickly to gain some advantage from this chance meeting, I turned to Kahlia and said. 'Kahlia, this is Mr Perron, the Northern Territory Attorney-General.' I then called Reagan and Aidan over to meet him. Perron did not look impressed.

'Aidan and Reagan, this is Mr Perron, the Attorney-General of the Northern Territory.' He looked extremely uncomfortable.

'What else could I do now?' I thought, as he remained there, a captive audience before my three children.

'Mr Perron,' I said, 'I wish you to know that on the matter of my wife's conviction and imprisonment I am available to answer any questions at any time.' I took my children's' hands and turned on my heel.

'I will note your comment,' he called out. Perron's face was unmoved and unemotional.

So incomprehensible was it for our children that their mother was in jail, that it was too ridiculous for words and too painful for all of us to relive. If we had, we would have just burst out crying in rage. But the problem for us was that very few, perhaps no one, could ever understand the intense ongoing trauma we had all endured. Can people in prison who have been savagely abused, talk about it? Our situation was in effect little different. No one could possibly understand.

Back outside, I tried to look composed as we joined the tourists watching the fish feeding in awe. Liz Noonan pointed out Marshall Perron's wife to me. She was attractive with a pleasant demeanour. I took the cue.

'Hello. Are your Mrs Perron?'

'Yes', she replied in a friendly tone.

'Oh. Well, you probably don't know me but I'm Michael Chamberlain.'

'Yes, I do know you,' she replied unruffled.

'Somehow, I don't think you do, really,' I responded. I then quickly changed the topic fearing I would say too much. 'This is a wonderful place,' I observed with some enthusiasm.

Oh God, I cried silently in my heart, how can I continue to shut up?

I saw Lindy for the last time in Berrimah Prison on Saturday 11 January, 1986. I had almost persuaded myself, that come what may, I would live in Darwin to be close to her. I would deal somehow with the hostile people, intransigent politicians, prejudiced police, the creepy flies and the eternal humidity.

When I arrived at the jail, Lindy had returned to her old self, talking almost incessantly about dresses, wool, lot numbers, crafts, patterns, crochet jumpers measurements and more. With five minutes to go I decided I should interrupt. If I did not speak now I would forever have to hold my peace.

'Lindy', I said in an earnest tone, 'Do you want me to live in Darwin? I could fight more effectively for your innocence here.'

Her reply was firm, her mouth set. 'Never! I'm not going to stay in this jail much longer. My boys are never going to live in Darwin. So, don't bother to make plans. If the worst comes, I'll transfer to a New South Wales jail. I might even get day leave. Anyway, you will get at least two hours a week visiting rights.'

We left on emotional terms again.

I headed for *The Northern Territory News* office to see Gary Shipway with whom I had struck up a friendly rapport. It was a cheeky move but I was on a 'fishing expedition' so see what I could stir up. I wanted to talk to someone about the refusal of Brian Martin to open an inquiry. Shipway was out, but as I strode through that stifling newspaper building, the newsroom buzzing with gossip, the chatter was suddenly reduced to whispers as I moved past the journalist stations. As I left, silence blanketed the office.

Bob Collins phoned me on 29 January to tell me that prosecution blood evidence witness, Dr Andrew Scott, had completed his written rebuttal of The Martin Report and would be seeing the National Executive in Canberra the next day. 'Scott's boss thought he would have political issues to face with the critical content of his report,' Collins said confidentially. 'He thought he would face some stiff opposition from his Attorney-General, Mr Sumner, in South Australia. But when this happened, Sumner washed his hands of it.'

Collins then outlined his strategy to me. 'I am going to run the report in stages rather than take it immediately to Caucus.'

My mind was running overtime. I wonder if this phone is still being tapped, I thought. It hasn't been dropping out shortly after making STD calls recently. Anyhow, I didn't care. They can't stop us now.

'The first stage will be to obtain the green light from the three Labor factions led by Senators Cook, Duncan and Richardson,' Collins continued. 'Bob Brown will oversee the formation of a Caucus subcommittee that specialises in legal matters. Here, they can call people before it. Everyone is in horror about a Royal Commission, though. It is better to go through a special select committee of Parliament that is bipartisan and to get a Royal Commission by ambush.'

'The concept of 'ambush' appeals to me,' I replied. 'Do unto others as they would do unto you. It almost fits.'

'Michael, this report was better than I could have ever expected,' Collins chuckled. 'In fact, it's quite excellent. It even has the imprimatur of Scott's laboratory. Andrew states that The Martin's Report is 'selective', that it contains 'inaccuracies and errors'.

'You know,' said Collins reflectively, 'I think your good wife could have been out before Christmas if Perron could have had his way.'

'Oh, how's that?' I asked.

'The editor of the *Territorian* Frank Alcorta is planning to run a strong 'Release Lindy' campaign in the New Year and this is all about his newspaper getting exclusives.'

17. An Ayers Rock Shock

Bob Collins knew that in his possession was a 'bombshell', with the potential to 'blow the case wide open'. (*Northern Territory News*, (2/2/1986). But his sensational information was about to be eclipsed by an event, stranger than fiction, guaranteed to shock the nation.

At around 4pm on 26 January 1986, it was reported that a lone Englishman had hiked into the Ayers Rock reserve. The temperature at the Rock was said to be like an oven. Dust and flies permeated the atmosphere. When a female park ranger saw the Englishman she was alarmed at what he was carrying. It was camping gear. 'You can't bring that in,' she said. 'Camping is forbidden by the traditional owners of the land, the Aborigines.'

This visitor was about to act out an even bigger no-no. At 7.50pm he was seen climbing the Rock in a forbidden area by two Aborigines. When the park rangers were alerted, they looked for him but he was nowhere to be found.

A very animated Mike Lester from the *Adelaide News* rang me at 4.30pm on Tuesday 4 February, 1986.

'Guess what, Michael,' he said. 'You aren't going to believe this, but a guy who has been missing for a few days has been found at the foot of Ayers Rock. It seems he fell off between the climbing trail and some lichen. In the search they think they've found Azaria's missing jacket!'

Although I trusted Mike, I would have to get confirmation to believe this. After six years in the desert, what were the odds of this being true?

A report in the *Advertiser* (7/2/1986) read: 'The maximum air temperature in the shade was 41 degrees here yesterday. The red earth baked. The heat penetrated relentlessly through the coolest, the sturdiest footwear. Tar in the asphalt road which circles the Rock melted. And the heat radiating from the spectacular monolith was remarkable. As one approached the restricted area, 33 metres from the Rock, the temperature increased noticeably. An immediate reaction was to turn around and walk back towards the sticky road.'

Enter David Brett, an English tourist who first arrived in Australia in 1980. Living in Perth, West Australia, he was drawn to the paranormal and psychic phenomena. On 26 January 1986, two Aborigines observed Brett in a dangerous and prohibited area on top of the Rock. Brett had seen a cave in the lichen-encrusted area of the Rock and had tried to get to it. Instead, he slid to his death, breaking his back and neck in the fall. It was claimed that he had been impressed with the notion that he should sacrifice his life for the Devil and had chosen Ayers Rock as the most appropriate location. The press spread a rumour that Azaria's name was tattooed over his body, but this was without foundation. But in the vicinity where he was found was something else so unexpected that it would produce even bigger headlines than the terrible Brett affair.

Dr Norman Young described the aftermath: 'A Victorian tourist guided by the stench of decaying (human) tissue found a partly decomposed and mutilated body at the base of Ayers Rock. It was later identified as the corpse of 31-year-old missing tourist, David Brett. A hand, an arm and part of one leg had been chewed from Brett's body. A police search was organised on the same day, to comb the area for the other missing body parts.' Here was proof that something at the Rock had an undeniable taste for human flesh.

Searcher John Beasy was looking for the missing limbs of Brett, when he noticed a partially submerged sleeve and collar of a small jacket. He reached down and raised it out of its crumbly russet-brown earthen state. A policeman was in the searchline nearby. Beasy called out. 'Hey, look at this. The only thing that was never found was a little baby's jacket.' An infant's grubby white matinee jacket now lay in Beasy's sweaty hand 140 metres below where Azaria's other clothing had been found. It was Azaria's missing piece, the matinee jacket, described by Lindy; the existence of which the prosecution had claimed was a lie.

Cartoonist Mitchell, interpreting events for *The Australian* (10/2/1986), was led to represent the whole shocking episode by drawing a mystified tourist peering over the cliff face where Brett had just plunged to his death, and exclaim: 'The Lord moves in mysterious ways.' Cartoonist Yahyey caricatured two bemoaning dingoes in his *Daily Telegraph* (6/2/1986) cartoon in which one comforted the other with the words: 'Don't look so unhappy dear, you'll find another jacket.'

Bernier, on the following day, backed up the theme in his *Daily Sun* cartoon, picturing two mean and threatening dingoes perched high above the matinee jacket location admonishing themselves: 'This time, by jingo—we're going to get ourselves a good lawyer.'

On an ABC *Four Corners* program (9/5/1981) I told the presenter that had the matinee jacket, with a Marquis brand name and a yellow thread woven through it, been discovered with Azaria's jumpsuit, it would have greatly assisted the investigation. A number of wrong assumptions and interpretations would have been corrected. The reasons for this included the blood 'specialists' attitude to pooling of blood around the neck region of the jumpsuit, especially Cameron's erroneous conclusion derived from the denial of the jacket covering the jumpsuit. It had caused him to think that Azaria must have had a cut throat. The pooling of the blood around the neck, he said, indicated a faster flow of blood. Severe head wounds alone, inflicted by a dingo, might not have resulted in a concentration unless there was another garment to restrict the blood flow.

Lindy had referred to the matinee jacket in her Mount Isa interview on 30 September 1980 when interviewed by Detective Charlwood. She had described the jacket in photographic detail. 'It had a zigzag knit design edged in pale lemon around the sleeves, collar and bottom edge, about six rows'.

Joy Kuhl immediately put her hand up for the forensic testing, to identify the authenticity of the jacket. She claimed that her forensic laboratory in

Darwin, where she had been seconded by the Northern Territory Police, was 'as good as anywhere in Australia'. Thankfully, the Victorian forensic police laboratory got the nod to carry out the investigation.

There were no surprises in the Territory police and Country Liberal Party politicians being in damage control and conveniently dismissing the find. Despite reports that the jacket was found 13 kilometres away from the campsite, in fact it was only four kilometres away. *The Northern Territory News* reported erroneously that the jumpsuit was turned inside out.

Peter McAulay, formerly the Northern Territory Police Chief and now the Federal Police Commissioner, stressed to the media that in 1980 the area where Azaria's jacket was found had been thoroughly combed and that it was not possible for it to have been missed. He was obviously hoping that it would be seen as a plant. The *Melbourne Truth* newspaper swung into action following his remarks with the headline 'Jacket a Plant'. McAulay's assistant, Andy McNeill, briefed by his superior, declared that 'there were no grounds whatsoever to link the jacket' with Azaria's disappearance. Paul Everingham chimed in: 'It is difficult to see the jacket being of any help to Mrs Chamberlain.' (Brisbane *Daily Sun*, 13/2/1986).

Hoping that Lindy would still be judged guilty in an inquiry, McAulay now accepted the need for an investigation. Northern Territory Solicitor-General, Brian Martin, was not so sure. On 7 February 1986 at 8.15am, McAulay met with Martin and then with Chief Minister Tuxworth at 9.30 am. Tuxworth was shell-shocked by the news. As he admitted to the Northern Territory Assembly later (4/6/1987), 'he was not aware of any facts connected to this piece of evidence which affected the veracity of the prosecution's original case,' so was stunned when McAulay came into his office to inform him that the matinee jacket was indeed substantial new evidence. A hastily arranged Cabinet meeting at 10am resulted in a quick communiqué that would significantly change our lives. Police Chief McAulay informed the Chief Minister: 'I recommend to the Attorney-General that the Northern Territory immediately institute such proceedings that are necessary to facilitate the establishment of a judicial inquiry into the new evidence' (*Daily Sun* 8/2/1986).

The nation was about to see an amazing about face by Marshall Perron. Perron's refusal to reconsider Lindy's release on compassionate grounds, two months before, suddenly evaporated when Collins confronted *The Northern Territory News* office with sensational evidence. The Territory justice system was about to be subjected to a devastating front-page headline, discrediting the Martin Report, set to roll at 2pm. Marshall Perron had to think quickly to head off this crippling news. Lindy would be released from Berrimah Prison, Darwin on the same day, 6 February 1986 at 2pm, and would be listed as never to return whether any inquiry found her guilty or not. Perron told the world:

'I can advise that a short time ago, the Administrator, Commodore Eric Johnston, accepted advice of the Executive Council that the balance of Mrs Chamberlain's sentence be remitted... She had suffered enough' (*Northern Territory News* 7/2/1986).

I was mowing the lawns at the time and a friend tapped me on the shoulder to come inside and listen to the breaking news. Dazed for a moment by the unbelievable turn around, I immediately sent a press release to all media stations. 'I am stunned and thrilled by Lindy's release. We are halfway to a just conclusion. An inquiry is now pending and any further comment is not appropriate.'

The boys and Kahlia could hardly believe it, but a huge smile emerged across their strained little faces.

The radio stations now flooded the country with the dramatic news. John Bryson reported in *The Age* (8/2/1986) that, 'when he last saw Lindy in jail, she was thin, gaunt, and her face was so incapable of colour of its own that it took on the hues of her prison smock—a lost and vagrant blue'.

In England, Richard Shears, later to write the second book entitled *Azaria*, described the event as a new battle for the 'Dingo baby mother' or 'Dingo Woman' (*Manchester Guardian*, 8/2/1986). Other press headlines appeared: 'Dingo baby mum freed'. (*The Sun*, 8/2/1986) and 'Dingo Mum Freed' (*The Echo*, 7/2/1986). One Seventh-day Adventist is alleged to have said 'it was if she had done penance'. The paper recorded that the 'Northern Territory Government had swung open her dormitory door in Darwin's bleak Berrimah Prison last night and allowed the devout worshipper to step to freedom... Now the stunning discovery (of the matinee jacket) has weakened the Crown case and strengthened Lindy's claims.' But even before this latest twist, it seemed inevitable that Lindy Chamberlain, the 'small town girl from New Zealand, who married the handsome student pastor would not spend the rest of her life in jail,' (*Daily Mail*, 8/2/1986). A common theme that pervaded all the papers was that the fight to clear our names was now on.

Senator Bob Collins had a new take on the release. Collins told *The Australian* Magazine journalist: 'It was not God, science, inquests, politics, pardons or public opinion that saved Lindy but an 'out-of-his-head lunatic' from England.' Then again, God did play a part. David Brett had crossed the world to visit the desert, and brought his mental illness with him. 'God told him to go to Australia and climb Ayers Rock, where he was to be transported to heaven', said Collins. 'He falls off to his death into the desert. The police go to recover his body. A foot away from his body, the copper sees a little bit of cloth sticking out of the dirt'.' (*The Australian* Magazine, 15–16/7/2000). It had turned the tables on a cocky Crown who said this jacket was a fiction and that scissors don't salivate. The defence had advocated there was no saliva on the jumpsuit because that matinee jacket had covered it.

The release of Lindy set Darwin alight with rumour and speculation. According to Malcolm Brown, in his report for the *Sydney Morning Herald*, headlined: 'Lindy Inc: an industry resurrected', Darwin was in a state of 'fierce resentment, irritation and uncertainty.' The case had 'come alive with undiminished intensity,' he said.

TV camera crews were approaching my spokesperson, Avondale College Senior Lecturer, Dr Norman Young, 'like tin soldiers'. I reiterated to the television stations that: 'Lindy and I are unconditionally innocent of the charges laid on us and that we will accept nothing less than full exoneration. I would rather face the grave than give up the fight to clear my name and that of my wife.' *Sydney Morning Herald* (8/2/1986).

On the same day, the *Daily Telegraph* cartoonist, Yahyeh, published a wicked cartoon of Northern Territory justice represented as a caricature of a dingo apologising to all the jury, also represented as dingo caricatures, now looking hang dog. Its response to the saddened jury, in failing to prevent the 'Free Lindy' juggernaut from winning, was the legal system's response...'Ahem, Sorry.'

But if there was jubilation in many quarters of Australia and New Zealand, Stuart Tipple was reflective in the huge victory that he had supervised. He told the *Melbourne Age* that his involvement over the past five years had taken a heavy toll on his family and career. 'People say it's probably one of the best things to happen but quite frankly it's probably one of the worst things as far as I am concerned...It was just a shame that it has taken so long to find (the matinee jacket)' (*The Age* 8/2/1986).

Senator Mason advised fellow Senators that they were in danger of appearing to the public as obstructers of 'simple justice to all our people'. He warned the Senate of his intention to bring up the bill again on 11 February 1986, the day after the Federal Caucus meeting. In the meantime, scientists from Avondale College visited various parliamentary members over the school holidays. Senator Publick confided in Dr Norman Young that although the conscience vote was still not an option for the Liberals, more of them were now persuaded to get behind Mason's Bill. Senator Sir John Carrick had now read the Tipple submission and the Northern Territory's Martin Report rebuttal and showed considerable interest in Tipple's response. But despite the growing host of Parliamentarians indicating their support, the big guns, Ian Sinclair (National), Stephen Spender and John Howard (Liberal shadow leader) were opposed to intervention, believing that the politics of non-intervention was more expedient than cutting through the red tape to enact justice.

Everingham, when challenged by the Territory press to make a reply in Federal Parliament, chose a different route. Avoiding debate, he released a letter to Federal Attorney Lionel Bowen and the media. He told the press that, 'indeed, the Chamberlains had a fair trial. Why should they complain? The experts were not Territorians. They had come from all over the world and this proved their independent reasoning. The trial by jury had been replaced by a trial by the Sydney press.' Instead of silencing the debate, The Martin Report had fuelled it. The Chamberlain Innocence

Committee, Stuart Tipple, the Support Groups from around Australia and New Zealand had done their job.

Former editor of *The Northern Territory News*, Jim Bowditch, described the Territory's parliamentarians as 'amateurs' in the way they had responded to our cry for justice. In a 180-degree turnaround, Marshall Perron introduced into the Northern Territory Parliament legislation setting up the powers of a Royal Commission to examine Lindy's and my convictions. I looked forward to our new day in court but outside the administration of Northern Territory 'justice'. But the end was yet a long way off. The temple of hate was alive and festering. The Territory rednecks would now work harder than ever. A T-shirt was hastily prepared in Darwin symbolising the hostility of this frontier. Beneath scissors dripping with blood was the slogan, 'Watch out Kahlia, Mummy's coming home.'

The Third Wave:
The Royal Commission

18. The Homecoming

The waiting press headlined it as 'A cat and mouse game to elude the media' (*Daily Sun* 10/02/1986), admitting that 'Lindy had evaded the hounds of the news media'. They reported: 'Lindy Chamberlain was last night whisked from the Sydney Airport with a Federal Police escort after eluding the media three times in one afternoon.' Now, it was 'a thinner, more elusive Lindy that was flying home.' (Brisbane *Courier-Mail*, (10/2/1986). In another paper, Lindy was described as 'thin and fashionably dressed'. She was wearing a royal blue dress, in fact, the same one she had worn three years before, when she walked in the dusk light at Brisbane airport, several days after Kahlia's birth. 'You may not recognise her now' was another headline that explained how Lindy's transformation had come through a very overweight woman 'having lost more than 30kg'. (*Daily Mirror*, 28/2/1986). Lindy was attracting as much, if not more detailed attention than Princess Diana.

Lindy's minders had played their own ace by having the media board the wrong plane from Darwin to Sydney. So different did Lindy now look that the press mistook her female minder for Lindy. They had not been able to publish a true photo of her for three years. The only photograph of 'Lindy' in the jail published on the front pages of the *Daily Telegraph* and *The Age* on 25 January 1984 to name a few, showed a well-upholstered woman with short black hair named 'Lindy'. Only problem was, it wasn't her. A journalist had claimed that he had photographed Mrs Alice Lynne

Chamberlain hanging out her washing, but it was another prisoner.

Lindy was driven to an Ansett cargo shed and hidden there until her 2.15pm aircraft was ready to load. She had then been ferried to the rear gangway of her plane in an Ansett cargo van. Now secure on the plane, Lindy took a glass of tomato juice. Stuart had to ward off a very persistent photographer in the plane and eventually took out his camera and took a shot of the antagonist. But photographer Ray Cash for the Brisbane *Sun*, (10/2/1986), who was able to observe Lindy for a short time in the plane, was shocked. He said she looked drawn and emaciated. Her previously round face was now angular and her ears stuck out from her severe jail haircut.

The Brisbane *Sun*, in a front-page headline, described Lindy's flight as an escape from 'a city of hate'. It was reported that Lindy had told friends, 'I hope I never see the place again' (*Sydney Morning Herald*, 10/2/1986). To add to the trauma, there had been a fear that some Darwin residents might try to harm Lindy, and the Darwin SDA Church responded by rostering a 24-hour patrol around her safe house. A member of that patrol, local resident, Gordon Feitz, told the *Sydney Morning Herald* that they had done this because 'they feared that 'ratbags' might try to harm her'.

When Aidan learned the sensational news by telephone that his mother was coming home, tears had welled up in his eyes. Reagan had looked dazed and it took a little longer to sink in. Kahlia had immediately picked the news up and had laughed for joy.

There was someone else at Ayers Rock who was also thrilled that Lindy had been freed, never to return to jail. Nipper Winmatti, the Ayers Rock Elder, wanted to deliver a message personally to Lindy: 'I am very happy you get out, very glad you free now.' Nipper remembered the time he tracked the dingo that took Azaria. 'I saw her crying, she was crying a lot. It was very sad, dingo take her baby.' He recalled his tracking experience the next morning. 'It (the dingo) was dragging something heavy (Brisbane *Sun*, (10/2/1986)'.

Lindy's arrival in Sydney was cloaked in remarkable secrecy, aided by the night. Lindy's security check was waived. There was no customs, no media, of which a contingent had been waiting at the airport all day and must have been very disappointed. A miffed *Daily Telegraph* reporter, Jeremy Scott, had no idea what had happened to Lindy after she got off the plane. He had to make up a story by claiming Lindy 'was hustled into a van and whisked to the flight facilities area' and then 'flown to Newcastle by charter aircraft' (*Daily Telegraph*, 10/2/1986). In fact, from the plane sitting on the tarmac, she jumped into a waiting car chauffeured by 'John' in his shiny new silver BMW 730. Into her arms I pressed a large bunch of fresh red, sweetly scented roses. The encounter was as electric as the day of our wedding when as one we had slid into our white HR Holden 149 ex-taxi in November, 1969 headed for our honeymoon. We hugged and kissed passionately and freely for the first time in almost three years. We were just elated to be together away from prying eyes.

As we sped by the throng of journalists, too fast to be photographed, Sydney airport security conveniently blocked their exit. Our getaway was a classic lesson for any would-be celebrity and it has since reminded me of the horrific tragedy that beset Princess Diana in a French tunnel while being chased by crazed paparazzi. Stuart Tipple had accompanied Lindy by request from Darwin where he declared to the media, smiling broadly, 'We believe we have won the decisive battle. We've now got a mopping-up exercise to carry out to win the war.' (*Daily Sun*, 10/2/1986).

There wasn't a better word for it than 'war'. We now had to wait to be heard. The only hope was to get a non-adversarial system, without lawyers who could win by their theatrics before a jury. This was the only way an angry and understandably bitter Lindy could now get justice. She told Bob Collins, 'I have some scores to settle,' (*The Sunday Telegraph*, 9/2/1986) and 'I am bitter at my treatment.' (*Sunday Mail*, (9/2/1986). Regardless of what Lindy had said or intimated, I knew this was only the first step and we were only half way to a just conclusion. We might have a long way to go, possibly years. Nothing less than exoneration would satisfy me in any upcoming inquiry. The day before Lindy's homecoming I said in answer to Malcolm Brown's question, about my feelings: 'Am I emotional about her coming home? I have been emotional for the last four or five years. Now I'm out of my mind! I am not going to Darwin. We have a contingency plan and I'll be waiting for her here.' (*Sydney Morning Herald*, 8/2/1986).

Here was a tough talking woman who vehemently hated 'the Screws', a term I thought was a rather distasteful one for prison officers. Because of her notorious public persona and the fact that she was the oldest and longest-sentenced prisoner in Berrimah, she had emerged as the 'Queen Bee' and had become even tougher, more cynical and more controlling. Now I had to get used to sharing my life with a woman I had not experienced any real intimacy with for four years and who was more independent now than I could ever imagine. I had not bargained that separation over many years empowers a person's independence. We would have to get to know each other all over again.

Lindy's jail friend, a self-confessed lesbian and man-hater, had become her protector and confidante in the jail. Her friend had been in and out of jail since the age of ten. I had tried very hard to be friendly to this short, young muscle-bound woman who had claimed she was so bad as a child, that her parents had tied her up with a chain and left her out at a kennel in an effort to try and subdue her. It sounded bizarre but as I got to know her, I could see a sophisticated criminal mind under that happy-go lucky dare-devil exterior. Frankly, this woman unnerved me, and while she could be very helpful and she worshipped Lindy as though she was a goddess, she was competing against me for Lindy's time and affection. One thing I knew for sure; one would have to think very carefully before you crossed her. Lindy, plainly wouldn't.

Paul Everingham disassociated himself from Marshall Perron's apparent haste in releasing Lindy with no possibility of returning to jail as a result of finding the matinee jacket. Frank Alcorta described the mood with the headline, 'Government to dismiss Royal Probe'. There was 'no chance the Territory Government will agree to a Royal Commission to handle the Lindy Chamberlain case,' Alcorta roared. One of the outcomes of Lindy's release was the exchange between Labor Senator Bob Collins and Northern Territory Attorney-General Marshall Perron to determine the terms of reference for any upcoming inquiry. That inquiry had to exclude the Solicitor-General, Brian Martin, because Martin 'should not be the Attorney-General's principal advisor on the Chamberlain case' (*Northern Territory News* 8/02/1986). New South Wales Premier Neville Wran's stinging comment several days later, that he was 'not too impressed with the way they conduct their affairs' in the Northern Territory, caused further embarrassment.

The Northern Territory's Police Association President, Gowan Carter, angrily struck back: 'Territorians are sick and tired of the continuous and unwarranted attacks on its police, administration and judiciary by those who think that the country begins and ends south of Newcastle...The Territory's public administration is clean—not at all like New South Wales. It should be a Territory inquiry—whether Wran and the rest like it or not. To do otherwise, would lend credence to the Territory's critics' (*Sunday Territorian* 16/2/1986).

Such was our fight for justice that now we had been elevated to the status of threatening the Northern Territory's aspirations for statehood. In a classic case of the use of hyperbole to inflame the Territory public, Frank Alcorta blamed us for stopping the Northern Territory in their tracks to gain statehood. The *Sunday Territorian* claimed that 'Statehood is now in the balance' and that 'The Chamberlain affair has done incalculable harm to the Territory's bid for Statehood and has hurt the foundations of the Territory's society.'

But the hallowed paper did not stop there. Alcorta turned on the incompetence of the Northern Territory Government. 'It had handled this issue with such mind-boggling incompetence (in releasing Lindy from jail) that it deserves much of the flak coming its way...The reality is that nothing is wrong, but our earnest southern critics are not interested in realities, they are far more interested in perceptions...The Territory will just have to live with those perceptions. They will take a long time to disappear...' Alcorta had attacked Perron's decision to let Lindy out of jail, merely on the pretext that a matinee jacket, found at Ayers Rock, which Lindy claimed, was Azaria's, but had not been proven. That garment, Alcorta moaned, had not even arrived at the Victorian Forensic Laboratory for examination, nor had it been explained why it was so significant a find. Obviously Alcorta was ignorant about the prosecution's reasons why Lindy was guilty; one of which was that her story about Azaria having worn a matinee jacket when she died which was claimed by

Barker as another 'fanciful lie'.

The real reasons behind Lindy's release were based on new and more powerful forensic evidence delivered by former trial prosecution witness, Dr Andrew Scott and the German anti-serum blood supplier, Behringwerke, concerning the incompetence of Joy Kuhl's testing. The physical discovery of the matinee jacket, claimed Alcorta, as sensational as that was, was really a convenient cover for the real problem that could reopen an inquiry. Alcorta then tried to promote the idea of suspicious behaviour, telling the world that 'the state of the garment and the manner of its finding probably indicates human involvement in its original disposal'. This unwitting remark had the potential to discredit certain rangers and a police account that they had nothing to do with 'a burial'. Alcorta concluded with brave media spin: 'All is not lost. The fact is that Territory institutions such as the police, the judiciary or the administration of law are sound and will be found so by any inquiry. And despite its hopeless fumblings and disastrous public relations, the Territory Government has also been impeccable in the whole affair.' (*Northern Territory News*).

While the rest of the media headed for the Avondale College owned aerodrome around midnight, the local NBN Television crew had a hunch that we were about to come through the gates of the College. That hunch proved right, as we hid behind a decoy white panel van before we suddenly peeled off from Freemans Drive and sped through the College gates. 'Well,' said one reporter ruefully, who missed us: 'The plane never arrived but I got a consolation prize... At least we now know where the aerodrome is.'

It reminded me of a Le Mans car race. The reporters dropped their cigarettes and the shout went up as they raced for their vehicles to career down College Drive after us. As we passed the newly erected barrier and guard box created for our security, they screeched to a halt. It was too dark to see clearly but it did not prevent Lindy from being ecstatic at the welcome home. The whole of College Drive had been festooned with yellow ribbons. The media raced from their cars and tried to sprint up the College Drive puffing and panting, with sound recordists tripping over themselves to catch up. But the security guards stopped them.

At midnight on Sunday 9 February, Lindy and I had arrived home to 5

College Drive. But the national media could not sleep, it was out in force and focused on the town. Avondale College was again under siege, just like the weeks after 19 September 1981, when all media station choppers circled my home, attempting to get exclusive sightings of us under police investigation. There was considerable inconvenience for the local workers at the Sanitarium Health Food factory. They were asked to show due cause next morning before they entered the super security zone of Avondale College. 'But I work here,' one man implored after it appeared he might be delayed for work. He pointed to his sterile white cap and overalls to prove it.

Aidan was excitedly crying out, 'Mum, Mum', uninhibited for the first time in nearly three years. Kahlia and Reagan returned in the morning from Jan and Owen Hughes' home and our family was complete.

But there could be no allusions for us, as Lindy and I attempted to pick up the pieces of our marriage and try to start again. On top of the entire trauma we had experienced, I found that her faith and my faith were quite different. She had a cast-iron faith in God but I wondered how intimate that faith was. I had a deep and abiding assurance of the grace of Jesus Christ, which I had experienced first-hand at 15 years of age while a Methodist. Lindy, was born into the Seventh-day Adventist Church, which promoted loyalty to standards, its 'way marks,' and what the institutionalised organisation of the Church leaders decreed. The iconic Methodist Church at Durham Street, Christchurch, had no such standards or organisational loyalty except a set of values from the Bible and the Spirit of Jesus Christ that guided you. Despite this, I felt optimistic that our marriage would survive.

Darwin Adventist Pastor, Bob Donaldson, was perceptive when he suggested that Lindy would, as a result of the long enforced separation from her children and husband, find re-establishing relationships difficult and traumatic (Brisbane *Sun* (10/2/1986). I had tried to do some preparation on what to expect from my wife after three years in an institution. Eighteen months was generally recognised as the cutoff point where people crossed over in becoming different. President of the Darwin Support Group, Rosslyn King, did not discount the possibility of 'problems adjusting to a life of mother and wife...Our Northern Territory Penal system would be to blame if the marriage was in difficulties,' she said. 'Her husband and children got only three to four hours every four months and one phone call every twelve months' (*The Sunday Telegraph* 9/2/1986). It was frightening to have my life and Lindy's life so openly dissected by the press. I would never get used to it. Lindy told me that she had a gutful of selfishness in her trapped environment and was determined never to be like the inmates she mixed with again.

'I have learned', she told me, 'why these people go to jail. They are so selfish; all they can think of is themselves'.

19. The Fight for a Royal Commission

Coming under fire for allegedly misleading parliament was Solicitor-General, Brian Martin. Professor Barry Boettcher, Head of Biological Sciences at Newcastle University, said that he 'had supplied Mr Martin with crucial evidence on three occasions prior to the release of the (Martin) Report indicating that methods used to determine the blood types found in the Chamberlain car were wrong... There is no doubt whatsoever that he had been informed by me of the new evidence and had acknowledged it. Yet his statements (to the Northern Territory Parliament) were completely and utterly wrong. The only interpretation of the Martin Report was that it misled Parliament.' (*The Sunday Telegraph* 9/2/1986).

Dr Andrew Scott was reported as having been quite dissatisfied with Brian Martin's handling of the forensic evidence. Dismissing the Chamberlain Innocence Committee's evidence, led by Retired Supreme Court Judge, Sir Reginald Sholl, was in his words, 'preposterous' (*The Sunday Telegraph* 9/2/1986).

Northern Territory's Senior Sergeant Henry Huggins, in charge of examining the area where the matinee jacket was found, was asked what he thought of Lindy's release: 'If you start to get involved in side issues of law and politics it affects your work at the crime scene.' Another police officer went one step further. 'The whole thing has been political all along. This is a political decision' (*Weekend Australian* 8/2/1986).

To shore up the Solicitor-General's position, the Territory Bar Association denied reports that Brian Martin's job was on the line. His resignation would not be appropriate unless there has been 'proven misconduct' on his part, they said. The Northern Territory Law Department had found another supporter of Joy Kuhl's methodology in Professor Herbert McDonnell, 'a leading American blood spatter expert' who was in Sydney for a police forensic conference. He told the media that 'the "blood" spatter marks in the car were vital to the case' and that he was 'completely satisfied that Mrs Kuhl's results were accurate' (*Northern Territory News* 11/2/1986).

Eugene St John, writing for the *Daily Mirror*, was one of the more fanciful journalists who had difficulty discerning fact from fiction. St John reported that my 'Seventh-day Adventist minister' father living at 'Springston in the North Island,' had a telephone conversation with Lindy who had 'begged father-in-law Ivan Chamberlain', 'Please Dad, I want to come back. They've ruined my life. I can't pack my bags quick enough—I want a new start.' And, according to St John, my father had said: 'She is very bitter—very upset at how their lives have been destroyed. She told us she hated Australia.' But the truth of the matter was that my father did not live at Springston, nor did he live in the North Island. He wasn't a Seventh-day Adventist, let alone a Seventh-day Adventist minister, and the reported conversation was a total fabrication. This kind of thing happened far too often in the press. Stuart Tipple, as our spokesperson, immediately responded to the spurious allegations. Lindy was not bitter and we had higher priorities than just compensation. Clearing our names was at the top of the list (*Courier-Mail* 11/2/1986).

Many irate members of the public began writing to various state papers blasting the Northern Territory Government for its travesty of justice in allowing Lindy out at all 'after serving a fraction of her sentence'. G.F. Donavan in 'Letters to the Editor' exclaimed in horror: 'Just what is justice coming to in this country for such a thing to happen?' Donavan concluded: 'How can governments expect to deter crime and maintain respect for the court system...I lament this sad day for the Australian judicial system' (*Sydney Morning Herald* 12/2/1986). Headlines from

'Letters to the Editor' continued. 'Our justice under threat' (*Brisbane Telegraph* 18/6/1986) and 'Backfire on Collins' (*Weekend Australian* 15/2/1986) were just two of many to fill the editor's letterboxes. In this latter letter, Dave Nason, apparently a Territorian, wrote: 'Political observers are almost unanimous of their assessment of the (Northern Territory) community feeling about Mrs Chamberlain which is that she is guilty of murdering her child, no matter what any inquiry may decide.'

Alice Springs *Centralian* newspaper journalist, Erwin Chlanda, reported the police take on the matinee jacket's find that 'the state of the jacket seems to rule out that a dingo or a dog had taken it off the baby: There are no tears nor rips although the garment is heavily bloodstained.' Stuart Tipple dismissed this diagnosis as 'pure speculation' and that nothing that had been found could exclude a dingo (*Centralian*, 14/2/1986).

Professor James Malcolm Cameron, the key prosecution's trial witness and 'top British medical expert', doggedly reasserted that his evidence at the trial was '...right. I know I was right. Nothing will change my mind. I will always be convinced that our thorough and extensive investigations were right' *(Sunday Mirror,* 16/2/1986). But Cameron did not know that things were about to unravel for him when he would be subpoenaed eight months later to defend his reliability as a witness. His colleague odontologist, Dr Kenneth Brown, would also be challenged following his concurrence with Cameron.

New legal comment appeared, defending the judicial process. Retired Supreme Court judge, the Honourable M.B. Hoare CMG, observed that the members of the general public should not be blamed for thinking that the account the Chamberlains gave was untrue. However, Judge Hoare castigated sources of information, describing them as 'monstrous in the campaign of vilification, lies and harassment directed at the Chamberlains' (*Courier-Mail*, 13/2/1986).

Bob Brown MP, made his feelings known to the *Newcastle Herald* (12/2/1986), boldly declaring that we were 'innocent of the charges' and that 'the traumas of that family would have been very, very damaging'. Brown told the Newcastle paper that it was quite probable the Federal

Government would assist in setting up the inquiry. He said Brian Martin's Report 'appeared to have sought evidence to support the prosecution'. Bob Brown, years later, described our situation in evocative terms, as we were confronted by an '...indiscriminate judicial system'. (Foreword by Bob Brown, *Cooranbong: First Town in Lake Macquarie 1826–1996,* Michael Chamberlain).

It seemed to us that Everingham, Perron and Martin were trying to avoid damage to their police force, forensic scientists and legal strategists. It was vital for the status quo that they remained as firmly in control as possible.

As a result of concern about the quality of a Northern Territory 'Judicial Review', as questioned by the *Sydney Morning Herald* editorial (11/2/1986), Labor's Federal Attorney-General, Lionel Bowen, announced: 'that it was more than fair comment as to the now very widespread concern across Australia as to what might have happened in the administration of justice in the Northern Territory, particularly in respect of this trial.' Bowen's concern was reflected in his comment about who should head such an inquiry. He welcomed the idea of the Territory to 'request a Federal judge or some other appropriate person to conduct an inquiry'. The Northern Territory had an 'obligation...to guarantee that the inquiry be far-reaching, wide-ranging and impartial'.

Cartoonist Bernier, for the *Daily Sun*, saw the inquiry as formidable as Lady Justice herself, leaving no stone unturned, having to raise up Ayers Rock to get to the truth. But Nicholson's cartoon saw it a different way. Northern Territory justice would indeed match the Federal claim to get to the bottom of the case but in lifting up Ayers Rock, would sweep the evidence under the carpet (Rock) (*The Age*, 12/2/1986).

The English *Guardian* alerted the public to the concern in Federal Parliament that a cover-up was a possible scenario. The newspaper reported that the Federal Government's Attorney-General, the Honourable Mr Lionel Bowen, might view the Northern Territory resistance to an inquiry as an attempt to cover up the real truth and to 'to avoid any cover-up charges'. In an address to Federal Parliament, Bowen told the members that the forensic evidence provided by the prosecution was questionable. 'Further, there are allegations that there has been an attempt to cover up for the administrators of justice in the Northern Territory in pursuing to get a conviction rather than looking at the fairness of the evidence.' (*Guardian* 13/2/1986). 'Actions of the individuals involved in producing the evidence' should be examined. 'It also must be related to the conduct of the officers concerned,' said Mr Bowen in the *Centralian* (14/2/1986).

Marshall Perron retaliated, accusing Lionel Bowen of having joined the 'sorry ranks of Labor politicians'.

From his seat in Federal Parliament, Paul Everingham joined in the chorus. He was reported to have lashed out at what he called Mr Bowen's 'wild allegations against the NT judicial system'. (*Centralian*, 14/2/1986). As 'Chief Minister and the Attorney-General responsible for prosecuting the Chamberlain case', Everingham 'denied accusations that Northern Territory authorities had blocked justice for Lindy Chamberlain' (*Courier-Mail* 13/12/1986).

The effectiveness of the jury system now came under the spotlight, with two academics, David Brown and David Neal, senior law lecturers from the University of New South Wales, speaking out in *Australian Society* magazine. *The Age* (13/2/1986) also reported that this 'widespread disquiet about the Chamberlain verdict had led to doubt about the ability of juries to deal with complex scientific evidence, with the implications that such cases should be taken away from a jury,' a matter that questioned High Court Justice Brennan's findings that a jury was capable of assessing hotly disputed and complex technical and scientific evidence.

Liberal Senator Sir John Carrick requested two days later that the inquiry should be of Royal Commission strength to have the legal right to force witnesses to appear and to require documents to be produced. Mr Bowen said this was a matter for the Northern Territory Government and that the inquiry should not only look at the evidence or lack of it but 'also the actions of individuals involved in producing that evidence'. Mr Perron did not reply (*Courier-Mail* 15/2/1986).

'Letters to the Editor' ran hot on the trial controversy for most newspapers. They ranged from the tragic and bizarre to the many misconceptions that kept people believing we were liars. *The Sunday Telegraph* floated an idea from a writer that was really a cruel joke. The letter, written by Miss Cam Pires from Bondi Beach, suggested that Australia was jumping to conclusions in thinking that Lindy was some kind of witch 'who wore the pants of the family'. The writer then floated the idea that there was no certainty that Azaria was actually dead (*The Sunday Telegraph* 23/2/1986).

The entirely false rumour, which began in the Northern Territory and spread across the nation, about the way Azaria's clothes were supposedly discovered 'folded in the crevice of a rock' was most effective in prejudicing the minds of the public. A letter writer to the press from Ettalong said that the matinee jacket find was an easy way for 'fanatical 'Free Lindy' campaigners to 'plant' an identical jacket a couple or more years ago.' (*Daily Telegraph*, 'Letters to the Editor', 21/2/1986). *The Sun Herald* (23/2/1986) published a letter which alleged, '...it was obvious that there had been human intervention in the way the clothes were folded'. This writer would not anytime soon consider that Lindy Chamberlain was innocent. Similarly, a person from Hornsby in their letter wrote: 'Lindy Chamberlain is not speaking for or representing me (as an Australian) when she says that the fight to clear her name is for the benefit of all Australians.' Another writer from Noosa Heads sought perhaps the most unrealistic wish of them all when he wrote to the Brisbane *Courier-Mail* in late February, hoping for 'The last word on Lindy'. 'Please let this be the last word on Lindy Chamberlain. My friends and I have long since reached the stage where we no longer know, or care, (if) Lindy was in fact guilty of an atrocious crime. All we earnestly desire is that this woman picks up her $250,000 or whatever for her "story" and quietly fades away.'

These views were typical examples of how a lie pedalled by the 'dingo media' had immunised a section of the community from ever rationally or objectively considering that Lindy might be innocent. It was information like this that created myths without ever being exposed to the searing light of fact. And it was this type of innuendo that cartoonists, comedians and satirists would feed off their prey; this included Barry Humphries as Dame Edna Everage and others.

The objective-thinking people of Australia had bitten their lips and waited for new evidence to challenge the verdict. Cruel and subjective minds had made hay while the media sun shone on the Seventh-day Adventist/Chamberlain demise. Twenty-eight-year-old comedian Austen Tayshus (Sandy Gutman), bedecked with long curly hair, underpants and with a penchant for dark glasses at night before his salivating audience, proceeded to shock them. 'Settle down, you bastards' he would admonish his audience, before treating them to a ferocious, ruthless, totally insulting tirade against the Chamberlains. One of Australia's newest and fast-rising comedians, the public was assaulted and insulted as Tayshus 'trapped Lindy and Michael Chamberlain in a merciless ambush' wherever he went. It was said that 'his staunchest followers were dingo lovers.' When interviewed, the funny man offered, as his raison d'être that audiences were inwardly angry and resentful about society and he knew how to 'tap into' that (*People* magazine).

20. The Media Circus Pays Us to Get it Right

From the moment Lindy arrived home, security was very serious at Avondale and as tight as the Church had ever seen. The new guards were never armed as implied by the media, or dangerous, except for the German Shepherd that walked with them. They merely carried walkie talkies. The Church's concern was that a crazy man might enter and try to shoot us (Lindy in particular), during a Church service or at some other time. Former President of South Australian Seventh-day Adventists, Pastor W.A. Townend, wrote in the Church newspaper, *The Australasian Record*, an account of the College Church service the following Sabbath Saturday:

'Lindy Chamberlain was back in her home church at Avondale College today, after being incarcerated in Darwin's Berrimah Prison for 136 Sabbaths and all the long days and nights between those lonely Sabbaths.

'We saw a Lindy looking rather thinner than the young wife and mother taken from her husband, children and the church, three years ago. Her strong face bore some traces of the effects of the horrors and cruelty she had suffered. But there was a certain radiance there, and many a warm smile, admittedly, sometimes through her tears. And not all the tears in this church this morning were from Lindy's brown eyes; not by any means.

'Tears notwithstanding, it was a Sabbath of rejoicing for the one thousand worshippers attending the very first service in the College's new church edifice.

'Before his sermon, Pastor Lyell Heise gave a concise review of some of the events through which Lindy had passed; events, which had touched a praying and caring congregation. There was a moment of deep feeling by all when in response to the Pastor's invitation, Lindy and her husband Michael came out from the congregation and went to the pulpit. Lindy's brief remarks were indeed a brave effort on her part. What happened next, as Lindy and Michael returned to their pews does not often take place in a (Adventist) church. But it was all so spontaneous that in its setting, it was none other than an expression of spiritual joy. The College congregation gave the Chamberlains a standing ovation.

'Today's service here in the College Church had one aspect I think I shall never forget. I stood in the foyer of the Church and watched Lindy, supported by Michael and their pastor, greet the members of the congregation with handshakes for all, warm words of thanks and for quite a few people a hug and a kiss. This went on for almost an hour.

'As Betty Hocking (Member for the Australian Capital Territory and executive member of the Chamberlain Innocence Committee) said to me today, 'Lindy's experience has done something special for all Christians and for all non-believers, too. We are being united in a common cause of justice. God is again beginning to count in our nation.''

Betty Hocking was herself a force to be reckoned with. Maintaining that forensic science had gone mad and taken the place of godly values, Hocking, as the president of the National Freedom Council, said that their significant assistance behind the scenes still had a long way to go in obtaining complete exoneration for us. 'The National Freedom Council would prefer to see a judicial inquiry outside the Northern Territory because we have no confidence in the integrity of those who are organising it' (*Sunday Sun*, 9/2/1986).

Our tiny three-bedroom home at 5 College Drive had been a wonderful place of refuge for us, courtesy of Avoldale College. However, we had now outgrown it and wanted to upgrade and buy our own place. We looked around the area for a property and settled on a relatively remote mountain ridge property in the Wattagan range overlooking Lake Macquarie. This would serve as our mountain retreat. It had a magnificent view across the lake but was also minutes away from the township of Cooranbong. We paid our money and took possession. We still had no home to live in that was our own, there wasn't enough money for that.

Events moved quickly after Lindy's release, especially in relation to the media. Every station and newspaper was desperate to get their share of Lindy's views after her three years of enforced silence. We came to an arrangement with Australian Consolidated Press (ACP). Supervising Producer, Anthony McClellan sent a chopper to Gosford to sign us up through a Stuart Tipple contract. With Malcolm Turnbull (recently Federal Opposition Leader) and Trevor Kennedy, they went to Turnbull's office to finalise details. It was a long meeting, with money not the only thing under discussion. Producer John Little in his book *Inside 60 Minutes,* described how Kennedy would occasionally exit and walk down the corridor to visit Kerry Packer to nut out a deal between Channel Nine and the *Australian Women's Weekly.* Little also accused us of upping the stakes in cheque-book journalism in Australia.

It was the iconic presenter Ray Martin who got our nod to create a *60 Minutes* full one-hour presentation for Kerry Packer's top rating Channel Nine network. Martin had been chosen over four other *60 Minutes* reporters: Jana Wendt, Jeff McMullen, Ian Leslie and George Negus. Jana would have gone a close second, but as professional as she was, I thought at the time that she lacked an empathetic presence and I did not want to go through another gruelling and unnecessary interrogation while a Royal Commission was in the pipeline. You can tell the truth to the best of your ability, but you will always get some prosecutor-like interrogator who will attempt to abuse the essence of your meaning.

Gerald Stone, the *60 Minutes* director, would not have countenanced our demand normally but had to accept the reality that we were in control for now. He stated: 'We'll be sniped at again for attempting to lift our ratings by paying for the Chamberlain story. That is bull. *60 Minutes* is the number one program in Australia. I could get away with not running a Lindy Chamberlain story in ratings terms, quite happily. But I feel that we'd be cheating our audience of one of the most talked-about stories in Australian history.' Stone certainly had no reason to complain. The story boosted the profile of his current affairs program beyond expectations for both Sunday nights.

George Negus seemed to have got his knickers in a knot about chequebook journalism and might have started asking offensive questions of us. He appeared to think he was a cut above us when he spoke to the *Sun Herald* (16/2/1986), 'Let's say I'm glad I wasn't asked to do the interview.' But then he back-flipped, saying, 'I don't like the idea of paying for stories unless it's the only way to get an important story.' The implication being that he did not regard our story as important—perhaps because he presumed he was talking to a murderess and an accessory after the fact, who were both blatant liars.

Lindy's and my position were quite clear on the payment issue. We had been victims of the media who had boosted their sales and ratings, often in a negative and hostile way, especially leading up to the second inquest. The Northern Territory Chief Minister, police and justice system had harnessed the media to drive negative and often vicious publicity that had prejudiced our trial badly. Now that the tide seemed to be turning, it was our time to collect. Our legal costs had been astronomical and our debt was great. The media owed us. But of greater importance was our determination to be free of media domination. For too long they had had unfettered control of dismantling our reputations and credibility. The way to curb this was to charge them for access to our information, and we employed experts in their field to make it happen.

So, why Ray Martin, you might ask? Martin had the track record. His image was that a man of integrity, he had an open face and questioned his interviewees sincerely. What you saw was what you got. It didn't stop with an image. He was real. His skills as an investigator were not those of a prosecutor or defence lawyer: Martin presented in the style of a Royal Commissioner. Dr Belinda Middleweek remarked: 'Scholars writing in the field of media studies regard Martin as a pivotal figure in the transformation of Australian current affairs journalism... Martin is a consummate celebrity news figure, whose ability to speak on behalf of his audience embodied the reputation of the Nine Network and proved crucial factors in his career success.'

Indeed the 'Still the One' top commercial television network in Australia, during the heady eighties and nineties, under the guidance of Kerry Packer, which generally reported on us with measured accounts, was part of the reason why I still had some trust in any media outlet to report reality with some balance. I found that Ray Martin constructed and presented his questions in an open manner, probing but not intrusive or obnoxious. Referring to our first major national interview, Dr Middleweek suggested that Martin seemed to ask 'what every Australian would ask you' but at the same time 'was probing and at times seemed to exploit the case's emotive potential'.

However, Ray Martin had his detractors also and was strongly criticised by Mike Gibson when Martin interviewed our son Aidan, then aged nine, with his trail bike in tow. Gibson anguished over the way Martin interviewed Aidan. Apart from Martin neglecting to recognise that Aidan was also my son, Gibson wrote: 'Ray Martin badgering Lindy Chamberlain's son, young Aidan, about the disappearance of his baby sister, Azaria...Ray kept at him hammer and tongs, forcing a sobbing youngster to relive the painful memories of what he saw on that fateful night.' Gibson then took the higher moral ground to include Martin in his list of colleagues that had embarrassed him through their unprofessionalism. Gibson opined that in his 37 years as a journalist, 'I never cease to be embarrassed at the levels to which some of my colleagues will descend to pursue a story' (*Daily Telegraph Mirror* 1/6/1994).

But Gibson was ignorant of the fact that Aidan wanted to talk to Ray Martin. Aidan did what he could not do at the trial or the High Court; tell the world that he was with his mother during the time she was alleged to have committed a crime and that this was rubbish. Amongst the three major gaps of evidence in the case that may have changed the verdict, the High Court judged that the absence of Aidan's testimony was one of the vital missing links. Now Aidan had his chance and he wanted to take it. The interview was done in several different takes between tears getting in the way. Aidan now had his day in the media 'court'.

Ray Martin's *60 Minutes* interview with us, taken over nearly five days, renewed the fierce controversy. The Murdoch-owned *Daily Telegraph* (3/3/1986) reported 'Hundreds of angry TV viewers jammed the station's switchboards all night as the row raged on over the innocence of Lindy Chamberlain. Many callers sneered at her version of the disappearance of baby Azaria and claimed she was crying crocodile tears for the benefit of the camera. There was fury on both sides as the calls—which went on throughout the night following the interviews... (and which) grew more heated.'

The public's perception that we were innocent now ran about 52 per cent, a far cry from 10 per cent following the second inquest, five years before. But with 48 per cent still considering we were guilty, we still had a long way to go, a very long way.

When asked by Ray Martin about what I thought about the trial verdict, I replied: 'I saw those jurors almost skulking, heads down, not looking at us...And then I looked across and saw the judge, whose face seemed to go from an ashen grey to a ruddy red and I thought, 'Yes, I know what you are feeling'—exactly the way we thought.'

I told Ray Martin: 'A lot of people don't realise how important innocence is to innocent people.' One senior journalist had suggested: 'Look, why don't you give it away? Walk away from it now. Just find a new place for Lindy to live and put it behind you.' But for me, this was unthinkable and in hindsight, because this journalist, we discovered, was a secret crusader for our justice, he was just testing us. We had to fight on to expose the lie. Our names and the names of our children must not be tarnished by a verdict falsely condemning the Chamberlains. The truth had to come out, no matter what the cost. If you know you are right in your fight for justice and freedom, and you can bank your life on it, then, never ever give up the dream for the truth to be told, I vowed.

According to John Little in *Inside 60 Minutes*, the interview, consisting of comments from virtually all our family, had 42 per cent of the total TV audience watching in Sydney and 50 per cent of all TV viewers in Melbourne. The second part of the interview ran the following week with equally spectacular ratings results. This was as high as it had ever been for audience viewing of the station. It set a benchmark for current affairs reporting for the rest of the twentieth century. An estimated six million viewers sat through the interview.

Martin was challenged on Lindy's alleged manipulation of him in order to win public sympathy for herself. The *Daily Telegraph* (3/3/1986) led a front-page story, saying that he had been taken for a sucker by Lindy. Martin told the paper that he spent five days with us, talking and questioning us, 'looking for an Achilles heel', but that he had never found one. He added: 'After three days, people usually start to become erratic if they have things to hide but I am not likely to fall for a sucker punch.' He flatly rejected claims that he had been duped.

John Laws, the 'golden tonsils' of Australian talk back radio, used the *TV Week* magazine to vent his spleen on Ray Martin also. Agreeing that our interview was watched by more Australians than all the other programs put together on the night, Laws had expected a 'tepid interview' with Martin presenting the questions, and would presumably not give us too much of a hard time. He would show Lindy in denial of guilt, crying and the 'contradictions in her character'. Laws complained that 'I hovered in the background, cutting in just at the right time to push Lindy forward to make her tearful speech to her church friends'. He then criticised Lindy for allowing Aidan to be 'attacked by the most savage question: 'Do you want to tell me what you saw?'' It was what the High Court judges asked of Aidan and was surprised he had not been asked at the trial. Appearances fool people, even the self-proclaimed wise men of the land who interview people just for the entertainment value. Aidan held the key to Lindy's innocence, and Laws, along with Gibson, was unable to comprehend the significance of Aidan's testimony.

It was not Lindy or Ray who encouraged Aidan to try and tell his story; it was my idea. But six years later it seemed that it was still too raw for Aidan to reveal his part in the saga. Laws' acidic tirade then shafted the authenticity of the *60 Minutes* program. 'Like many of us outside the Seventh-day Adventist Church, he (Aidan) had a gutful of the entire shabby business. The shots of the blond Aidan roaring through the scrub on his revved up trail bike probably told more about his inner turmoil than anything he could have said' (*TV Week* 22/3/1986). It seemed that Laws had missed the point completely.

The *Women's Weekly* was accused of writing 'soppy, sentimental stuff' about us, but that is what sells this type of magazine and in our case the magazine was telling the story directly from the horses' mouths.

The Sun Herald (3/3/1986) predicted that there would be an inquiry 'so abrasive to so many that it would be tantamount to conducting an operation without anesthetic.'

My father was ready and waiting when the press knocked on the door of his home on the Selwyn River in Canterbury, New Zealand. The *Christchurch Star* recorded that he believed there had been 'a number of people in authority in the Northern Territory' who had lied in the case. He was also furious that because Lindy had been in jail for 12 months or more her criminal record prevented her from visiting her family in New Zealand (*Northern Territory News*, 3/3/1986).

A search to dig into our past now started, with three journalists investigating our paths for five years in Tasmania between 1970 and 1975. Did we have any skeletons rattling in the cupboard? People who either knew us or knew of us were interrogated about any aberrations of character or behaviour in the three locations we served across the Northern Coast. The press, namely the *Sunday Examiner*, sought to bust open any chink in Lindy's armour, wherever she had been or had worked. These reporters spoke to Church members, non-Church members and employers in the community. The verdict was that: 'Those who knew Lindy (and Michael Chamberlain) will not hear a bad word about the family' (9/3/1986). One- -time radio announcer at Scottsdale's radio station, 7SD North Eastern Tasmania, Sheila Ryan, was never a Church member but her anger over our convictions was expressed in the *Launceston Examiner* when she became the leader of the Launceston Chamberlain Justice Committee support group. She recounted to a *Sunday Examiner* reporter: 'I am not a Seventh-day Adventist, but I got to know them when I was an announcer at 7SD Scottsdale. Michael Chamberlain took a regular religious session and he helped me give up smoking...To me they were a delightful couple—there were no stories then. That's why I am so appalled at the current wave of rumour and innuendo. It is not just the rumours but the hate letters to us, individuals and local politicians.'

Sir Reginald Sholl came out fighting on behalf of the Chamberlain Innocence Committee again. He took aim this time at the fairer sex in Australia, many of whom, he claimed judged Lindy guilty without knowing the facts. For that reason he had concerns that some women on juries might not be capable of objectivity. But if this wasn't enough to stir the pot of women's issues over equality, the Northern Territory Government's ban on our legal team from any involvement in a judicial inquiry struck again at the heart of Northern Territory justice. Furthermore, a poll in Darwin indicated that if Lindy was proven innocent after a judicial inquiry most Darwinians would still continue to condemn her as guilty (*Brisbane Daily Sun* 5/3/1986).

One of the significant factors that had brought on the Royal Commission was the constant publications of the *Azaria Newsletter*, from 1984 to 1986. It had been conceived of, run and conscientiously managed by Nonie Hodgson, an unsung hero for this cause. Nonie was a very tall and happy student who had attended Avondale College and had married an inventor. She regularly supervised the bi-monthly publication containing various editorials and allowed me, as its unofficial executive editor, to keep the news train rolling while Lindy was in jail. I adopted the role to assist in keeping informed the various support groups in Australasia. The first issue left Cooranbong on 1 April 1984. In my first editorial letter, as the executive editor, I said that the Information Service should be used as a resource and not as a directive. 'Local support groups have shown amazing initiatives and strength in their endeavours' (*Azaria Newsletter*, 1/4/1984). It was not for me to dictate who should do what or where. The support groups would do their best work with their own armour and in their own time and for this I would be indebted for life. Generally, Nonie acted as the resource person, but gradually gained confidence to write copy. It was one of the most proactive things I could have done to relieve the anxiety that was my constant companion.

But not everything ran smoothly. Some of Lindy's letters from jail were so angry that I had to rewrite them into more public relations-like communiqués to prevent a public backlash. Despite Nonie and Stuart Tipple's support on this, it did not go down at all well with Lindy. It became a festering sore in our relationship. Lindy was her own woman and she would not permit anyone to overrule her from her jail vantage point. I feared that if some of her material had gone public, unedited, she might have served longer, but the work of others and the matinee jacket find overruled this fear.

Malcolm Brown's article, 'How the media convicted Lindy Chamberlain', added fuel to the drive for an inquiry, along with the works of John Bryson, Guy Boyd, George Rollo, Veronica Flanigan, Dr Bill Peddie, and Dr Glenn Rosendahl. In Rosendahl's book, *The Dark Side of the Law,* (1984) he referred to the 'cheap debating tricks' of the Crown that were: 'a prospect as pleasant, a taste as delectable, a smell as sweet as pus frothing from a gangrenous and putrefying limb.'

The power of the protesting support groups to bring together a record number of 131,000 signatures to alert the Federal Parliament, also caused people to recognise that this movement for justice was not going away. In December 1985, the Governor-General, Sir Ninian Stephen, was overwhelmed by dozens of boxes of signatures at Government House Canberra. It added one more reminder to the Northern Territory that a Royal Commission was coming, ready or not.

The Royal Commission into our case was at last approved by the Northern Territory Government and was locked in to commence with the preliminary hearing on 19 March 1986. For me this was a huge milestone in our fight for justice, but it also heralded alot of work ahead for us. Justice Trevor Morling, who was selected by the Territory

Government, was virtually unknown to the media up until now. It seemed that, following his employment by the Northern Territory to sit on the bench of an Australasian Meat Employees Union dispute at Mudginberri Station, his finding in favour of the Government may have been a signal to the Territory he was a safe choice in presiding over our matter.

Morling would be given authority under the dual umbrella of Northern Territory Law and the Commonwealth Royal Commissions Act, but the local view was that, as a religious conservative, he would protect the Territory from any adverse effects. We were anxious about Morling, but at the same time we had our Royal Commission. At least the way we presented our case was in our control.

The Federal Attorney-General, Mr Lionel Bowen, indicated that the Commission would sit in Darwin and Sydney. Marshall Perron ratified this through an introduction of a Bill into the Northern Territory Parliament. He appeared to have had a remarkable change of heart, considering that only a month before he wanted to challenge Bowen on the steps of Federal Parliament over the claim that the Northern Territory was incapable of conducting an impartial inquiry. It was clear that Bowen, who wanted the Royal Commission, would have to examine not only the 'safety' of the guilty verdicts but the handling of the case by the Northern Territory Police and Government. The major worry lay in the way the police, tabloid media and key forensic scientists had colluded in the past. (*Sydney Morning Herald*, 20/3/1986). But recognising the fierce resistance that an angry police force could wield, I feared that at best only partial justice could be achieved.

Another problem had now emerged. We had no legal counsel for the Royal Commission. One thing was sure, we would not tolerate any further abuse by the media to break into our privacy. Lindy and I decided to accept media celebrity agent, Harry M Miller's offer to be our buffer and agent to manage our public responses. Under his umbrella we would have an advocate to shield us from the media. Mr Ellicot QC, had been suggested as a likely candidate to be our Royal Commission counsel, but he was busy until August. Family friend Denise Roy was harassing me for not already choosing a counsel, but it was easier said than done.

Whoever took on the role would have to master the forensic science maze of blood and fabric damage, have a cool and methodical head and be a strategist in cross-examination of the trial prosecution witnesses. Joy Kuhl, Professors Malcolm Cameron and Malcolm Chaikin would have to be demolished.

On 1 April 1986, Stuart Tipple advised us that neither Tony Fitzgerald nor Tom Hughes, two other leading Australian QCs, could represent us. It was less than two months before the Commission was due to commence. Hector Crawford was also dogging us with pressure to create a press release about a proposed upcoming drama series. Interest in the case had been hotting up with Crawford's Channel 7 film studios, first suggesting on 15 January 1986 that a documentary, docudrama or telemovie could be made. After discussions with Mr Crawford it was agreed that more research was needed and that a serialised telemovie might be the best road to take.

By 7pm that same night, there seemed to be a breakthrough in our Royal Commission counsel dilemma. Stephen Charles QC had informed us that he was interested in our case and wished to take us on. Another barrister and specialist in medical matters, Ken Crispin, had thrown his hat in the ring, bringing medical expertise to the team. Mr Crispin was a significant find and a memorable figure. His thick, wavy, raven hair and affable appeal exuded confidence. His deep brown eyes and engaging smile gave us a feeling that here was a terrier for truth. He could have passed for an Italian or Greek, but after making that assumption, Crispin informed me, 'I'm pure Aussie,' with a smile. 'I get it a lot, but they're all wrong.' Things were looking good. With Brind Woinarski, a tall blonde Melbourne barrister supported by good references, Crispin would be our second junior counsel.

A few days earlier, Northern Territory Solicitor-General, Brian Martin, requested details of our meagre funds in order to make a determination about our eligibility for our own legal counsel, other than the Royal Commission Counsel. Mr Martin argued that although the Northern Territory would have their own legal counsel, funded by the Territory Government to defend their prosecution witnesses, there should be no

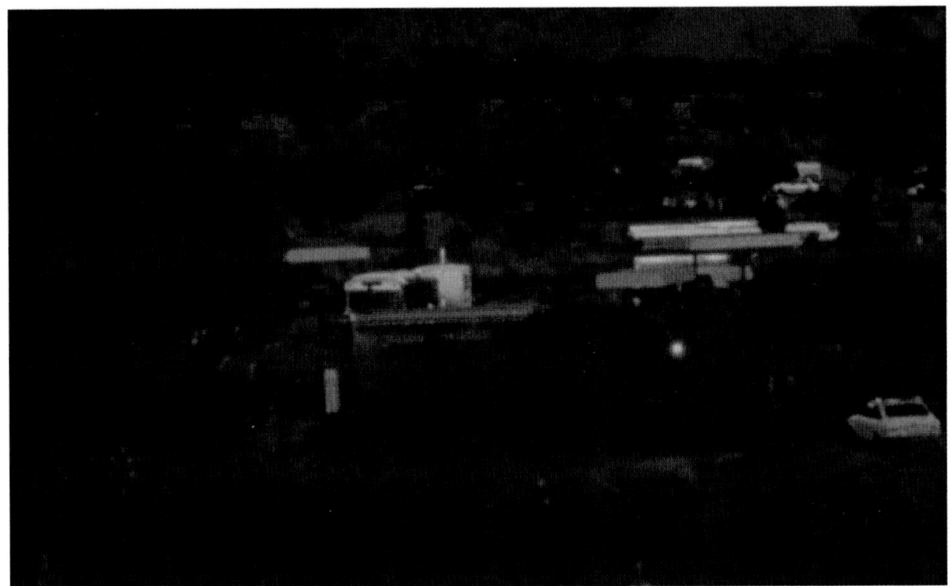

Above: Ayers Rock camping ground, 6am on 17 August, 1980. The Torana hatchback is pictured far right. The light shows the barbecue area, and how close we were camping to it.

Below: Our car at Ayers Rock climb around 1.30pm, 17 August, 1980.

Above: 'Where is our Azaria?' I took this picture with tears in my eyes, of Aidan and Reagan in front of our tent after Azaria went missing, about 10am, 18 August, 1980. It was the toughest picture I have ever taken but I felt it was an important record to help warn others of the potential danger of camping at Ayers Rock.

Opposite page: (From left) Peter Dean, myself, Phil Rice QC and Lindy at night during the first inquest, December 1980.

Below: A dingo photographed at Ayers Rock camping ground.

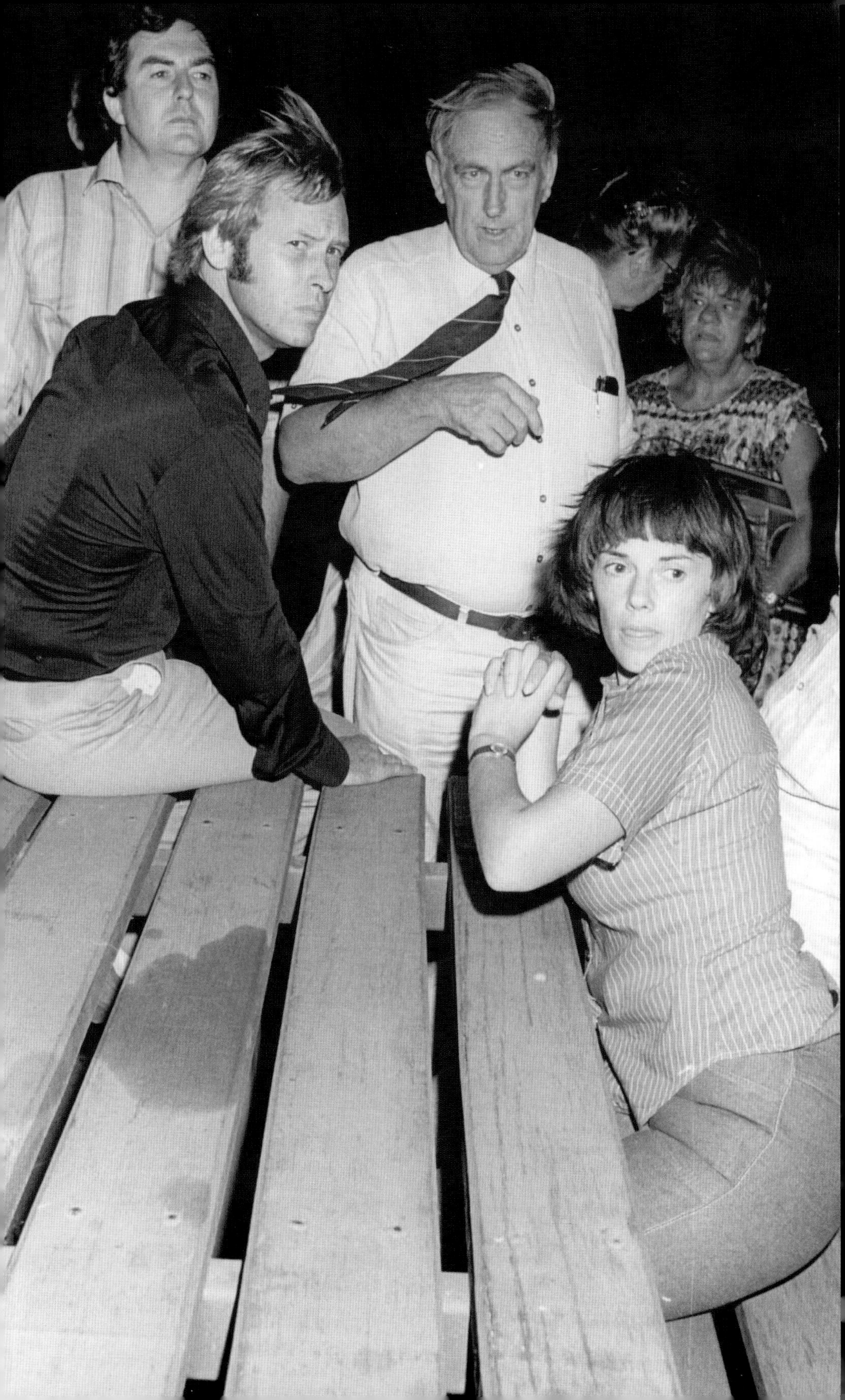

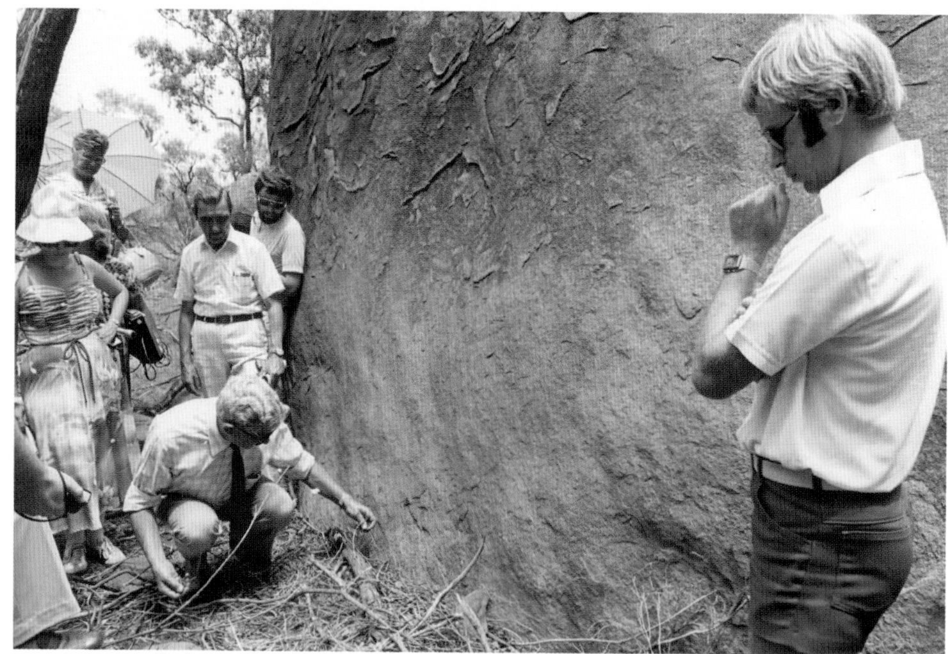

Fairfax

Above: At the site where Azaria's clothing was found during the first inquest.

Opposite page: Lindy and I with Snr Constable Frank Gibson, discussing the route that the Aboriginal Elders and Chief Ranger Roff followed up the sandhill, tracking the dingo during the first inquest.

Below: Snr Constable Frank Morris (centre) pointing to the area where the dingo tracks would lead, along the ridge south of our tent, at the first inquest.

News Limited

Fairfax / Nicholson Cartoons

Above: Cartoon commentary about the jury and the influence of television, in the *Melbourne Age*, published 1 November, 1982.

Opposite page: Irene Heron, Snr Constable Gibson, Lindy and Peter Dean heading for the place where Azaria's clothes were found. Six years later, the matinee jacket that the Crown suggested Lindy had invented, was found just a few metres ahead of where these walkers were.

Below: A cartoon from the *Northern Territory News* by Tony Dean, Tuesday 26 November, 1985, commenting on Northern Territory attitudes towards Lindy and my fight for an inquiry.

News Limited / Tony Dean

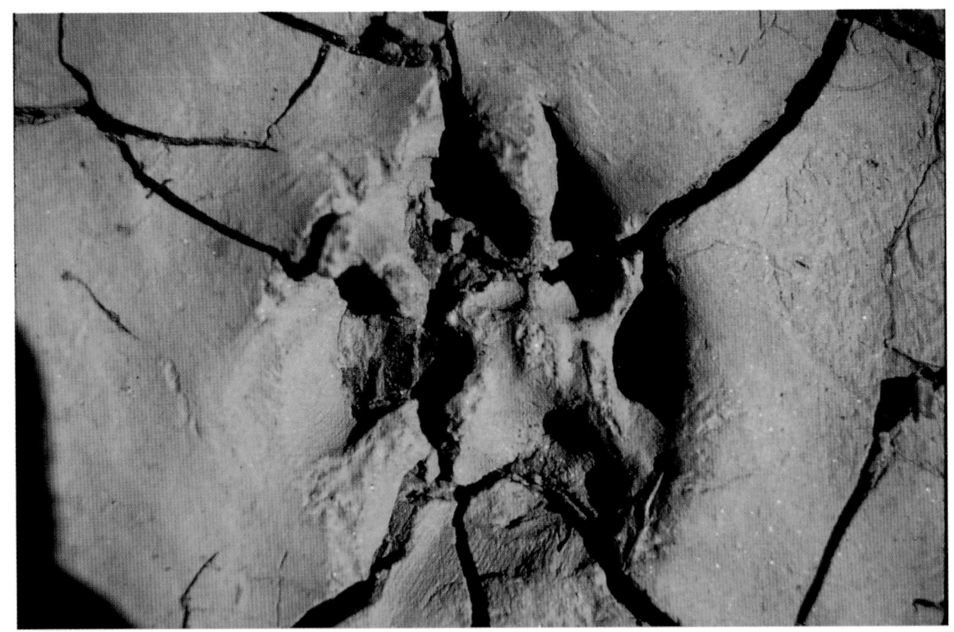

Above: The tell tale paw print of an Ayers Rock dingo, 18 August, 1980.

Below: Myself, Peter Dean and the Deputy Principal of Alice Springs High School exercising during timeout at the first inquest.

News Limited

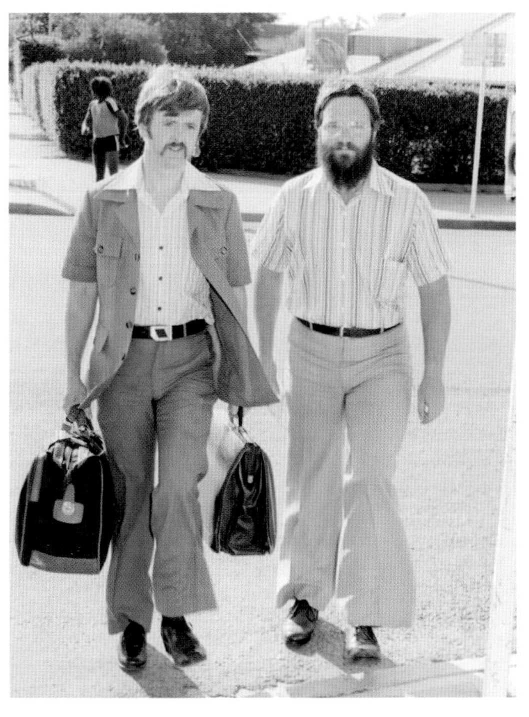

Left: Dr Andrew Scott (left) and Dr Tony Jones, blood experts for the prosecution at the trial. Dr Scott later supported the our push for an inquiry after realising the blood evidence was flawed.

Below: Expert blood witness for the prosecution, Joy Kuhl, photographed supposedly finding 'blood' in my Torana. It was, amongst other things, a spilt milkshake, copper dust and bitument-based sound deadener spray.

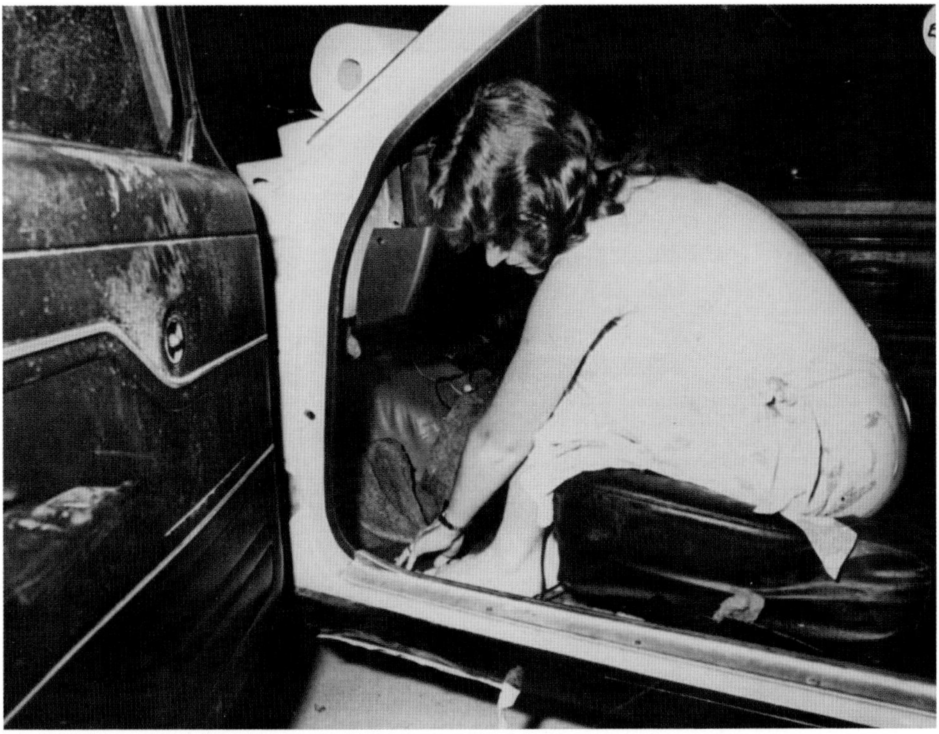

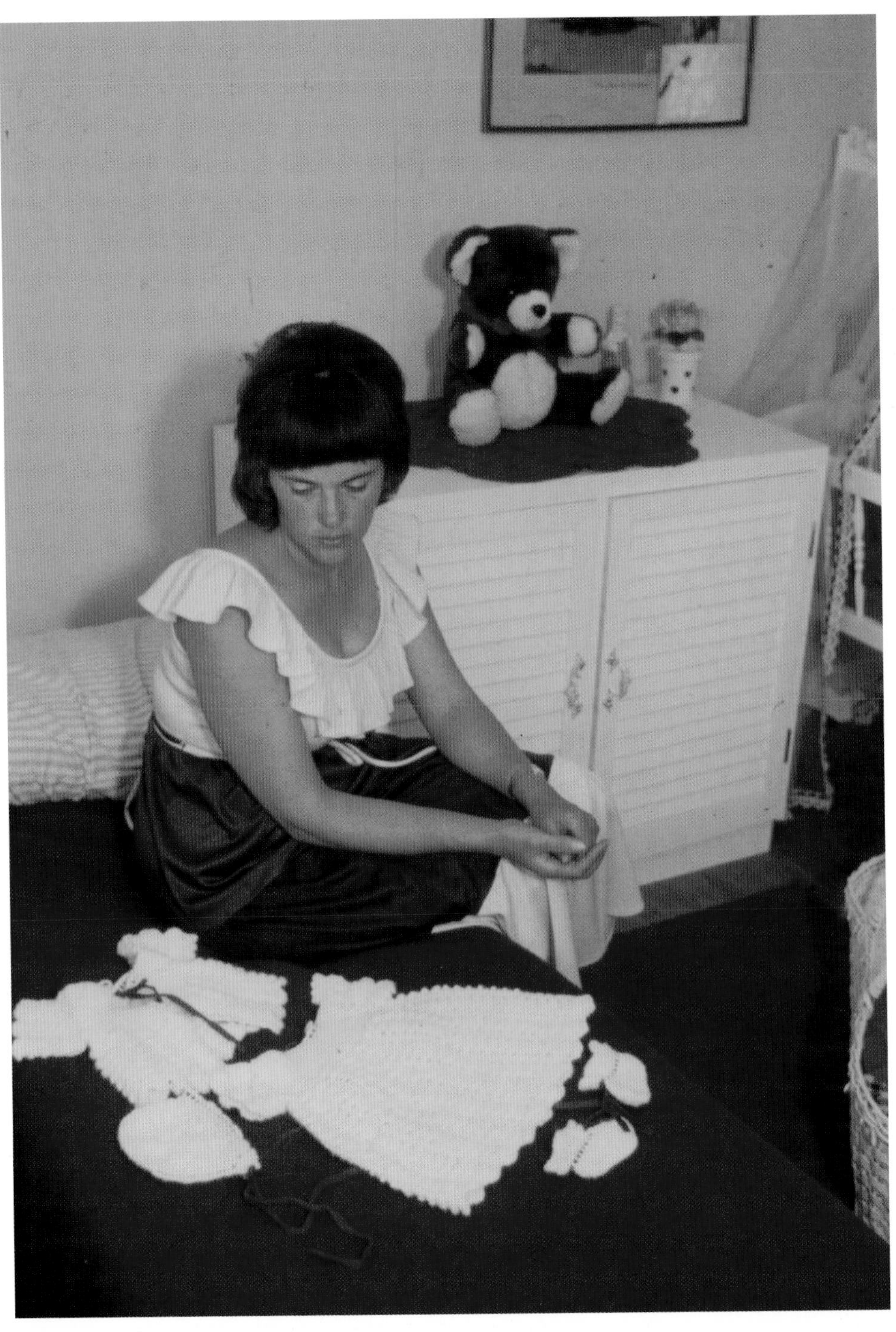

Above: Lindy after returning home from Ayers Rock and remembering Azaria, 22 August, 1980.

Right: The T-shirt dehumanisation of Azaria, and an example of the Northern Territory's obscene responses during and after the trial.

TASTY CRITTERS BUT THEY'RE A BUGGER TO PEEL!

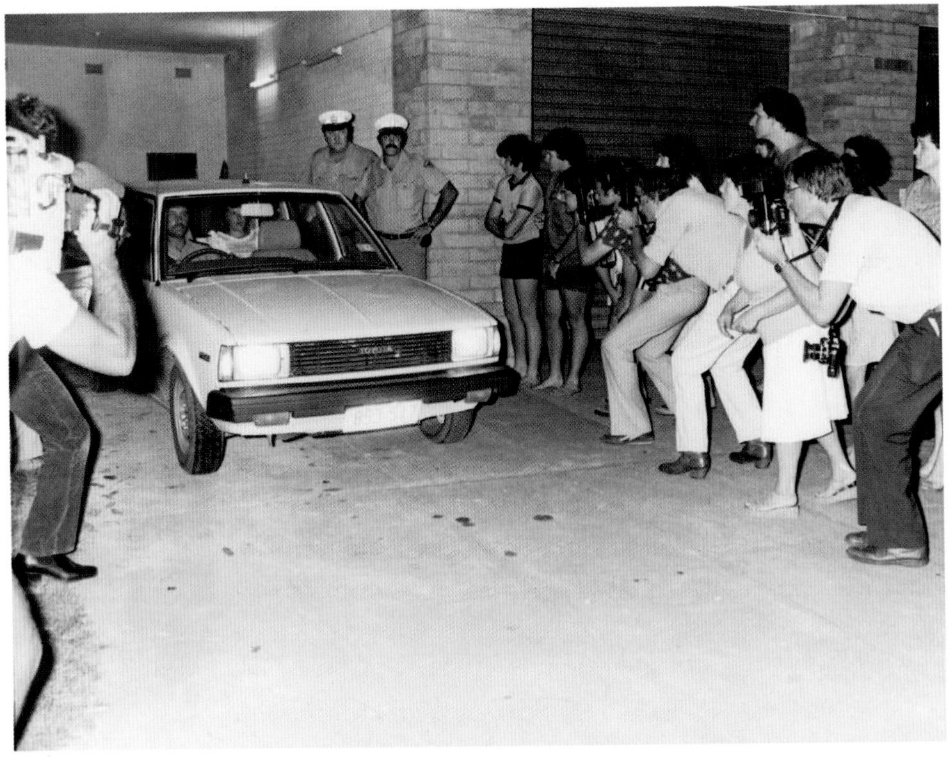

Above: Lindy leaves the Supreme Court building for Berrimah Prison on 19 October after being given a life sentence with hard labour.

Opposite: Organising my campaign, from my kitchen, to lobby federal parliament MPs and Senators, 1985.

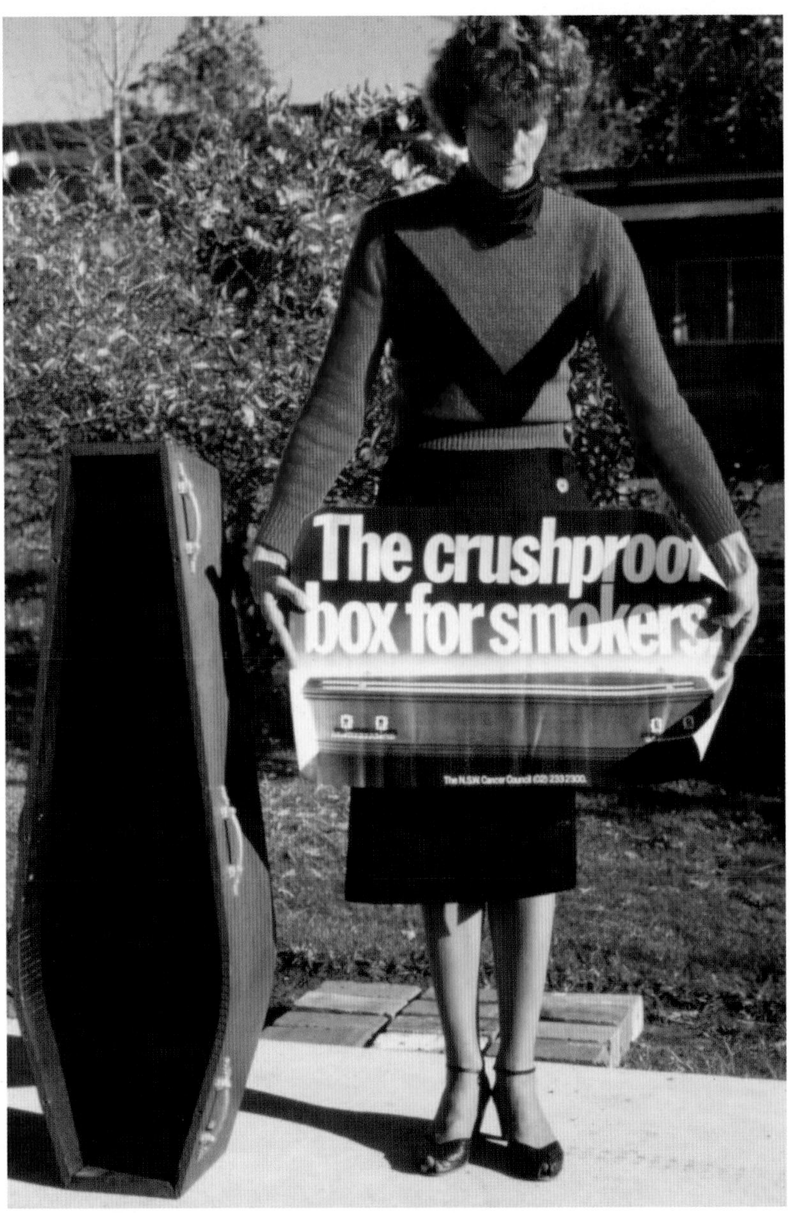

The crushproo
box for smokers
The N.S.W. Cancer Council (02) 233 2300.

Above: One of the 'quit smoking' props I used between 1977-1980 at Innisfail, North Queensland. This was not the first time this idea had been used in health services. It had been promoted at the Sydney Adventist Hospital in Wahroonga in its own quit smoking program. The catchline was: 'Throw your cigarettes in before they throw you in.'

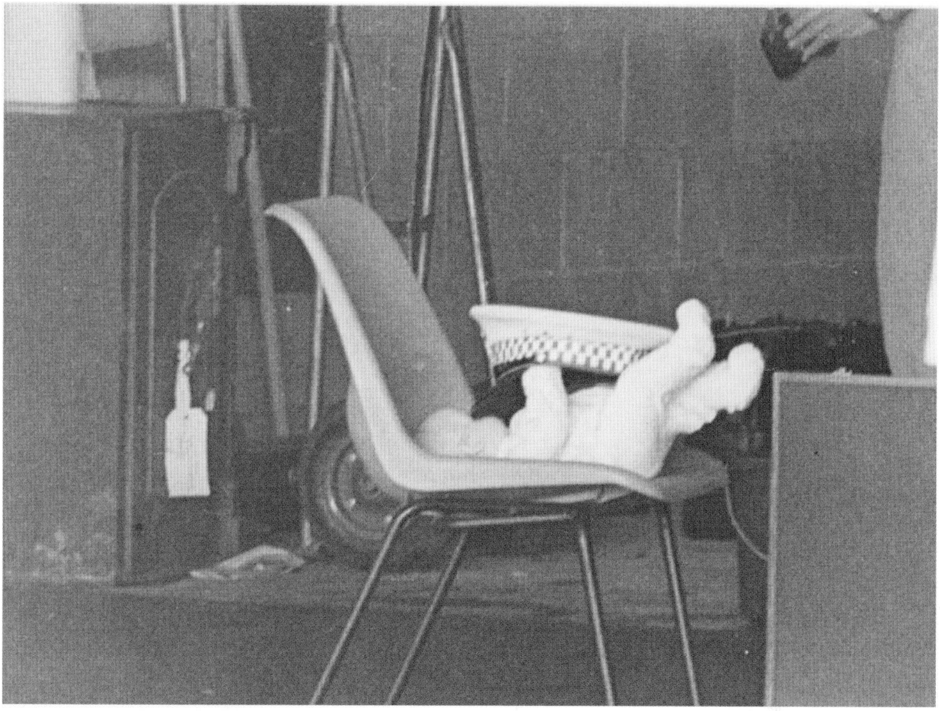

Above: 1982 Supreme Court jury room. Note the effigy of Azaria with the police hat sitting on top of it.

Below: The forbidden photo: Lindy gives birth to Kahlia in jail conditions on 17 November, 1982.

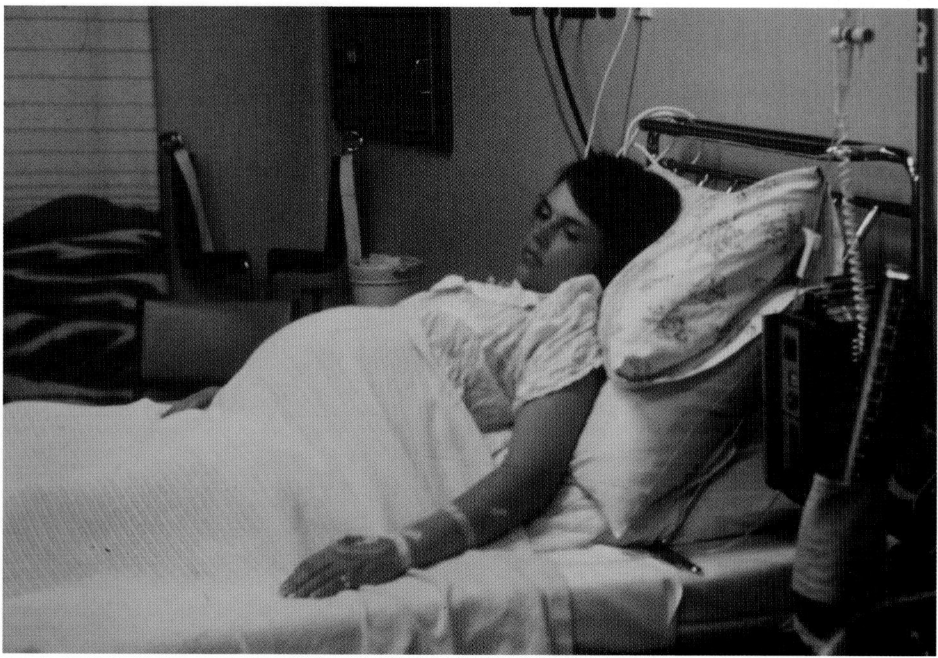

Two weeks after I was convicted, I graduated from an MA (in Religion) from Andrews University, Avondale Campus, November 1982.

need for funding our counsel as we shouldn't need one! (Letter from Northern Territory Solicitor-General's office, 15/4/1984). Stuart Tipple replied that if it was the intention of the Northern Territory legal system to irrevocably undermine the Royal Commission in refusing us legal counsel, Martin was doing a pretty good job. The Royal Commission's advice from the Commission's solicitor, Mr Davis, had been 'that it was imperative that we be represented' by good legal counsel. Stuart Tipple wrote back to Martin, telling him to reconsider very carefully (Tipple letter to Northern Territory Solicitor-General, Brian Martin, 17/4/1986). Right down to the wire, it seemed that at every turn, and in every response to our plea for justice and a fair go, the Northern Territory Government would thwart our chances.

The Darwin public's anti-Chamberlain attitude was also alive and well. Our Northern Territory friend and stalwart, Liz Noonan, was casually browsing the shops in the Darwin Mall some days later when she came across a large mobile display of T-shirts. The trader called himself 'Bazza's Bizarre'. Liz was suddenly stopped in her tracks. Before her eyes were four T-shirts that contained a chilling message. Deeply incensed, she was compelled to purchase them as evidence of the twisted mindset still pervading Darwin. Liz described the T-shirt in her letter to us, dated 21/5/1986.

'The first had the large word 'Azaria' with the 'A' being formed in the shape of a scissors dripping with blood. The second had a 'bikie' dingo astride his motorbike with Ayers Rock as a backdrop and the words: 'Let's split. I've had a gutful of babes around here'. A third T-shirt showed a crocodile poised ready to eat, napkin in place, holding a fork. A dingo is sawing off a human leg and is saying. 'How come they always blame us?' Suspended on a spit over the fire is a baby, head obscured, with the spit entering the baby via its rectum. The final T-shirt illustrates a dingo leaning on a fence holding a little jacket with Ayers Rock in the background. The dingo is saying: 'Tasty critters but they're a bugger to peel!' The third and fourth T-shirt had a copyright insignia to 1986 Smutty Printz Design.'

Two weeks later, on 28 April 1986, Lindy and I flew to Melbourne, still without a QC, because Stephen Charles was no longer available. Lindy was excited for many reasons. She wanted to show the world her gutsy spirit of grit and control. This included her pride in her new figure. Her black skintight leggings, quite appropriate for a fresh Melbourne autumn morning, revealed that despite three years of tropical incarceration she was a woman with a lion's roar and on a mission. The press, amazingly, did not focus on her attire and certainly no overt or derogatory comments were made about it now.

But it did not go unnoticed by some of the conservative Chamberlain Support Group members from the Wahroonga Adventist community. They issued Lindy with two books on how to dress appropriately. They were American publications having been printed in 1975. Inside one of the books, the well-meaning faithful had carefully underlined for Lindy the relevant parts about inappropriate attire. The instruction about the type of clothing she must wear to court, (including woollen fabrics in the tropics) was as subtle as a flying brick. No one was very impressed. But this kind of censure was becoming increasingly rare.

The attitudes by the press to Lindy's body and apparel before her jail sentence, now three years later, had changed dramatically as Belinda Middleweek in her doctoral thesis on 'Dingo Media' observed: 'The number and range of discourses on Lindy's body...gave audiences an opportunity to read her appearance in alternate and sometimes contradictory ways. From the outset, descriptions of her physical appearance were the subject of newsprint, radio talkback, current affairs programs and television broadcasts. At the second inquest one press report noted she wore 'an orange and purple patterned dress...her shoulders, bare except for the thin straps of her dress, showed the pink tint of sunburn'. From a desirable feminine representation she was now transformed into a maternal figure just six months later 'in billowing frocks, heavily pregnant with her fourth child' (Dr Belinda Middleweek, Dingo Media? R v Chamberlain as a model for an Australian event, PhD Thesis, University of Sydney, 2007).

The press now figured, erroneously, that Lindy had been reined in by the Church. *The Sun Herald* purported that: 'The Chamberlains have been tightly controlled. Mrs Chamberlain has continued her dress sense in the maternity mode. She has had a new maternity dress each day' *(Sun Herald* 19/9/1982). There was little substance to this. Certainly I hadn't been told to conduct myself any differently.

Lindy's imprisonment had heralded the changing of the media tide. A guilty woman outside of jail now became, to many, the problem of an innocent girl in jail. Within days of Lindy being jailed, the media focused on a new aspect of her physical appearance in her 'secret childhood' where she is described as 'a beautiful little girl, so natural, a little fairy'.

When *Northern Territory News* editor Gary Shipway visited Lindy in jail during October 1985 he recorded the moment in an amazing about-face observation: 'The slight five-foot nothing, smiling woman... did not look at all like the Lindy Chamberlain of the inquests and trial. Gone were the hard eyes and sullen gesture, the chubby face with petulant mouth, and the rolling gait of a woman accused of murdering her baby...Instead we were greeted by an attractive, petite and healthy woman looking much younger than her 37 years' (*Sunday Territorian* 27/10/1985).

From that time on the press never seemed to focus on, or evoke, a derogatory response about her attire again. She would be described as 'attractive, stylish or trendy'. Lindy now met the requirements for film star appeal and had shaken off the vestiges of a witch. Whether one could have ever construed a female with 'tanned shoulders', 'petite figure' or 'eye catching frame' as a representation of a witch is highly conjectural but Belinda Wilson in *The Making of a Modern Myth* has argued that: 'In effect...the Australian media with the public in tow, decided Lindy was a witch, hunted her as one, and then, symbolically, led her into her cart through the jeering mobs to the stake, just as it happened to witches in the Middle Ages.'

Lindy had returned to the status that James Simmonds once described her in his book *Azaria: Wednesday's Child*. Her femininity was 'self evident' in her 'beautiful...darkly vivacious good looks'. No more commentary on the woman who was 'hard faced',' impassive', 'cold' or the 'Mother who killed Azaria'. In her coming out of jail debut, the *Australian Woman's Weekly* (March 1986) described her as: 'tiny, bird-like, sharp featured, with a modified punk brushed-back hairstyle, trim waist, shapely legs with fashionable black and gold sandals, and a beaming smile'. The mindset of the media had crafted her into a character that, now, could do no wrong.

Lindy's body had in effect been politicised and used as a means of positioning her as an 'evil woman' in media. But had women been in control of the media, I wondered, if I had been the focus of attention, would their interest in the male body have been different?

Lindy did receive advice from professionals about how to dress conservatively, yet smartly, and all were satisfied after that.

We were now bound to meet our trial QC, John Harbor Phillips, in his new chambers and elected to his new office as a Supreme Court Judge of Victoria. He would eventually become Victoria's Chief Justice of the Supreme Court. He told us, with some pride, that a new independent forensic laboratory in Melbourne had been set up at the cost of $28 million, and that he had helped in its establishment. This new service, to be used jointly by police and civilians, would remove the problem of perceived vested interest and lack of precision and record keeping, as experienced in the blood evidence tested in New South Wales Health Laboratories for the Northern Territory Police.

John Winneke QC had been recommended to us by John Phillips QC. We went to see him in action, where he was defending Derryn Hinch, a television and radio presenter. Hinch had preconceived notions that we were guilty, but on this day, 28 April 1986, it was his turn in the dock in the Melbourne courtroom. He had been charged with contempt of court. Winneke was an imposing tall gentleman, approaching middle age, relaxed and good-humoured, oozing confidence. But beneath the surface was a sharp, ferret-like instinct and capacity to dig. He had been a Royal Commissioner and had been Counsel assisting numerous inquiries. As we sat at the back of the courtroom listening to Winneke's summing up, I decided that this was our man. As the case wound up, we came out a side door of the court with Derryn Hinch behind us.

At that moment it all began to feel surreal. The press was not interested in Hinch or his 3AW Melbourne station. They were hot on our heels trying to find out why we were in the same court and indeed in Melbourne. We had not been seen since Lindy's release from jail and our appearance in public was like a lightning rod after the *60 Minutes* interview with Ray Martin. One particularly aggressive female radio reporter was so keen for an interview she tried to stuff her microphone into our mouths hoping to badger a response. But her action only gagged us.

Two months earlier, unbeknown to us, two witnesses not called at any inquest or the Darwin trial by the prosecution had come forward to speak to the *Melbourne Age* (27/2/1986). They were Max and Phyllis Cranwell with their daughter, four-year-old Amanda, and they had been at Ayers Rock on the night of 22 June 1980, seven weeks before Azaria was attacked. Amanda had been dragged from their car on 23 June by a dingo allegedly shot by Ranger Ian Cawood. It turned out that it was his pet. The Cranwells knew that Cawood had told the police about the incident at the Rock and that the police had their address, but no phone call ever came to investigate it, nor were they interviewed for the trial.

This report drew Chief Ranger Roff of Ayers Rock to make a statement that would not have pleased the Northern Territory Conservation Commission. Derek Roff, in his letter to *The Australian* (18/4/1984), told the world that with the Cranwells' evidence it was time that 'certain experts (should) give the Chamberlain case a more detailed consideration'. Roff took the view that if the Cranwell's evidence had been allowed at the trial the jury might have been more likely to have believed our story. Roff stated: 'Having lived at Ayers Rock for 16 years, I know that the dingoes of this area are conditioned by and to people. Consequently their behaviour is not that of a true wild animal and not fully understood by anyone...I do not think any of us should feel comfortable with the present situation'.

As if by fate, the media reported an increasing trend of dingoes attacking children. If they did not reveal themselves as 'man eaters', as Ian Barker represented them at the trial, on each occasion there were parents or adults on hand who were able to quickly intervene.

Had these victims not been rescued, death may have been an outcome. In June 1984, two-year-old Debbie Cowlishaw visited the Auckland's Whangarata Zoo Park dingoes. She left with gaping wounds to her arms and required 60 stitches to sew them up. Mrs Sheryl Cowlishaw told the *Auckland Star*, ('NZ park horror: Dingoes maul baby') that the dingoes were close to her throat when she rescued her daughter in a collapsed state. Little Debbie was rushed to hospital.

Five-year-old Christy Corney will never forget the day she was attacked by a pack of dingoes on 10 April 1986, at Cooloola National Park, Queensland. Christy had to 'fight for her life' after sustaining 'deep wounds to her neck and back'. The ambulance officer described her as having deep lacerations and puncture marks everywhere...There were four-inch gashes on her legs and a puncture the size of a 20 cent piece on her back, one gash on her neck just missed the jugular vein.' (*Daily Sun* 11/4/1986).

Back home, on 1 May 1986, we had an unwanted skirmish with Pastor Ron Craig, the Seventh-day Adventist Church Secretary-treasurer for Eastern Australia. He told us that there was no guarantee that the Church would back our legal counsel at the Royal Commission. In jeopardy was our claim to having Tipple, Winneke and Crispin to conduct our legal representation, and even our accommodation and travel to and from court. At this revelation, Lindy became hysterical and during the day she wept inconsolably. We had learned that from now on we needed to record all relevant conversations with the Church to avoid misunderstandings. Fortunately, a little later, the Church, seeing the dire consequences of not supporting us, quietly accepted the onerous task to cover our costs.

The following day, 2 May, brought with it new hope to our financially and legally- strapped status. At 1.15pm in Woolloomoolloo, an inner suburb of Sydney, Lindy and I signed up with Australia's shrewdest and most powerful entrepreneur in media management, New Zealand-born, Harry M. Miller. John Behm was used as our go-between solicitor, but not before consulting with a few of Miller's clients including Ita Buttrose. Miller was also looking after Graeme 'The King of Comedy' Kennedy.

Former Federal Minister for Aboriginal Affairs, Bill Wentworth, telephoned me on 4 May 1986 about a letter from the manager of the Ayers Rock cooperative store, who was now living in the United States. 'I just think you should be aware that contrary to a Territory rumour to discredit Nipper Winmatti, he was observed by this manager to be out searching that night, after all.'

'Ah huh,' I replied. 'As an independent witness that might have been helpful at the first inquest. Why didn't he call earlier?'

'Well, he said Nipper was apparently telling everyone who would listen that a dingo had taken Azaria to Ian Cawoods.'

Lindy and I met with Winneke and the new legal recruit, Brind Woinarski. We discussed an incoming submission brought on by Ian Barker, advocating that Professor Malcolm Chaikin, Dr Simon Baxter and Constable James Metcalf supervise the control of the new evidence.

'You have to be joking. What provocative, cheeky bastards,' I told Winneke, in disbelief.

'Well,' Winneke replied, smiling expansively. 'The Victoria Forensic Unit is going to get first bite, excuse the pun.'

'Hmmm,' I replied, 'Thank God for that.'

Having said our goodbyes to Aidan and Reagan before their travel to Byron Bay Youth Camp and then to Melbourne for holidays, and leaving Kahlia with her foster parents, we packed for our trip to Darwin in preparation for the Royal Commission.

On my 36th plane trip to Darwin we were accompanied by Stuart Tipple, John Winneke and Brind Woinarski. Winneke had put the case together extremely well. We would spend two days at the preliminary hearing for the Royal Commission before returning to Brisbane. Lindy remarked that I was looking as weary as she had ever seen me. Australia's *Mode* magazine had voted me as one of Australia's worst-dressed men for 1985. Apparently it was the way I brushed my hair that had annoyed the magazine!

Three weeks later we would return to Darwin. While on a trip around Darwin, I noticed the Yarrawonga Zoo had the same danger sign (a red and white triangle) on the high fence in 1986 for crocodiles and dingoes.

The most amazing thing about the Church communication, or lack of it, was that Stuart Tipple was still back in Gosford, not aware that the Royal Commission was about to commence in Darwin, just 24 hours later. We were advised that the Commission would run for approximately 10 days between 10am and 4.15pm. The police witness evidence at the Rock and interviews with us would be called first, followed by evidence, for the first time, from the Aboriginal trackers.

We were indeed fortunate that first weekend of this inquiry, 9–10 June, was one of the most enjoyable I could remember. Recognising the great ordeal we would have to endure in court for the next year, Dr Tony Noonan, Lindy and I, with his small son, travelled to Corroboree Lagoon where we spent the day fishing for barramundi. It was only my second visit to the 'Top End' to fish and I had no expectations about my catch. I would be lucky to hook a catfish, I mused and was just a bit concerned about the state of hunger of the crocodiles that lurked the lagoon. However, fortune smiled that day and much to the pleasure of the Noonan's, I hooked into two magnificent barramundi, one that weighed more than three kilograms and the other over six kilograms. It took the 'catch of the day' award. Lindy, an avowed vegetarian, was constrained to eat a small morsel of the catch after being cooked in a fried onion and buttered pan with a topping of coconut milk by the Travel Lodge Chinese chef. With all five lawyers, Winneke, Woinarski, Crispin and Kirkham, including Stuart and Cherie Tipple, Lindy and I enjoyed the night, believing that this might just be the omen of good things to come.

21. The Royal Commission Opens: The Aboriginals' Day in Court

Time magazine depicted the Northern Territory Parliament as having one of two kinds of representatives: the 'redneck cowboy' addicted to development at any cost, with little sympathy for Aboriginal people and their desire for land rights; or the 'bleeding heart wimp', effeminate and un-Territorian. The Northern Territory, the magazine reported, had gained self-government just two years before we lost our daughter at Ayers Rock. It had a population of less than 160,000, smaller than the City of Lake Macquarie in the lower Hunter Valley. One Federal Government minister, Senator John Kerin, had described the Territory as '140,000 people being run by an Apex Club'. In terms of entities this state was 'one of the smallest in the world in population–smaller than most Pacific Island electorates'. Each member was responsible for around 3000 voters, less than 10 per cent of the Australian average.

The Wild West ethos went with the Territory psyche and with a vision of the growth to come. Every Territorian cowboy politician wanted a slice of it. This was around the time when the plight of the Aborigine was being reviewed. Although Aboriginal people had gained the right to vote in 1967, other insidious evils were growing in the name of good government. The Territory Government chafed under the Federal Land

Rights Act in 1976, which allowed the Aboriginal 22 per cent of the population to claim more than 35 per cent of the Territory, a significant amount since the Northern Territory was several times the size of England. The government appeared determined to oppose any further gains by Aboriginal people.

In Darwin, the climate was perfect, with a day's maximum temperature of 26°C, when the Assistant to Commissioner Trevor Morling, a grey-faced, deeply intoned Chester Porter, stood to his feet and addressed the hushed Commission Courtroom. It was 5 June 1986, the first day of the Chamberlain Royal Commission into the death of Azaria Chamberlain. Lindy and I sat expectantly, waiting to hear a non-adversarial approach to our quest for truth. But I was deeply concerned about the original references for this inquiry. Although it was rightfully about determining our innocence or guilt, the Northern Territory had rejected the Lionel Bowen concern about an investigation into who caused this and why this all happened in the first place. Of even more concern for me was that this Royal Commission had no mandate to determine if the dingo was guilty of killing Azaria. A headline in *The Age* (27/2/1986) telling the world that 'The dingo goes on trial again' was sadly misleading. This Royal Commission was not about establishing the dingo's guilt, but only the status of the guilty verdicts and our 'innocence'.

Chester Porter's address (Royal Commission Transcript, pp26-133) was comprehensive. It ran for a day and a half and set a tone much less adversarial to our situation. Porter announced: 'I am here to assist Your Honour into inquiring into both aspects of the case, guilt or innocence... In our (extensive) enquiries no possible motive has turned up for Mrs Chamberlain to kill her baby...

'The position therefore as at the time she went to Ayers Rock was that she was an apparently loving mother, happy with her child and no motive to kill it...the evidence of the witnesses who saw Mrs Chamberlain (at the Rock) that day with her baby is certainly inconsistent with any intention then in her mind of killing the child.

'Rather they give the impression of an affectionate mother. Both of the Chamberlains were persons of excellent character. Michael

Chamberlain, I think as everyone knows, was then a pastor of the Seventh-day Adventist Church. I think this should be said, although it must be obvious to most people, that there is absolutely nothing in the doctrine of the Seventh-day Adventist Church which would in any way suggest the killing of young children. The doctrines of that church are very similar to the evangelical doctrines of many Protestant churches, and they involve a belief in life after death. The doctrines involve various matters that might give comfort to those who lose a relative, and that may become relevant.'

Further in our defence, John Winneke QC stated in his introduction (Royal Commission Transcript, pp144-166): 'We venture to suggest to Your Honour that their trial was unique in this regard in the history of Australian criminal law, in that it fuelled rumour, speculation and innuendo. Very little of that was favourable to the Chamberlains. Rumour, as your Honour will be told, had them as religious fanatics, sorcerers, callous and cunning liars, and notwithstanding the well-motivated intentions of the first coroner in seeking to quell those rumours by announcing his findings on national television, Your Honour will be invited to conclude that the probabilities are that it had the opposite effect.

'Your Honour, our law prides itself on being able to bring people to trial in circumstances of fairness and before a jury free from preconceptions, but we will be submitting that the equipment the law has to ensure a fair trial did not operate in the case of the Chamberlains and that it was impossible, no matter how much care had been taken, to be satisfied that this trial took place in a climate free from preconception.'

On the same morning Winneke delivered this message, a member of the public had approached Porter with the T-shirt 'Darwin's Answer: Lindy is guilty', she had bought in the mall that morning. Morling responded by concluding that these were in the poorest taste possible and requested that the shop responsible would stop selling them immediately. The request was ignored and the sales continued.

Among the first to be called in the Royal Commission were the Aboriginal witnesses, Daisy Walkabout (Royal Commission Transcript, pp217-221) and Barbara Tyikadu, Nipper Winmatti's wife (Royal Commission Transcript, pp283-314). It was virtually six years to the day (10/6/1986) after Azaria was born on 11 June 1980, that Daisy and Barbara would take the stand, at last, using the appropriate protocols with a female interpreter. On the night before this witness presentation I had awoken in a lather of sweat after a nightmare about the Aboriginal trackers. I dreamed that their testimony had been discredited by some clever cross-examination by Ian Barker, who found conflicting testimonies between the Aboriginal witnesses. It was not to be however, to my great relief. Assistant to the Northern Territory Government team was Michael Adams, who commenced an exasperating cross-examination of Daisy. Adams was a large garrulous man. His dark-blue woollen serge pinstripe suit, his bow tie, straw hat and dark glasses made a memorable spectacle.

Daisy stated on oath that when she got to our tent on the night of 17 August 1980: 'What I saw myself was just tracks, the dog's tracks. They were at the tent and then went back. It had been walking around the tent. It was not a camp dog but a wild dingo. The camp dog has short claws; the dingo has sharp ones. These were large.'

Barbara Tyikadu's testimony followed. She was an impressive and convincing presenter on the dingo tracks. She stated: 'The tracks I saw went to the east until we came to the sand hill. The tracks went on where we tracked it, and we could see where he stopped and put down something on the ground where he had a rest. He picked it up and then he went at a fast speed. That's as far as we went and then went back home.'

What the dingo put down, Barbara described as having 'a lot of weight in it' and that: 'I was thinking it was the baby'. The question was then asked of her: 'How do you know the difference between a dingo and a camp dog?' She replied: 'Camp dogs have short nails or claws, whatever they call it, and a dingo has sharp ones and long.'

Barbara's swore on oath that when she went to the place where the clothing was found, a week later, that she 'saw the same dingo tracks' at the dingo den site 'as she saw at the tent...(It was) the big male dingo'.

When asked if Barbara had ever seen those large tracks before she said: 'Yes'.

The interpreter then engaged with Mr Adams, appearing for the Northern Territory Government. Adams strongly argued that the dingo may have been carrying a joey (baby kangaroo) in its mouth and not the baby.

Barbara replied through an interpreter: 'I know it was the child.'

When Mr Adams stood up and asked Barbara if she was sure it wasn't a joey in the dingo's mouth, Barbara and the interpreter became angry with him.

'You are talking your way with your ideas,' Barbara said.

The Commissioner then asked Barbara the question that clearly further annoyed her.

'Could the dingo have been carrying a joey?' he enquired.

After so much tedious examination Barbara now scowled at Justice Morling and said; 'Was there a kangaroo living in the tent?'

The court applauded with laughter.

The testimony of the Aboriginal trackers was the backbone to this case. If they were lying, there was a serious missing link in the evidence to support our stand. If they were right, despite the prosecution conveniently choosing to ignore them, no one dared to say their witness was flawed. Their evidence was prima facie from responsible, credible experts and Barbara was generally acknowledged as the best of the best. Barbara's leadership was later seen when she became a leading land rights exponent for the Territory. They had nothing to gain by their testimony. In any other case their evidence would have been deemed of great importance.

The governments and police forces of Australia have long history in using Aboriginal trackers to capture their quarry. Furthermore, traditional Aborigines don't have a history of telling lies. It does not seem to be in their psyche or thinking. Even if the truth was only through their eyes and not factual, the possibility that they were mistaken was not demonstrated at the Royal Commission.

The *Sunday Press* magazine had already checked out the capabilities of Aboriginal trackers at the Rock in August of 1983, when its reporters, in similar conditions to those three years before, went to the Rock and checked out the now 70-year-old Nipper Winmatti. In his article, 'Nipper knows all the tricks', feature reporter Dennis Williams described him as 'the grizzled tribal elder of the Pitjantjatjara people,' who 'still' believes that a dingo killed Azaria Chamberlain.

Williams decided to try and trick the elders' tracking powers and expertise by concocting an elaborate scheme to clamber over rocks, sand dunes and scrubland surrounding the Ayers Rock campsite from where Azaria disappeared. Changing his shoes several times (even alternating left and right pairs), concealing his shirt in a hole at the rock face, kneeling and dragging himself along the ground and, at one stage wiping away his own tracks, Williams was later surprised to discover that Nipper could show him the scuff marks and tracks he had made across the sand and even locate the writer's hidden shirt. Williams confirmed that Nipper was a 'key figure in the (Azaria) drama' and 'one of the last masters of the age-old bush craft' *(Sunday Press* 21/8/1983).

Following Mr Adams' examination of Nipper Winmatti the Commissioner thanked Nipper for his testimony. The Aboriginal interpreter for the women, a slim, dark-haired Aboriginal lass, Marlene Cousins, had been impressive throughout. Her quiet expressionless face, and determined but vulnerable strength, set against a brutalising and blustering examination of an imposing Adams, evoked a strange power over the large fat man. He had met his match. Such was my admiration, I considered her one of the heroes of the inquiry.

Adams was a fascinating man to watch in action. When John Winneke rose to his feet to cross-examine any former prosecution witness, Adams would sometimes start flapping his knees in and out, his trouser cuffs waving, as if touched by a gentle breeze. It appeared to be a sign of his nervousness. The flapping seemed to accelerate when Winneke was getting close to the bone, raising a touchy point or an area of contradiction that the witness was about to reveal. Adams would then rise to his feet and object, his irritation unmasked.

With the backdrop of Aboriginal testimony setting the scene for dingo involvement, on 13 June we faced the hostility of Darwin's residents. Former Federal Minister for the Aboriginals, Bill Wentworth, had described the hysteria in the city at the time as 'paranoid'. On our lunch break we found it necessary to take refuge in a milk bar near Casey's Corner and ordered a milkshake. A young female attendant served us and decided to sit on the order for 15 minutes. The Northern Territory Parliament also remained hostile. We were warned: 'If they find you innocent they will demonstrate in Darwin'.

Ayers Rock Store manager, Mr Ferguson, blamed the problem on the media misinformation about the way the clothes were found, allegedly 'folded' or 'stuffed in the crevice of a rock'. We knew we had to be vigilant at all times.

Five dingo experts were called to the Royal Commission to testify about the chances of a dingo snatching and killing Azaria. They were: Ranger Cawood, Chief Ranger Roff, Dingo Foundation President, Les Harris, Dr Lionel Corbett and Dr Alan Newsome. Ken Crispin in his book *The Crown versus Chamberlain, 1980-1987*, (pp271-282) summarised their observations after the QC assisting the Commissioner put the following questions:

'In or about August 1980, was it within the bounds of reasonable possibility that a dingo might attack a human baby?

Ranger Cawood: Yes.

Head Ranger Roff: Yes.

Dingo Foundation President Harris: Yes, Given the increased need for food, possible reduction of food, I would say that it is...an outright acquisition of prey.

Dr Corbett: Yes I think it is possible, but unlikely. (The Northern Territory Police had led Corbett to believe that Azaria was already dead when the dingo took her out of the tent.)

Dr Newsome, CSIRO scientist: Yes.

Was it within reasonable bounds that a dingo might carry away the baby for consumption of food?

Cawood: Yes.

Roff: Yes.

Harris: Well, at the risk of sounding silly, it would not have taken the baby for any other reason whatsoever but food...It would have removed it to a place where it was unlikely to be challenged for possession.

Dr Corbett: I think it is possible; but again, unlikely.

Dr Newsome: Yes.

Would the dingo have the ability to carry the weight of a nine-and-a-half-pound baby?

Cawood: Yes.

Roff: Yes.

Harris: Yes, quite easily.

Dr Corbett: A dingo can move a nine-and-a-half pound baby from A to B, yes.

Dr Newsome: That would depend on the distance.

Assuming a den is four to six kilometres away, would it be able to carry a baby that far?

Cawood: It could take the baby near to where the clothes were found.

Roff: Right to the den...It would be a reasonable range... to where it was seeking to feed its puppies.

Harris: I can only draw on my general observations over more than a decade in the field and in captivity, and my opinion that a distance of four to five kilometres and the weigh of about 10 pounds would present absolutely no problem for a dingo.

Dr Corbett: It would get the baby that far, yes.

Dr Newsome: I'd imagine that it wouldn't be able to carry that kind of weight clear of the ground the entire way.

Does a dingo normally or occasionally bury its prey?

Cawood: Yes, for various reasons (at Ayers Rock) but it is not its normal habit.

Roff: Yes, dingoes in the vicinity of Ayers Rock do.

Harris: This seems to vary...but the answer is yes, the dingo does seem to bury its prey from time to time...

Dr Corbett: I have not seen dingoes burying prey.

Dr Newsome was not asked this question.

Would a dingo be reluctant to enter a tent at Ayers Rock?

The answers given by Ayers Rock tourists and members of the public, including Richard Dare, Rohan Delgliesh, Peter Elston and Derek Roff, indicated that 'dingoes frequently entered tents at camping areas near Ayers Rock.'

Were puppies in existence at Ayers Rock during July and August of 1980?

To this question all five dingo experts answered, Yes.'

The senior police constable confirmed this when he was asked:

'Was at any time a dingo seen near where the clothes were found?

Constable Morris stated: "Yes, a lactating bitch was shot."'

Dr Corbett agreed that his knowledge of Ayers Rock dingoes was very limited and 'readily conceded that Chief Ranger Roff would be well informed about contacts between dingoes and humans at Ayers Rock at the relevant time.' Despite this, the Crown relied more heavily on Corbett and Newsome at the Darwin trial.

If Ian Barker had satirised the 'dexterous dingo' notion it was now becoming plain how cunning, adaptive and manipulative dingoes could be in tourist situations where hunger and familiarity with humans was a key factor.

Corbett, Harris and Tony Raymond, a new key expert on various issues in our case, indicated that dingoes were unpredictable. The Crown's contentions were flawed in their a priori views about what their 'experts' would expect and not expect a dingo to do. The Royal Commission was drawing evidence on what dingoes have been observed to do in specific and general contexts. When the father of the Attorney-General, Marshall Perron, gave evidence at the Commission a new dimension was added: the taking of Aboriginal babies by dingoes, were never recorded because the British Government did not require it.

This was all very well, but the major conundrum was how a dingo might leave its evidence on attacking and killing a small human. So far, the Crown forensic evidence had been totally unenlightening–in fact, worse, misleading; since it had failed to understand that any dingo attack on Azaria would have been possible. Was this failure due to genuine incompetence or was it more sinister in its desire to not want to find the truth?

The vital area for any enlightening new evidence was Azaria's clothing. Tony Raymond made the observation that in doll experiments at the Healsville sanctuary in Victoria, dingoes could pick up the doll and make no observable damage to any clothing. But when they took on a dead animal Raymond observed, 'They would go for the head first', just as a real dingo expert had told him.

Richard Dare described how a dingo could 'gently unwrap' a cake sealed in aluminum foil with no significant tears.

Derek Roff had observed a dingo unwrap a bar of chocolate. He described this as 'extremely amazing the way it did it, without ripping and tearing'. When dingoes were not aware of being observed, they became 'very fastidious...and extremely efficient'.

Les Harris described dingoes as 'thoughtful and methodical', able to 'unwrap things with care and consideration'.

Dr Corbett agreed that dingoes could easily open press-studs with their nose or teeth.

Neither Corbett nor London odontologist Bernard Sims, giving evidence at the Darwin trial, had been privy to the Adelaide experiment with dingoes. When the jumpsuit was opened, with no damage to the clothing and just two press-studs undone, it was identical to the way Azaria's clothing was left at a dingo lair at Ayers Rock. But the Northern Territory police and forensic division ignored this remarkable behaviour.

In Wally Goodwin's description of finding Azaria's clothing, the jumpsuit lay on its back with the feet in the air and the neck of the garment facing a large rock; the feet pointed towards the road from where his family had walked down a worn animal track; the singlet was inside the jumpsuit, with the nappy lying to the right with torn pieces of nappy lining scattered about; the mystery, including the booties left in the jumpsuit, was about to be solved.

When Tony Raymond watched dingoes removing clothing from life-sized dolls, the dingoes pulled on the extremities of the jumpsuit, which parted company with the doll with the booties still left in the jumpsuit. This was identical to the manner in which Azaria's booties were found in her jumpsuit. Raymond was satisfied he had the answer.

The Crown in the Darwin trial had dismissed these initial experiments as 'failures' because the results 'looked wrong'. It did not fit their theory. The prosecution had used 'dingo experts', pathologists from London and Canada, places that contained a paucity of dingoes. Corbett and Cawood did have behavioural knowledge of dingoes but had never seen evidence of their damage to clothing. With Newsome, they had expressed surprise at the small amount of damage done to the clothing. Sims had been the only odontologist among them and he expressed the view that more 'florid' damage should have been done. It was theoretical knowledge, out of touch with the reality of the wild (Ken Crispin, *The Crown versus Chamberlain, 1980-1987*, pp271-282).

Our excursion to Darwin's Gunpoint Beach afforded us a much-needed rest. Across the endless sand line we could just make out through the smoky bushfire haze an image of Darwin's landmark Casuarina hospital. Here Kahlia had been born under prison guard. The flashback of media in hot pursuit, a one-week-old baby in tow, the dash to the airport and the war of words with the jail and Northern Territory authorities still felt like a ridiculous dream. I turned to Lindy. She looked attractive, wise and serene, her gently tanned olive skin contrasting pleasingly against a clear sunset deep blue sky.

Next day, we drove a tired late model red Falcon, to the Royal Commission. This was the unimpressive vehicle that the honourable gentlemen in the Northern Territory Law Department had chosen to provide my legal counsel with. At the parking bay in the Darwin police station there was a sign marked, 'Chamberlain Inquiry Counsel'. Rubbish in the form of plastic bags, cigarette cartons, beer cans and the odd smashed brown beer bottle were strewn over the parking bay; red carpet treatment, Territory Police-style.

By our final day in Darwin, Friday 20 June 1986, we were just glad to get out of the place. Several journalists had dinner with us the night before at the Darwin Beaufort Japanese Restaurant, including a young female reporter from the *Australian*, Steven Fennelly from Channel 9 and Kevin Hitchcock, Channel 10. This was undeniably their reconnaissance mission to see what sort of people we really were. We were not particularly worried about them reporting on us, but they were asked not to bring their film crews nor their notebooks. It was a wonderful night for us and we did not return home until late.

As we arrived at the Darwin Air Terminal, all the now-familiar court faces were clamouring to get home to the south on a special direct plane from Darwin to Sydney. Commissioner Morling, his assistant Chester Porter, and their assistants were all present. 'Dear God,' I whispered, 'please don't let anything unfortunate befall this plane.'

To add to the flavour of the trip, Stuart Tipple said: 'Now Michael, the judge is going on the same plane so you will have to pay special attention to your dietary habits. (He had already regaled me on an earlier trip for eating blueberry yogurt with cornflakes). He will be watching you, so it will be terribly important to be careful.'

'I thought judges were objective and were more interested in what eats you than what you ate,' I replied dryly.

'They are also human, mate,' he retorted.

I don't know if Stuart had known anything of the plane's seating arrangements, but to my horror Morling sat in the second back row of the plane while Lindy and I were allocated in the back seats, just behind him. He may not know what I ate but he could hear everything I said.

22. *Forensic Evidence Feels the Dingo's Breath*

We had just purchased our mountainous property in Lake Macquarie, adjacent to Forestry Commission lands. While our financial state was no longer precarious, we still owed a couple of hundred thousand dollars. Nevertheless, it was a fresh start. In honour of Kahlia and her second name we called it 'Nikari Park'. Lindy was quite tired and strained and not looking forward to returning to the Commission in Darwin, where all the spurious forensic evidence would be dredged up again. We worked hard on the property to plant seedlings and cacti, before our long journey back to the Commission hearing scheduled for 4 August 1986. I was worried about leaving our children for a month while we sat in court. This and my regular nocturnal trips to the refrigerator, due to an insomnia condition, created strain and premature ageing. My fitness regime had given way to providing assistance and advice to our very alert legal team.

Aidan, now nearly 12 years old, would get his day in court this time and was looking forward to it. His special moment would come when Ian Barker would cross-examine him and he was keen to bring this on.

My thirty-eighth trip to Darwin on Ansett 64 via Alice Springs had been in first class to Darwin's Travel Lodge Hotel. It was a sign of the times. It was quite an improvement on the refurbished fowl house at the back of the Adventist Pastor's residence, which we stayed in during the 1982 trial. But the exclusivity of a first-class ticket came with isolation and the need to be in a secure place.

The Crown's trial prosecution evidence in 1982 was about to be investigated in a way the Northern Territory Government, Police and Law Department would have nightmares about. The Aboriginal evidence discriminated against and discarded by the Northern Territory Police had revealed a dark side of Territory law.

All the Ayers Rock lay witnesses present on 17 August 1980 would be re-examined; some with a vengeance. The Northern Territory Crown tried to allege that the baby in the picture with Lindy taken at Ayers Rock on Sunday at around 3pm, was someone else's child, and not Azaria! However, Judy West, the camper next door to our tent on that night, was adamant they were one and the same person in Lindy's care. Chester Porter announced that he was satisfied with Azaria's identification. 'Phew,' exclaimed Winneke loudly for all the court to hear and then ponder what would be the Territory's next desperate tactic.

Just a few minutes later in court, Michael Adams lent back in his chair too far. All heard the unmistakable crack as it fell apart. For the third time Adams' weight had managed to demolish a courtroom chair. It did him no harm, it seemed. Later in his career he was elevated to a judge's chair.

It was now 17 August 1986. Azaria would have been six years and three months old today. The Northern Territory Support group, Liz Noonan, Annette Bailey and the Support Group sent flowers to our hotel. During our conversation the hotel phone in our room continued to make annoying noises, as if wires were crossed. What was new? Our phones had been behaving strangely for years.

The Royal Commission inquiry evidence resumed on 1 October 1986, this time at the Federal Court Building in Little Bourke Street, Sydney. Having covered all the witness testimony and the expert evidence on dingoes, in Darwin, it was now time to shine the spotlight on the maze of forensic evidence that had cast doubt on our truthfulness. I couldn't wait.

The inherent danger of the police being the primary and authoritative agents in collecting evidence in this case was their partiality and the worry that they may have excluded vital evidence. The confusion and lack of expert coordination in our case remained a source of constant pain in the search for the right answers. Had an independent specialist task force been initially considered as the supervisory body and an independent scientific forensic laboratory used from the beginning, the truth could have been found much sooner, and at a fraction of the expense. At last this was happening and a host of independent scientists were about to be called to analyse essentially the secret evidence that had been used to quash the first inquest and to railroad us to trial.

There were a few moments of joy with a number of friends and associates greeting me at court. Among them was Pastor Peter Joseit, my old German roommate from Avondale College, from my ministerial student days in the 1960s. I also meet Sir Reginald Sholl and author John Bryson. These were treasured moments for Lindy and me. The mood was changing in the street—a far cry from the Darwin experience. People were stopping us and wishing us good luck. The courtroom, usually packed with journalists and legal people, was now filling with well-wishers and friends.

Ian Barker seemed to recognise that the writing was on the wall for the Northern Territory and in a moment of wry humour, signalled to my legal team the possible demise of the London forensic evidence given by Professor James Cameron and Brian Culliford. (Cameron, we had heard was in a wheelchair, and he was not keen to return to Australia.) In 1982, the jury was treated to a Dorothy Dix question from Ian Barker about whether there was the slightest chance of a dingo killing Azaria. Professor Cameron answered, poker-faced, that he 'could not contemplate a situation where a dingo could wield a sharp instrument for the purpose of cutting a child's throat.' (*Northern Territory News* 2/11/1982).

New and formidable odontologists were in court to give evidence at this session of the Royal Commission. Cameron was about to learn how good his work had really been. These new world experts understood the nature of canine teeth and the cutting effects on Azaria's jumpsuit, something that wasn't available at the trial. One of these men was Professor Gustafson, described as 'the father of forensic odontology'. He had written the first book on the subject in 1966 and was still widely regarded as the leading expert on forensic odontological matters. This white-haired, 80-year-old's eyes still sparkled and his knowledge remained encyclopedic. His testimony was that he had observed the 'shearing action' of canine teeth and that the alleged scissor cuts on Azaria's jumpsuit were also capable of being duplicated by the shearing action of dingo teeth.

The misunderstanding of such evidence by Professor Malcolm Chaikin had been one of the main causes of our guilty verdict. It was amazing how this professional expert, with high academic credentials, could persuade a jury that he really knew what he was talking about. They had given a big tick to Chaikin despite the vigorous cross-examination by John Phillips QC in the Darwin trial. Chaikin had claimed that he was an expert in dingo-cut material, but Phillips was on to him when it became apparent that he knew much less than it appeared.

During the 1982 Supreme Court trial (Transcript, pp1113-1134), under cross-examination, Phillips had asked Chaikin:

'Can we just return to the question I asked you? Apart from the zoo jumpsuit, you have not examined any clothing that's been bitten by a dingo?

Chaikin: Correct.

Phillips: Have you examined the body of any person that has been bitten by a dingo?

Chaikin: No.

Phillips: Have you seen a living dingo bite anything?

Chaikin: No.

Phillips: Have you seen a live dingo?

Chaikin: Yes.

Phillips: Where?

Chaikin: Ayers Rock.

Phillips: Right. That didn't bite anything in your presence?

Chaikin: No.

Phillips: Well, in uttering the opinion that you have, you do it without having seen any of the matters we have just discussed, don't you?

Chaikin: Well, I claim that I have some expertise in the interaction between various objects with various properties and fabrics, and fibre assemblies, and I base my opinion and conclusions on that.

Phillips: I will repeat the question. In stating the opinion that you have, that it is not a dingo tooth that produced the damage, you do that without ever seeing a live dingo bite anything, don't you?

Chaikin: That's correct.

Phillips: Yes or no, please?

Chaikin: Yes.

Phillips: You state it without ever having examined the clothing of a person who has been bitten by a dingo, don't you?

Chaikin: 'I have as I said, carried out experiments with dingo teeth on this particular fabric.'

Phillips: Will you please answer my question? You state that opinion without ever having examined the clothing of a person who has been bitten by a dingo?

Chaikin: That's correct.'

Now at the Royal Commission, (Transcript, pp5183-338; 5511-39; 6490-7025) Chaikin came up with a new technical term that he called 'planar array' which meant 'all in a line'. The term had not been used in any scientific publications that I know of prior to his Commission appearance. Chaikin claimed that one could determine the difference between a dingo incisor cut and a scissor cut alone, through 'planar array'. Professor Gustafson and Professor Fernhead, now a Chair of a Japanese university and formerly a Professor at London and Hong Kong University, both rejected Chaikin's interpretation. Fernhead, who had taught Dr Bernard Sims (who had sided with Dr Kenneth Brown in his determination to prove that no teeth mark evidence was present on the jumpsuit) was in strong disagreement with Sims and Brown. Another eminent odontologist, Dr Hector Orams, rated as Australia's foremost expert on the odontological discipline, also gave evidence agreeing that the 214 millimetres of cutting damage to Azaria's jumpsuit was 'quite consistent with causation by the teeth of a dingo'.

That these eminent men unanimously agreed that it was dingo damage to the jumpsuit was based largely on the ground-breaking work of the unheralded and unknown scientists, Les Smith and Ken Chapman. Smith and Chapman's extensive experiments and analysis found that two types of products could be produced from observing Azaria's jumpsuit. These were 'tufts' and 'snippets'. In analysis of other dingoes' canine action of material consistent with Azaria's jumpsuit, the same tufts and snippets were identified.

Chaikin had maintained that only scissors could create this. But the experiments of Smith and Chapman were confirmed in the laboratories of the Victorian Forensic Science unit and had proven Chaikin wrong. The thrust of the Darwin trial that dingo teeth could not cut but only tear, had now become irrelevant. During Professor Fernhead's evidence, Barker had slumped into his chair, red pen in his mouth, eyes closed and shaking his head. It seemed as if he was not happy. Barker and the Northern Territory Attorney-General's Department now requested permission to find new evidence to the contrary to shore up their 'murder' claims.

The Crown had come up against another problem in 'array' which had caused considerable 'disarray' in their ranks. They were unsure whether to back a cut by scissors, a knife, a hammer or something else. The defence at the Royal Commission also felt the need to do more research but unlike the Crown, was refused any money for travel. Fortunately, the Church came to the party and my lawyers were also able to travel to Europe over the new year of 1987 for new information.

The Crown, in desperation, now sought to subpoena all our letters and my diaries. At midday on 23 January, the Royal Commission staff flew to the Avondale Airfield and proceeded to our house in College Drive and took my diaries and other written material. In the final analysis, there was nothing of any significance that the diaries could add to the court's evidence that was not already known.

The Royal Commission was not always a place of high drama and intrigue. It had tested the abilities of some of the reporters, causing daydreams and glazed eyes. When a new ABC reporter arrived at court, he drew attention to himself early in the proceedings, dropping off to sleep, head cocked back and his mouth wide open. His notebook was full of doodles. From time to time he sat bolt upright. But within minutes his head began to droop and his eyes would close again. But he wasn't the only person to create a stir. Occasionally a female assistant to the Northern Territory Crown would look over at my legal team and at me and smirk as if to say, 'Gotcha that time'.

Lindy would now get her chance to give her evidence again but away from the prejudiced context of a Darwin jury. Porter proceeded to lead in an emotionally charged examination of her and it seemed that Morling, at one stage, was fighting to hold his emotions. Even the stony-faced Ms Fullerton, assisting Michael Adams and Ian Barker for the Northern Territory, appeared to wipe a tear from her eyes, but then I might have been imagining it. While Lindy was in the witness box being examined by Porter, Adams and Barker sat slumped in their chairs with heads down. It was different from giving evidence before a captivated, parochial jury.

On cue, when Barker stood up to cross-examine Lindy, she was rehearsed and ready. Barker's cross-examination and the price she had paid for this was ringing in her ears. In her strident no-holds barred attack, she fired a salvo across the bows of an astonished Barker with the exclamation: 'I do not like you, Mr Barker. I never have and I never will'. This extraordinary outburst recorded the desired effect: a perfect front-page headline for the *Daily Telegraph* (11/2/1987) on the following day.

I had also planned to express my dissatisfaction in court at Barker's methods but that had been trumped by Lindy. Yet, I did not begrudge her the chance to get even on that memorable day in 1987. I don't think I would have said what she said but it was her day in court and she would get away with it. Justice Morling might have cheered inside but he had to maintain courtroom decorum. He rebuked Lindy for her outburst and warned her that the court would not allow this to continue.

Ian Barker's wife came in to court for the first time, perhaps as a show of strength for her husband or just to see some fireworks. I thought at one stage that I saw a long stare from her in our direction. I returned the stare, not realising at the time who she was. But Lindy said what she wanted to say, and Morling's rebuke seemed little more than a formality.

Barker's case at the trial was that if Lindy had seen the dingo leave the tent and if Les Harris's claim that dingoes hold their heads up high when carrying prey, why did she not see what was in its mouth? It seemed a fair question. Lindy maintained that all she had seen was a dingo with its head low shaking something. She admitted seeing nothing in its mouth. If Lindy could meticulously describe its head and ears to a jury why could she not say anything about its mouth? The answer may lie in the fact that the tent had a triangular entrance with the narrowest point at the top. For a dingo to negotiate a load, the lower it held it, considering that the flap was wider at the base, the easier the animal could have executed its departure with its head down at the lowest point.

Lindy's response was that there had been a low railing in front of the tent that had created a shadow from a 100-watt lamp 20 metres away at the barbecue area. That answer was verifiable, as I remember the railing and the light myself. Speculation was rife after this point, as no one had ever witnessed a dingo move through tent flaps with a live baby in its jaws in similar conditions. If there had been two dingoes, a view that both Derek Roff and Dr Newsome considered a possibility, then Lindy had seen the wrong animal.

But to make too much of this was to attempt to stereotype human behaviour when plainly every individual has potentially a different way of reacting. 'To know something is true and to accept it, are two different things,' she reflected, under inquiry examination. To add weight to her thinking, three other witnesses at Ayers Rock, shortly after Azaria's disappearance, did exactly the same thing. Derek Roff, Frank Morris and I, all disbelievingly checked the tent to see if Lindy had been mistaken about Azaria's absence.

In the matter of Lindy having enough time to accomplish the horrendous deed, in an estimated ten minutes, a time and motion study, with the added problem of Aidan present, was deemed ridiculous (Transcript, pp8051-8375). According to Dr Norman Young, Chester Porter was not fooled in being able to discriminate between Lindy's 'natural tendency toward vivid and perhaps exaggerated storytelling, so that by the time she told the story at least 20 or 30 times so as to put it on the record with the media and police, it was really quite surprising how few variations there were between the numerous versions of the story.' If Barker had mistaken her for being 'a fanciful liar', other witnesses had severely disappointed him in this accusation.

Another misconception that the Crown attempted to get away with were the observations made of Azaria's purple woollen-nylon blend blanket before its trip to Ayers Rock. I was not aware of any damage to this item nor were Lindy or the dry cleaner, Mrs Hansell, at Mount Isa. But after the Ayers Rock attack on Azaria I maintain to this day there were rip or cut-like marks in this item. When I saw it after it had been in the hands of the Crown forensic scientists it looked like it had been shrunk or washed. It was claimed by the police-controlled forensic team that 'insects' had created the marks. The blanket was of a synthetic/woollen mix and, because of the way we stored our blankets, it would have been highly unlikely that any 'insect' would have got anywhere near them, let alone have been desperate enough to attack an unpalatable synthetic blend. Certainly the 'cut marks' appeared to have shrunk. I was shocked. Hillary Tabrett, a witness at the Royal Commission, saw what she said were 'cuts' in the blanket days after it had been to the Rock. When forensic odontologist Dr Pelton examined it he was also sceptical of insect damage being the cause.

The onerous and irksome task of describing and defending my own comments and reactions to questions and responses to the events on that night seen in a negative light by the Crown should be dealt with here. At the trial, I was criticised on a number of contexts. Firstly, that I did not do much searching on the night. The answer: I made three or four sweeps in the first hour to hour and a half within 200 metres of the base of the Rock, to satisfy my feelings that all close areas had been covered. My torch was marginal and I could not have seen more than a few metres into the pitch-black moonless night. My first attempt to search with Greg Lowe and its futility are well documented. In the end, I was told to remain close to the search base at our tent after 9.30pm for any information about Azaria's whereabouts. I was following instructions from the police or rangers to remain with Lindy and the children.

One of the officials remarked that if I looked to the south there were a hundred or so people with torches and I should take comfort that if anything could be found, it would be. Therefore I should stay with Lindy because there was really nothing else useful that I could do. Unfortunately, on the night there was no news, and no news the next day or up until we were advised to leave the Rock. Later, when I was told by the police that they had no information I thought this was odd. Aboriginal trackers and witnesses who had seen dingo paw print material impressions in the sand on the night, and dingo tracks that showed a dingo was carrying something in its mouth were not passed on to me by the police during our stay. Detective Sergeant John Lincoln also saw evidence of dingo attack and this information wasn't communicated either.

Any alleged failure by me to rigorously enquire about the progress of the search was answered by the fact that we were told to wait for any answers by Senior Constable Frank Morris, of which there was none while we stayed at the Rock.

The body language, and looks on the faces of the searchers, police and rangers conveyed an answer that defied any question of hope. But what was really strange, now looking back, was why Senior Constable Frank Morris told us nothing when there was plainly information out there to be declared to us and that we had every right to be told the next morning, and weren't. It was not me who should have been interrogated about the efficacy of my searching, but Morris for failing to disclose relevant information. While at the Rock during the first inquest, Morris came up to me and apologised for our travail. His words: 'Sorry Mr Chamberlain. I was only doing my duty', were strange. It was an uncomfortable moment.

Another fault I was accused of at the trial was that I gave varying descriptions of the nature of Azaria's cry shortly before Lindy saw the dingo; the various minor changes in the descriptions of her cry were ultimately analysed as: 'slight differences...of no great consequence.' Along with Sally Lowe there was confirmation that Azaria was heard to give a short cry, sounding squeezed and cut off.

I was accused of a failure to exhibit 'sufficient grief' in the 24 hours following Azaria's disappearance, and failure to exhibit sufficient hope in her being found alive or in any shape that could be saved, was explained by our gut conviction. We were both in a state of shock and denial. Azaria had gone and all we could do was reflect with a brave face and stoic attitude. To accuse Lindy or me of faking anything was preposterous. Not one close friend or family member thought we had reacted out of character or disingenuously.

I was also criticised for my description of a large amount of blood in the tent. I had been accused in the Crown's summing up that my description had been 'patently ridiculous.' In this the Crown relied on the jury to find me to be a 'liar' and they seemed to have been successful. There was, in fact, a large amount of blood in the tent on a foam mattress, which had seeped into the material covering and the foam of that bedding. The blood covered the area, overall, of that of a saucer. The amount of blood I saw was far in excess of any other quantity ever verified as blood.

Finally, my questions to Derek Roff some 40 minutes after Azaria's loss, that I did not expect to find Azaria alive, was based on several obvious facts: the temperature was at freezing point. Dogs make a real mess of small animals in a short time. Greg Lowe said: 'There's not going to be any joy for you, mate, if you find her'. I felt instinctively that I had to be prepared to face the worst possible scenario if she were found, and I would not have wanted to see her body, so horrific would be the damage. As a hunter and farmer's son I had seen enough evidence of animal attacks on lambs. In my question to Roff, I was hoping to find solace that Azaria's death would not have involved any pain or suffering. I had put him in a difficult position. Later, he wrote a letter to Lindy and me offering his deepest sympathy for our loss, an act by a former policeman and senior ranger one would not expect had there been the slightest doubt in his mind about Azaria's cause of death. In these matters, my responses at the Royal Commission to Justice Morling, in principle, found no fault in my answers.

In Crispin's summary of the Royal Commission evidence, what had been determined was that: 'Many of the grounds for suggesting that Lindy and I had lied, were based on serious misconceptions (used against us at the trial). We were now vindicated (by the Royal Commission) from those misguided attempts to accuse us.' Any evidence that we might have tried to keep people away from our car, just a metre from the side of our tent, and the alleged place where Lindy was supposed to have killed Azaria, had not been forthcoming. In fact, we had invited people to the car shortly after Azaria's disappearance.

Other important facts emerging from the Commission included:

- There was strong evidence that dog 'guard hairs' (hairs that surround the mouths of dingoes) were present on the jumpsuit.
- The tears in the baby's blanket could no longer be attributed to insect damage.
- Any marks or alleged 'handprints' on the back of Azaria's jumpsuit were not caused by a bloody handprint, but by red sand.
- There was indeed a matinee jacket on Azaria that without having been worn, might have confused scientists into thinking the flow of blood was more indicative of a cut throat than a bleeding and crushed head.
- The blood on the jumpsuit appeared to have been post-mortem bleeding. Consequently, death was less likely to have been caused by an incised 'cut to the throat', as stated on Azaria's death certificate.
- Paw prints had been seen on a silver space blanket, the thermal sheet placed over Azaria at night.
- The teeth of dingoes could duplicate the cuts on Azaria's jumpsuit in creating both 'tufts' and 'snippets'.

Sergeant Barry William Graham, who was stationed at Mount Isa Police on 30 September 1980 and was now a retired police detective was subpoenaed to the Royal Commission (Transcript, pp2056-287). The unearthing of this witness proved to be a very important jigsaw piece for the puzzle of the prosecution's strategy. His examination of my car for blood for nearly three hours in 1980 at Mount Isa was now exposed by Chester Porter's examination.

'Porter: Is it correct that you were examining substantially for bloodstains?

Graham: That's correct.

Porter: Did you examine the interior of the vehicle?

Graham: Yes.

Porter: The front?

Graham: Yes.

Porter: The rear?

Graham: Yes.

Porter: The seats?

Graham: Yes.

Porter: The console?

Graham: Yes.

Porter: The dashboard?

Graham: Yes.

Porter: The hood?

Graham: Yes.

Porter: The underfelt?

Graham: Yes.

Porter: The luggage compartment?

Porter: Yes.'

Porter: Did you find any suspicious staining whatsoever?

Graham: No, Sir.'

I had to pinch myself at this revelation. Where was this evidence at the trial? Why hadn't it been presented?

Had there been any blood in the car at all, it was certainly not Azaria's. Small amounts may have been found as a result of nosebleeds from either Aidan or Reagan, post Ayers Rock in 1980, and there was the possibility that small amounts of Keyth Lenehan's blood might have been in the car. But no blood was found.

The stains on Lindy's tracksuit pants, to which she had alerted others, were not proven to be blood.

Any blood in the car, including the carpets, had not been detectable at all.

The much-publicised 'arterial spurt of foetal blood' under the dashboard of my Torana was proven to be bitumen sound deadener used in all Holden Toranas. In 1986 General Motors Holden (GMH) informed us that it was in fact Dufix 101 sound deadener from the spray of a GMH paint gun. The rest of the blood 'awash in the car' was, among other corrupted things, a spilled milkshake. The fine blood spray on the tent wall where Azaria had slept that night would remain a 'mystery' to the Commission.

23. The Morling Royal Commission Report

We travelled from Sydney to Darwin on 3 March 1987, hopefully the last trip for a very long time. I think Lindy was now anticipating a positive ending. I was almost in the mood to joke with the team, for they were certainly very relaxed with me. I even began to detect a change in direction from the Northern Territory Crown.

Chester Porter QC opened the final submissions to the Royal Commission with a two-hour address. He stated that because it could not be demonstrated beyond reasonable doubt that there was foetal blood in the car, therefore the inference of guilt could not be drawn. Porter also revealed, 'although the majority of three (High Court) judges to five did in fact hold that there was evidence to support the jury's verdict, that does not mean that the majority held that the jury's verdict was in fact right'. Porter admitted that the evidence given to the High Court (by the prosecution) had changed 'quite dramatically'.

John Winneke QC's summing up of the Commission evidence on 10 March, 1987 gave no grounds for the Crown to feel good. He took five days to explain why the trial verdict was 'unsafe and unsound' (Transcript, pp9396-9449). Barker was there in body but to my observation not in spirit. Most of the time he was slumped in his chair, his eyes closed. Occasionally he would wake up and jot down a note.

Winneke continued: 'This is not a case where an alleged murder victim had disappeared in circumstances of isolation with opportunities to kill and dispose of a body that are obvious; rather this was a case where the alleged victim disappeared from a public camping area within metres of persons known to be there by Mrs Chamberlain and where hundreds of people responded within minutes to her call for help.

'It was, accordingly, not a case where there was a shortage of reliable and independent witnesses to the events surrounding the disappearance of the victim. On the contrary, there were campers, locals, police, rangers and Aboriginal trackers. These people, we submit, have almost universally supported the Chamberlains—and with good reason.

'It must, indeed, be a very strange murder case, giving rise to very strong doubts, when the chief ranger of the National Park...maintains and has always maintained that not only was the mother's explanation for the disappearance of her child an inherently believable one because of the behavioural patterns that had been established by dingoes at the time, but that...he has absolutely no doubt that, tragic and unusual though it may have been, Azaria Chamberlain was, in fact, taken by a dingo... He does not stand alone. Every person closely associated with the Chamberlains on that night and who assisted in the search for their child, entertained no doubt as to the truth of the mother's explanation.'

The morning session of 10 March finished with some of the most telling remarks of the Commission, and some moments of humour. Winneke at one stage suggested that Professor Cameron's testimony was about as useful as 'Freddy the Frog's' evidence. It provoked the reply from Barker: 'If it had been Freddy the Frog's evidence you would have jumped at it.' In the afternoon Winneke read High Court Justice Brennan's evidence and at the end of it Morling exclaimed: 'I have already told Justice Brennan that this is the only chance I will probably ever have to overrule a High Court.'

Winneke continued: 'It (the Crown) predicates that they (the Chamberlains), one or either of them, sat down in the early hours of the morning with an armoury of equipment, be it scissors, tweezers, knives, sharp-pointed instruments or any other variety of weapons for the purposes of inflicting a variety of damage to the jumpsuit, singlet and nappy. The case postulates that quite coincidentally they were able to inflict upon the jumpsuit damage in the manner, which the evidence suggests that no layperson could have foreseen. It suggests that in doing this they studiously avoided the outer garment, the matinee jacket, and inflicted damage solely on the undergarment...(and) that they were able to inflict damage upon the nappy, which parallels, we submit the evidence shows, in the minutest way (in the dark), known dog damage.

'It (the Crown) postulates that they then jogged three kilometres in the dark, found a dingo den that even Roff and Cawood did not know existed, that they flattened the vegetation in a manner consistent with a way it would look if a dog had lain there and managed to do it in a way so as to ensure that it was still seen a week later, and on the way they dropped off the matinee jacket, having dragged it around at ground height so as to collect the ground-hugging calotis seed; that they then ran on with the remainder of the clothes and picked out a rare species of paretaria and rubbed the jumpsuit and singlet in it and in the course of doing this or some other time they rubbed the clothes so heavily in soil so as to thoroughly impregnate the garment and collect a teaspoonful of soil inside it, but making sure that they got that soil from different locations.'

In further describing the expert opinion evidence in the trial presented by the prosecution, Winneke said that Lindy and I would have needed had the combined skills of odontologists, textile experts, botanists and bush walkers to understand it. 'Having so meticulously planned and executed this operation they then simply drop the clothes in a heap, leaving booties within the jumpsuit in a manner which any layman would think was quite inconsistent with the way a dog would leave them...As if to put the icing on the cake, (they) threw a few dog hairs in for good measure.'

Winneke concluded: 'The Chamberlains were the victims of it (the Northern Territory investigation) and suffered a gross miscarriage of justice on account of it...the Crown skated from one hypothesis to another...It is not, we submit, a murder case. It is rather a chameleon and a nightmare for the people charged.' (Royal Commission Transcript, pp9396-9449).

After the fifth day of Winneke's submissions on 13 March 1987, it was time to relax at our hotel. Fifteen people crowded into the Sheraton VIP room but not for a victory party—we still had to face Barker's wily defence, the judges seeming equivocating stance and Chester Porter's unwillingness to find a scapegoat except the one in the past—us. Senator Bob Collins was there also, now as the endorsed Federal Senator for the Northern Territory.

Lindy and I forgot our anxiety for four and a half hours and laughed about all the funny things that happened during the inquiry: flying in small single-engine planes; what we considered to be the inconsistencies and viciousness of some Northern Territory politicians; the police politics and the hopelessness of ever obtaining any fairness from a Northern Territory legal institution without the moderating factors from the federal spheres. I then went to the local Adventist church, still feeling shell-shocked.

Ian Barker again launched a scathing attack on our credibility in his summing up. His assistant, Michael Adams, dressed in a black and white straw hat, then led the charge. Adams commenced his presentation after lunch on 17 March, and sent Chester Porter to sleep for a time, gesticulating with his arms as if frustrated. Shortly afterwards, Morling stopped him and asked him if he was not heading into the realms of fantasy. In the end, Adams was thrashing around in a sea of words, hoping that he might find meaning—but it was not to be.

The following day Adams again arrived in a hot winter-weight pinstripe suit, wearing the black and white sun hat. On 19 March, Winneke stood up to address Adams' arguments. Adams often looked over at him, appearing astounded at Winneke's exegesis. Ms Fullerton had a look which appeared to say; 'How much more of this can we stand?'

But Barker sat stoic-like, his jaw set. For Barker the inquiry had been like trying to 'run through treacle'. (Ian Barker, 'Forensic Science and the Dingo' *Bar News Journal of the New South Wales Bar Association*, Summer 1987).

We flew out at 8.45am on 20 March 1987, from Darwin to return home in a direct flight to Sydney. We were confident this time that justice would be done, but we had been waiting for seven years. The media thought we were ahead on points—well ahead—but we had been there before.

At the terminal we were all in first class. There was Justice Trevor Morling again but this time with his wife; his assistants, Chester Porter, and Mr Caldwell, Michael Adams, all the Crown associates, and Ian Barker. I looked for signs of security but it was thin on the plane. Some men were upstairs in the lounge but the only noticeable police presence was a Commonwealth sergeant who stood stoically nearby. But I was sure that two other men close by, who smoked, were also Commonwealth police. I looked for concealed weapons but saw none. The one surprising thing for me was the ease with which the Crown lawyers chatted with the Commission staff. Ian Barker spent considerable time talking to Chester Porter. Michael Adams spent some time with the Judge's assistant. Beaming smiles and the cracking of hearty jokes were a regular feature. I felt both sensitive and paranoid about this. It was the end of the Royal Commission hearings. Was I being too anxious? I attempted to look cool and confident but on the inside I was a nervous wreck. It was as though a dozen odontologists were examining me and I would have to wait to find out the state of health of my teeth.

We were never sure if someone was going to try and 'take us out'. I was paranoid about our personal security, but this was rooted in the threats we had received. On our arrival home, we changed our silent number, but that did not stop some press finding us. How did they know? One journalist was Malcolm Brown, who rang for an 'off the record chat'. I did not have to test this notion of 'off the record' as Brown and I had been there before, and he had kept his word. But I was only part right. Brown quoted 20 of my words in the *Sydney Morning Herald*. When Harry M. Miller, read the five columned article, on page three, he scowled. His eyes glowed, then he snarled: 'What were you thinking, Michael? If you think you owe him for seven years good reporting I don't care if you have known Malcolm Brown 70 years.

Don't talk to them. Don't say a word to them. If you must be polite, say, 'Sorry no comment''. He was right.

My comments to Brown did not prevent Miller from bluffing Channel Seven into paying a six-figure sum to interview us after the Royal Commission, when other channels were not rising to the bait. It was Channel Seven's turn. There was a smirk on Miller's face as he clinched the deal and a wry smile on our faces, which still could not erase the knowledge that we were potentially a million dollars in debt for legal expenses to the Church.

On 1 June 1987 we woke after a long sleep, knowing that the Royal Commissioner would bring down his finding, which would be made public the following day, but not knowing how the new day would unfold. As usual, we were trying to avoid the press. The Murdoch-owned *Daily Telegraph* knew this, but still declared that we were 'in hiding'. It sounded good, but who were we in hiding from? We were walking around our home town with gay abandon before we shopped at the next town, Morisset.

Harry M. Miller had laid down some general rules for us to follow in times like this. The local Adventists might shudder at our association with this style of businessman, but for us it was a pragmatic and necessary decision. Plainly we needed a good public relations minder to play catch-up, but I disliked being categorised as 'entertainment' for the masses. Having a celebrity agent was a necessary evil; we had tried going it alone with the media, and had ended up lambs to the tabloid slaughter.

Harry M Miller's presence made us feel good. He oozed charisma and confidence. He was the man at the helm, to shield us from the bullying and harassing media, and to steer us to financial catch-up, without us having to explain the whys and wherefores. It worked well, with Stuart Tipple drawing up the media contracts to protect us from double-cross. The media were livid with the way we had now buffered ourselves from inaccurate reporting, 'back to back' interviews and negative sensationalism.

To my mind, the Court had to get an objective clearing and vindication of our names before another inquest could be demanded.

That night was nerve-racking. We got little more than three hours sleep thinking about the next day's events, when the finding of the Royal Commission would be made public. I rose to watch the rich orange sunrise over the Sydney Harbour Bridge and took some photographs from the 21st floor of the Boulevard Hotel to celebrate the momentous time. Today, I hoped, our criminal shackles would be unlocked. Lindy and I had booked in as Mr and Mrs Peet with our 'daughter'—in reality my attractive 20-something cousin, Nerolie Hills. The security was tight—very tight. Then we were handed the day's edition of *The Australian* newspaper. The headline on page three read: 'NT confident of Azaria inquest'. I was being constantly overwhelmed by waves of horror and insecurity in facing the day.

The Murdoch press, had, as a general rule, taken a stand against our innocence and was now doing it again. The Northern Territory had thought that Morling, as a constitutional and institutional sympathiser, would protect them and possibly confirm again that we were the cause of Azaria's death. There was an old saying among politically astute observers that a wise government should never call for a Royal Commission if they thought they would come out worst. But on the other hand the Northern Territory Law Department had been dragged, kicking and screaming to this Commission. Errol Simper, writing for *The Australian*, I thought, should have been the Northern Territory's public relations man. Here, in this article, he presented a last ditch beat-up to make the Territory feel good.

I clearly remember breakfast at the Boulevard. Lindy's tomato juice was either spiked or off. She complained in typical Lindy fashion and an embarrassed waiter brought fresh juice in a larger glass. Our breakfast egg and toast order had to be replaced after a fried cold rubber version arrived on our plates. In the lift I met a photographer who extracted more than the usual 'no comment' when he asked if I was 'having a holiday'?

It was 9am on 2 June, 1987, and the anticipation of the Morling Report that was killing me, was now over. At the Federal Court Chambers in Sydney, the 379-page report prepared by Royal Commissioner, His Honour Justice Trevor Morling, was released within minutes. To my surprise, Morling had written 108 pages on the crucial blood evidence alone. The window of opportunity for Lindy to have killed Azaria and clean up the blood, all in a matter of five to ten minutes, he observed, gave her 'little or no opportunity'. In addition, not one witness, and there were many, had even hinted that they were suspicious of her behaviour.

The most likely person to have detected anything untoward in the car was the registered nurse, Bobby Downs. She had travelled with me in the passenger seat, the area it was alleged Lindy killed Azaria, and testified that she 'did not see, feel or smell any blood and she did not pick up any blood on her clothing'. Secondly the people who packed the car to travel from the tent to the motel did not see, feel or smell anything. This included the Ayers Rock policeman, Constable Noble. On the following morning Bobby Downs spent 'some time in the driver's seat' of my car, but again had not seen or smelled any blood, nor did she get any on her clothing.

The investigation by Sergeant Graham on 1 October 1980, which was not presented in the second inquest, was addressed by Morling. In Graham's 'lengthy inspection of the car', Justice Morling was satisfied 'that Graham was able to carry out a proper and thorough inspection of the car for the purposes described'. Morling stated that Graham: 'would have expected to have been able to identify signs of removal of blood from the vinyl or metal surfaces of the car, since there would have been variations in surface textures and colours if stains had been removed without using the same method on the whole surface. He did not detect any sign of blood having been removed from the car.'

In terms of the evidence of Joy Kuhl, Justice Morling stated that errors in her work were caused by the fact that 'certain important controls were lacking'. The sensation in the media concerning the 'under-dash spray', created by Professor Anthony Jones in the 1981 second inquest, had in Joy Kuhl's notes become a spray of baby blood. Justice Morling stated that the pathologists and biologists who had re-examined this spray with either the naked eye or under microscopes: 'now agree that it does not look like blood, in either the shape of the droplets or the pattern of the spray'. There was no evidence that any blood ever covered the area or that any blood was underneath the spray. In reporting that this spray was foetal blood, Joy Kuhl had done something quite unusual, said Morling.

'(Her) result book disclosed 12 occasions when the recorded results of the tests of these three examples were crossed out or changed. In contrast it is quite unusual to find results crossed out or changed in the rest of the book.'

The Royal Commissioner continued to be concerned about Kuhl's unsatisfactory methodology and reporting. In referring to her testing of two other samples from under the dashboard area she had found one result to be 'non-specific' and the other 'negative'. Of this selective answering tactic by Kuhl, Morling again expressed his deep concern in the following comments.

'It was unsatisfactory that neither of these tests was mentioned in the work notes which were produced at the trial and which were represented to be a complete record. It was also unsatisfactory that they were not mentioned by Mrs Kuhl when she was questioned about these matters in the witness box.

For Joy Kuhl to come up with such a preposterous finding of foetal blood in this under-dash sample defied imagination. Justice Morling concluded she was dead wrong. In polite legal terms he observed: 'The strong probability is that any sample lifted out of this spray pattern on the metal plate was sound-deadening compound and contained no blood at all... The fact that she (Kuhl) could come to such a conclusion about something, which was, very probably, sound-deadener, casts doubt upon the efficacy of her testing generally and upon the accuracy of her other results.'

At the Supreme Court trial (Transcript, pp1302-1688), Mrs Kuhl said that she used adult and foetal controls for all her tube precipitin tests. However, they are not recorded in her work notes, there is no laboratory result book record of these tests at all, and before the

Commission, she said that her evidence at the trial was incorrect and there were no adult controls in these tests.

The notion about my camera bag having been allegedly the transport item for Azaria's body was anathema. In finding 'evidence' of foetal blood on the clasp of my camera bag, Kuhl had implied that someone had 'washed this bag' prior to her receiving it in October 1981. The High Court Chief Justice, Harry Gibbs and Justice Anthony Mason also agreed with this idea in the dismissal of our appeal. But others, who had examined the bag before the second inquest, saw no evidence of guilt attached to the bag.

Dr Andrew Scott had used various tests to examine for blood but this Crown witness at the Royal Commission 'saw nothing that would indicate blood on it (the camera bag)'. Furthermore, Scott determined that there was 'nothing (that) appeared to him to indicate that the bag had been washed'. Another expert who had examined the bag was Dr Lincoln, who confirmed Dr Scott's finding. When examined by the Royal Commission, Joy Kuhl backed away from her washing notion and that she had found foetal blood in it after it was suggested that her orthotolidine tests also reacted to copper dust and that this bag had been down a Mount Isa copper mine.

The hand-written reports that emanated from the testing of this bag were to be signed off by Dr Baxter. For some reason only three of the five reports had his signature. This led Justice Morling to conclude that Mrs Kuhl 'lacked the considerable experience required to enable her to plan and to carry out these complex and difficult testing procedures, at least without careful guidance from a more experienced biologist'. Furthermore, such investigation should not have been undertaken 'without extensive consultation with leaders in immunological research'.

In addressing the general question about any blood in my car, Justice Morling was unconvinced of the reliability that the Crown sought credit for. The suggestion that my 'car floor had been awash with blood', was, in Justice Morling's conclusion, absurd. He stated: 'If there was any blood present in the car, it was present only in small quantities in the area of the hinge of the passenger's seat and the floor beneath. I conclude that none of Mrs Kuhl's tests established that any such blood was Azaria's.'

The blood caused by a dingo was seen in a different light. Concerning the evidence of blood found in our tent on bedding and other items based on the evidence of a host of dingo experts, odontologists and others, including Professor Bradley and Dr William Rose, Justice Morling concluded that, 'the quantity of blood found in the tent is not inconsistent with dingo involvement'.

Bearing in mind that the reference point in the Royal Commission was to determine principally whether the convictions against us were 'unsafe or unsound', Morling could not investigate as a matter whether or not a dingo killed our daughter. But Morling did say this, about the nature of the attack on Azaria:

'It was the Crown case that Azaria was killed in the car. It seems absurd to suggest that Mrs Chamberlain carried Azaria's bleeding body from the car back to the tent when she would have been under Aidan's observation. The presence of Azaria's blood in the tent, unless it be shown to have been transferred there from Mrs Chamberlain's personal clothing, is inconsistent with the Crown case... It has not been shown by the Crown that the blood in the tent was transferred there by the clothing or person of Mrs Chamberlain. On the contrary, the evidence points to this being an unlikely occurrence.'

On the matter of Professor Cameron's supposed evidence of a bloodied handprint on Azaria's jumpsuit, Morling concluded that Cameron had no support for his opinion. On the failure of Dr Scott to find dingo saliva on Azaria's clothing and to conclude that indeed this meant the absence of any dingo activity was for Justice Morling, 'not a proper inference to draw'. Morling focused on evidence of damage to Azaria's left sleeve (ignored by the Crown), where the stain, 'apparently from a biological fluid', was 'more consistent with canine damage' than an attempt to simulate it.

In summarising Dr Hans Brunner and Dr Harding's evidence about hairs on Azaria's clothing and in our tent, Morling accepted that these were in fact dog dingo hairs. The two dog hairs found in the tent might well have been many more if a collection of these had have been possible before the contents of the tent was removed to the Uluru Motel. Dr Brunner author of a textbook, *The Identification of Mammalian Hair*, was arguably a world expert on animal hairs and had no difficulty in the differentiation between cat and dog hair. Brunner had originally offered his services as a hair expert, but the prosecution refused his help. Dr Harding, for the Crown, eventually agreed with Brunner's diagnosis. At the Commission, when asked about where the rest of the vacuumed hairs that had been on Azaria's jumpsuit had gone, Harding answered, 'It had been lost sometime after the trial, never to be seen again'.

The position of the clothing, Roff observed, was not inconsistent with dingo activity. According to Ranger Cawood, the flattening of the foliage where the clothes were found was 'not inconsistent with an animal having lain down'. Justice Morling was impressed with Chief Ranger Derek Roff's evidence. He was a 'practical man with much knowledge and experience of dingoes'. Morling saw Roff as a valuable source because: '...he is a disinterested witness. As a Senior Ranger at Uluru National Park it is not in his interest to support an allegation that a dingo had taken a child from a camping area within the park for which he had general responsibility...I conclude that, although a dingo would have had difficulty in removing Azaria's body without causing more damage to it, it was possible for it to have done so.'

The Crown had conveniently seen the tracking by the Aborigines, when trying to find Azaria, as of little use, suggesting that tracks seen on the following morning were fresher than those seen the night before by Roff and tracker Nui Minyintiri. Justice Morling observed: 'Mr Roff said that they (the tracks) were remarkably well preserved next morning when he showed them to the Winmattis. The fact is that this is quite surprising, as Roff himself said, is no reason for rejecting his evidence. I found Roff to be an impressive witness, not given to exaggeration. His veracity was not attacked and is beyond question.'

Nui Minyintiri, who gave evidence for the first time at the Royal Commission, was assessed by Justice Morling as 'an impressive witness' and the other key witness, Barbara Tjikadu, Nipper Winmatti's wife, 'had the reputation of being an excellent tracker'. Their involvement, according to Justice Morling, had given 'greater credence to dingo involvement in Azaria's death'.

A further example of remarkable incompetence was in the sad tale of Mount Isa policeman Sergeant Brown and his notebook. He had taken a vital piece of evidence, in the form of the silver space blanket or thermal sheet that was placed over Azaria to keep her warm in our Ayers Rock tent on 17 August 1980. Its significance, according to several family witnesses, was that it contained a partial dingo imprint. Owing to the loss of his notebook, Brown alleged that he had no knowledge of picking up the blanket. Morling regarded this loss as 'less than satisfactory', and that his inability to write down that he had collected the blanket was 'surprising'. The three witnesses, Lindy's mother, brother and former sister-in-law, were 'all honest witnesses and they all saw marks on the space blanket that they thought may be made by a dingo.'

In relation to Aidan's testimony, Morling accepted the record of interview made at Mount Isa in 1980 as a reliable guide to what took place. Aidan, at the age of turning seven, was credited with having had 'good powers of recall of events that occurred six weeks previously'. Justice Morling noted Police Officer Scott's reaction to the interview who indicated that there was no evidence that his mother might have prompted him about what he should say.

'I find it difficult to accept that a seven-year-old child could be so well coached in his answers that an experienced police officer would be unable during the course of an interview, exceeding one hour in duration, to satisfy himself that the child had no independent recollection of the events of which he was speaking.' Morling concluded.

Justice Morling also understood that Aidan had cared deeply for his little sister. In his summation of Aidan's encounter with his mother in the tent on the fateful night, Commissioner Morling said: 'Finally, I think it is probable that if Mrs Chamberlain took Azaria to the car and returned alone, Aidan would have noticed this and would not have assented to his mother's statement that a dingo had taken the child.'

Justice Morling then turned his attention to Sally Lowe's evidence. According to the prosecution, Azaria had to be already dead when Mrs Lowe heard a cry from the tent around 8pm. Their desire to either change Sally Lowe's story or discredit her as a witness, was noted by Morling. He stated that in any event, had this been explicitly alleged, he 'would, in any event, reject such a suggestion'. But a third party that I was unaware of for nearly six years was Ayers Rock camper, Mrs Dawson, and of her testimony Justice Morling said this: 'She (Mrs Dawson) did not appear to be unduly sympathetic to the Chamberlains and, indeed, some of her evidence as to her observations of the Chamberlains' conduct during the day of 17 August is mildly critical of them. Her inability to fix the night of 17 August as the time when she heard the baby's cry deprives her evidence of the weight which otherwise might have attached to it. However, her evidence is at least consistent with Mrs Lowe's evidence that she heard a baby cry shortly after Mrs Chamberlain returned to the barbecue and affords some marginal support for Mrs Lowe's evidence.'

In assessing the Crown case at the trial, which alleged Azaria's death took place in the car and that the dingo story was a fanciful lie, Justice Morling said: 'The effect of the new evidence on the first strand of the Crown's case is to leave it in considerable disarray...Taken in its entirety, the evidence falls far short of proving that there was any blood in the car for which there was not an innocent explanation...The doubt cast upon the findings of blood in the car is of more importance than might first appear...The new evidence shows that it cannot be safely concluded that there was more blood in the car than was in the tent. Moreover, the Crown's inability to prove that there was any of Azaria's blood in the car leaves the hypothesis that the blood found in the tent was transferred from the car was without any factual foundation.'

Justice Morling concluded that Professor Cameron's horrific allegations had now been severely weakened, 'if not totally destroyed'.

On the soil evidence used to discredit dingo activity at the trial, Morling concluded. 'The new soil evidence on the jumpsuit given (at the Royal Commission) by Dr Andrew Scott, the first Crown expert to examine the jumpsuit, had not weakened evidence of dingo involvement.' The 'quantity and distribution of sand on it might well have been the result of it being dragged through sand'.

In the analysis of Ken Crispin, in his book *The Crown Versus the Chamberlains*: 'It had become clear that a reasonable match of the soil found in the jumpsuit could be found under bushes which were widespread in the sand dune country and other desert oak trees, (throughout the Ayers Rock region).'

Justice Morling now turned the evidence, presented by Rex Kuchell at the trial, which implied that we had buried Azaria somewhere, into evidence more consistent with dingo attack. 'Moreover, the new evidence concerning plant fragments on the clothing is consistent with the clothed body of the baby being dragged through the low vegetation of kinds, which grew in the dune country and on the plains between the camping area and the Rock.'

In the light of this new evidence, it is difficult to conceive how Azaria's clothing could have collected the quantity and variety of plant material found upon it if it had been merely taken from the car, buried, disinterred and later placed near the base of the Rock. 'It is more consistent with the new plant and soil evidence that Azaria's body was carried and dragged by an animal from the campsite to near the base of the rock rather than it was buried on the dune and later buried there'.

The evidence for a dingo attack and that the 'tracks of a dingo carrying a load which might have been Azaria's body' had become stronger, Justice Morling stated: 'The Crown expert has conceded that the hairs found in the tent and on the jumpsuit which were said to be probably cat hairs were either dingo or dog hairs. Dog hairs are indistinguishable from dingo hairs. The Chamberlains had not owned a dog for some years (six) prior to August 1980.'

If the Crown's case at the trial had been correct, Justice Morling said that: 'It is extraordinary that the persons present at the barbecue area at the time of and immediately after Azaria's disappearance accepted Mrs Chamberlain's story and noticed nothing about her appearance or conduct suggesting that she had suddenly killed her daughter and nothing about Mr Chamberlain's conduct suggesting that he knew she had done so.

'It is indeed fortuitous that a dog or dingo should have been heard to growl and a dingo should have been seen not far from the tent very shortly before Azaria disappeared and that on the night of the 17th August a canid's track should have been found hard up against the tent.

'It is surprising that, if Mrs Chamberlain had blood on her clothing, nobody noticed it in the hours after Azaria's disappearance. If Azaria's body had have been left in the car after the alleged murder, it was foolhardy for Mrs Chamberlain, in the presence of the Demaines and their dog, too, to open the car door and give the dog the scent of Azaria's clothing.

'Further, it was bravado of a high order for Mr Chamberlain to tell the police at Cooranbong that they had taken possession of the wrong camera bag if Azaria's body had been secreted in the one that he then produced.'

It is also notable that Justice Morling did not consider intervention by a third party a probability.

'It is difficult but not impossible to imagine circumstances in which such intervention could have occurred. It is not inconceivable that the owner of a domestic dog intervened to cover up its involvement in the tragedy or that a tourist, acting irrationally, interfered with the clothes before they were later discovered by others.'

I refer to Justice Morling's final words, typically couched in legal terms, but blunt. 'It follows from what I have written that there are serious doubts and questions as to the Chamberlains' guilt and as to the evidence in the trial leading to their conviction. In my opinion, if the evidence before the Commission had been given at the trial, the trial judge would have been obliged to direct the jury to acquit the Chamberlains on the ground that the evidence could not justify their conviction.'

I looked out of my hotel window after the finding and it was as if I could see eternity or a heavenly sight across the northern direction of Sydney Harbour Bridge. I took a photo as a celebration of the event.

As grateful as we were for this Court's findings, we were not yet vindicated or exonerated. The cause of death by a dingo attack was not admitted by the Northern Territory Government and no apology had been discussed.

Following the Morling Report in June 1987, the Northern Territory's new Attorney-General, Darryl Manzie, misstated the context of the Commission. In his speech, the former Northern Territory police sergeant said: 'Mr Speaker, the Commission's Report will not satisfy everyone...it makes no declaration of innocence, but points rather to doubts and problems in the way of proving guilt. The Report stops a long way from saying that a dingo took Azaria... (it simply) says that the contrary has not been proved.'

Manzie had a golden opportunity at this significant time to have acted impartially by stating that with guilt not having been proven, the Chamberlains were entitled to have been declared innocent. He had tried to shut the door to clear our names. True, a 'pardon' was offered, but unlike a New Zealand pardon the granting of one would mean we had not been declared innocent, only forgiven.

For us, Manzie's offer was an insult. We vowed never to give up and for now push ahead for legislation to create a court of law that would hear our call for the quashing of our convictions and make available a total exoneration.

Dr Norman Young summarised the whole fiasco well: 'The Crown seemed to be prepared to belittle the Chamberlains as liars, the black trackers as incompetent deceivers, the eyewitnesses as fanciful romantics and the defence scientists as biased fools while attributing to its own experts an aura of infallibility.'

24. *Exoneration*

Finally on Monday, 29 February 1988, we turned up to the Darwin Supreme Court Building at 10am, to appear before a Northern Territory Criminal Court of Appeal sitting. Three judges: Chief Justice Keith John Asche, Justice John Nader and Justice Sir William Kearney, would listen to the Northern Territory submission into why we should not be exonerated as a result of the findings of the Royal Commission. According to Michael Adams, the Chamberlains could come and be represented in this appeal but we should not be allowed our own legal representation. This ploy had become monotonous. After all that had happened, how could our own interests be fully protected without proper legal representation?

With the opening of the court I thought Justice Nader looking bored and almost disdainful. He spent a considerable amount of time with his head propped up by his arm, trying to listen to Adams. The second judge, Justice Sir William Kearney, launched into some rather pointed questions as to the use and practicality of some of Adams' contentions. We knew something of Kearney's background. He had issues with the way the Territory had misinterpreted the Commission finding. The third judge, Chief Justice Asche, was an unknown quantity and we were a little worried about his demeanour. By the end of the afternoon's session I left with a splitting headache. Lindy donned her dark glasses, crying almost hysterically and very angry at Adams' rant.

On the flight home, we stopped over at Alice Springs for half an hour and met up with the first inquest staff. Senior Constable Frank Gibson, who had been ostracised after the second inquest for his belief in our honesty and integrity, told us how he had been subject to an unpleasant mix of threat and harassment.

The announcement of the death of Guy Boyd came to our attention and was a terrible blow for us. I learned about it when rung by Dr Norman Young late at night on 26 April 1988. If there was any man on earth who I prayed would live forever, it was Guy Boyd.

Guy Boyd had an utterly unerring belief in our innocence. And it was this gratitude for his trust in us that often triggered moments of high emotion in remembering how he defended our cause.

John Winneke presented to the Federal Court of Criminal Appeal a 109-page response to Darryl Manzie, Northern Territory Attorney-General. If Perron had set up the Royal Commission, Manzie would vigorously contest Justice Morling's finding to protect his police force and his government's past behaviour. He instructed Michael Adams and Elizabeth Fullerton to submit a 105-page document dated 27 June 1988. The document was tendered 11 days later than set by the Appeal Court.

In an audacious report, Adams argued that there were legal objections to the way Morling had provided his conclusion. Thirty-three pages were devoted to defending the infallibility of Professor Chaikin's report and 50 pages trying to tear down the veracity of our testimony to the court. Adams sought to float a new hypothesis that Lindy 'was covering up the death of the child from another cause, falling short of murder but for which she may have felt responsible'. He had told the media that the other cause of death was suffocation. Winneke could hardly contain himself. Adams had gone on a fishing expedition with the Appeal Court, despite not having a shred of evidence to show for it.

John Winneke renewed his attack on Professor Cameron for his careless investigation. Cameron, he said, could not 'sustain even one of the damaging opinions which he had expressed at the trial'. Winneke then described Joy Kuhl's work and person, perhaps euphemistically, as 'an unreliable witness, a person whose integrity is entitled to be questioned with regard to the manner in which her records or tests were compiled, and a person who was prepared to compromise herself as a scientist in order to accommodate the police'.

As for Malcolm Chaikin, the Crown's unassailable expert, Winneke described him as 'a very careless and very inexpert witness'. He demonstrated the Crown's incompetence and time-wasting tactics in providing 'argumentative submissions to the Court about matters in respect of which the Court is in no position to form a conclusion'. Rather its role should be to seek the Court to quash the convictions.

In mid-August 1988 another warrior for justice fell—Sir Reginald Sholl. This was a very sad and somewhat guilt-ridden event for me. Sad because I wanted very much to see him again before he died; guilt-ridden, because I had not thanked him personally in a way that really showed my gratitude to a man who was not afraid to be criticised, despite his high social status.

It was now time for the much-anticipated decision by the judges. On 13 September 1988, we took off from Sydney for Darwin to hear the Appeal Court's finding. The *Daily Telegraph* (14/9/1988) reporter observed our arrival in Darwin describing me wearing 'a casual white linen suit and sporting a new short hairstyle'. The journalists had picked up on the change of heart and pace, and that I was obviously upbeat in demeanour.

It had been a long haul since 29 February, when Adams had first fronted the Federal Judges. Now he wanted a second chance like some school student realising that he was about to score a zero for a late assessment task. The Crown was still pedalling the 'Chamberlains are liars' trial prosecution line. Kuhl, Chaikin and Cameron were still the invincibles, said Adams.

At two minutes to twelve on Wednesday 14 September, Adams presented a 50-page document to the Federal Court judges on the prosecution's attack on Morling's Commission findings. John Winneke was beside himself with disbelief and rage. It was apparent to me that here was the last desperate and ridiculous attempt to try and protect the forensic scientists from adverse scrutiny or investigation into ethical conduct, and the administration of justice.

At 10am on 15 September 1988, Lindy and I were invited to walk up the steps of the same Darwin Courthouse that had shattered and shackled our lives, six years and two days before. Not knowing the verdict, we were ready to take the new finding of a Northern Territory Federal Appeals Court on the chin. Within a minute of our entry the same three judges: Chief Justice Asche, Justice Nader and Justice Kearney, resplendent in their crimson red gowns, sat down. They had come with faint smiles on their faces, a good sign, I hoped. In the audience were my legal team, John Winneke QC, Ken Crispin, my solicitor Stuart Tipple, Senator Bob Collins and the Seventh-day Adventist Church representative, Pastor Ron Craig. Sixteen media members sat in the jury box, searching every feature of our faces for the slightest reaction. Adams was sitting directly in front of us and appeared distinctly uncomfortable.

What happened next happened very quickly. The three judges brought down their finding in just one minute and ten seconds. It was a unanimous ruling and one of the most resounding events in Australian legal history. I heard the judges tell the world that we were 'innocent'. I blinked, stunned at what I heard. People gasped. Lindy and I embraced. The mood was jubilant.

Ken Crispin, sitting close by, recorded it well: 'Justice Nader (as with the other two judges) accepted the chief findings of the Morling Report and quoted with basic approval, Justice Morling's conclusions. From this acceptance Justice Nader concluded, 'therefore, the convictions of the Chamberlains ought to be quashed and verdicts and judgments of acquittal, entered. Not to do so would be unsafe and would allow an unacceptable risk of perpetuating a miscarriage of justice.' Nader was concerned that the legal language of 'reasonable doubt' into our convictions might not be understood by the public, so he took the unusual step of adding an explanatory excursus...Justice Nader said he 'would categorise that doubt as grave doubt'. The addition of the adjective 'grave' is significant. Since innocence is presumed by a court until proven otherwise, Justice Nader emphasised that 'the convictions having been wiped away, the law of the land holds the Chamberlains to be innocent''.

After seven years' punishment for a crime that did not occur, we had been vindicated and exonerated. As the moment of truth hit, I instantly felt my old boyish self return. Seven years of being a criminal was now obliterated, blotted out. I was clean again. I smiled at the world and with my arm around Lindy, who felt like she was about to collapse, walked out into the bright sunshine and raised my arm in salute to Jesus Christ.

25. The Good, The Bad and the Ugly

Bill Hitchings, the journalist for the *Melbourne Herald,* had covered the case from almost day one. He told the world the next day '...on a cold night in August 1980 (and ever since has)...baffled and divided Australia, been through eight different court cases in as many years and cost tens of millions of dollars... But, while as one who has watched, listened and recorded every nuance, every mood and every shift in direction of this amazing affair, I find it impossible to resist the temptation to say—thank God it's virtually almost over.'

'For a few minutes it was the old Lindy Chamberlain—tiny, vulnerable, and terribly ordinary as she tried in vain to stop the flood of tears, her jaw quivering with the effort. Alongside her and just as distraught was her blond-haired husband, Michael. He too, sighed at the declaration. He too, looked his old self as he smiled through his tears and put his arm out for his wife, who was near to collapse. They had put up the veneer of remoteness but now it was all gone.'

Hitchings then gave a brief account of our changing demeanour during the early years of travail. 'From the outset, for instance, they were quite different. Lindy (at the Rock), her bobbed raven black hair and ankle socks gave her girlish buoyancy. Michael though serious and almost dour had a pleasing dullness about him.

'They knew nothing of the harsh world of the law and what it could mean to them. But then at the first inquest came their first harsh act of reality. Someone threatened to kill them and for the first time in their lives, they were given an armed bodyguard.

'Naturally they tried to protect themselves by going into their shell. It was an act that could have easily been mistaken for harshness.

'Their faces became expressionless masks—that is, in public. In the privacy of their hotel room Mrs Chamberlain nearly became hysterical with worry and fear. But their proclivity for what others might call odd behaviour--a trait which to some extent got them into trouble—showed itself at the end of the first inquest.'

With the Appeal Court out, Hitchings, a man who I had never been sure of, now gave me an assurance I would have been grateful for many years ago. He had actually trusted our testimony. His report continued:

'As they were crushed by well-wishers from the packed court and the crowd gathered outside, one felt that old twinge of sadness and yet a reflective triumph that two such ordinary people could have dredged the depths of unfathomable determination, fought a seemingly unbeatable system, and won.

'I, myself, had the indulgence of a brief twinge of excitement on hearing the judges' verdict. And if you will excuse the mild boast it is something I have believed should (have been) the case for a long, long time.

'Perhaps it is the fact that at last you no longer have to witness the indelible wrongs. Perhaps it is because you no longer have to be the onlooker of the wrenching of two lives...the remarkable transformation it has wreaked on them... It is, with all the drama and with all the tragedy, a relief for it to be all over.' It was if one might conclude: This is the day when we could say 'and justice for all''.

But it was not all over. Compensation aside, the whole story had not yet been told. The real comfort of subsequent vindication and exoneration would only be complete when the dingo was given its day in court and shown conclusively as the killer of my baby girl. 'Red centre' or not, it was the 'dead centre' for Azaria and for her it had not been rectified.

Many wanted to congratulate us. Among the first was Bob Collins and

Channel 10's second in charge, Kevin Hitchcock. Hani, the Northern Territory Aboriginal Art Gallery proprietor, followed them. But her behaviour was unacceptable to the Northern Territory Police–one of them rang her shortly after the court verdict and told her that he would not be purchasing any more art from her and this would be the stand of all his Northern Territory Police friends.

Our aircraft's stop at Alice Springs brought mixed reactions at the terminal. Some people smiled at us, others looked on with stony faces, curt replies or officious behaviour. Of course, once the new evidence of the Royal Commission was revealed, and the Appeal Court's endorsement of our innocence was told, a new era of attitudes and perceptions among the public would emerge.

Jana Wendt was the next presenter to interview us, on Channel 9 on 16 September 1988 and I remember visiting the studio through a back door. Once again it had to be a covert act, for the fear was that, as hot property, we might be 'zapped' by some other media organisation. Jana was much warmer in the flesh than on television. She was also more supportive than I imagined and her manner off-camera was surprisingly empathetic.

The legacy of this legal nightmare had to be unpacked, because it was seen as 'the most famous, complex and strange criminal case in Australia.' (*Advertiser* 16/9/1988). Dr Belinda Middleweek observed in her doctoral thesis on the media's portrayal of us, that the total vindication and official exoneration over any crime committed, for Lindy and myself, was momentously timed. It coincided with an Azaria collection in the National Museum of Australia, the international release of the first feature-length film about the loss of Azaria, the 1988 Bicentenary of Australia, and the imminent decision to hand Ayers Rock over to Aboriginal jurisdiction.

Such had been the impact of this case on the Australian (and New Zealand) psyche it was now senior journalist, Malcolm Brown's observation, which went back as far as 1982 that: 'It is rather difficult for anyone who has been with the Chamberlain case from the start to imagine a post-Azaria world–without the mystery, the Rock, the church, the dingoes' (*Sun Herald* 26/9/1982). Now we had to brace ourselves for the period of reinvention through the patterns of 'repetition, renewal and reinvigoration' from the media as Middleweek observed of our saga.

Memorable investigative reporters often create nightmares by bullying their quarry into feeling trapped into making statements to get rid of them. One of the worst types of reporter is the one who thinks he or she knows better and that after the article is printed they will be available to justify their nasty sensationalism. There is a case for some people in society being hounded by the media because it is genuinely in the public interest to have them exposed for what they are, have done, or might do in the future. These societal types, who have a psychopathic-like bent to hurt or destroy others, need to be exposed and brought to justice. On the other side, however, once in a while, the media gets it terribly wrong, and false information is published about people. When the information is later found to be wrong and the people innocent, the effects can be devastating. They result in exacting the highest price and the most unjust punishments on earth. I give thanks to those journalists and news managers who have soul and are prepared to use their own moral and ethical judgment to give space and objective consideration to a situation, rather than slavishly fulfilling their editor's demands.

Malcolm Brown was one of these. He had smelt a rat all along and had first become aware of something really bad in the Northern Territory Government's method of pursuing us before the second inquest. He told me that: 'The leaking of alleged evidence after the raid on your home (on 19 September 1981) was so sensational and graphic, it was as if the Northern Territory were out to bury you without you ever saying a word. The way the information came out, leaked into the *The Northern Territory News*, was shocking'. This included the notion that 'Lindy had 12 minutes (police time) to take Azaria's life'; the invention by Cameron of the alleged bloody handprint; the decapitation theory, another invention by Cameron through the *Sydney Sun*.'

Then there were the gossiping journalists who were snickering about the Northern Territory Police branding Denis Barritt as the 'Ding-a-Ling Coroner'. They had forgotten he was once one of them and knew the character and behaviour of detectives in the force. This is not to mention the great expense and resources used to pin a murder on a woman. Mothers convicted of infanticide had never been treated so harshly. Most convicted mothers were given a good behaviour bond when post-natal depression was evident. In 2010, the *Herald Sun* reported juror Yvonne Cain's comments in 1985 when she said she was 'ashamed at having sent to jail a person she believed to be innocent.'

What about the great expense of digging up the desert; and the huge cost of the large number of police involved?

Malcolm Brown further complained: 'The magnitude of the police investigation both shocked and appalled me. The entire Crown case had been publicised in a hysterical manner. There was sensation after sensation, misconceptions about your religion, Azaria's (Reagan's) black dress, the Five Day Plan smoker's coffin, the old family Bible and the stupid misinterpretation of Azaria's name. The police had a free run at convicting you long before any justice could be achieved. I realised that the Chamberlains were being burned alive.'

It seemed that a safety principle was emerging here. In cases that were technical or had sustained long-term media publicity, an alternative or modified method of making judgment should be available to the defence. At the jury's decision there were tears, flowers and remorse for some, indicating a highly emotional state of mind. John Fairbanks Kerr, in his book, *A Presumption of Wisdom*, suggested that this could often be a sign that there is confusion and a lack of objective decision-making. There are five main reasons for a jury getting it wrong: pre-trial publicity; emotional take-over; technical evidence; minority group misunderstanding or stereotyping; and the inability of juries to discuss difficult evidence objectively.

For Malcolm Brown, the greatest shock had been the way the Northern Territory jury system had been conducted. He remarked: 'I became aware early on how impossible it would be to obtain a jury that could be remotely objective. The jury was yapping their heads off all over Darwin. I knew that they could not speak to the media and that we could not approach them, but it was my friends in Darwin who told me that after Boettcher's forensic blood evidence, the jury thought he was an idiot. It was purely a superficial assessment.'

This wave of observations sent journalist Brown into 'profound despair' and from then on, he fought his ever-present hostility to maintain objectivity towards the accusors and the incarcerators.

Brown's worst nightmare and ethical agony came through his conscience nagging him that he had to help Lindy to freedom, knowing that at the same time any further reporting of the injustice could keep her longer in prison. Brown believed that by the end of the Supreme Court trial, he had 'stepped across the line' (from being capable of 'doing the dirty' on me when he wrote about our jog together) to becoming a participant in the 'Free Lindy' campaign.

As a result, Malcolm Brown was convinced that he had been placed in a queue and would be targeted by and worn down through the Northern Territory's intransigence towards him and all others coming to help Lindy's cause. (Malcolm Brown, Letter to Michael Chamberlain 2/12/2008).

In 1988, following our exoneration, Malcolm Brown wrote a 'constrained' letter in late September, congratulating me on being vindicated against the Northern Territory's shoddy lies and miscarriage of justice.

'You will no doubt end up on your feet. The SDA Church must surely, within its empire, have a place for you. You've shown such steadfastness in the face of the massive pressures brought against you that I know you are not going to throw in the towel now. I think ultimately, when the academics and historians have thoroughly sifted this case, the suffering of all of you will turn out to be a great benefit to society.' (Letter from Malcolm Brown to Michael Chamberlain, 24/9/1988).

His letter reminded me of the austere and uncompromising way I had to play a strategic game with the media and at all costs keep them at bay. But it also told me that this journalist had earned my respect and would in future dealings be treated accordingly. I put him on the list to attend our vindication celebrations at Avondale College in October 1988.

The positive change in news reporting in the later part of this decade grew with the probability of our innocence and the questions now being raised in the national and international conscience. Dr Belinda Middleweek noted that: 'further questions were raised about Australia's international reputation, Michael and Lindy's regard for the nation and its people and the sanctity of the legal system in the face of investigative, forensic and judicial error'.

The major problem in this trial for me was accountability. Police and forensic scientists had made unwise judgments and called on their subjective observations to make rumour, innuendo and waste huge amounts of taxpayers' money often driven by prejudice. People in responsible positions for making expert comments should recognise that facts and the truth are of supreme importance. Nothing, absolutely nothing, should stop them from being frank and earnest in their quest.

There was a perception that this had been a travesty of justice. This came without the Royal Commission explicitly saying there was an unsafe verdict. The Northern Territory had avoided any scrutiny about its own administration of justice. They not only avoided an examination of the new measures that should have been put in place, but the persons who should have been disciplined for the debacle.

While the Crown demonstrated that some of their forensic scientists had ability and integrity, like Dr Andrew Scott, they were also riddled with experts who were either incompetent or naïve.

Another troubling area was the relationship Joy Kuhl had with the Northern Territory police. In the mind of Justice Morling, certain Northern Territory police had placed pressure on forensic scientists. Royal Commissioner, Trevor Morling, observed: 'This was illustrated in the Chamberlain case by evidence of numerous telephone conversations between police officers in which they expressed their anxiety to obtain the results of Mrs Kuhl's testing and their hope that it would support the Crown case'. It was quite evident that the notion of certain Crown experts purported to have been disinterested and objective participants in our case was questionable. ('Experts and Evidence' *Bulletin*, March 1988.)

Under the headline 'Guilt-Edged Justice', at the end of the Darwin Supreme Court trial, James Oram, in the *Sunday Sun* (9/2/1986), described a stricken Lindy wearing a 'mask moulded from her belief in God and justice'. As Oram reflected on that trial, he began to understand for the first time that 'there was more on trial than just a woman who was said to have killed her baby. Was it prejudice?...No case had been so cluttered with prejudice...' Oram, who had covered the case from 1980, asked himself at the first inquest: 'Had politics become involved? Were the police capable of, if not rigging evidence, at least of twisting it to their advantage and therefore betraying truth?' (*Sunday Sun* 9/2/1986).

What made a crowd of nightclub revellers cheer the news that the dingo was innocent and a young mother of three children was going to jail for life? Wasn't this a case about scientific evidence? Oram noted that in propping up the Northern Territory Police's collecting of evidence was their insistence on fanning Seventh-day Adventists' alleged dark deeds of human sacrifice and bizarre rites. 'The Northern Territory police had to be protected. Governments have fallen over smaller issues than suggestions of a police incompetence.' (*Sunday Sun* 9/2/1986).

Murdoch reporter Errol Simper claimed our case remained a 'murder case that would never die...The system—so often questioned, insulted and vilified—can be said, after a fashion, to have worked.' It was 'the circumstances (of finding the matinee jacket) and not loud voices that triggered a change for Lindy Chamberlain'. Simper said that he was not looking forward to the 'tiresome cinematic hype to come' referring to the film *Evil Angels* (*The Australian* 16/9/1988). Clearly Simper was toeing the Northern Territory line, still having nothing of the dingo's involvement. While I considered him to have been half asleep during the coverage of the case, there was one thing on which we were in agreement. It was dealing with the fundamental question about 'What happened to Azaria?' If the parents were innocent, it was the question to clear up, and the sooner the better.

Following the quashing of the convictions I was interviewed by Alan Jones on Radio 2UE in Sydney. I argued that an element of 'social guilt' had taken hold of the nation amongst the many who had mistakenly believed in our guilt. Belinda Middleweek concurred, aligning our experience with the 'disavowed collective guilt over the past and present treatment of Australia's Indigenous population—a struggle which continues over both settler–colonial legitimacy and Aboriginal land rights.'

General Secretary for the Northern Territory Police Association, Mr Gowan Carter, presented on Channel Nine's *Today* program, the Territory's version about why we should never be awarded any compensation for injustices from the Territory Government. Ken Crispin observed that Carter was adamant that his Government had 'paid out enough in securing justice for the Chamberlains and that the Government's money could be more effectively used on projects like housing and the Aborigines'. Carter, in a breathtaking performance, rejected Liz Hayes' assertion that the Chamberlains 'had been declared innocent'. The police did not adhere to the presumption of innocence that their own Federal Court of Appeal had declared. The antipathy towards us by some senior members in the police force remained alive and well. The choice of some of them to believe with fanatical preoccupation in science fiction was very disappointing.

It was profoundly untrue to say that we cost the Northern Territory Government anything. Were we not the victims the night Azaria disappeared in a Government-protected camping site? We assumed that we were safe from wild creatures. We paid our camping dues in good faith and were subsequently predated upon by a wily dingo (or perhaps two). To this day, Lindy, myself and our family remain sufferers of that failure to adequately warn us.

Another breathtaking statement from Gowan Carter concerned the use of the media for which Carter 'had to congratulate the Chamberlains. They had conducted a magnificent media campaign and it had succeeded'. That comment was both hypercritical and laughable. Wave upon wave of undesirable front-page headlines leading to the second inquest assaulted the Australian reader, and the Northern Territory had driven it.

Actor Sam Neill, who played me in the film *Evil Angels*, told me that one of the scary experiences was his observation of the power of the media. 'That was the frightening thing,' he reflected. 'If you are in the media and deal with them all the time you can become quite professional, but clearly at the beginning all the attention for you guys was bewildering.'

With reference to the first inquest finding, Padraic McGuinness said it was the journalists who were the 'evil angels', but also 'victims' (*Australian Financial Review* 4/11/1988). McGuinness saw the real need was to now confront how this dreadful injustice was propagated. 'What is really needed now is a careful analysis of the origins and propagations of the story...with a careful telling of who reported and said what and when.' McGuinness further opined: 'Probably we will have to wait until the records of the Northern Territory Police and especially the Government are available to the public.'

The Age newspaper editorial (16/9/1988) supported this notion with a rather memorable cartoon about the law used by the Northern Territory to prosecute us. The law, it said, had emerged 'looking a little worse for wear'. A cartoon supporting the editorial text depicted jurors, judge, scientists, and journalists with bleeding injuries to their legs. The caption was poignant. 'Wild dog horror: Australian institutions mauled.' The *Courier-Mail* added: 'It is obvious that the Chamberlains have suffered badly from the (legal) system.' But it was in shock that I read *The Northern Territory News* (16/9/1988). The editorial stated: 'Our claim for compensation should not just cover legal expenses but 'for the obvious injustice done to Mr and Mrs Chamberlain'.

With reference to the first inquest finding, that a dingo took Azaria, Padraic McGuinness (*Australian Financial Review* 4/11/1988) asked the most significant question: 'Why couldn't the Northern Territory Government leave it at that? ...Having discussed the matter with a couple of very senior ministers of the Northern Territory Government I was at a loss to understand why they were so emotionally involved in the case. They could not leave it alone. What was wrong with them and the police? It has been suggested that they were worried about an adverse impact on tourism in the Ayers Rock (Uluru) area. But surely such a relatively trivial matter could not account for their passion?'

The day after the handover ceremony of Ayers Rock back to its traditional owners and the renaming of it as Uluru, in October 1985, the *Sunday Territorian* ran a story about Lindy's cry for truth, juxtaposed on the front page with the headline: 'Chief jeered at Rock' recounting Ian Tuxworth's unfavourable reception at this ceremony and Lindy's demand: 'The truth...that's all I want'. (*Sunday Territorian* 27/10/1985).

Tuxworth's predessor, Everingham, had been reported in the *Sydney Morning Herald* saying that he 'feared the Commonwealth's decision would jeopardise the future of the $150 million development planned for Ayers Rock' (*Sydney Morning Herald,* 12/11/1983). The Yulara development would eventually cost more than $150 million. Officially it was put at around $380 million, but unofficial sources believe it was nearer $600 million.

The tourism industry around Uluru/Ayers Rock has never abated. The Northern Territory Government sold its 60 per cent stake in Yulara in 1997 for $220 million. Annual visitor numbers, according to *Alice Spring News*, went from 100,000 when it opened in 1984, to 350,000 in 1996. It is calculated that 63 percent of the visitors are from overseas.

As in the case (and film) of the Erin Brockovich revelation concerning the toxic chemical chromium six and the shocking secret big business had tried to hide, Lindy and I wondered if we were a sacrifice to cover up the potential flow on to big business. Such ethics would forever block any official declaration that Azaria was killed by a dingo. This deduction should come as no great surprise. Governments and corporations the world over have been jealous about their profits and will do what it takes to remove impediments to their success. For them, the word 'unconscionable' does not exist.

The *Brisbane Sun* editor noted that the Northern Territory Government went after us with almost 'fanatical preoccupation'. The *Adelaide Advertiser*, in a sobering headline 'It could be any of us'... asserted that 'the way the Northern Territory pursued the Chamberlains smacked of petty revenge for the disturbance of some cosy Territorian notions'.

Padraic McGuinness observed that a lot of people were easily led in abandoning the safe British tradition that you are innocent until proven guilty. Lindy was quickly condemned.

Oddest of all was the line that became increasingly prevalent among the greenies and those with a conservation bent that the dingoes were being unjustly accused, and had to be defended lest there be a campaign to wipe them out. One would have thought that babies would have been given the benefit of the doubt any day. Environmentalists and 'green' people have remained quite sceptical, if not biased, about the ability of dingoes to kill humans. A dingo could not have killed Azaria, they say. They are paranoid that on the false assumption that dingoes are an endangered species, they must be protected from being seen to do wrong.

In Peter Van Noorden's high-school textbook, *Living Geography*, he asks a simplistic question to ill-prepared pupils on the topic of dingo behaviour: 'Could a dingo kill and eat a human?' The author, according to Dr Norman Young, is short on information about dingoes and wills the student to answer in the negative.

We wondered why several key witness accounts had not been taken seriously. This included Greg and Sally Lowe's account, key witnesses at Ayers Rock on the night, Max and Amy Whittacker's account of Lindy's grief at the loss of Azaria and Max and Phyllis Cranwell's account of their own three-year-old daughter, who was attacked on the back of her neck, leaving blood and bite marks, and then dragged from their family car by a dingo, weeks before Azaria's disappearance.

Why was this? Was it a hatred for Seventh-day Adventists? Was it a prejudice against Aboriginals? Was it a lust for power? Was it a fear that the Northern Territory tourist economy would suffer at Ayers Rock?

Professor Stuart Piggin of the University of Wollongong's History Department, nominated us as the most hated persons in Australia's 200 years of history. Sir Allan Walker, director of World Evangelism for the Uniting Church claimed that we were clearly the 'victims of religious prejudice and discrimination...because we were members of a small and little understood Christian church'.

The now-deceased James Oram was one of the most sensational reporters of our case. He had been writing about us since 1980. I did not become aware of this until late December 1981 when he wrote an obscenely coloured article about my Torana which I instantly resented. In his review about the case (*The Sunday Telegraph* 6/11/1988), Oram claimed that he had no opinion about Azaria's death up until the Darwin trial. He claimed, 'the media were merely recording the events that allegedly transpired...No; the media in general were not to blame. If the blame lies anywhere it was with the legal profession, through the eyes of the politicians; too smart by half on the side of the prosecution, not so, on the part of the defence.' Was Oram trying to tell us something?

Taking a glass or two in a Darwin pub with a stereotypical Northern Territory policeman: 'tough, intelligent, and not too keen on the blacks', Oram recorded a shocking dialogue he had with a policeman.

'"You know," the policeman said, "there's no doubt it was a sacrifice. It's one of the rituals of their mob. They sacrifice babies to cleanse the sins of all of them."

'I laughed. He had to be joking.

'"It's true," he said, his face serious and a little pained that I should be amused by his remarks. "That's what happened to Azaria. You can't tell me any different" (*The Sunday Telegraph* 6/11/1988).

'I suspect he holds the same view today...So unbelievable was this stuff concocted by this police force, I personally started to think that it was a nasty clumsy ruse to deflect the truth. As a mascot and icon of the Territory this underdog, the dingo, had to win and had, hands down.'

Within a short time after our exoneration, the leading journalist of television's current affairs at the time, Jana Wendt, interviewed Lindy and myself on Channel Nine's *A Current Affair*. At the end of Jana's interview she was shocked to hear the hostile reaction of some callers who had jammed the switchboard, seeking to 'get that murdering woman off the screen'. The threats were clearly defamatory, but while the manner in which Azaria was killed was left up in the air, nothing could be done.

John Bryson, when asked during a national television interview, what the most significant cause of injustice inflicted upon us was, answered: 'I think it could be described in just one word—bigotry.'

Former President of the New South Wales Court of Appeal and now distinguished retired High Court Judge, Michael Kirby, considered that the only trial that probably attracted as much or more attention in Australia than our case was the trial of Ned Kelly. Kirby pointed out that the normal courts did not save us. Right up until the High Court Appeal we appeared to be irrevocably determined as guilty persons. Justice Kirby continued:

'It took extraordinary, extra-curial steps to be taken to rescue (Lindy from prison) to secure a Royal Commission and to provide amending legislation to permit the quashing of the convictions...

'After all, this is a story which, upon one view, ended happily ever after. Would the original coroner's findings have been challenged and set aside, but for a feeling in some official quarters that it impugned the integrity of some government officials? Would there have been an indictment and trial in such a case at all but for the tremendous media coverage and the 'beat-up' of the story provided by the media, reaching as it did into the very coroner's courtroom?

'Would Mrs Chamberlain and her husband have been convicted if there had not been so much media coverage intruding every night into the living rooms from which the jury would be eventually drawn? Did the fact that the Chamberlains belonged to a minority religion or came from a different part of Australia in anyway influence the jury's or the community's opinion as to their guilt? Would there have been quite the same energy put into fighting their case through three levels of courts in Australia but for the support they had from the institutional church, which stood behind them? How would an ordinary unsupported citizen have gone in such straits? Would the exceptional steps of the Royal Commission, the amending legislation and the compensation have been provided if the Chamberlains had stood alone? Or would a lonely Mrs Chamberlain still be sitting in a Darwin Jail as I write this?' (an excerpt of a letter written by Michael Kirby at the Court of Criminal Appeal 1 June 1989, published in *Innocence Regained* (1989) by Dr Norman

Young).

Lowell Tarling summarised the situation incisively after the secret quashing of the first inquest: 'The forensic criminologists made their memorable comeback, proving beyond doubt that the Australian public had faith in the unseen if it is packaged as science rather than religion' (*Rolling Stone* March 1984). It was upon Azaria's Rock that they have stumbled.

When the whole of a government system marshalls itself to go out and get you, and drag you through the courts to put you away, what chance do you have?

Dingoes could not possibly kill white, Australian, female, Caucasian babies, only unfortunate Aboriginal ones. And, of course, Lindy's angry denial delivered the message the press wanted.

Yet it was also incredible the way people came to the fore, seeing us under this terrible siege in the legal and political world, and stand up and said, 'Enough is enough. We won't put up with this injustice any longer'.

Few people have ever been accused of a serious crime, and while relatively unknown, been able to draw the support that accrued to us. So, why did we receive so much support? Was it the overwhelming shock and enormity of the subsequent injustice that aroused latent justice inside every moral human being?

We were just normal, everyday, law-abiding people going about our daily routines, unnoticed, who had suddenly become the 'wrong people at the wrong time in the wrong place'. We were caught up in an event that engulfed us and caused enormous damage to all who were related to us through lineage, religion or friendship.

The first thing that incensed many people was that it eventually emerged that the rumours, the charges, trials and the convictions were all based on misconception and human error. From only days after Azaria's disappearance, until the end of the Royal Commission in June 1987, Lindy and I had the power to silence a whole room, simply by walking through the door. We were both pariahs and refugees in our own land.

Yes, we were, and are flawed people, who had difficulty at times recounting in minute detail the events surrounding the loss of Azaria. Lindy in her detailed recounts was not always a consistent witness, according to Morling. But she told the truth to the best of her ability. I did not come out of this legal wash as a pristine and sharp recorder of what I saw either, even though I tried to be very measured in recounting events, and as a result, was probably considered quite boring at times. We both exhibited our own unique responses during extreme moments before the glare of the media world.

We had very different emotional responses. Lindy in private shed a good deal more tears than me. I dreaded her coming to me and talking at length about our precious daughter because I would just as easily become teary eyed and men don't do that! I was more abbreviated in my recount of events. Lindy was full of details in her responses. She seemed to take ages to get through the introductory comments. On the other hand, I was a concept-focused person perhaps as a result of the theoretical and philosophical training that grew out of my student education.

Although she was clearly quite capable, Lindy never went on with her Bachelor of Education, commenced after Azaria disappeared, because everything else seemed to overwhelm her. Could you imagine her conducting her life as a teacher in an educational institution and surviving with people always asking questions? I later attempted an institutional job for five years and almost succeeded. An experience like this was for me during 1980 to 1987, according to psychiatrists, like going through four lifetimes worth of stress.

The members of the Seventh-day Adventist Church, in general, rallied in a wonderful way, the way New Testament Christians care for each other. Despite their involvement in our ignominy, the Church administration provided a secure haven for us in their College grounds. They provided an income that put bread on our table and clothes on our backs. They allowed my children to attend the Church school at Avondale, fee-free, and were vigilant about their protection from outside harm or media skirmish. It was a credit to the Avondale Primary School;

so good was their security that no photographs were ever taken by the press while my children were in its care. The Seventh-day Adventist Church administration ultimately demonstrated their belief in us when they shelled out hundreds of thousands of dollars in legal fees, plane fares and accommodation for some eight years until the legal engagements had largely subsided. Various church members sent cheques and cash donations, which paid for fuel and food and the occasional outing for the children, as difficult as this was under the spotlight of the press.

Even so, while the Wattagan mountain property had provided a wonderful playground for the kids, we needed a proper house. Avondale College was making noises to us to move on and live in our own place. I had a bulldozer and driver sculpt new roads, build dams and get ready for us to build a new home.

In Australia, New Zealand and in the wider world we received countless expressions of support and love from almost every Christian group imaginable. There were religious groups, regarded by most as fringe dwellers, which sent expressions of support. Jehovah's Witnesses, Mormons, and even various Brethren members offered condolences. If these souls had vested their faith and prayers in our vindication, there were equally persons who wore no observable faith on their sleeve or held any religious views or spiritual philosophy who expressed their yearning for the truth to come out in our case.

Of special note was Professor Barry Boettcher, who endured domestic pain as well as some professional malignment at the Darwin trial and even at the Royal Commission made huge sacrifices of time and emotional energy to stand up for us. This physically powerful and fit man had true grit. He would never say die in pursuing the cause of scientific truth. Professor Boettcher later presented a paper to the journal *Medicine, Science and the Law* titled: 'Contaminating Antibodies May Produce Unexpected Reactions in Counter-Current Immunoelectrophoresis'. It was with some irony that the authority accepting this research, driven by the ignorance of some of the prosecution blood scientists was 'Professor James Cameron'. The trial jury chose to believe Cameron over Professor Boettcher.

Another tireless defender of the truth, one who was also a shrewd politician, was Senator Bob Collins. Brian Johnstone, formerly 'the only Northern Territory journalist working for a national news agency' worked with Bob Collins during his fight to obtain a Royal Commission. Johnstone had covered the whole case, and said that the story was now 'seared into my memory'. He was angered how 'the front page stories down south from the yellow press' was often mirrored in *The Northern Territory News*. The hostility against us remained so intense in 1985–86 that no one in his or her right mind would have voted for Bob Collins as the Chief Minister of the Northern Territory. As a result, the media-fuelled hatred caused serious debate as to whether the death penalty for Lindy by hanging was appropriate.

Collins had been up, night after night, papers strewn over his desk, digesting the forensic evidence and planning his next move in the Federal Parliament. The attack on the Northern Territory Country and Federal Liberal Party had attracted flak from within his own Labor party. It was claimed that his behaviour and stance had been electorally damaging and that he had not represented the feelings of his Labor supporters in the Territory. Ken Crispin observed, 'His colleagues were right'. He was asked to resign as Leader of the Northern Territory Opposition.

Two scientists who really stuck their neck out and remain publicly unsung heroes in the quest to find the meaning behind the Crown's blood and alleged scissor cutting evidence, were Les Smith and Ken Chapman. When they took on the forensic establishment, neither man had any former experience in the discipline of forensic science. Both were employed at the Sanitarium Health Food Company. Their ingenuity, resourcefulness and lateral thinking in applications, were remarkable. To summarise their stamp on the case: Les Smith cracked the code of the meaning of the under-dash spray. He and Chapman jointly unravelled the mystery of the dingo's ability to create 'tufts' through the shearing action of its teeth on fabric identical to Azaria's jumpsuit. He took on Professor Malcolm Chaikin, the most knowledgeable forensic expert in Australia on material cuts, and won through tenacity, logic and observational brilliance.

A number of people, either in law, politics or the arts, made some very significant contributions to bring into being the Morling Royal Commission. These included the late Sir Reginald Sholl, Senator Colin Mason, Bob Brown (local Labor Member), Betty Hocking, (Canberra ACT politician), the late Guy Boyd and artist Pro Hart and High Court Justice Michael Kirby. Guy Boyd and his wife Phyllis sent a number of letters between 1984 and 1987, which renewed our hope in human nature. Boyd's bronze work was amongst the most aesthetically pleasing I have ever seen, and Justice Kirby came to Avondale College and presented a College Graduation speech in which he made reference to the injustices in our case.

In December 1984, famous Australian painter Pro Hart sent me four remarkable paintings based on the Ayers Rock saga. Photographs of them were published in *On Being* magazine in May 1986. Hart was so passionate about exposing the injustice that he sent them to us to highlight major cultural aspects of the case. The four works of art told four different stories with a theme of intrigue and cover-up. The first painting highlighted the theme of 'Insulted Elders' at Ayers Rock when their testimony about how a dingo took and killed Azaria, and then was tracked, wasn't believed by the Northern Territory Government. The second painting, 'Discussion for Burial' symbolised the rumour that four unnamed residents of Ayers Rock had intercepted a pet dingo and had taken Azaria's body and buried her using a shovel. The third painting, 'Tracker at the Window' illustrated an Aboriginal looking into a Northern Territory house owned by a ranger and seeing a pet dingo. The fourth painting, 'Judgment at Ayers Rock', illustrated the courtroom trial in Darwin with the 12 jurors, a blindfolded judge and the dingo taking central place as the revered underdog of the Northern Territory. Both the late Pro Hart and his wife Kaylee, sent letters of encouragement which spurred us on. Like Guy Boyd, and later the adventurer and businessman Dick Smith who sent a significant donation to aid in our fight for justice, these people put their money and efforts where their mouths were and helped us in our journey to justice.

The moment our legal status returned to that of innocent citizens, overnight we became celebrities on the international speaker circuit. In particular, the Church was keen to present us as their trophy, now clean, now victorious and now icons of what good Adventists should be under extreme adversity. Lindy and I grasped the opportunity to fly to New Zealand and to the United States for this purpose. Another highlight was a presentation at a Canadian university, where we fielded some very animated questioning from their law students.

I had by this time collected, filed and accumulated documents, photographs, letters, cards and materials about our cases.

From 1985-86, I helped set up the Australian SDA Church's Archives based at Avondale College. It was also ironic that I was elected to become a professional member of the prestigious Australian Society of Archivists through the Northern Territory Government's examination of my work by their own archivists. For that I was extremely grateful. Little did I know at that time that this material collated by me would form part of a collection now held at the Australian National Museum (Eternity Series, prepared by Dr Robert N Moles).

And so it came to pass, that on 15 October 1988, I thought it fitting to hold an acquittal celebration at Avondale College. Over 300 people from all walks of life and vocations assembled for one of the most wonderful nights of praise and gratitude you could ever imagine.

On Wednesday 19 October 1988, three days after our exoneration celebration, I felt empowered to give back to my community some of the help they had offered me. The morning sun felt particularly refreshing and the temperature was bracing. The sky was an unusually pristine blue. Perhaps I was buoyed by the Northern Territory Appellate Court decision and I thought it time to repay my community for all their prayers, tears and lobbying to obtain justice on our behalf. I decided to work in the community to offer my services and try to fix local shortcomings and injustices in the Cooranbong and Lake Macquarie community. This decision to crack open my frozen self-imposed wasteland of anger and hostility towards the Northern Territory. I had buried myself, vowing to never do anything for the general public until my name was cleared.

Fortuitously, my town, through a local real estate agent, wanted to set up a small newsletter. I put up my hand to edit it, which would mean that I would be the reporter and general all-rounder. So the first edition of this humble news sheet, with me as its fledgling editor, consisted of four pages typed on a typewriter. It was published as *The Cooranbong Newsletter.* My reporting motto would be based on Thomas Jefferson's words: 'Our Liberty depends on the freedom of the press and that cannot be limited without being lost'. If this seemed incongruous coming from one who had suffered trial by media first hand, I still believed in the integrity of some journalists, and it was these men I sought to emulate in my reporting. Over two years of my editorship, *The Cooranbong Newsletter* grew to a modest 16 pages, much to the concern of the local real estate boss who felt it was becoming too much like a local newspaper. Instead of growing it even more I resigned from the position. It was taken over by the Avondale College Librarian, Brian Townend. It was only ever going to be an honorary non-profit production, but at the time of writing it has become a healthy 48-page local news magazine called *The Cooranbong Gazette*, ably controlled by the local printer, John Duffy.

Despite the celebrations, I was still deeply unsatisfied that the truth about Azaria's death was still to be acknowledged in public.

The Fourth Wave: Confession Time

26. *Evil Angels: the Film*

In 1988, Lindy and I were described dubiously by the Church's most authoritative academic magazine as 'the best known Adventists in the world' (*Spectrum*, vol. 19, no.3 1988). The editors declared that: 'the response of the Australian public to Lindy and Michael was significantly bound up with their feelings about Seventh-day Adventists.' The Church was anxious to learn if there had been any shift in the public's opinion about it. But there were players other than the Church, anxious to find meaning in the case and to analyse it, post 1988, from a national and international perspective.

Then something quite unexpected turned up. Verity Lambert from Cinema Verity sought our assistance for her proposed film, *Evil Angels*. I had first heard of this two years earlier when a journalist, Kevin Childs, interviewed Ms Lambert, describing her as 'an outstanding producer of British television and films'.

Childs was incensed by the depths the British and European tabloid press had sunk to in their treatment of us, and by the brutal manner in which they dealt with sensitive issues. This film was designed to expose the irresponsible press and their fictitious information, all too frequently peddled to damage people's lives and livelihoods. My interest in seeing this film get off the ground grew as it became apparent that perhaps a lesson could be learned from a genuine tragedy—our loss of Azaria—being unravelled and exploited by the different power groups who were threatened by it.

I wondered how a feature film, of the average 95 minutes in length, would be able to convey the truth of our story. John Bryson had sold the film rights to his book, *Evil Angels,* to Cinema Verity. His book was a great start from which to develop the film. A dramatised documentary-style film could create a 'true' and 'real' production of the facts (rather than based on or inspired by the truth) and would need a treatment far in excess of 95 minutes, I believed. The second hurdle concerned the actors. Casting the right actors for this film to provide an authentic and accurate representation would be no mean feat, especially in view of the contemporary context, with the events still being fresh in people's minds. At the time, the finding of the Royal Commission was still a future event, but after she had read and purchased the film rights to Bryson's book, Ms Lambert was convinced that she was doing the right thing.

According to Dr Belinda Middleweek's analysis, 'films like *Evil Angels* were part of the new phase of cinematic nationalism in which the Australian Government under Gough Whitlam implemented a range of initiatives to promote the arts,' in order 'to develop a national identity through artistic expression and to protect Australia's image in other countries by means of the arts'.

Evil Angels, however, would express a very different side to Australia to films like *Crocodile Dundee* and in turn provide 'an absorbing, disturbing drama that gives the Aussie Office of Tourism fits' (Belinda Middleweek, Dingo Media? R v Chamberlain as a model for an Australian event PhD Thesis, University of Sydney, 2007). *Crocodile Dundee* was a tourism advertiser's dream; *Evil Angels* would present the dark side of Australia's social milieu of the 1980s. This would not be good news for Gough Whitlam's promotion of a 'national identity through artistic expression and to protect Australia's image in other countries by means of the arts'. Would the portrayal of a biased police force and a flawed forensic system improve a nation's identity?

Dr Belinda Middleweek makes the point: 'In making belated amends for the trauma Lindy and Michael suffered, the film constructs a discourse of blame around the Australian public, which it represents as gossipy, larrikin, and preoccupied by the (lies surrounding) the 'dingo baby' case. Not unlike the Bicentenary which projected a multicultural vision of Australia and coincided with the film's release, *Evil Angels* presents a narrative of (a) nation that is about redressing the injustices of the past, in order to assert the cultural and social progress of a nation by the late 1980s.'

For the part of Lindy, the actor had to look like her and, of course, take her off as closely as possible. After going through a couple of Australian actresses, Meryl Streep was finally cast. She had just completed the Oscar-acclaimed film *Out of Africa*. This was exciting news. It was rare for Meryl Streep to make a decision so quickly, but Bryson's sensational 550-page book impressed her. When she came to Melbourne to live for a few months, she found the intense media interest extremely taxing. This gave her an insight into the media glare we continually faced and probably assisted in her empathy towards us.

Director, Fred Schepisi, noted for successfully directing several films including *Roxanne*, was elated to get Meryl on board. When interviewed by Sally Ogle Davis he glowed about his star. 'Without Meryl, I would not, I could not, have made this picture. I needed someone with that sort of intelligence around to give me another viewpoint—not just on her character but on the whole picture. I would work with her again anytime' (*The Sunday Telegraph* 20/11/1988).

On 4 October 1987 we flew to Melbourne and locked ourselves away in the Park Royal to spend two days reading a film script draft given to us by Fred Schepisi and Verity Lambert. Bryson's book had less than a modicum of information about us as characters. His book wasn't about diagnosing the Chamberlains, and the film would need a good deal more than what was in Bryson's book. I had carefully documented most of the significant feelings and events that had gone on behind closed doors, and those diaries might be called upon—and it made me nervous just thinking about the prospect. (My mother had always thought I was too honest and open for my own good.) So what did the boyishly jubilant screenwriter, Robert Caswell, selected to write the screenplay, have in store? He had just written an Australian television series on justice and corruption. I found him accepting and helpful, but he was about to leave for America to work on a film script titled, *The Magic Pudding*.

Schepisi would have the ultimate say on what was in and what was not. The pressure of having to read this document made me cranky, but I should not have been. Why be unhappy when you had a chance to be let loose on editorial input for the sake of accuracy in an upcoming feature film? It seemed a little crazy and churlish, but Lindy and I were reacting like a pair of cut snakes and sleeping poorly. We had very different ways of analysing things. Lindy's eye for detail and minutiae was sometimes irritating. My concentration on making the big picture right made her feel I was too accepting and sloppy. If the flow and coherence of the film was disjointed, I would have been unnerved by the lack of professionalism, but for Lindy, just one word out of place or a description lacking on a point of colour or design brought unrest. What should have been an affirming experience had become divisive between us.

At 10am the following day we met Fred and Verity again to present our analysis. We were making good progress with the corrections. Fred was subtle in his comments but very clear in his direction. Lindy was having a fine time of explaining her focus on intricate detail and Fred was becoming a little flabbergasted. 'I'll make the notes and corrections so that there is no confusion,' Verity said. It seemed to solve the problem for now. From time to time she would receive a mild rebuke from Lindy, but she carried on with her note-taking undaunted.

What came next was totally unexpected. A flash across the double doors, then with the steadying of a windswept flushed face, the radiant being of Meryl Streep burst in. I gasped inwardly. I could not quite believe my eyes but it really was the lady herself. She seemed quite shy, and was very apologetic about being late. Instinctively, I stood to attention. I was in the presence of a screen goddess. The others turned around as if a little stunned. The introductions were magic. Yes, she surely was just as I had seen her on screen in *Out of Africa* with Robert Redford. We had all lost sleep thinking about this moment. So human in her intuition yet so perfect in her responses, Meryl was perceptive and sensitive, and seemed totally unaffected by her fame. Of the people you meet in life, those who you can feel utterly at ease with are very few and far between. Meryl Streep was the epitome of unpretentiousness.

If people thought Lindy could be cold and remote, Meryl Steep did not. 'I did not find her the least bit cold although she does carry everything inside. She carries her religion around like she carries a purse' (*The Sunday Telegraph* 20/11/1988). Meryl worked hard on getting Lindy's voice perfect and apart from a couple of lines in the film, when I think Meryl momentarily forgot and played Meryl, it was a masterful production. She carried tapes around of Lindy and practised words and phrases. It seemed a never-ending task to get that half-Queensland, half-nasal Strine accent, cute in one way but in the words of Sam Neill, 'at times sounded like a finger nail on a blackboard'. According to Sam, 'Meryl caught all that'. *Time* magazine (15/6/1987) asked a facetious question, 'Can Meryl Streep simulate a truly convincing nasal strine whine? Is Robert Redford handsome enough? Why not Paul Hogan?'

In finding an actor that might play my character, the names Michael York and Robert Redford were tossed around, even Richard Chamberlain. Redford was my first choice, but he was seen as too old and Richard Chamberlain did not seem interested in further acting. Coincidentally, it was felt that a New Zealand actor, Sam Neill, had a similar voice and speech patterns, was about the right height, and could portray a serious disposition.

Dusk, and the Sydney to Newcastle flier had just pulled into Morisset rail station, built about 100 years before, on a late September day in 1988. I got there early in case my mystery guest lost his way. My emotional scars from the case still showed. I knew this by the nervous way I was treating this encounter. I also wanted to survey the demeanour, body language and attitude of the man who was going to portray my person and character on the world screen. In short, I wanted to know something more about my special guest than he knew about me. Was I intimidated by him? Probably, but I should not have been. Was I anxious to meet him? Definitely. The eight-car silver electric train arrived on time. The 15 or so passengers alighted and then I saw him. I can't recall what he wore, something grey and unassuming, but I know I was nervous. He stood and waited a minute or so longer while I composed myself. Then from the corner of his eye, my guest spotted me.

'Have you just arrived?' Sam Neill enquired.

'Oh no,' I replied while shaking hands. 'I have been here for a while waiting for you.'

I think Sam was as anxious about coming into our lives as we were. After all, he was not going to represent a deceased person who could not come back from the grave to haunt him. Accuracy was all I wanted. Don't portray me as someone I am not.

The next day, the pastor took the actor for a walk. I took him to the place of my belief and courage: the College Church sometimes dubbed the 'College Cathedral'. We discussed the contexts of our upbringing. Sam had an Irish background and had been involved in acting from an early age. I had English ancestry from Devon on Dad's farming side of the family, while my mother held up a proud Norwegian background, which she was never going to let me forget. But I was also interested to see if Sam had any spark of faith. Origins and childhood contexts have a bearing on people's thinking. It would be helpful if he could identify with me on some spiritual plane. He couldn't. I did not mean to put him on the spot or embarrass him but there were a few awkward gaps in our conversation. As Sam later said: 'This sort of threw me a bit, because I didn't have any good answers and I was starting to backpedal furiously, so I said I could probably call myself a spiritual person. I certainly could not call myself a Christian or a religious person.'

After three days of talking and conviviality, we parted on good terms, knowing and respecting the power and responsibility of our own approaches to the values of life. We had both studied each other intensely in order to understand and make the most of our professional backgrounds and activities. Sam was dedicated to objectivity and truthfulness to the essence, rather than a 'music hall' impersonation.

If Sam Neill was concerned that I was a person 'too meek and wishy-washy for my own good' as John Laws had once described me, Sam later told me: 'You are a lot stronger than you are given credit for...You have had your faith severely shaken. It's a wonder you have any faith left at all. Frankly, I don't know how you made it this far. So I want to be very clear on how I portray you. I want to make sure you are done justice. I'm not going to make you look any better than you are, just simply how you are.'

One of the highlights of my short time with Sam was when I was alerted to a fire in the Wattagan Mountains, not far from where our property was. It was westerly and about 10 kilometres away, I estimated, as I looked out the back porch of my College home, and saw the billowing smoke.

'Better go and take a look,' I said to Sam. 'Do you want to come?' I needn't have asked. He was dead keen.

As we climbed the steep long ridgeline in my ex-Air Force, camouflage green Toyota 4WD, it was becoming increasingly clear that the property owner beneath me had 'done it again'. In order to clear the forest floor in preparation for the summer bushfires, the old farmer of Martinsville pioneering stock, had lit his side of the mountain, and now mine, and the fire was racing up the slope to my ridge. Sam was undaunted. He watched our techniques of bush-fire reduction, broke off some green saplings with a prolific growth of eucalypt leaves and started pounding the flames.

Sam wanted to know what lay below our land, so Lindy and I half-walked, half-slid down the slope with Sam, ever nearer to the old man's domain. I knew the property, an almost deserted orange farm, left to grow wild for years and abounding with sweet juicy fruit. Sam had a fierce thirst and, without asking, rushed to the nearest tree and started gorging the 'forbidden' fruit, juice streaming over his parched lips and down his chiselled chin. He recalled later how he 'was like a pig in heaven on all these oranges—you know, kids in orchards—and I realised I was the only one doing this...indicating they should pick a few, I said 'Go on, these are fantastic' but she (Lindy) wouldn't, because they were someone else's oranges.'

Sam picked a whole bag of these little orange beauties. 'That's no big deal,' he defended himself; 'look at the hundreds and thousands of them going to waste.' Of course, he was right. It was a wicked waste, but Lindy stuck to her guns. No way was she going to allow one morsel of orange flesh between her teeth. 'Me too,' I said. I wasn't thirsty, and I did not know if and when the old grumpy firebug farmer would turn up and turn us into front-page fodder in the *Daily Telegraph*.

Sam said he wanted to buy the man out if the orchard ever came up for sale. But it never did.

The intricacies of understanding each other, I think, made *Evil Angels* an emotional journey for Sam. In representing me as the deeply wounded and confused person that I was, he was prevented from being detached or entirely objective, or even being able to assess how well he had portrayed me. I know this from when he watched it, because I think the whole story became quite overwhelming for him. The missing ingredient he could not fathom was my unerring trust in Jesus Christ to take me through this ordeal.

One of my most anxious moments was in meeting dingo handler and trainer, Evanne Chesson, contracted for the film. Dingoes, she told me, chew through all types of materials and are surprisingly dexterous with their mouth and paws. 'Once they ate a pet rabbit,' she told me, 'and actually skinned the whole animal with their paws' (*Newcastle Herald* 3/11/1987).

By 5 October 1987, the script was now more or less complete. The emendations were few, the tone cohesive and warming to us both. Warner Brothers had wanted a film with sensation; Fred had opted for truth and humanity. That was powerful enough. Any more real than this and the public might leave in disbelief, Fred warned. Along with Sam Neill, we left for Meryl's temporary home in South Yarra to dine with her husband, Don Gummer, and their children, Gracie, Marnie and Henry. It was a delicious vegetarian meal, with the addition of chicken for those not ready for the 'food of angels', vegetarian cooking.

The following day we concentrated on the film studio at Broadmeadow just out of the Melbourne CBD. My first impression of this massive building, dubbed 'Hollymeadows' or 'Broadwood' by the locals, was that of a rundown warehouse. I was armed with my prize toy, a Sony Umatic ¾-inch film camera. I had bought it to film the 1988 Bicentenary at the Sydney Harbour Bridge and also to film Sam and Meryl together in the film. I was quite surprised that no restrictions were placed on me in my selection of film topics but then I tried not to be intrusive and probably recorded nothing of any lasting value. I have never revisited this film since the day I shot it; however that day was memorable all the same.

We were ushered into the 'white room', a restaurant with totally white décor: white table, chairs, walls and ceiling, and white plastic cups and cutlery. I was amazed by the stark conditions under which rich and famous people worked. There were Meryl, Fred, Lindy and myself, and Sam with his bodyguard with Sam's attractive partner, Japanese-born Noriko and five-year-old daughter, Micha. Out of gratitude for allowing Sam to act me, I presented Noriko with a pot of orchids, her favourite flower. But we would have to wait another half hour for Verity Lambert to arrive and were informed that the actual filming of Meryl and Sam in film dialogue would make them too nervous with Lindy and me present.

During this mid-afternoon lunch we exchanged our experiences in an informal workman-like atmosphere. Lindy and Meryl selected clothes that Lindy might choose to wear in real life. Sam was about to get his hair colour lightened to match mine after exposure in the hot desert environment of 1980. The attention to detail was impressive. Sam had taken time to get used to my dark 1980 sideburns, conservative for that time, but now, in 1987, a bit out of fashion.

Some weeks later I was treated to the long-awaited scenes where Sam and Meryl had to act out their version of romantic love between Lindy and I. Sam invited me to be his double with Meryl and teased me about being filmed in bed with her. I was at once in shock and awe. There was no telling what that might have done to Lindy's and my fragile relationship!

The stills photographer for the film, a smart-looking American accented woman in her early thirties was zealous to protect the secrecy of the film set. She spied us trailing the film crew with our own security guards and stopped us.

'Excuse me', she said officiously, interrupting my conversation with Lindy. 'What are you doing here?'

I looked at her blankly and before I could answer, she fired a second staccato-like shot, 'Who are you representing?'

'Er... myself?' I replied.

'What media organisation do you represent?'

I tried to explain who we were and our reason for being there but it took several minutes for the penny to drop.

'You need some local knowledge,' I said humorously. 'Have you heard of Lindy and Michael Chamberlain?'

'Oh dear', she replied and stared at us as if she had seen a ghost. 'I am so sorry.' She repeated her apology several times, terribly embarrassed.

Surprisingly, I ended up with two full 20-minute tapes of the proceedings. The most challenging moments came when I was able to film Sam and Meryl in their prospective studios having makeup applied. I took my stills camera and captured several shots of Meryl with Lindy and then Meryl with my boys. I guess the filming was allowed out of deep trust, and I was impressed by the discretion they allowed me for our own personal memories.

The manner in which *Evil Angels* was being created came as a surprise. Only one camera was used at a time with a three-man film crew working feverishly in extremely tight conditions. The camera, a Panaflex Platinum 70 mm, said to cost $250,000, was very quiet and expensive. There were two of them on the set. As the angle of the camera changed, a bevy of up to 10 builders would remove and remake walls in front of us.

Sometime later, the *Melbourne Truth* tried to get an angle on our fraternising with Sam and Meryl. I was described as the 'dominated husband' in Meryl's eyes. I asked Meryl in private about this notion, but she declined to comment. 'I have never expressed my thoughts to anyone about it,' she told me. Meryl was diplomatic. Another newspaper ran a headlined story on 4 January 1988, suggesting that we were about to go into partnership with Meryl and purchase a block of land in Melany for $1.5 million. A pleasant thought, but a pity that it was fictitious.

When interviewed by *The Australian Magazine* Sam said he was unable to fathom what had driven this unnecessary legal battle in the first place. 'Why did it all happen?' he wanted to know. One thing that came out of this saga was the raw nature of people. He was shocked to have been in the middle of an experience illustrating how primitive humanity was; where a whole set of rumours could take hold of a community and drove its negative judgments. 'Whether we are English, New Zealanders, Australians or whatever, we are not as sophisticated as we like to think,' he said. It was a conclusion I had now long held following the second inquest. An irresponsible media publishes material that is purely of entertainment value. It is calculated to divide the community and to stir emotions, fire prejudices and endorse stereotypes. This engages more readers to buy more papers and satisfies the advertisers who are dependent on circulation statistics.

I believe that ultimately Sam and I had an understanding that was based on the all-important value of trust. I sent him several messages, thanking him for his confidence in me and for not skewing the ethos and integrity of our story. It probably hampered his creative acting skills a bit, because the film ended up more as a docudrama rather than a full-blown feature film. I doubted if Sam would ever wish to be involved with this type of movie again and I didn't blame him—I was still trying to believe that this had happened to me, and was still happening eight years after.

Putting the media aside, Sam had done a good job on me, I believed. In himself and behind the scenes he was a relatively quiet, confident and somewhat retiring personality. He had done his utmost in his unobtrusive way to get inside my skin. Representing a boyish young man with a dose of naiveté, I was seen as an embattled true believer in God's plan, experiencing heart-rendering stress through courtroom and media glare (*Sydney Morning Herald* 10/11/1988). Sam's rendition of me as 'a highly intuitive and ultimately very moving performance (was) a portrait of a man confident of his faith and in his own pastoral abilities, yet strangely awkward with the language of intimacy' (*The Bulletin* 15/10/1988),

On 19 September 1988 we were ushered in to see a private screening of the film that encompassed seven years of our lives. Some of the scenes were uncomfortable. Other scenes I had wanted in were left out. All sorts of people were consulted for this film, including ardent critics and the people who loved to hate us, and those who desperately wanted to see us go down and stay down. We were warned to bring an adequate supply of tissues. It was called a 'six hanky event' by Verity Lambert. It was a intensely private and exciting event for us.

Evil Angels (called *A Cry in the Dark* in the United States) would have happened with or without our help. Our personal information was, according to my mother, generous—too generous. 'You are very brave', she said in a tone which might have been a gentle rebuke. 'I don't know how you did it. I couldn't have done it.' My father was silent. It did not seem as if he could comprehend what went on in my mind and we rarely talked about personal matters.

The film evoked many reviews from some prestigious quarters. David Anson from *Newsweek* described it as 'a hair-raising, absorbing drama'. *People Magazine* said it was 'Streep at her bold and brilliant best'; *Time* called it an 'Awesomely tough-minded performance by Streep'. *The New York Times* described the film as a 'celebration of personal triumph'. On *Today*, NBC TV, Gene Shalit thought 'Sam Neill was brilliant; Meryl Streep destined for another Oscar'. However, the *Weekend Australian* (22–23/8/1988) said it all about Meryl. 'Magnificent Meryl was a master of 'living' every character she portrays. She is so absorbed in her work and so adept at shedding her own skin and stepping into another that she is often unrecognised on the set.'

But it wasn't all praise. Journalist Susan Geason in an acidic letter to the *Sydney Morning Herald* (3/11/1988), described Meryl as a 'black Streep', the 'self-righteous posturing of the celluloid moralists, whose haste in condemning the Australian media's role in the Chamberlain case is matched only by their speed in turning the episode into box office profits.' Another detractor described the alluring Streep in mimicking Lindy, as wearing a 'brutal helmet' of black hair.

Yet Meryl Streep made the film live in an otherwise 'dull' movie wrote Geoffrey Himes, in the *Columbia Flier*. Schepisi did not show how the innocent Chamberlains came to be convicted. The problem about how on earth two obviously innocent people could get into such a mess was not explored. The reviewer thought that it should not have been told through our eyes. However, on this point Himes was wrong. The narrative was based on the Royal Commission's findings and John Bryson's incisive mind.

The film, according to Himes, had not built the antagonist's scenario of allegedly finding blood in the car or determining that Azaria's throat had been cut; in other words, to sufficiently or equally engage the audience 'into questions of guilt and innocence or reality and perception'. He said there was no mystery or intrigue or the suggestion that a Government would quash an inquest secretly and controversially. The audience did not have to ask the question: is she really guilty or innocent? Neither did it portray the magnitude of hostility or strength of the political forces against us. At best, Himes declared the film would work for those who had a firm grasp of the background, explaining Australian culture and how we were targets for misunderstanding and prejudice. Himes may have been intuitive in his critique, but seemed to miss the point that there had been horrendous overexposure by an Australian media to a darkly conceived, forensic lie.

What would make the film an extremely difficult task for Schepisi was the 'embarrassment of riches' described by *The Bulletin* film reviewer, Sandra Hall, as having available, several powerful themes. To provide 'great cinema' and not just a 'painstakingly accurate film', the director had several films within the film to choose from: an expose of the fallibility of the Northern Territory justice system; the study of a media machine in frenzy; or an emotional account of 'a woman forced by the cruellest of circumstances to discover a new and less comfortable self–one whose abrasive stubbornness is complemented by tough talking humour and resilience' (*The Bulletin* 15/10/1988). There were simply too many good things going in this film and not enough time or resources to expand on all of them. More elements were put together than could be developed. It could have been a masterpiece but instead became 'the movie of the week'. The film had all the integrity needed but it did not dig deep enough for it to become a Hollywood blockbuster. According to an American viewpoint, you came out of the film, 'moved—even shaken—yet not quite certain what you have been watching' (*The New Yorker* 28/11/1988). But what seemed to strike a universal tone was the final line of the film, when Sam Neill took a line from my words in the *60 Minutes* documentary: 'People forget how important innocence is to innocent people'.

The film *Evil Angels* became part of the 'myth' itself. *Newsweek* film reviewer, Dave Hansen, suggested that we, as Seventh-day Adventists, had been 'ripe candidates for a mean streak of religious bigotry'. In its most powerful representation, Meryl Streep presented Lindy at her worst; 'a prickly, intransigently unglamorous Lindy Chamberlain...the focus of a lurid media thunderstorm...Lindy became the ideal scapegoat for all their (the public's) fears about human nature'.

On his own critique of the media, film director Fred Schepisi, said: 'We get the media we deserve because we want our news quick, and we want it juicy...unfortunately, people think it's information they are getting—they don't understand that it's entertainment. Nor do they understand that the people producing this stuff on the television, radio and press do it because they want to make money not because they want to disseminate information. The critical question in this case is: How much information didn't we get?'

Some critics accused Schepisi of being biased in his belief of the Chamberlains, accusing him of only presenting our side of the story. But Schepisi was adamant. He had sat on the fence and presented the facts of the story from all sides, and in his words, 'let them speak for themselves' (*The Sunday Telegraph* 20/11/1988). In the following years, particularly since 2000, the film seems to have been more difficult to face due to its uncomplimentary expose of Australian social culture.

In his daily radio broadcasts, Alan Jones on 2UE Sydney suggested that the quashing of the verdict had placed the media in the dock (*The Sun Herald* 18/9/1988). The media, in my view, generally were well behaved when it came to the evidence coming out of the Royal

Commission. Pity that this caution was not observed during the second inquest and the events leading to it. Of course, the media are conduits and purveyors of reports rather than objective processors. I saw the media as really accessories after the fact. The real culprits for the dock were those government officials and strategists who manipulated the media to bring on a trial by media.

The late Padraic McGuinness saw the journalists themselves not only as the 'evil angels' but also as the 'victims'. 'What is really needed now is a careful analysis of the origins and propagations of the story...with a careful telling of who reported and said what and when'.

McGuinness further opined: 'Probably we will have to wait until the records of the Northern Territory Police and especially the Government are available to the public. We can be sure that much has been destroyed and will be destroyed before that day. There is a lot the authorities of the Territory have to hide' (*Australian Financial Review* 4/11/1988).

27. The Third Inquest Whitewash

All we need for evil to triumph is for good men to do nothing.
Edmund Burke

With unfinished business remaining in our quest for Azaria's justice at Ayers Rock, by 1994 it had been declared, ironically, as a 'major health hazard'. So said Barry Hailstone, a medical reporter, on behalf of the *Medical Journal of Australia* (*Advertiser* 10/12/1994). In one 18-month period there were 255 recorded incidents on or near the Rock. Six people died and the others were injured, some seriously. The 1.6-kilometre, 348-metre summit was 'associated with a high incidence of heart attack'. This was not welcome news for Northern Territory Tourism. Their tourism, 'as a growth industry, (was) now earning $120 million a year' (*Weekend Australian* 10–11/12/1994).

I now sought the quashing of the second inquest finding. We had received a compensation payout. The first inquest Coroner, Denis Barritt, accepted my mission to quash the second inquest. 'I can understand Mr Chamberlain's reasons for seeking a quashing,' he told the *Weekend Australian*.

My dad, ever true blue to fighting for justice, again asserted his disgust at the Northern Territory ploy to keep the case alive by allowing the second inquest 'murder' implication to stand. 'For goodness sake, it's a very hard thing to understand why they were so quick to overturn the initial inquest but have never overturned the second,' my father told the *Christchurch Star* (14/12/1994).

My push for the need for another inquest had gone on for nearly six months, without a result, since mid-1994. Despite Lindy and I being divorced I was still continuing the quest for justice for Azaria. It was my own quest, a father's task in memory of his daughter. It did not look like the Territory had any enthusiasm for the idea. Then suddenly without warning, Chief Coroner for the Northern Territory, John Allan Lowndes, declared that there should be a response to 'complete outstanding obligations' and to 'finalise the manner and cause of death of Azaria Chamberlain'. The decision 'to consider and record appropriate findings in the light of the findings of the Royal Commission and the Court of Criminal Appeal decision' was welcome.

My only concern was whether the Northern Territory Justice Department would present the two options stated clearly and unequivocally by Ian Barker in his introduction to the prosecution case at the 1982 trial: 'Either Mrs Chamberlain killed her baby or it was a dingo' . There should be no problem with understanding such a clear directive as this.

On 12 September 1995, I instructed Stuart Tipple to distribute a press release declaring our position on Azaria's death. We stated that she died 'accidentally as the result of being taken by a dingo from her tent at Ayers Rock in harmony with the findings of the Royal Commission as adopted by the Northern Territory Court of Criminal Appeal' (Brennan Blair and Tipple Submission for third inquest letter 12/9/1995).

As a result, *The Northern Territory News* (27/9/1995) announced that: 'Michael Chamberlain has moved to have the 1982 Coronial finding (second inquest) struck from the record to leave the way clear for him to have a plaque erected at Uluru in Azaria's memory.'

I looked forward to the third inquest and a memorial service for Azaria where I wanted to have a plaque placed on the Rock in remembrance of her death.

Senator Don Chipp, founder of the Australian Democrats and the dictum that he would be 'keeping the bastards honest', wrote a scathing attack early in October 1995 on Australian and Northern Territory prejudice. He said: 'I recall the mockery of justice, which falsely convicted Michael and Lindy Chamberlain in the Northern Territory 13 years ago. Every screening in the US of the film *Evil Angels* starring Meryl Streep and Sam Neill was greeted with sustained jeering and palpable loathing for the Australian justice system.

'It should have not led to a manic pursuit for vengeance that ended in a life sentence and made us the laughing stock of the free world. The actions of the Northern Territory politicians and those who supported them in pursing this tragic woman were revolting to me' ('Insight', *The Sunday Telegraph* 8/10/1995).

On 16 October 1995, I sent a letter to Kristen Marlow, General Manager of Channel 10 programs, expressing my anger at the use of satire to depict Azaria's death in the production of *The Simpsons Down Under–Bart Versus Australia*, shown on Channel 10 on 11 October 1995. I informed her of my deep concern at the show being presented in children's prime time and that 'the remarks made about a dingo in relationship to a baby were extremely hurtful and in very poor taste'. I viewed it as a means to 'damage our reputation and imply that my (then) wife was a liar at the trial and the Royal Commission, or something worse'.

A reply came back from Charles P. Williams, Director of Broadcasting Policy. 'As you would be aware, *The Simpsons* is an animated situation-comedy series about a dysfunctional American family and their mischievous disobedient and ill-informed son Bart. The series regularly uses topics of contemporary and public interest as the basis of parody and satirical comment...Indeed the accents used by the voiceovers in the episode appear to be a parody of the unfortunate Australian accent adopted by Ms Meryl Streep in the movie *Evil Angels*...

'While appreciating your views and your family's sensitivity to this matter, we do not believe that the particular section of dialogue denigrated either you or your former wife.'

Okay well that was a fight I could have in the future. But for now my focus was on the inquest. Perhaps it was pie in the sky, perhaps not, if I ever get the truth out of the Northern Territory. To do it I realised I would have to upskill myself with some high-powered training to make a difference.

I knew that I needed to keep pushing for a new inquest to quash the second inquest allegation that Lindy had murdered Azaria with 'a cut throat'. If Azaria's death certificate could be altered that a dingo had killed my daughter, it would assist us with some moral and legal protection against future exploiters of our loss and grief.

Greg Wendt from the *Newcastle Herald* (14/11/1995) assessed the case as 'Australia's longest and most expensive legal saga', noting that our legal status as innocent persons was not in dispute. I felt sure that this new thrust would be the last—and the most resounding victory for Azaria. Here was the watershed test of the Northern Territory's integrity, to demonstrate an unbiased and 'fair dinkum' conclusion and closure to the case. I made this clear to the *Newcastle Herald,* that 'I was looking forward to the opening of the inquest at the Darwin Magistrates Court on 29 November. I want the Northern Territory to bite the bullet and do it right.' The *Adelaide Advertiser* reported my additional comments on 8 November: 'The truth must be told. The moral fibre in a human being demanded that justice be done...This will leave the way clear for my daughter—at long last—to have a proper burial at Ayers Rock. ...For the last five or six years... the thing that has stuck in our gizzard is the result of the Second inquiry.' *The Advertiser* (9/11/1995) repeated the fact that the 'Royal Commission five years later effectively cleared the Chamberlains and the Full Bench of the Court of Criminal Appeal quashed their convictions a year later.'

As the new inquiry date approached, I accepted an invitation to address a forum at the New South Wales State Parliament on 23 November, the topic to be addressed: 'The fabrication of evidence and the review of wrongful convictions' *(Newcastle Herald* 15/11/1995). The panel I was on included ex-Detective Sergeant from NSW Police

Trevor Haken and Terry O'Gorman, the President of the Australian Council for Civil Liberties. Other speakers include: John Akister, NSW Corrective Services Minister, and Professor David Brown, a leading criminal academic.

In the opening address to the public forum I stated: 'In 1980, our exceedingly tragic and fatal stay at Ayers Rock was one which has remained with me like a heart of stone. After 18,000 pages of transcript, a $20 million price tag, almost a year wasted in court in attending nine separate hearings, I am persuaded that the expert who presents forensic evidence is in need of a serious code of conduct. Anyone in an authoritative position, whether police, doctors or teachers, is accountable. Somehow, the forensic scientist has slipped through the net. What I have experienced has not gone away. It will not go away and why should it?

'Our vindication is still only a Pyrrhic victory. Selective evidence, hidden evidence, discrimination of minority groups—racism, it is all here and needs to be talked about. But this is in no way a denigration of those objective, honest police or forensic scientists who don't have a heart of stone. These people listen to their conscience. They are fearless in their objective pursuit of truth. They can be trusted. Some of the Crown forensic scientists could not be relied upon. In my view, that is why they secretly quashed the first inquest and then conducted a trial by media campaign to try and break us.

'The Crown tried to shore up the testimony of Joy Kuhl, their weakest link. At the trial she said it was foetal blood, and Barker said, "I suggest to you that she ought to know, and Dr Baxter ought to know what he is dealing with, because you know really, if the negative suggestion made about their work in this court has any substance, people in New South Wales are in constant danger of being wrongfully convicted whenever there is some blood involved...

"What we ask you to do is respect her opinions. She didn't come here for her greater glory. She is a biologist we say, who does an honest and competent day's work. She goes to court to offer her honest opinion and finds herself confronted with the criticisms of academics who have probably never in their lives entered a forensic science laboratory... and have never experienced the dirty side of the profession, the sex crimes, the murders, the old blood stains...the difficulties which the poor old practical hard-working forensic biologist is confronted with."

'Joy Kuhl had testified in court: 'I used up all the dry flakes (of the blood) for example. I have also extensively swabbed and scraped from the hinge and the base of the hinge. I was not requested to keep any of the samples.'

'In cross-examination, (Supreme Court Trial Transcript, pp1572-1684) John Phillips QC asked the $64,000 question: "Did you take any slides or photographs of the tests that you conducted on each of those items found in the car?"

Joy Kuhl: No.

Phillips: None at all?

Joy Kuhl: No.

Phillips: So that when you gave your evidence, you relied then on your work notes and the comments were made in the work notes?

Joy Kuhl: Yes."'

We need a code of practice in court cases to prevent juries from being bamboozled, where (disputed) technical forensic evidence is produced.

Parts of my speech were reported on in *The Australian* (24/11/1995). 'Neither forgiven nor forgotten' was the response in the *Daily Telegraph* from journalist Rachel Morris, but that was only half the truth. I had forgiven the perpetrators but I had not forgotten who they were. Justice had not yet been done. The dingo had to have its day in court.

The Australian Council for Civil Liberties endorsed my comments. Terry O'Gorman called for such a body to be established in the light of the recent findings of the (Wood) Police Royal Commission which had been established to investigate police corruption in the NSW Police Force.

Professor Barry Boettcher called for scientific evidence to be more fairly and transparently presented in Australian criminal trials. He wrote to Professor D Craig of the Australian Academy of Science on

18 August 1993, appealing to him to approach the Australian Law Reform Commission to facilitate a safer process in presenting such evidence. Lay witnesses should only have to address facts in experts' testimony. Scientific experts could give opinions and be believed by juries unless there is general consensus agreement on the scientific evidence provided.

The danger lay in the interpretation of these experts' evidence, which could be utterly wrong and yet they had the power to persuade a court. In the adversarial trial jury system, unlike a Royal Commission collaborative system, the prosecution could promote Joy Kuhl as a competent expert who analysed blood as a matter of daily routine. She had provided an appealing and comforting testimony. At the trial, Ian Barker contrasted this with 'ivory towered' scientists who had been the forensic science lecturers and supervisors, but supposedly knew less about the theory behind the forensic analysis.

Boettcher said in his appeal to Professor Craig, that: 'prosecution expert scientific evidence, as presented in the Darwin Court, was flawed and demonstrated poor technical competence, prejudice and incorrect facts being given to the (Darwin) court.' As in the American Supreme Court system, it seemed reasonable to make judges responsible for ensuring that 'any and all scientific testimony or evidence admitted (to a jury) is not only relevant but reliable.'

Melbourne Herald writer Bill Hitchings described the case as 'ragged tangents of conjecture, mischief and myth', giving it 'the texture of smashed jaffa'. He suggested that the biggest initial mistake was when the police believed and propounded the idea that Azaria meant 'sacrifice in the wilderness', causing the public imagination to run wild with gossip and prejudice. Furthermore, the recognition that a dingo and a domestic dog were unequal in their dexterity, the dingo more like a cat in cunning and dexterity, was either misunderstood or ignored. Hitchings described the double-jointed nature of a dingo's jaws, able to completely enclose a baby's head in its mouth; the extremely sharp teeth with their scissor-like action. A dingo could 'curl back its upper and lower lip and use its teeth like miniature pincers to pick delicately at its food' (*The Advertiser* 30/11/1995).

For Bill Hitchings, the third inquest was the last chance to lay the case to rest in what he described as 'the most confounding, divisive and, on anyone's terms, the most intriguing and sensational case in Australia's legal history'. It was the moment for 'Ending the Age of Intrigue'. The moment when it would be shown that 'all along the Chamberlains had been telling the truth. But then, so had everyone else...?'

Gold Walkley Award winner for journalism, David Bentley's report on the case (*Sunday Mail* 3/12/1995), continued to promulgate myths. Bentley's first mistake came in his first sentence when he alleged that I had been on a charge for murdering Azaria. I had only been charged as 'an accessory after the fact'. Secondly, he invented the story that 'Lindy would give evidence (at the third inquest) watched from the press gallery by many of the same reporters who covered the original court cases'. This inquest involved paperwork only and no witnesses would be called. His third mistake came from his remark that 'Lindy hotly disputed' the news reports that 'the baby clothes had been neatly folded at the scene where the Azaria was disrobed.' It was never alleged by either the prosecution or the defence that this had ever occurred. Someone, other than Wally Goodwin, the first on the scene where the clothes were found, (followed by the police) had invented the idea, and the media had without foundation spread the lie. I was entitled to ask: who spread this lie?

In his final piece of creative writing David Bentley claimed that 'Lindy was convicted at the second inquest and, heavy with child, sent to Darwin's Berrimah Prison to begin her life sentence' (*Sunday Mail* 3/12/1995).

On 13 December 1995, Chief Coroner Lowndes, was scheduled to hand down the findings of the third inquest into how Azaria died. Stuart Tipple had expressed our manifesto in simple terms. We had submitted that there should be two findings: the first one was that there should be a formal recording that the Chamberlains had nothing to do with Azaria's death. The second was that Azaria died accidentally after being taken by a dingo from our tent (*Sydney Morning Herald* 30/11/1995).

We wanted this to be the last court case. I had pushed for it and driven it. It was Lowndes' task to correct the Galvin second inquest finding, following all the overwhelming new evidence that had dismantled that finding, including that there was 'a lack of objective evidence or no positive evidence, or to support the view that any dingo could be involved. On the contrary there was considerable evidence to show that a dingo could not be involved' (Galvin, Inquest II pp. 9-19).

The press turned up in force. So, coming together on the day when the Coroner's finding was handed down, sitting within several metres of each other it all felt wrong. Lindy did not speak to me nor did I want to speak to her. She was with her new husband, John Hampton Creighton IV as we had finally divorced in 1991.

To our complete amazement and disappointment, Lowndes' finding brought down an 'open' verdict into Azaria's death. He ignored the fact that in *Fisher v Stuart* in 1979, Chief Justice Foster of the Northern Territory Supreme Court declared: 'I am satisfied that the dingo is by nature...inherently dangerous to man'.

But two weeks before Azaria died, Derek Roff, Chief Ranger at Ayers Rock, stated in a letter to the Northern Territory Conservation Commission (Lewis R., The Chamberlain Case: was justice done? HTAV 1920 at p.20) '...Children and babies ought to be considered possible prey.'

Lowndes, in conceding that there was 'considerable support for the view that a dingo may have taken Azaria' made the incredible leap to state that: 'the evidence is not sufficiently clear, cogent or exact to reasonably support such a finding (of a dingo attack) on the balance of probabilities...the cause of Azaria's death cannot be determined and must remain unknown.'

I began to shake with rage. This inquest had not brought closure to the final minutes of Azaria's life at all. It had been a whitewash and not worth the time or effort to attend. I doubt that Lindy felt any different. This finding had flown in the face of Justice Morling's acceptance that intervention by a third party was not a viable prospect. It also flew in the face of Ian Barker's Trial opening address that only two scenarios could be open for a jury to decide: either it was Lindy or a dingo that killed Azaria.

Derek Roff had given compelling dingo track evidence at the trial. The Royal Commission described him as an impressive witness. He saw the tracks of a dingo carrying a load, which may have been Azaria's body. This is corroborated by Mr (Nui) Minyintiri, Daisy Walkabout and Barbara Tjikadu. Roff described Daisy and Barbara as 'very, very good' trackers (p. 803). Justice Morling described Roff and the Aboriginals as 'experienced trackers and familiar with dingo behaviour'. Dingo tracks found close to the tent on the southern side just after the attack were then evidenced similar tracks of a dingo carrying a load, which they believed was Azaria.

Morling stated: 'It was within the bounds of reasonable possibility that a dingo might have attacked a baby and carried it away for consumption as food. A dingo would have been capable of carrying Azaria's body to the place where the clothing was found. Had a dingo taken Azaria it is likely that, on occasions, it would have put the load down and dragged it.'

Roff stated at the Royal Commission (Transcript, p775) that after tracking the dingo with the Aboriginals, seeing the drag marks and witnessing the dreadful moment of seeing the crepe-like cloth imprint on the sand: 'I am convinced—and I think I have been consistent in the trial—that the marks that I was following were associated with the child being taken by an animal and on the night in question I had no doubt whatsoever that it was a dingo.'

Lowndes had got it wrong, very wrong.

His finding, in my view, was plainly weak.

Now we would have to wait for an apology, again. We would have to grieve Azaria without consummating that grief at her place of death at the Rock. There would be no memorial funeral service until the spirit of Azaria had received justice from this heart of stone.

Many were of the same view as Tom Coulthard, a Woodville

pensioner from South Australia, and an ordinary Aussie you might say. Yet Tom was a thinker with a keen mind when on a just cause and was most uneasy about the inaction on our case. His ideas about Azaria had not meshed with the findings of this Coroner. He had read every morsel of information about Azaria's disappearance that he could place his hands on: the Court transcripts, letters, newspaper articles—the lot—and he had been to Ayers Rock and camped close to where we had been. 'Some people are so bloody ignorant,' he declared. 'All they know is what they feel. This case will never go away—not until the Northern Territory Government comes to its senses—until they officially declare with no strings attached that a dingo did it' (*Adelaide Advertiser* 15/12/1995).

The third inquest's 'inability' and 'unwillingness' to close the case 'had done great damage to the credibility of the Australian legal system', and inflicted 'double injustice' on the Chamberlains, said the *Sydney Morning Herald* editorial (16/12/1995). Yes, I mused, truth had been trampled in the streets. An *Age* newspaper journalist thought that the gates had been flung wide open: 'An open finding now gives us licence to speculate—probably forever' (*The Age* 14/12/1995). Dr Middleweek considered that the Azaria case would now remain the 'cultural benchmark against which all acts of injustice are measured'.

Coroner Denis Barritt, then 68 years of age, stated: 'After studying all the facts of the case there was just no evidence (that Lindy and I were to blame) and that was all there was to it... It was entirely due to allegations of suspicion and innuendo...All it boiled down to was that there was something wrong because the Chamberlains had this funny religion which wasn't all that funny anyway' (*Newcastle Herald,* 'Life After Azaria', 28/11/1995).

Even *The Northern Territory News* writing on the Northern Territory Government agencies, was less defensive than usual. The paper reported, 'the Chamberlains are smouldering with resentment' (*Northern Territory News* 19/12/1995).

In this article, Barritt criticised the second inquest Coroner, Gerry Galvin, for placing us on the stand first when he knew that the inquest would result in a committal for trial. 'Their evidence should come last so that they can answer the allegations...As for the Chamberlains' convictions I was thoroughly disgusted. There are still many people who believe the Chamberlains are guilty.'

Writing *Evil Angels* had given John Bryson an insight into the real world that provided a lesson for believers in the humanistic view of the goodness of man. 'The case certainly changed the way I saw much of the world. It proved the extraordinary degree to which we believe what we want to believe rather than what we should believe and what influences others–scientists, police, journalists, everybody.' Coroner Denis Barritt agreed. 'When you strike some people's attitudes, people who are prepared to make dogmatic claims without any evidence, you understand how witches got burnt' (*Newcastle Herald,* 'Life After Azaria' 28/11/95).

Four days after the 'Whitewash third inquest', on 17 December 1995, an agitated James Oram wrote a satirical attack on the Northern Territory justice system, headlined, 'Why the bitch had no chance'. Writing for the Murdoch-owned *Herald Sun* (17/12/1995), he said that despite the Royal Commission and the Northern Territory Appeals Court finding, Lindy was still a 'murdering bitch'. Powerful 'social pressures' had overwhelmed the justice of the case.

With still no chance of burying doubt and getting the truth, I left the (inquest) courtroom alone, saying nothing. Despite being buffeted and cajoled by agitated pressmen, I shoved my way through to a waiting car, my lips sealed in grief and despair.

I later signalled to the press that this might not be the end of the case after all. You may hear from me again, was the message I left with the following day. In an interview with Channel 7 *Today Tonight* show on 16 December 1995, I argued: 'Forensic science must learn yet to be accountable for its actions of putting people away in jail, falsely and cruelly in prison...'

John Bryson summarised the forensic and police view exactly. 'You see what you want to see, and find what you want to find. No modern (legal) event illustrates this so vividly as does the Chamberlain case.'

In the *Sydney Morning Herald* (18/12/1995) Bryson argued that this (third) inquest 'flew in the face of all the evidence'. 'Do you remember the search of the Chamberlains' tent for dingo hairs? Suspicious investigators found none. Aha. And do you remember the courtroom laughter when the scientific methodology came to light (in the first inquest)?

'The 'forensic' laboratory task had fallen to a new police constable. She was given a microscope. Provided with no hair samples for comparison, she pulled a strand from her own head. Any hair which did not look like this she threw out. So the Northern Territory Forensic Science Unit had collected five human hairs and three strands of wool. But headlines read: 'No dingo hair in Chamberlain tent'.

'Now we have another finding. A third Coroner, magistrate John Lowndes has concluded the inquest that began with Coroner (and former Detective Sergeant) Denis Barritt who found the dingo was the agency of death...Coroner John Lowndes chose to find that a dingo was not the likely culprit not even on the balance of probabilities.

'Justice Morling (the Royal Commissioner) said this: 'Having seen Mr and Mrs Chamberlain in the witness box I am not convinced that either of them was lying...I am far from being persuaded that Mrs Chamberlain's account of having seen a dingo near the tent was false.'

'So, why now did the (third inquest) Coroner choose to disbelieve the Chamberlains? Why now choose to disbelieve the other campsite witnesses (and the chief ranger Derek Roff)? (*Sydney Morning Herald* 18/12/1995).

Why was this culture so powerful, I wondered?

The Morling Inquiry, Bryson continued, came about when 'the Northern Territory Government was not keen to reopen the case, even after Azaria's jacket was found. The Federal Government decided to hold the Commission, which the Northern Territory was politely invited to join. Justice Morling was appointed by Letters Patent issued by Federal authority, so lines of responsibility were clear (*Sydney Morning Herald* 18/12/1995).

The battle between the Federal and Territory systems was spanning a crevasse. *The Bulletin* (18/2/1986) confirmed this nine years earlier with its diagnosis that 'flimsy evidence had cost Lindy her freedom' and had damaged Territory justice. 'Territory authorities', *The Bulletin* writer stated, 'have become excessively defensive, as though every attack on the verdict has an attack on the local justice system's ability to deal with a big case'... but which 'the key evidence was very simple.'

When Max Whittacker heard about the verdict, he rose up in indignation. The Whitackers told the *Melbourne Age* (23/12/1995): 'We were aghast at the Coroner's finding. The two main concerns are the evidence that came from us and that from other witnesses on and around the night of the event...

'Rangers told us to look out for dingoes which were hungry because of the drought. Dingoes were seen prowling around just before the event. A dingo growl was heard at the time...

'My wife's observation (she was a double certificated nurse and a qualified practising social worker), of the distraught parents over several hours of the night, while comforting them, saw them behaving totally consistently with the shock and emotions of losing a much loved baby...

'I naively believed that the police and lawyers would only have one motive–pursuit of the truth. However, I discovered to my dismay that when the police questioned me before the second inquest, they were interested only in answers that supported the murder theory... I was not called to any inquest.'

John Bryson suggested that: 'The culture of John Lowndes' delivery was seen as a jibe at the Chamberlains' solicitor, Stuart Tipple, whose submission relied on the view of the Morling Report which the Coroner sees as a fundamental misconception. This is a term that goes beyond error, beyond fallacy. It's a term used when a judge wants to be scathing. Does it also reflect irritation over a Commission with which the culture is unable to deal?'

Bryson concluded: 'Do you remember the car stickers popular in Darwin at trial time? These were not the cars of Greenies, but they read: 'Save the Dingo'. The T-shirt flaunted at the court (this was contempt of court) 'The Dingo is innocent'. This too was an expression of a culture.' It suited Lowndes to bring down his finding. It had little to do with justice. It was all about culture; a culture that cannot be changed easily. 'Oh yes. The search for a culprit will go on, and on', Bryson concluded (*Sydney Morning Herald* 18/12/1995).

Journalist James Oram's report concluded with an explicit message that I had waited a long time to hear: 'What the Chamberlain saga did was expose the fallibility of forensic science. Some world-renowned scientific figures from Australia and Britain have been left with their reputations in tatters. Yet they have not been brought to account for their part in sending an innocent woman to jail. Nor have the police ('Why the bitch had no chance', *Herald Sun* 17/12/1995).

That was about it. Mr David Farquhar told the *Adelaide Advertiser* that there was 'unlimited time available to lodge an appeal. The Chamberlain case could be reopened through the Supreme Court. They could direct a different magistrate to hold a new inquest or they could reopen John Lowndes' hearing and reexamine his findings.'

But not surprisingly, Fred Finch, Acting Northern Territory Attorney-General, told the *Advertiser*: 'As far as we are concerned, the final chapter has been written, the book is closed and it's time for the Chamberlains to get on with their life...A decision by the Chamberlains to appeal would be 'rather sad''. Yes, I thought, but a just man welcomes the sunlight. An unjust man runs for the shadows.

Was it, and is it 'inherently unlikely' that a dingo would take and kill a child? Lowndes selectively took his lead from Morling's remark that 'it was an event for which there was no known precedent' for a dingo to kill a baby. Was Lowndes then justified to say that the notion of an inherent unlikelihood of a dingo killing a child changed when Derek Roff called for dingoes to be shot in the fear that small children 'could become prey'? Did not Lowndes fail to use a wider interpretation as a result of 'failing to consider evidence that should have been considered'?

Had Lowndes made further inquiries, he would have realised that dingoes do approach humans and act aggressively towards them under a given set of conditions. Marshall Perron's own father testified at the Royal Commission of his experiences with dingoes killing Aboriginal kids. Lowndes' term, 'the dingo theory' should have been modified to: 'the dingo threat'.

Why had Lowndes ignored the Supreme Court Case in Darwin a year before Azaria was killed when Chief Justice Foster declared: 'I am satisfied that the dingo is by its nature...inherently dangerous to man' (*Fisher v Stuart* 1979 25 ALR 336).

Lowndes, it could be argued on this basis, ignored the public interest, failing to give sufficient consideration to the role and purpose of a Coronial investigation. That role is to 'act as a watchdog for public dangers and to offer recommendations in the public's interest to prevent avoidable deaths.'

The Park authorities at Ayers Rock (Uluru) informed us through the media that we would not be allowed to erect a memorial there (*Advertiser* 15/12/1995).

Through a letter from Stuart Tipple, dated 4 March 1996 (vv: 120428), I was advised that in the light of the third inquest finding, a senior Victorian judge (name withheld by request), said he was disgusted with the Northern Territory Coronial verdict, and recommended not proceeding with the Supreme Court appeal as he considered that I would 'never get justice in a Northern Territory jurisdiction'. It was a moment of extreme despair and angst and it has taken me many years to come to grips with this shocking view. But it was also a moment when I heard another sound. It was the sound of something that endorsed the fact that with proper skilling of my research and analysis tools I might somehow be equal to turning around the Northern Territory injustice.

Bob Collins exclaimed in 1997: 'I believe the Chamberlain story is the worst miscarriage of justice the country has ever seen—and still do. There is no media event like the Chamberlain case. It was top of the tree' (ABC National Radio 11/1/1997).

On 17 August 2000, it was the 20th anniversary of Azaria's death and *Good Weekend* Magazine examined the ongoing lie. That article repeated the myth that Azaria 'was slaughtered in a religious rite on top of Ayers Rock the night before (16 August) she was reported missing'. This was despite the acknowledgement that there were a number of campers who swore that they saw Azaria alive the next day on 17 August 1980, including 'Mrs Gwen Eccles who dandled the baby on her knee because Azaria was crying'. But there were those who maintain to this day that all 'were hoodwinked by an effigy in swaddling'.

28. *An Opera and TV miniseries*

After an escalation in friction between Lindy and myself, brewing during the writing of her book, and our inability to communicate empathetically anymore, we drifted apart. The woman who accompanied me to Ayers Rock in 1980 was not the same woman who came home from Berrimah Prison six years later. In 1991 we divorced. Lindy married in 1992, to an American Adventist nine years her junior, John Hampton (Rick) Creighton IV. I remarried two years later, in April 1994, to Ingrid Bergner, also an Adventist, who had just graduated from a teaching degree.

If Moorhouse's *The Disappearance of Azaria Chamberlain* and Cinema Verity's *Evil Angels*, had attempted to represent the truth, Lindy's image and her defiance in the male-dominated institutions of law was now resonating with feminists. The opera *Lindy*, driven by Moya Henderson, a former Roman Catholic nun, and a strong feminist, clearly focused on Lindy's side of the story with her involvement and her blessing. I well remember the warm introduction by Senator Bronwyn Bishop, a Federal MP, as my wife Ingrid and I arrived at the Sydney Opera House with our complimentary tickets in hand. I had to brace myself, as I had no idea what I would be watching.

My only potential involvement in the crafting of this opera occurred when I was asked if my Ayers Rock V8 Torana hatchback was available as a stage prop. That meant the car would have to be pulled apart

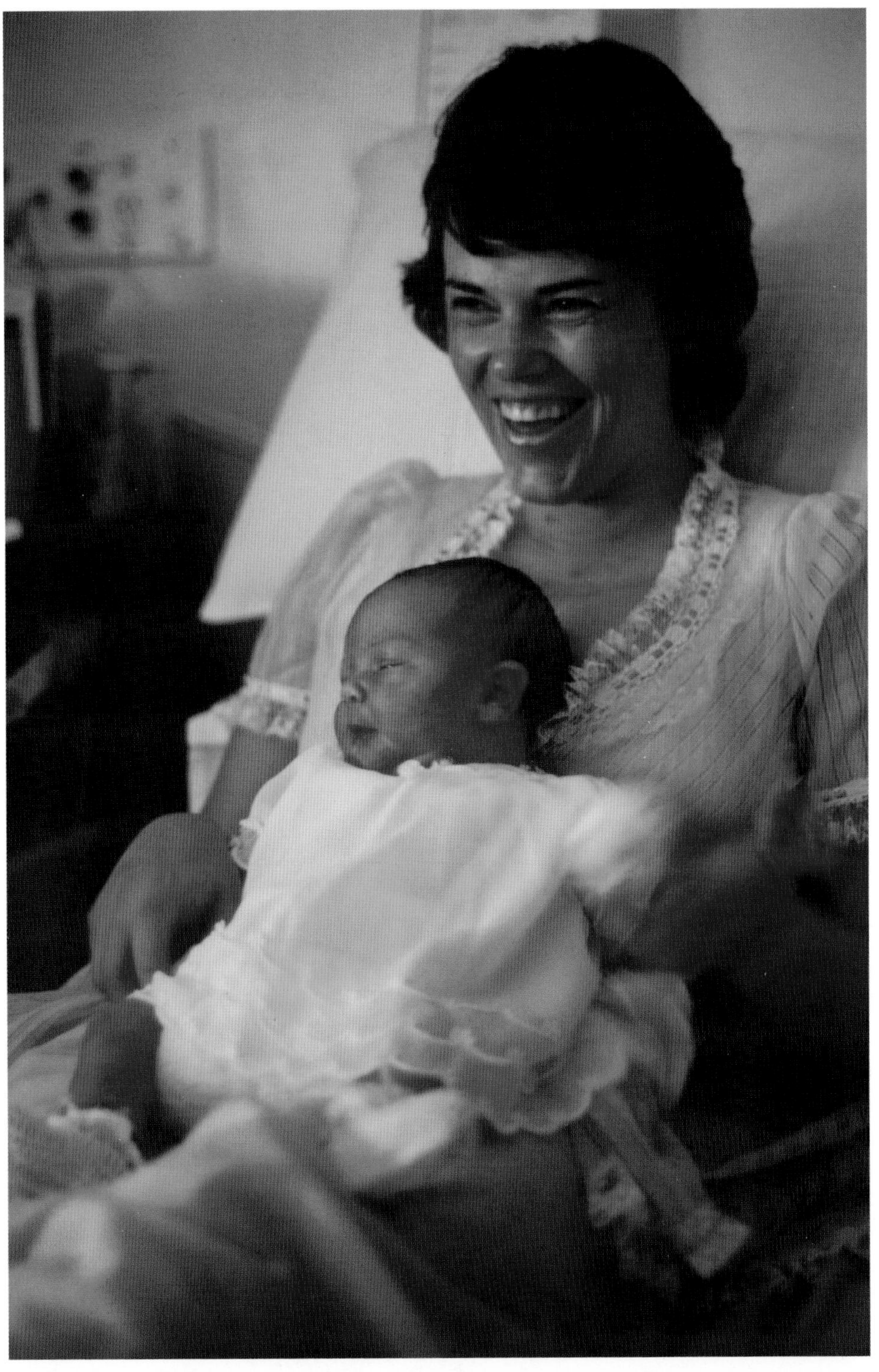

Lindy with Kahlia in Casuarina hospital, hours after being bailed from prison.

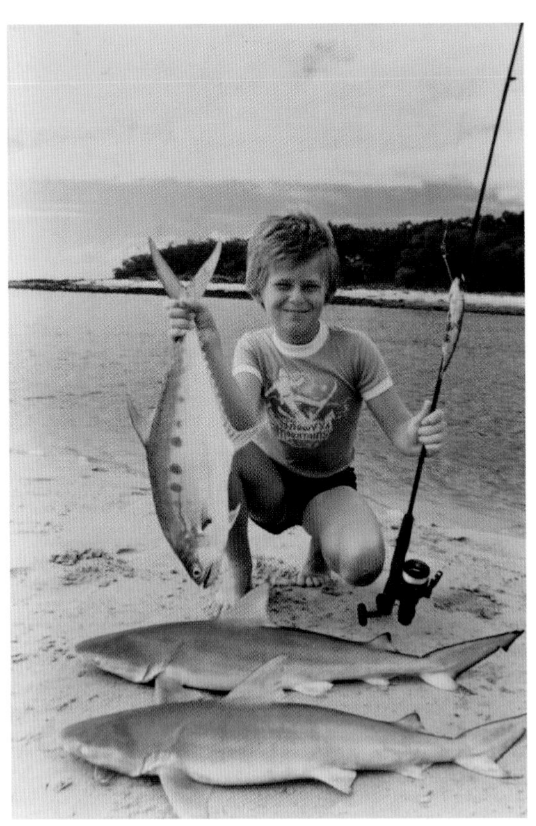

Left: A proud Reagan aged 10, with his morning catch at Gove, Northern Territory.

Below: The new Royal Commission legal team (left to right) John Winneke QC, myself, Lindy and Stuart Tipple.

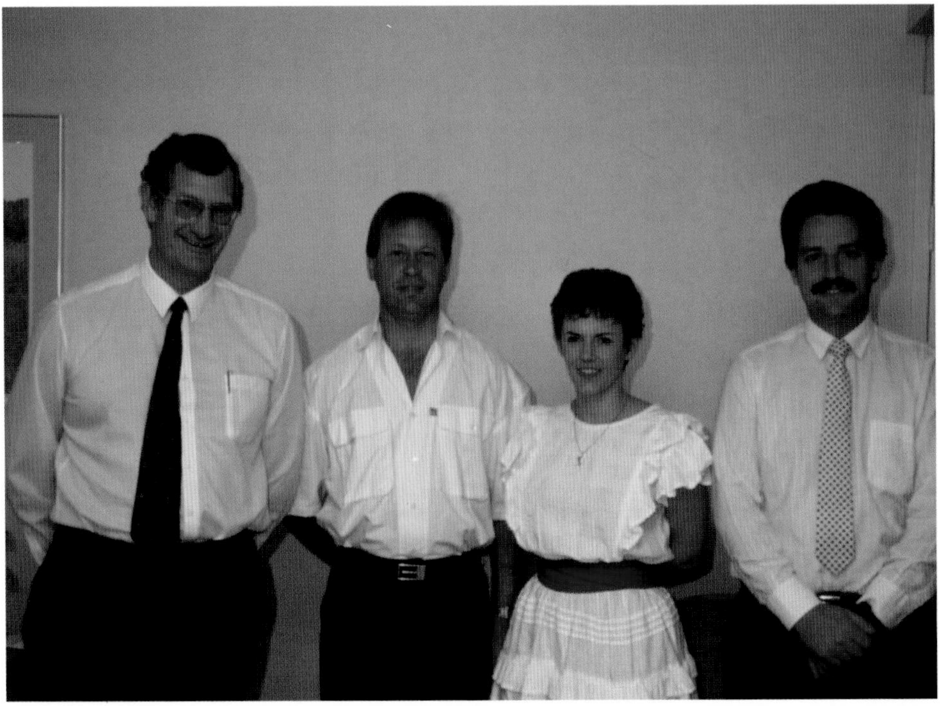

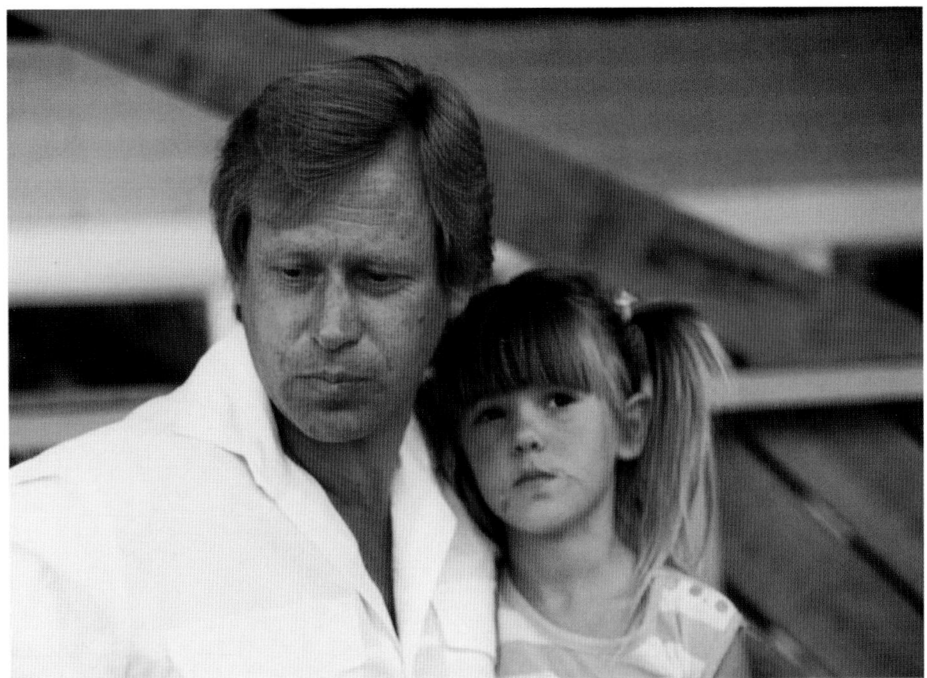

Above: A sad Kahlia sits on my lap, photographed just weeks before Lindy's release from Berrimah Prison, 6 February, 1986.

Below: Reunited with Lindy and Aidan: Avondale College Church in late February, 1986 at the *60 Minutes* interview with Ray Martin.

*Above: (*From left) Myself, Lindy, Kahlia, Aidan and Reagan in February 1987, twelve months after Lindy's release from Berrimah Prison.

Below: Reagan (left) and Aidan with Meryl Streep dressed as Lindy, in the back room during the filming of *Evil Angels* in 1987.

*Above: (*From left) Lindy, Meryl's husband Don Gummer, Meryl Streep, Sam Neil, Noriko (Sam's partner) and myself at Meryl's home, 1987.

Below: (From left) Lindy, Fred Schepisi, Meryl Streep and myself having dinner at Meryl's home, 1987.

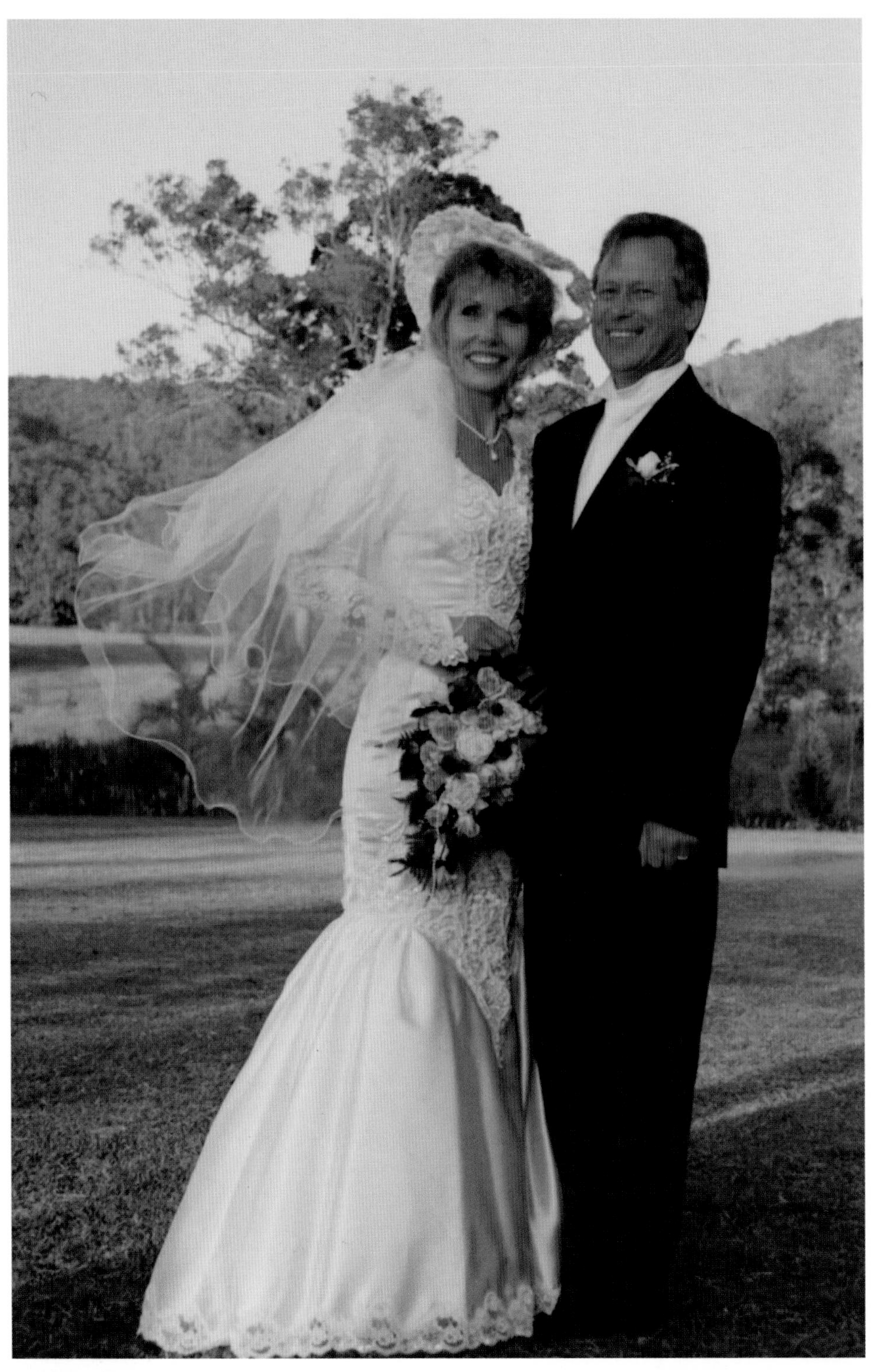

My new wife Ingrid and our wedding day in the Hunter Valley on 4 April, 1994.

(From left) Ingrid, Zahra and myself at my parents home in Christchurch, 2001.

Ray Martin (left), Zahra aged 4 and myself at Ayers Rock on August 18, 2000.

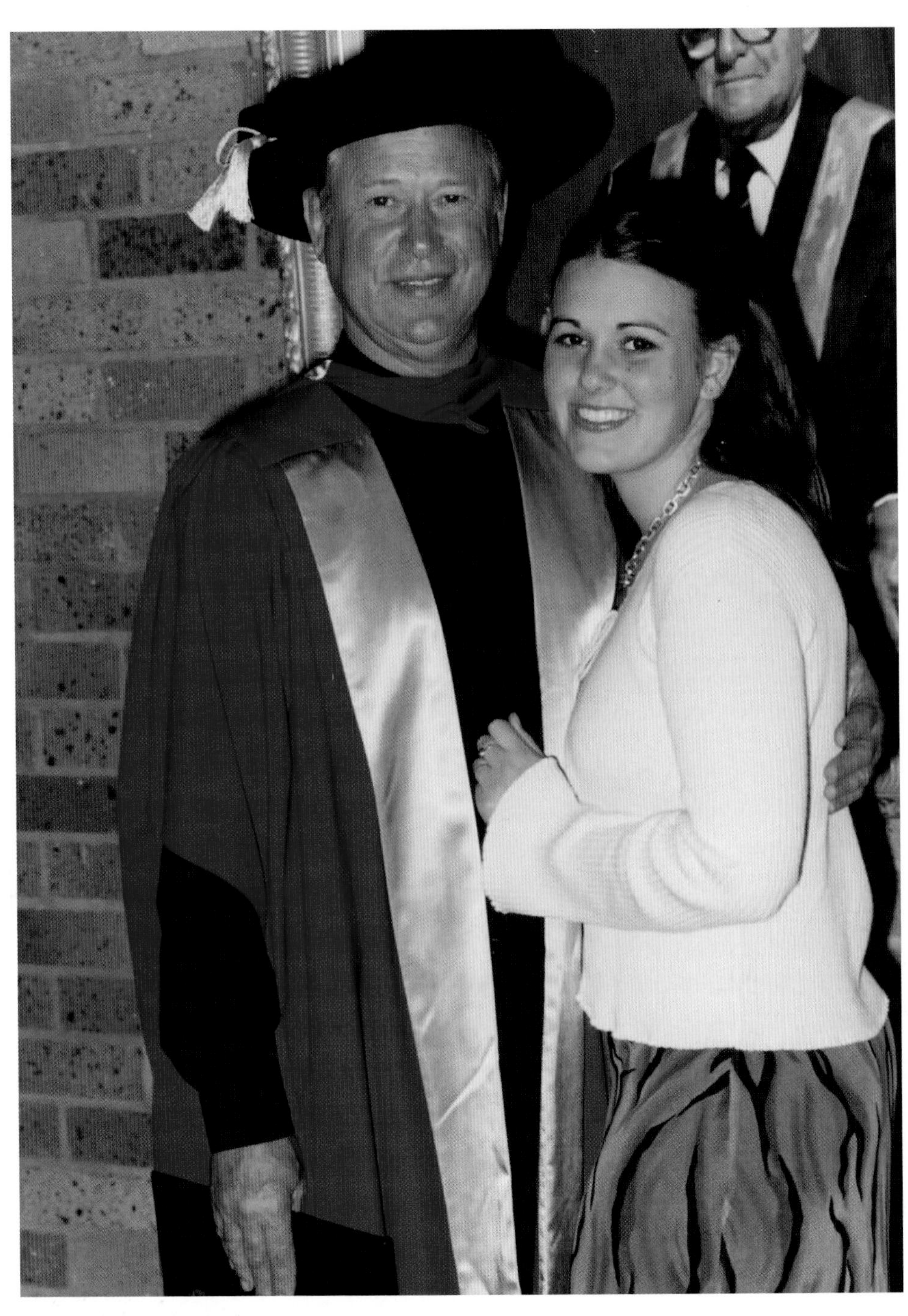

Kahlia and me at my PhD graduation ceremony at the University of Newcastle, 2 May, 2002.

to its forensic investigation status again and I wasn't about to let the refurbished vehicle with the plate, '4ENSIC' (Forensic) attached to it, suffer that indignity. I owned another similar absinth yellow V8 Torana hatchback, bought from the *Evil Angels* film producers, but I did not feel like refurbishing that car again either. I eventually sold this car to my son, Aidan, who reworked it, registering with the number plate, '4MOVIE', and later used it with '4ENSIC' in his wedding.

Lindy, the opera, was certainly an emotional experience for me. I was particularly struck by the impressive three-octave range and stage presence of local Lithgow soprano, Joanna Cole. But this was only the beginning. If 37 years of being a church member had reduced my exposure to opera (I think I had only been to half a dozen performances in my lifetime) this one had whetted my appetite. Ms Henderson created a fine production. The musical accompaniment was particularly dramatic, as the jangled and discordant impact of brass instruments represented the horror of finding Azaria missing from the tent, and the subsequent disbelief, disillusionment and despair that Lindy experienced. The production was clearly from a feminist perspective. My role was severely reduced, which didn't faze me. The opera focused on the courtroom battle between a pure and perfect Lindy and a cunning Crown prosecutor, who describes himself as 'an absolute bastard'.

The Lindy Chamberlain TV miniseries, *Through My Eyes,* screened in 2004 on the TV Seven Network, was driven by producers, Simone North and Tony Cavanaugh. It was my view that, if as a commercial venture Lindy had legal backing for her stance, as far as I was concerned, she had no moral justification. Lindy, I believed, had taken complete and exclusive ownership of Azaria and her life.

Through My Eyes was reported to cost $8 million and was a four-hour television drama based loosely on some of Lindy's book. This miniseries was one that I wasn't looking forward to. I was told by Lindy: 'there would be things in there that I would not like'. It was billed as a definitive and complete story designed to upstage all past renditions. It would be headed by 'the most outstanding Australian cast ever assembled' and would be 'the true and untold story of Lindy Chamberlain'. Strong viewing results of 1.29 million occurred in the 16–24 year-old bracket. The following night it drew back to 1.09 million viewers. It was seen as a considerable success, with director Di Drew claiming in *Inside Film* magazine that it was 'probably one of the biggest miniseries we've done in the country...the design and structure of the film (was) very complex'.

Belinda Middleweek analysed the Tony Cavanaugh and Simone North production as: 'a simulacrum that feigns the historical existence of the real'. She said portions of the film made it 'difficult to discern where 'truth' begins and fabrication ends'. This was despite Cavanaugh suggesting that, 'This is a drama based on true events.' There were at least two fictional characters introduced: Chris, the government advisor and Trevor, the political advisor.

The film's portrayal of Lindy through Miranda Otto was that of a 'brave' but 'flawed' person. She is 'slightly anti-social' and 'doesn't fit' into the stereotype of a grieving mother—the major reason for Australians convicting her. Her personality and behaviour was described as 'unacceptable to the majority of heterosexuals'. Lindy was impressed with Otto's performance. Despite Meryl Streep's fame, Lindy opined: 'The way Miranda plays me, I can almost hear what she's thinking in some places. She's a lot better than Meryl Streep. Meryl acted me, but (Miranda Otto's) got the essence of me.' It was at this point that I knew Lindy had opted for the more romanticised Otto version rather than what I thought was the more real portrayal of her by Meryl.

If the miniseries portrayal of Lindy, predictably, dealt kindly with her, I was satirised as some kind of religious goof or nut case. My portrayal could best be described as a parody of a clergyman. I felt demeaned by it and considered that it slandered the Adventist clergy. As a close friend observed: 'This has not gone unnoticed by a lot of people who know you.'

Acting my part was Craig McLachlan, who became well known during this era starring opposite Kylie Minogue in the long-running Australian TV soap opera, *Neighbours*. McLachlan 'relished' this opportunity to play a pastor, and although he portrayed me as 'physically very fit—broad of shoulder, skinny of waist—a very fit cat', his interpretation was of someone I was not. I was represented as a man out of touch with the world, a sectarian zealot. In the women's tabloid weekly magazine *New Idea*, Patrice Fidgeon purported to have special knowledge about my actions on the night of Azaria's death, claiming that it was my behaviour that caused us to be branded as weird, following Barker's trial prosecution line, which somehow justified McLachlan's representation of me.

James Simmonds, in the first book published on the Azaria case, *Wednesday's Child*, said: 'I can understand his reaction to the loss of a child. People say that the parents seem not really upset but the main reason for that is their faith, a strong belief in the hereafter, a very strong faith. I hope I would react in the same way. That child was loved and wanted.'

Through My Eyes was a clear illustration of how reality and truth can be fabricated by people who have not the faintest notion of the appropriateness and authenticity of my response about Azaria in my prayers, with, and for others. I felt it was a shabby and cynical attempt to degrade the authentic nature of a person who had a legitimate and authentic belief system. Cavanaugh and North had succumbed to the tongue-wagging and gossip-mongering majority who believed that Seventh-day Adventism was some kind of weird sectarian-style or cultic belief system.

A large circulation national magazine contacted me through Stuart Tipple several weeks before the film's release, offering me $40,000 for a few thoughts on the film. I declined the invitation, as I felt it was Cavanaugh's ploy to improve the ratings with my criticism of it. Apart from revealing the significant inaccuracies of the film—especially some prejudicial stuff on the producer's part—the other thing I wondered was, 'Why didn't they talk to me in a professional manner?' Cavanaugh and North ignored me, declined to meet, apart from a reconnaissance meeting to mine me for information and details, which I gave them.

In 2005, with the 25th anniversary of our daughter's death, a closed conference on 'Nation, Media and Myth', was held at Macquarie University by Lindy and her academic acquaintances, including Associate Professor

Adrian Howe and Dr Deborah Staines. According to Dr Middleweek, Lindy was seen as a cultural icon, an '...elder stateswoman, the figure to whom others frequently defer as exemplified in the part she played in this 25th anniversary'. Academics, writers on the case, curators, the campsite witnesses from August 1980, and advocates of the cause were all invited to this conference. I was not. A father's pain, grief and perspective about his daughter was considered not relevant. In dismay, I fired off a satirical email to Dr Adrian Howe, which probably sounded like one of those angry shots from a grumpy old man. Predictably, there was no acknowledgement from the academic. It was a deeply saddening experience to be ignored as the other authentic voice concerning my daughter Azaria Chamberlain.

In the meantime, entertainers, particularly comedians, continued to play with Azaria's death like a dog with a rag doll.

One such entertainer was the Aussie comedian, Barry Humphries who again wowed a Sydney ABC TV audience on the evening of Monday 13 December 1999. I had been sitting back, relaxing in the lounge, when the very funny Humphries, skilfully using his satirical characters, engaged his audience in a delightful show. But I was in for a shock when I sat bolt upright to comments clearly directed at me and my family.

Humphries must have considered us powerful persons in the community to have been the focus of his sarcasm. The essence of his snide remark lay in his belief that of course a dingo killed Azaria, just as a koala had stolen his own daughter. Humphries' satire, which is world-renowned and mostly at the expense of others, had struck a very raw nerve. I felt he was attacking the integrity of my life and my former wife's, and that this was well below the belt. I could hear the groans from his attentive audience from his highly offensive hit. Humphries was eroding my integrity, my work and livelihood. I found his satire sickening.

We were still victims of a grave Australian miscarriage of justice. The private agony of a loss of a child is sacrosanct and should have been off limits. I felt that only a fourth inquest would put this type of person on notice.

Likewise, Paul McDermott, star of the ABC TV comedy *Good News Week* in 1999 successfully swaddled Azaria's death in a dehumanising manner, demonising us as her parents. I wrote a scathing letter to the ABC and showed it to journalist Malcolm Brown, to consider it before sending it. He told me not to be so sensitive. 'Get over it Michael, you are being too precious about public comment and will face this kind of behaviour for the rest of your life', he seemed to be saying. I was in no mood for a fight, for I was in the middle of trying to research a PhD at the University of Newcastle. On reflection, I think I should have stuck to my guns, and sent it. We were convicted on a 'black comedy' of scientific errors and the black comedy and misconceptions paraded by satirists and comedians were endorsed by the Lowndes' open finding.

29. *More Dingo Attacks on Children*

The third inquest finding that the disappearance of my daughter was an 'unsolved major crime in the Northern Territory' was still hanging over our heads.

I still could not understand why the behaviour of dingoes in the Northern Territory was so different to the others around Australia. Or was it? Would our baby have been at risk at other tourist sites in Australia? In a letter to me, the late RA 'Birdie' Swift, a Chamberlain campaigner before his death, thought there was a 'clear imbalance of attacks by dingoes emanating from the Northern Territory relative to other states (except West Australia).'

In the Northern Territory dingoes were protected. Swift believed that there were 'unusual Conservation and Tourism policies, especially at Ayers Rock, during the 20 years leading up to Azaria's death', in particular the policy prohibiting the culling of dingoes.

Also at Ayers Rock in 1980, two weeks before Azaria's death, Derek Roff stated in a letter to the Northern Territory Conservation Commission (*The Australian*, 1984) 'Children and babies ought to be considered possible prey.' In contrast to the Northern Territory, all other states had a decree that dingoes were vermin and 'should be shot on sight' (Kirsty Dixon, Clinical Legal Practice Paper, Newcastle University 1998). One exception was on Queensland's Fraser Island. During the 1990s, dingo attacks were increasing, but according to the

National Park's authorities, it was the victims who were to blame for the animals' behaviour.

I began to monitor activities on Fraser Island. Tourism was big business on Fraser Island—just as it was at Ayers Rock. I personally knew people who had a few close calls, one of whom lived just a couple of doors down from me. I had grave concerns for the children of parents who holidayed there. In 1996, on my behalf, Tom Coulthard started corresponding with the Fraser Island authorities. Their replies angered me deeply.

In a letter to the Hon. B. Davidson, Queensland Minister for Tourism, Coulthard cited the Fraser Island tourist magazine (produced by the Fraser Coast-South Burnett Regional Tourist Board): 'Isolation has ensured that the Fraser Island dingoes are the purest breed in eastern Australia and consequently no domestic dogs are allowed on the Island.' Coulthard then referred to the attacks on the Island that were beginning to worry the local tourist operators, who still chose to seal their lips about the increasing dingo attacks on humans.

Christy Corney, Cooloola National Park, April 1986

Reported in the Brisbane *Courier-Mail* (11/4/1986) five-year-old Christy was pursued by dingoes which attacked her, causing gaping wounds around her eyes, ears, throat, chest, arms and legs.

Andrew Bartram, Fraser Island, 1997

In March 1997 (*Australian Women's Weekly*, March 1997), five-year-old Andrew Bartram, son of Peter and Jane Bartram, 'let out a blood curdling scream that chilled his mother Jane to the core. Frantically, she ran to the shrubbery from where the terrifying sound had come. On her hands and knees in the darkness of early evening, she thrashed around until she felt her son in her hands, then pulled him out of the dingo's jaws'. The parents noted that it had been a nightmare reminder of the way Azaria was killed in August 1980. 'If those dingoes could drag my 25 kilogram son four metres, I don't see why they'd have any trouble with a new born (4 kilogram) baby,' said Peter Bartram, a veterinary surgeon from Victoria. Dr Bartram told the magazine that he had no doubt that the two dingoes, had they have been older and more experienced, would have killed his son.

That dingo attack on Andrew Bartram caused a departmental manager for the Great Sandy Region, in August 1997, to inform visitors of a brochure that would warn them not to feed dingoes. Non-compliance would attract a $50 on-the-spot fine. But the diminishing food sources on the island, including the supply of human scraps, had actually made the situation critical for the increasingly desperate population of 200 dingoes. It seemed strange that authorities thought it preferable that the dingo would now have to focus on the native wildlife, including one of Australia's rarest birds, the ground parrot. Coulthard, who had read the transcripts of all the events at Ayers Rock and the subsequent trials, recognised the similarities at the Rock leading up to the death of Azaria. 'It wasn't until Azaria was taken that the Ayers Rock authorities realised that the situation had become intolerable. All the (six) dingoes were shot.' The boy had large wounds to his legs, one of which was four centimetres long.

Tom Tolhurst, Director General for the Queensland Department of the Environment, replied to Coulthard (Letter 9715833-10/12/97) and explained that the cause of the attacks was the familiarity and loss of fear of dingoes due to humans feeling sorry for them and feeding them. However, there was also an acknowledgement that 'aggressive behaviour' from dingoes would result in the removal and/or destruction of the offending animal by the rangers. Coulthard became increasingly upset by the lack of a more direct response from the Minister for Tourism. He sent a communiqué to Bruce Davidson on 9 February 1998 with relevant material relating to Ayers Rock dingoes, warning them of my predictions that signs telling visitors not to feed dingoes were inadequate and would result in duplicating the Ayers Rock experience, which had led to my daughter's death.

Coulthard added: 'I ask you again to heed the clear warning provided by the tragedy at Ayers Rock. Indeed, the measures in place on Fraser Island designed, according to your colleagues Littleproud and Tolhurst for the Department of the Environment; 'to prevent interaction between visitors and dingoes' have been proved wrong. A series of attacks by dingoes (from January 1994 onwards) including an attack on a nine-year-old boy on his legs which required 22 stitches', was a warning for Coulthard that, like it or not, dingoes had to be removed or culled severely.

Coulthard wrote a scathing letter to Mr Littleproud (12/2/1998) stating: 'Mr Davidson, Mr Tolhurst and you have so far been heedless of the clear warning provided by the happenings at Ayers Rock...You state: 'Only individual dingoes, positively identified as responsible for an attack on a person (or where the potential for an attack is highly likely) will be considered for destruction.' Apart from the obvious 'shutting the gate after the horse has bolted', are you seriously suggesting that none of the other 199 dingoes would make such an attack?' Minister for Tourism, Bruce Davidson, replied. 'The position of the Queensland State Government remains unchanged,' he said (ref T1448-13/3/1998).

Kasey Rowles, Fraser Island, 1998

'When you pitch a tent under the stars (in Australia), you can expect to rest peacefully,' wrote Greg Roberts for a *Sydney Morning Herald* (8/4/1998) feature article 'Wild at Heart'. 'When you pitch a tent under the stars (in Australia), you can expect to rest peacefully, danger was the last thing that should be on your mind.' Roberts told the story of a family just after dusk at Waddy Point camping ground on Queensland's World Heritage-listed Fraser Island:

'The sausages sizzled as the seven children from the three families, travelling together on a camping holiday, played in the sand. They had just pitched their tents after arriving for a one-week stay.

'The youngest child, 13-month-old, Kasey Rowles, was playing three metres from her parents when she was suddenly grabbed by a dingo.

'He grabbed her, shook her a bit then started dragging her away into the dark' (*The Australian* 7/4/1998).

'It dragged her for two metres before her father, Alan, alerted by the baby's screams, rushed at the animal forcing it to release its grip and flee into the nearby wallum scrub.'

Alan Rowles said he heard a 'crunch' sound as their daughter screamed and that it shook her before trying to drag her away.

Kasey was wearing a thick jumpsuit and her attacker was an old dog with a limp and a few blunt teeth. A fortunate event for the toddler, who could have been severely injured, or even worse, had the father not taken immediate action.

The Australian court reporter and entrenched dingo sceptic, Errol Simper, changed his mind in 1998, following the Kasey Rowles dingo attack. After following the Azaria case since 1982, the attack moved Errol Simper to remark in *The Australian* (7/4/1998): 'Evidence 18 years too late'.

His comments struck directly at Coroner Lowndes third inquest findings that there is no evidence of dingoes having a propensity to kill humans or babies. He said: 'It is difficult to say precisely how badly Lindy Chamberlain's cause was damaged at her trial by the overriding certainty among many observers that dingoes simply don't drag babies away and eat them...If you didn't accept a dingo could do all that then you drifted towards the prosecution's version of events. Now a toddler has been seized by the shoulder by a Fraser Island dingo and, arguably, saved from serious harm only by an alert father.'

It seemed that suddenly the light had been switched on for Simper, enabling him to conclude 'Lindy's case has taken an enormous leap forward. Unfortunately for her it is 18 years too late. There's only the consolation that even the most entrenched sceptic would now concede her imprisonment, between May 1983 and February 1986, was a miscarriage of justice.'

Sarah Challands and Kim Richings, Fraser Island, 1998

Two British backpackers, Sarah Challands and Kim Richings were washing their camping utensils in the sea when without warning a dingo attacked them. The *Sydney Morning Herald* reported: 'Challands needed hospital treatment after being bitten 14 times and having her shorts ripped from her...Both were shocked at the animal's ferocity and its refusal to be intimidated by their efforts to protect themselves' (8/4/1998).

30. The Fraser Island Disaster

Dingoes continued to trouble the tourists at Fraser Island, but it was kept off the front pages of the newspapers until the last day of April 2001. At midday, Tim Martin, from the Queensland Media and Public Relations Branch, Queensland Police Service, posted a media release on the web, euphemistically titled: 'Fraser Island incident' (30/4/2001).

The first I heard about the details was from John Healy from Channel Seven who phoned me about the shocking news. 'A nine-year-old boy is dead and a seven-year-old boy hurt in a dingo attack on Fraser Island.'

It took a few minutes for the news to sink in. I asked Healy to send me anything he had in writing and he faxed me the police media release, which was later posted on their website. It revealed that a 'Mr Atkinson (The Queensland Police Commissioner) said that the nine-year-old boy was walking with a seven-year-old companion early this morning when it is believed he was set upon by the dingoes ... An air exclusion zone had been established one kilometre around and 700 metres above the incident's location at Waddy Point to assist in preserving the scene.'

The following day the newspapers flooded their front pages with headlines of the horrific fatal mauling by dingoes of nine-year-old Clinton Gage. The grief from this stopped me in my tracks. I could not go on. In anguish, I felt finally the truth would come out in my own daughter's case.

The Australian (1/5/2001), the Murdoch paper that had published all the hysteria about Azaria's death, reported: 'The death of a nine year-old boy has tragically laid the question to rest: These dogs do kill children.'

The funeral in the Dural Baptist Church Hall for this innocent victim drew more than a thousand people and outpourings of grief from the four corners of the earth. A large photo of a smiling Clinton was projected on the wall. My wife Ingrid and I were among the mourners who paid tribute to the Gage family (*Daily Telegraph* 5/5/2001).

When interviewed by a media outlet later I referred to the shocking event as an unspeakable tragedy from which I doubted the parents and relatives would ever fully recover. Given the way Clinton died, the last moments would have been excruciating and beyond words. I knew shell-shocked parents would never get over this tragedy and would need counselling, despite their Baptist Christian beliefs. That they sought to pass up a Coroner's inquest on the basis that they felt too traumatised to go through it, was evidence of the effect it had on the parents, but even more so on the younger seven-year-old son, Dillon, who saw his brother killed by the two ferocious predators.

Clinton's Gage's uncle, Kelvin Gage, read a statement to the media on behalf of Clinton's parents, Ross and Annette Gage. 'Our beautiful and precious son Clinton was taken from us and rests in God's arms.' Fraser Island Wilderness club spokesperson Dean Monaghan stated: 'I'd prefer to see 100 dead dingoes than one dead kid' (*Who Weekly* 14/5/2001).

The Newcastle Herald (5/5/2001) reported that: 'At that he (Ross Gage, Clinton's father) heard the screams of his seven-year-old and turned around and saw the dingo on him, so he left the dead boy Clinton and raced back and kicked the dingo from the seven-year-old who was bleeding. And the dingo even had a go at Ross. So he carried the seven-year-old back to the dead boy and the dingo was back on the dead boy, trying to eat his face away.'

'The killing evoked memories of the famous case of Azaria Chamberlain, who disappeared in a suspected attack at Uluru in the Northern Territory almost 21 years ago' (*Newcastle Herald* 5/5/2001).

The Sunday Telegraph (6/6/2001) headlined the Fraser Island dingo feature 'Portrait of a killer' and 'Natural born killers'. The *Daily Telegraph* in the feature 'Killer Instinct' recorded on 5/5/2001 this comment. 'Indeed harking back to Uluru on the 17 August 1980, one wonders what might have happened if Azaria Chamberlain's death was treated not as a murder mystery but as a genuine dingo death...as Fraser island locals, who have seen dingoes run off with objects as big as full grown wallabies, are convinced it was. Had the lesson of her death been learned, that dingoes are wild animals that must be treated as such, Clinton Gage might still be alive today, another little happy camper on Fraser Island.'

No public inquest was ever held into the fatal dingo attack on nine-year-old Clinton Gage (presumably at the request of the parents). It is, however, gratifying that recommendations preceding the Coroner's report were accepted by the Queensland Government, which has since provided a comprehensive guide (2002) informing tourists entering Fraser Island to be very vigilant of dingo behaviour and to treat them as potentially lethal animals.

Since 2001 there have been many other incidents with dingoes and children on and off Fraser Island.

Georgie Corke, Fraser Island, November 2004

Two young girls were stalked by a dingo inside a hotel bedroom at Fraser Island's Kingfisher Bay resort in November 2004. The *Christchurch Press* (11/11/2004) reported that Georgia Corke, the older of the two girls snatched her 14 week-old sister away just in time. Until the father arrived, the dingo had stood its ground but he was able to frighten it out of the building.

Nataya Boxall, Eden, South Coast NSW, December 2005

On 27 December 2005, two-year-old Nataya was playing in her back yard at Nullica, 10 minutes south of Eden on the South Coast of New South Wales. Her 'playmate', the family dog turned on her at around 11.50am. The chained dog, a pet dingo crossbreed, attacked Nataya without warning, bit her on the neck and ripped her throat. An ambulance came, but by the time it reached the Pambula hospital Nataya was dead. The family did not wish to be identified (*Daily Telegraph* 28/12/2005).

Port Macquarie, 2005

Just six months later, worried National Parks authorities at Point Plover, 20 kilometres north of Port Macquarie, New South Wales, elected to shoot four dingoes. The park rangers feared an escalation of threatening behaviour by dingoes to park visitors. 'The dingoes had been seen stalking children and anglers on the beach', Angela Kamper reported in the *Daily Telegraph* (13/6/2005).

Four-year-old girl, Fraser Island, August 2007

An attack on a four-year-old child at Eurong township, Fraser Island, late afternoon in August 2007, 'almost mirrored an attack at the same place in September 2006', according to the *Sydney Morning Herald*, who reported the girl's wounds occurred on her thighs, buttocks and back while she was playing next to her father's vehicle.

Three-year old girl, Fraser Island, September 2008

In September 2008, the *Courier-Mail* reported that a three-year-old girl was attacked and bitten on the back and buttocks, again at Eurong. It was now the fifth incident in the past year. Nick from Toowong posted one of many blogs on the Internet, asking the obvious question. 'I wonder how many people today still think Lindy Chamberlain was guilty?' Another view to the problem raised its head. One satirist stated: 'To the animal haters, you people need to be shot, not the animals.' Another said: 'Cull dingoes? Cull the people first.' And another not so 'wild' idea: 'Don't take children to Fraser Island!', 'Have your eyes open'. Finally, a reflection from a fisherman: 'Dingoes are a fact of life on Fraser Island and parents should take extreme caution when bringing children to such an environment. I am a 90kg man and am just short of six foot and was attacked by a lone dingo whilst fishing alone at Indian Head last August.' There is little doubt in most responsible people's minds now that Fraser Island is a place you take your small children holidaying at your 'peril' (*Courier-Mail* Readers Comments, 18/9/2008).

The supplementary feeding of these animals is also an issue and probably artificially inflated the population, at least to a small degree. As at Ayers Rock and now on Fraser Island there is simply not enough native food to go around for these animals and removing supplementary feeding appears to exacerbate the problem.

Rebecca Beale, Byron Bay, June 2010

A 'vicious attack' on Rebecca Beale, a pregnant Byron Bay woman, was reported in the *Northern Star* (15/6/2010). Ms Beale flagged concern for her unborn child when, after she took the rubbish out to the bin at her Bangalow road home last Tuesday when she saw a dingo in her front yard. As she stopped to pick up her cat, the dingo attacked her. She suffered a broken finger and lacerations to her arm.

She told the *Northern Star*, 'It pulled me to the ground and I was trying to get up as I was worried it was going to get to my face. The dingo was just hanging on to my hand, chewing on it. It was disgusting and really scary. I was trying to put my hand on the ground to protect my stomach.'

'Ms Beale was saved when her partner, Kirk Scarborough, heard her screaming and hit the dingo with a plank of wood. She was taken to hospital.

'Ms Beale, a barista, has had to take two weeks off work and has paid hundreds of dollars in medical bills for herself and veterinary bills for the cat, which suffered a sprained leg in the attack.' The dingo was not going to put down as it was 'a legal pet'.

'Firstly we want an apology from the dingo owner and secondly an agreement to compensate Rebecca for her expenses.'

The *Rural Lands Protection Act of NSW 1998* determined that dingoes were pests that must be eradicated.

The thirtieth anniversary of Azaria's death on 17 August 2010 again inspired a spiteful litany of 'guilty' accusations towards us in radio talkback shows around Australia. Some radio jocks fired up their faithful to ring in if they thought Lindy was guilty or innocent. This was in the face of the Federal Court decision and could have attracted defamation action.

Man takes on dingoes to save girl, Fraser Island, 26 April 2011

The Fraser Coast Chronicle 26 April, 2011 headlined: 'Man takes on dingoes to save girl'. This report again endorsed the importance of human intervention to save a child fatality. Two dingoes had followed a three-year-old up a sand dune, while the parents were unaware of her impending doom. Quick thinking by a Fraser Island resident David Law saved the girl when he thought that the three-year-old was facing certain death.

At the Manta Ray ferry, a Eurong resident, a Mr Law noticed a group of about eight adults, some children and three or four cars in front of the Kingfisher barge. Mr Law said, 'two dingoes prowled the water's edge further along the beach but were tranquil. I looked down the beach and saw this young child by herself going over the dune, up another dune and into the bush. The dingoes were wandering down the beach and got to a point where they saw the girl and began to trot in her direction. Nobody knew the girl had gone–I couldn't believe it.' Horrified, Mr Law began to sprint in the girl's direction as the dingoes moved into attack mode. Screaming 'dingo', he attracted the attention of another man who joined the race to save the girl. At the top of the foredune, Mr Law said he saw the girl fleeing ahead of the snapping dingoes then stumbling. From where she fell she was hidden from view in the dunes and at the dingoes' mercy.

'The male dog was on top of her and was attacking her for perhaps five seconds before me and another guy arrived to drive them off,' Mr Law said. 'I just ran my guts out–it's the only reason I got there in time. I'm just so glad she wasn't killed. We checked her to make sure no arteries had been severed and then her distraught mum arrived.'

Department of Environment and Resource Management Chief Terry Harper said one of the dingoes involved in the attack had been shot, and another had been trapped and would be put down. Harper stated:

'Our experience shows there is only a split second between a playful approach, a bite and fatal attack.'

The girl was sent to Gympie Hospital and was reported to be in a stable condition, according to a Queensland Health spokeswoman (*Fraser Coast Chronicle*, 16 April, 2011).

For those who think I have a vendetta to go and massacre every dingo within sight, I would say this: I don't. I don't believe in culling all dangerous game from anywhere. There has to be a balance, but in the context that humans are at the top of the chain. Their lives come first. You wouldn't let your children run around the veldt in Africa unattended and yet some people remain in denial that wild animals on Fraser Island or Uluru are somehow different. While we were the first to be in the public's eye to cry out 'A dingo's got my baby', we are not the last, and it is my task to help the governments of this country take steps to protect kids from future killings.

As part of my investigations, in 2006 I visited Fraser Island and acquired an eight-page, A3 sized, coloured brochure. It was produced by the Queensland Government's Parks and Wildlife Service. For the first time I found some useful information on dingoes and some remarkable admissions. The brochure stated: 'Dingoes have bitten visitors, occasionally quite severely and are capable of killing people.' Some 20 paragraphs on dingoes, under the heading 'Be Dingo safe', gave useful tips on how to protect oneself from them, if threatened. When it came to fatalities, Conservation Commissions seem to have had a problem distinguishing who should be conserved first, humans or animals. But here at Fraser Island the penny had dropped and the human stakes had risen.

The Northern Territory, likewise, had shown itself to be proactive about dingo danger. Its management plan in 2006 stated: 'Visitors to national parks will be informed that dingoes are different from domestic dogs—they are inherently aggressive and dangerous; problem dingoes will be destroyed and inappropriate behaviour by visitors and residents (such as deliberate feeding and inappropriate rubbish storage) is the ultimate cause of their deaths. This information will also be disseminated to privately-owned remote tourist establishments (and to the wider community) to inform them of the potential danger that dingoes pose to humans' (*A management plan for the dingo (Canis lupus dingo) in the Northern Territory of Australia 2006-2011* Parks and Wildlife Service Development of Natural Resources, Environment and the Arts).

There is also the issue of dingo fencing and whether that works. In showing its deep concern, the Queensland State Government finished building a controversial dingo fence around a Fraser Island township in 2008. The grids that allow vehicles to access the town of Eurong on Fraser Island were electrified. They were part of a dingo-proof fence system built around the Eurong and Happy Valley area. The Queensland Government said that the fences will help prevent a repeat of the fatal dingo attack that happened on the island in 2001.

Some residents are furious, however. They said that the electrified grids were dangerous and would not stop dingoes from getting into the towns or approaching people on the island's beaches. They were also worried about the impact of construction on the World Heritage listed sand island.

The Queensland Government stated on 12 January 2010 that their fences were working. They had no attacks since the fences went up. 'As with all our dingo management activities, our number one priority is public safety.'

Dingoes, like crocodiles and foxes, are wild predators at heart.

31. *My Fight for a Fourth Inquest*

From 1995 it became my mission to overturn the nefarious third inquest. It took no encouragement for me to do this. My short career in journalism for a Central Coast newspaper; the research and writing of my first book on Cooranbong to thank my town for caring for me; the invitation to research a PhD at the University of Newcastle as a result of that book in 1998; my graduation four years later; a second book; a screen play and a second teaching degree in 2002, had all sharpened my passion to create a submission for the Supreme Court in Darwin to overthrow the Lowndes inquest—but not just yet. I had a daughter at a private school, and teaching secondary English provided me with a secure income. I had wanted to teach History but English teachers seemed to be in higher demand.

Driven by my experience with the Aboriginal people at Uluru/Ayers Rock in August 1980 I had a yearning to serve an Aboriginal community. They had been fearless and frank in the Royal Commission and I wanted to honour this. My first teaching appointment with the NSW Department of Education was at a small, largely Aboriginal, community on the Barwon River at Brewarrina, north west New South Wales. The Aboriginal population was 1,000, the white population 200.

For the first three months from September 2003, I lived alone in the town. Every three to four weeks I would travel back to Cooranbong to see Ingrid and Zahra. It wasn't easy for them and it wasn't much better for me. The outback road to Brewarrina became quite challenging, where I would struggle not to fall asleep. It was an eerie road at night. The country is so flat and clear you could see the powerful spotlights of a B double 90-tonne semi-trailer 30 kilometres away. The severe drought at that time had drawn hundreds of eastern grey kangaroos to the road's edge to graze on the remaining morsels of greenery and lick the brief late night dew off the bitumen road in an otherwise impossibly barren sunburnt terrain resembling some outer world. Hundreds were hit by cars which was dangerous for drivers and not a pretty sight. The aroma of stench in the still hot air permeated even the best-sealed car with death and destruction.

I formed a love-hate relationship with my car, a black Holden Commodore wagon. I nicknamed it the black dog. I blew two transmisions and a motor during my three and a half year contract at the school.

Brewarrina felt like a third-world town. Dogs roamed the streets unabated and they were hungry. The Aboriginal community leaders and teachers maintained the town in coordination with the police and civic authorities with pride and responsibility.

My home there was an insignificant two-bedroomed bungalow in a quiet back street, across from the rugby union park, courtesy of the New South Wales Department of Education. It was surrounded by high colourbond fences and the doors were deadlocked. No one told me before I came to teach there that two years earlier a schoolteacher had been shot dead in his home by criminals still at large. Also two doors down from me, the boss of the Returned Services League (RSL) club was beaten up by two baseball-bat-wielding Aboriginal youths in his home.

Teaching English to Aboriginal children who didn't want to be there was a real challenge. And for them listening to a 59-year-old English teacher was a shock to their system. I hardly had a spare moment to myself, having come virtually straight out of university. I didn't start too well at this eight-point school (which was another way of saying a school with the maximum learning and behavioural difficulty in the State).

It was unnerving for many Aboriginals and some whites in the town, it seemed, to have the father of Azaria Chamberlain in their midst. Some were very welcoming. Some wanted to bash me. One in fact did give me a couple of punches to the head in the main street, where a small crowd of Aboriginal people had gathered, in broad daylight, presumably to watch my demise. This was a very different community to the traditional Aboriginal community at Uluru/Ayers Rock in 1980. Fortunately, I was able to swing out of his headlock and told him if he had real guts, to wait for my return. He didn't. Instead, he went for the corner pub and hid there. I returned, with a small search party. They were dressed in blue uniforms attached to NSW police insignias. It was the first time I had faced such an incident and probably the first time the Aboriginal community had seen such a swift response from a schoolteacher. After a court appearance the man received six months detention and an apprehended violence order (AVO). This the first time I had ever enlisted the help of the NSW police/or police in general, after my treatment by the Northern Territory Police.

A second man in the local RSL also threatened me and was taken to court for his labours, with an AVO issued to him as well. But this was a problem for the school, as this man was also an employee. Both AVOs were served on people who accused me of killing Azaria. I was offered a compassionate transfer to some other State school. I told them I would serve out my three-year contract. I doubt if the principal was too happy. The employee later apologised in writing and we became good friends.

The problem with violence in the community had infected their skilful and greatly feared town rugby union team, the Brewarrina Brumbies, who had been thrown out of the Western Plains Union 2004 competition. While playing in Bourke, Brumbies team members had smashed the jaw of an off-duty detective. The Brewarrina team thought it was a racist plot to deny them the championship. They were angry but had few allies among the Caucasians.

Late one evening, however, this was about to change. A 120kg Brewarrina Brumby forward came to me to seek a private audience. Tearfully he recounted how the Brumbies, the icon of their town, had been stripped of their right to play. He asked me if I would take charge as their chief executive officer. He said in essence: 'You know the law and you're not afraid to execute it and that is what we need'. I think that what he was really saying was that if I was on their side, I would take no rubbish from those adverse to the team. There were plenty of detractors, especially from Bourke. Rather anxious about this request, I rang Ray Martin for his advice. His response was: 'If I were asked, it would be an honour, especially for a black fella to approach a white guy out there.' The next day I accepted the privilege.

With the experienced coach, Matthew Slacksmith, a grazier and later town mayor, we set about to restructure the team with some proper ground rules. We took the team to new performance heights, making the finals in 2005. This was despite the team walking out on me at three matches because I sacked the captain for threatening a referee. I knew that not to do this would have resulted in the Brumbies being suspended from the Western Plains Union competition again for the rest of the year.

For me, being the CEO of the Brewarrina Brumbies was one of the most rewarding and privileged moments of my life.

Ingrid and Zahra came out to Brewarrina for 12 months. It was a steep learning curve for Zahra to go to the local Catholic Primary School. offensive language was the norm, but the local public school would have been worse, where no white child was welcome. I was extremely proud of Zahra for hanging in there in the Catholic system for a year and she left with high accolades and as the champion junior athlete of the town. I fulfillued my teaching contract during 2005-06, even though I missed Ingrid and Zahra to do that.

The thirtieth anniversary of Azaria's death arrived in 2010, always a quiet day of reflection for me. The usual round of beseeching from media outlets was considered and on 9 August, it was the ever-reliable Channel Nine network that got my nod with Tracy Grimshaw, presenter of popular news program, *A Current Affair*.

It must have triggered something because the Northern Territory Government wrote to Lindy and me on 19 August, indicating their interest in changing Azaria's death certificate. It was odd that this government could entertain such an idea without ordering a new inquest. I instructed Stuart Tipple to prepare, head on, for a new inquest and not cut any corners to get it right. He replied that I would have to do the research for him and compile material related to dingo attacks since 1995 to get him up to speed.

In late August 2010 I sent, through Stuart, the submission to the Northern Territory Attorney-General, Delia Lawrie, asking her for a new inquest on the grounds that we had sufficient evident to change the Lowndes third inquest finding. I had been writing my book, *Heart of Stone*, and was accumulating good evidence and material for another inquest. My research on dingo behaviour had become an important part of the book.

I took a call from Lindsay Murdoch, ABC Northern Territory reporter, who told me about a movement towards reopening the third inquest with the new evidence of dingo attacks in the context of the 1986 Royal Commission and the Federal Appeal Court of 1988. Murdoch was upbeat with the view that surely after 30 years it was time for the Territory to finally get it right. I was more cautious. 'There are still powerful people alive with long knives who have a vested interest in keeping the dingo out of court,' I replied. And besides, the third inquest ethos was predicated on the notion that it was 'inherently unlikely' that a dingo would kill a child.

The brief of material on dingo attacks for Tipple was delivered on 10 October. I had found that there had been three fatal attacks by dingoes, all on children considerably older than Azaria. Among the hundreds of grabbings or chasings by dingoes, there were dozens of serious attacks, with significant wounding.

The barrage of phone calls the next day started at 6.03am, mainly from ABC radio and a couple of TV stations. I took most of the ABC calls because I generally trusted them. Responsible and serious print media came first, then reliable radio stations, followed by TV stations and reporters who had a credible track record. I took one ABC Radio Australia call, focusing on the Aboriginal trackers for their honest and expert work. Apart from that, I was probably annoyingly minimal with my interviews.

We waited for a response for an inquest date to open. I prodded Stuart twice to remind the Attorney-General's Department of their commitment. I wondered what political and police battles were going on behind closed doors. Would the truth finally be coming out or would it again be hidden? After my second prodding of Stuart in November 2011, he wrote a 'please explain' letter to the coroner.

The reply came a month later: Elizabeth Morris was now willing to hold an inquest. It had taken 14 months more for the Coroner to inform me, but on 17 December I received the all-important letter. It was now open for further submissions; but when did they have to be sent in and upon what grounds? Feverishly I had to work toward getting my friend and coronial consultant, Professor Ray Watterson, briefed and up to speed. We wrote submissions together, trying to cover every base. He reworked the technical and legal reasons why Lowndes had failed.

It was a very different feel this time. I was alone in this task, without Lindy. Professor Watterson had been at the forefront of research into coronial procedures in the last ten years. To me he had been unstinting in his time, and unbounding in his critique and encouragement.

In my original draft, I prepared a document with 20 headings, supported by almost a hundred pages of reasoning.

On 9 January 2012 the Northern Territory's Coroner's office sent me a police brief of roughly 28 pages with annexures totalling another 600 odd pages. I had Ray Watterson review it as he had been on the case, monitoring it as far back as 2002, and was well placed to assess the Coroner's response since he was involved in helping to rewrite the books on how Coroners must be objective and exacting in their taking of evidence. He was also waiting for a response to a paper to the West Australian Government on how to reform their coronial system. I sent my final submission, along with Ray and Stuart's submissions, to Coroner Morris on 20 February 2012. It was simply titled *Submission to Coroner Elizabeth Morris*.

In it I state that: 'The new evidence about dingo danger reinforces the need for a new finding. The finding should not just be about deaths from dingoes but about the many near misses that could have become fatal had intervention by parents or observant people not been swift.'

In my report I state that the 'soil and plant evidence found on Azaria's clothing was varied and demonstrated material from a wide area from the campsite to its place 30 metres away from a dingo den unknown previously to park rangers. It was consistent with being carried and dragged from the campsite by an animal rather than it being buried on a dune and later carried there.'

I continue: 'Mr Roff (the senior park ranger) gave important dingo track evidence at the trial. The Royal Commission described him as an 'impressive witness'. He saw the tracks of a dingo carrying a load, which may have been Azaria's body. This was corroborated by Mr (Nui) Minyintiri, Daisy Walkabout and Barbara Tjikadu. Roff described Daisy and Barbara as 'very, very good' trackers. Justice Morling in the Royal Commission stated: 'It was within the bounds of reasonable possibility that a dingo might have attacked a baby and carried it away for consumption as food. A dingo would have been capable of carrying Azaria's body to the place where the clothing was found. Had a dingo taken Azaria, it is likely that, on occasions, it would have put the load down and dragged it.'

'The Crown's expert has conceded that the dog hairs found in the tent and on the jumpsuit were either dingo or dog hairs. It was noted that the Chamberlains had not owned a dog for some years prior to August 1980 (1974 in fact).

'Mrs Chamberlain's claim to have seen marks on a space blanket was supported by plausible new evidence before the Commission. The claim by Mrs Chamberlain that damage to a purple blanket covering Azaria in the basinet was not moth damage as claimed at the trial, but caused by a dingo, is more credible as a result of the new evidence before the Commission.

'Forensic material expert for the Crown Professor Malcolm Chaikin conceded that the opinion that he expressed at the trial that dingoes did not produce tufts when they sever fabric with their teeth was erroneous.

Chaikin had previously said that the cutting example was the strongest evidence that a dingo was not involved. It therefore cannot now be concluded that the damage was not caused by a dingo.

'Dingo experts Newsome and Corbett expected that Azaria's clothing as found might have been more scattered, but Mr Roff did not consider the appearance of the clothing as inconsistent with dingo activity.

'Although no blood was found on the nappy, the marks on the nappy were similar to marks made by a dingo on another nappy used for testing purposes. Derek Roff was asked: 'Have you seen in the vicinity of the camp site at Ayers Rock evidence of nappies being torn by animals?' This question was asked in response to Michael Chamberlain's observations of Azaria's shredded nappy laden with faeces and urine stuffed in the fire grate and pulled out on the Sunday morning. Roff replied, 'Yes and perhaps I can go a little bit further, I have found the remains of nappies and such like within—faeces—dropped by dingoes.'

In the Court of Criminal Appeal three judges concluded that 'it was indeed fortuitous that a dog or dingo should have been heard to growl (Mr West) and a dingo should have been seen (and photographed by Mr Haby) not far from the tent very shortly before Azaria disappeared and that on the night of the 17 August tracks should be found hard up against the tent.

'Evidence that dingoes were attacking and wounding children months before Azaria arrived had been reported at least five times and possibly many more. Evidence of Mr Roff's concern was indicated in his letter to the Conservation Commission with a request for .22 Hornet bullets to eradicate offending animals, but this was denied. Although the damage to humans was recorded as 'minor' none were as small or defenceless as Azaria.

'The growing body of evidence concerning dingo behaviour in tourist areas and their propensity to see children as prey, particularly at Fraser Island, over the past 20 years is quite compelling. The Northern Territory Government has now enacted a plan (2006–2011) for the management and control of dingoes on the basis that they are inherently dangerous to humans.'

Just before I sent my report, I was surprised to receive a letter to the Coroner from Greg Lowe, the camper who with his wife Sally, was with Lindy and I at a barbecue just before Lindy found Azaria missing from the tent and the man who first ran with me into the dark to search frantically. Greg wrote directly to the coroner, in a letter dated 17 February 2012 which I have extracted verbatim from here:

Dear Coroner,

I have never done this before to an inquest, but feel compelled as a very concerned citizen to make comment. It might be a last chance to do so. Legal input so far on this issue has only tended to nefariously cloud the original event beyond any semblance of reality. I am NOT being coerced or paid$ X per day to present or defend any position.

My then wife and I were tourists to Ayers Rock in August 1980, and per chance happened to be in the company of the Chamberlain family at Ayers Rock when their daughter disappeared.

As eyewitnesses to Azaria's disappearance we were unexpectedly called as Crown witnesses at the trial. Our knowledge totally contradicted Crown allegations.

We could never understand the outrageous claims against the Chamberlains.

It seems that no one at the time was prepared to believe us.

The times since have tended to shroud the original event in mystery in the eyes of many, but not to us.

Apart from the initial inquest, the legalese that has followed almost defies belief. It's really been a troppo trip!

One of my concerns is that (according to recent press reports, if they can be believed) (there is a belief that) there was human intervention subsequent to the initial tragedy. By aggregation, that puts all those involved in the initial search under scrutiny, including myself.

If that is truly their belief, why the heck didn't they devote resources toward finding the culprits? I really resent my taxpayer dollars being misused in such a manner.

It's a bloody disgrace.

3rd Coroner Lowndes, whose 1995? report I only recently delved into, seemed to cherry-pick the Inquiry Commissioner's report to support an open finding, regarding the possibility of later human intervention or potential irrational behaviour of a tourist, even though Commissioner Morling reported that there was no evidence at all to support it. As you would be aware, Mr Morling's terms of reference were very different to that of a coroner.

Regardless of the many past squirmishes, I personally do not want to see the official legal record forever stained with speculative get-out clauses regarding possible human intervention unless there is ample credible evidence to support such an hypothesis. To that end, and to potentially put such speculations out of reach, I suggest that a finite period of amnesty/ immunity be provided to anyone still alive (apart from the litany of kooks of course) who might be able to provide credible and cogent information that has not yet come to light.

I'll be happy to metaphorically resurrect Mr Barritt for a celebratory jar or two. He was indeed a practical and conscientious man.

Which brings me to a personal point!

Seeing that I was present at the original tragedy, I wouldn't mind being there at the potential end. It's been a very, very long journey.

Impecunious as I am, there is no hesitation in again selling up a weatherboard or two back to the bank in order to be able to fund a trip to 'see it through'. If there is any chance of prior warning of the coroner's public announcement, I'd like to know. Only takes a day or so to get to Darwin from Hobart.

I'd sincerely like to be safely there when the 4th coroner's decision is announced.

Who knows—apart from the child's parents, it could mean proper closure to me and many other campsite witnesses after a whole host of years of unnecessarily induced anxiety.

Your call! Greg Lowe, Eyewitness

I travelled up to Darwin and slept fitfully the night before the inquest, waking at least four times and switching on the ABC television around 3am to soothe my nerves. The tropical light of Darwin Harbour reawakened me around 6.30am.

The inquest commenced at 10am on 24 February 2012. The day was already sitting on 31°C with 90 per cent humidity. For some reason it was not oppressive for me. I made my way to the Court via a taxi ordered by my minder, South African former plain clothes policeman and military trained, Francois Shamley. Security is always on my mind. I had a job to do and I was trying to cover all the bases.

I arrived with the nuggety Professor Ray Watterson, a perspiring Greg Lowe and the bearded Francois. Press reporters and eight or nine TV cameras, all very strategically positioned outside the main door, apart from one or two who had rushed out to capture us, were respectful as we brushed past into the court foyer security area. The staff, including an African, who presented starkly at the security screen by contrast of his imposing height and very dark skin, looked ominous.

As the announcement to stand for Elizabeth Morris broke the silence, I stumbled to my feet knowing this was indeed my last chance for justice to be done. I felt exhausted but also exhilarated that this could be final closure.

Morris lived in the Northern Territory. I watched her intently as she walked to her seat at the bench. She sat quietly, highly focused on everything that was going on. As I thought about her task and her demeanour, I felt myself strangely warmed. I hoped that her judgment would be fairer if not bolder than Lowndes.

Rex Wild QC, counsel assisting the Coroner, opened by describing Lowndes' finding as 'reasonable' but that the balance had shifted with (my) submission on post-1995 dingo attacks. He motioned with his hands to illustrate that change in balance to about 30 degrees, presumably to demonstrate the shift in the scales of justice. This irked me. I wanted him to drop his hand much, much, lower. I would have to be patient. Stuart was yet to come.

The previous day, *The Northern Territory News* had published a provocative editorial suggesting that retired Detective Sergeant Denver Marchant's recount of the examination of Azaria's matinee jacket held a pivotal role in whether a dingo was involved. He claimed that in no way could Azaria have died without some form of human assistance. Marchant was described as a 'lead detective' by the paper in the case, but it seemed strange that neither Stuart nor I had heard of him or seen him at any court, including the Royal Commission. I rang Stuart after talking to Ray Watterson. I voiced my concern that we should have a meeting but he assured me that I wouldn't need to worry. 'Michael I can assure you that I have got this matter well covered. I have been up half the night tracking the Royal Commission expert testimony on this and I am ready.'

I rang and tried to allay Ray Watterson's fears with the affirming news. Recognising the tone of Stuart's voice, I knew that the editor of *The Northern Territory News* might wish he had never written anything about the importance of Denver Marchant. The editor had made a number of factual errors, including which inquest this was; he claimed it was the third!

Ann Lade, a sprightly police researcher and ex-Northern Territory detective sergeant, presented the police report into an investigation into attacks by dingoes on humans on Fraser Island. A total of 239 were described as either minor or requiring at least first aid, while some needed emergency hospitalisation. Three deaths were mentioned by her, and later described in some detail by Rex Wild.

When eventually I stood at the bar to address Coroner Morris, I wondered whether I would be able to finish without some help. I prepared Ray Watterson to give me backup after giving him a copy of my 530-word speech.

I started slowly and deliberately. I was confident but also nervous. I had to get this message out clearly. The coroner watched me intently. One half of my mind was on my paper, the other on how she was dealing with it because from teaching and preaching I had learned to recognise when everyone was hanging on every word. I studied her face carefully as I spoke, but not so much as to cause her to become uncomfortable. I began.

'In the eyes of a mother, a father, virtually all the Ayers Rock witnesses on 17 August 1980, and now the vast majority of forensic witnesses, a dingo stole a little girl from our humble tent and killed her. The propensity for dingoes to attack and kill children is no longer an hypothesis. It is a fact. This is why this inquest was called. To look at the evidence in the context of the propensity for dingoes to kill children, given the right circumstances.

I am grateful that such fine witnesses like chief ranger Derek Roff and the expertise of the Aboriginal trackers including the excellence of Barbara Tjikadu, Daisy Walkabout, Nipper Winmatti, and Nui Minyintiri were able to be heard in an appropriate court of law to present their truth.

Since the loss of Azaria I have had an abiding fear and paranoia about safety around dingoes. They send a shudder up my spine. It is a hell I have to endure, and for a former farmboy and alpine hunter, I wish I could be free from it, but it won't go away.

I have always maintained that dingoes in their own habitat, not conditioned to a human environment, deserve their life in the wild and are an important part of Australia's fauna. But dingoes and children are a toxic mix.

Clinton Gage, Nataya Boxall and Kara Compton in Victoria, and their parents, did not realise this until it was too late.

Now that the Queensland Government on Fraser Island and, more recently, the Northern Territory Government have put into practice management plans to protect humans from dingoes, it is our hope that people will heed the warnings from these deliberations and be saved from further fatalities.

This is the opportunity for all Australians, and indeed the world, to know what Lindy, our sons, Aidan and Reagan and I, Michael Chamberlain, have always known.

Although this will cause us to relive the terrible pain and suffering behind the scenes of our lives, we await the truth, in the eyes of the law, about how our daughter, Azaria Chantel Loren Chamberlain, died.'

Ray Watterson leaned over to me and said: 'Do you know what effect you have just had on this court?' he asked.

'I have no idea,' I replied.

'Half the people in the court had either misty eyes or they stopped writing.'

Rex Wild afterwards congratulated me on my speech. Lindy came up to me and said; 'That was a good speech; better than the submission you put in.'

After both sides had put their evidence and had agreed that on the balance of probabilities the dingo was the culprit that killed Azaria, the inquest was adjourned to a day when the finding would be brought down. Like the first Barritt inquest, again the decision of Ms Morris would be televised nationally. Did I think that this time she would get it right? If it wasn't a forgone conclusion until the fat lady sings, as they say, then I had to trust as the Psalmist (Psalm 95:15) promised: 'Justice will rturn to the upright and all the upright in heart will follow it.'

Despite being haunted by the advice I was once given, that 'I would never get justice in the Northern Territory', my answer in faith had now to be yes!

32. Justice for Azaria

There is a tide in the affairs of men,
Which taken at the flood, leads on to fortune;
Omitted, all the voyage of their life
Is bound in shallows and in miseries.
On such a full sea are we now afloat,
And we must take the current when it serves,
Or lose our ventures.
The Tragedy of Julius Caesar Act 4 Sc. 3

But because of your stubbornness and unrepentant heart you are storing up wrath for yourself in the day of wrath of the righteous judgement of God.
Romans 2:5 ASV

Twenty five years after Michael and Lindy Chamberlain's baby Azaria vanished, we still have a lot to learn about justice,' John Bryson wrote in *The Bulletin* (30/8/2005). I have to agree with him.

'Why, in the peacetime early 1980s, in Australia, would someone in government, or in its bureaucracy, strive to deny fairness in a trial to parents suspected of the murder of their swaddling baby? And why would a government like that, be so applauded on radio, in newspapers, in sports clubs, in hotel bars?

'Following the heart-rending shock of an interview with bewildered parents, the TV took control of the story, while word of mouth carried the rumours.'

The Bulletin traced the beginnings of the story back to naturalist author and editor of *Wildlife Australia* magazine, Vincent Serventy in *The Courier-Mail* (20/8/1980) when he said: 'Dingoes don't behave like that', and 'a dingo couldn't run with such a weight in its mouth'.

So began the allegation that I had made a sacrifice for the sins of the world, a notion still peddled by many, including the police.

John Bryson saw it clearly and linked it to the pop culture of the 1970s and early 1980s that was saturated in satanic horror films, including *The Exorcist*. It was alleged I had made a sacrifice for the sins of the world. That I had a healthy loathing for this kind of entertainment was irrelevant.

Coroner Denis Barritt's anger over the public hatred, so well orchestrated against us, caused his decision to televise the first inquest finding in an attempt to reveal the truth. Barritt identified the dingo as 'the slayer' but proposed that there had been some type of human interference or interception after Azaria's death. He apologised to us for the appalling public bigotry, catalysed in the Northern Territory.

Who authorised the massive expenditure to create, investigate and foster this story? The untested theories that Azaria's clothing bore a bloodied handprint purportedly the size of Lindy's and that her throat was cut, based on the blood flow pooling around her neck, was all disclosed in secret.

All of the Ayers Rock campers' cogent and compelling testimonies claimed without doubt that a dingo had killed Azaria. Every one of them were called at the trial. The expert Ayers Rock Aboriginal trackers' statement claimed that they had followed the four-legged killer from the tent. Forensic science, so called, had to convince a jury, against the odds, that this evidence was irrelevant.

Ayers Rock Chief Ranger, Derek Roff's report, dated several weeks before Azaria's disappearance 'warned of increasing danger to visitors from the current pack of dingoes around the campsite.' It advised a cull of the dingoes because, in its own chilling language, 'small children... can be considered possible prey.' This 'whistle blower' has vanished from public view.

A thorough three-hour investigation of our car at Mount Isa by Detective Sergeant Graham, a year and two weeks before the trial, found 'no blood in the car'. As Bryson states, 'Confiscation of the family car, and the removal for blood tests, began a rumour that the sedan was 'awash with blood', again wrong but useful in reassuring public prejudice.'

At the trial, the blood evidence looked suspect but could not be proved faulty. General Motors Holden (GMH) later informed us that the supposed 'blood spray' under my car's glove box, supposedly driven by an 'infant's beating heart', was in fact Dufix 101 sound deadener from the spray of a GMH paint gun. The rest of the supposed blood 'awash in the car' was, among other corrupted things, a spilled milkshake. I remember it myself. It was a cherry-ripe thick shake.

All the details of our life were scrutinised. A forensic interstate specialist was sent before the trial to North West Tasmania 'to locate a file recording child abuse by the Chamberlains when living in Tasmania, a folder rumoured to be as fat as a briefcase. He spent a long time fruitlessly searching.' A search was conducted of the sewer at the Uluru Motel, where we stayed, in the hope of finding the missing remains of a nine-week-old child. The desert around the tent site was dug up in searing heat with cameras focused intently to record the thoroughness of the Northern Territory police. A reconstruction of what Azaria's grow suit might have looked like, if a dingo had killed her, took place. The effigy of a small child, borne by a two-legged Territory policeman, was dragged over the top of bushes 'attached to a lanyard, paced by a news camera', in a highly unlikely route and then examined by the Australian public while 'bathed in floodlights'.

The tactic created suspicion in the public mind and pandemonium in ours. As parents we only discovered all this activity, alongside everyone else, through TV and newspapers. As Bryson says, 'Their alarmed lawyers asked (Northern Territory) detectives for information. They were refused. They asked (Northern Territory) Crown law for it. They were refused.' Our lawyers flew to London to interview Cameron only to be told that, 'he was forbidden from speaking'.

Bryson summarises the events: 'The Crown's application was made to the (Darwin) Supreme Court. No notice of it appeared in court lists, it was heard in secret and it was successful on every count.'

'The Chamberlain family was given notice that the case had reopened by the arrival of a crew in a helicopter over the house. Barritt was assigned to do urgent work in Darwin and Magistrate Gerry Galvin appointed Coroner in Alice Springs.'

'The usual practice of giving copies of statements to be given in evidence, to the parents of the deceased, was refused. The usual practice of giving copies of evidence to the parties concerned, in this case, the Chamberlains' lawyers, was refused. No new evidence from campsite witnesses would be taken. No evidence from the Aboriginal trackers would be taken.'

We were never made aware that, in effect, the second inquest placed Lindy and I on the stand for murder. It was not until the end of the second inquest, after all the damaging evidence had armed the media with relentless and unanswered accusations and proofs, in headline form and blasting the airwaves night after night, spraying the public, were we told that Lindy would be charged with murder and I, of being an accessory after the fact to murder. We would have to front up for a trial.

No Australian forensic expert was willing to back Professor Cameron's unsubstantiated notion of a cut throat or handprint on the jumpsuit.

There is no doubt that the jury were exposed to intense media coverage, prejudice and supposition. They could never make their decision separated from the effects of that.

Defence leader, John Phillips QC, returned to Melbourne to become Victoria's Public Prosecutor and later Chief Justice of the Supreme Court. He did not forget the experience of facing the Territory's rough justice and became the driving force to set up an independent forensic laboratory and science centre in Victoria.

A dingo killed Azaria, as the Barritt first inquest correctly found. The push for a fourth inquest is about the need for a Northern Territory Coroner to accept this truth to rectify her birth certificate for the official record.

The time is ripe to tell the truth behind the Northern Territory façade.

After the fourth inquest presentation, Errol Simper wrote the most definitive of all news reports about the cause of Azaria's death. Headlined, 'Time to reason on the fate of Azaria', Simper says 'It's close to extraordinary that 32 years after Azaria was kidnapped, then consumed, the (Northern Territory) legal system continues to wrestle with legal processes that will make a dingo guilty and absolve Azaria's parents for posterity. The evidence that a dingo took the child has built to an overwhelming level. Simultaneously, the cold science that in October 1982 convicted Lindy and Michael Chamberlain has been revealed as flawed and threadbare.

'An official finding that nine-week-old Azaria was taken by a dingo would represent a triumph for personal, eyewitness gut-feeling evidence as opposed to an over-reliance on pure science.

'The trial prosecution, brilliant as its courtroom performance was, produced no murder motive, no body and no plausible weapon. It has become increasingly obvious that a dingo did it. Officialdom should now simply say so' (*The Weekend Australian* 25–26/2/2012).

During 17 years Errol Simper had been a respectable and honourable Australian journalist and a national anchorman for the Northern Territory's point of view. His change of heart must surely rate as one of the most serious turnabouts. Why did he change his position? Although this has provided me with some personal satisfaction, it cannot change the need for accountability.

Mark Tedeschi QC, the Crown prosecutor in a high-profile New South Wales trial, was heavily criticised for his courtroom performance and his zeal to win the case at all costs. He was accused of engaging in 'speculative' argument where, 'A line is crossed from available inference being drawn from evidence and speculative submissions with no proper basis in the evidence'. There was a difference between prosecutors 'courageous enough' to pursue criminal allegations and those 'putting 'fanciful' allegations' (*Sydney Morning Herald*, 28/2/2012).

Malcolm Brown argues that it is the prosecution's role to 'defeat tactics by the accused, to obfuscate, evade and disassemble' (*Sydney Morning Herald*, 28/2/2012). What happens when evidence is lost or discussed in secret? When expert evidence is discredited and yet still upheld?

The Crown must have been aware of the Supreme Court case held in Darwin in 1979 before Mr Justice Forster, *Fisher vs Stuart* (1979, 25 ALR 336 at p338 Foster CJ). In this case the judge declared: 'I am satisfied that the dingo is by nature...inherently dangerous to man.'

In 2009 Justice Dean Mildren interviewed Ian Barker QC, and asked him what his view was now. Mildren recorded: 'If he had known at the time of the original trial what he now knows, he would have advised the government not to proceed with the trial' (personal interview with Ian Barker QC, 2/3/2009 by Justice Dean Mildren in *Big Boss Fella All Same Judge*, The Federation Press, 2011).

Natural justice had been denied us in a number of instances. Is it now time for a proper independent investigation, along the lines that the Federal Government sought in 1986, into the administration of justice?

Timeline of Main Events

11 June 1980: Azaria Chantelle Loren Chamberlain born, Mount Isa Public Hospital.

17 August 1980: Azaria taken by a dingo at Ayers Rock, Northern Territory.

December–February 1980-81: First inquest into the death of Azaria held at Ayers Rock by Denis Barritt, Coroner.

19 September 1981: Northern Territory police raid the Chamberlains' Cooranbong home in New South Wales.

18 November 1981 Supreme Court of Northern Territory quashes the findings of Denis Barritt, orders a second inquest.

December–February 1981–82: Second inquest into the death held in Darwin, by Gerry Galvin, Coroner, overturns the first inquest finding and commits Lindy and Michael for trial.

13 September 1982: Lindy Chamberlain and Michael Chamberlain on trial in Darwin for murder before Justice Muirhead.

19 October 1982: Lindy Chamberlain sentenced to life imprisonment for murder, Michael given suspended sentence for accessory after the fact to murder.

17 November 1982: Kahlia Chamberlain born in Berrimah Prison in Darwin.

19 November 1982:	Lindy released from prison on bail pending appeal.
30 April 1983:	Federal Court rejects appeal: Lindy again pronounced incarcerated for the term of her natural life.
22 February 1984:	High Court Appeal narrowly rejects the quashing of the Chamberlain's trial verdicts 3:2.
November 1985	Brian Martin's report for the Northern Territory rejects application of Chamberlain Innocence Committee for full judicial inquiry into the case.
25 November 1985	Northern Territory rejects application for early release from prison of Lindy.
2 February 1986:	Matinee jacket found at Ayers Rock.
7 February 1986:	Lindy released from prison on compassionate grounds.
April 1986:	Royal Commission ordered.
8 May 1986:	Royal Commission commences under Justice Morling.
2 June 1987:	Royal Commission finding delivered: trial verdicts found to be unsafe and unsound.
15 September 1988:	Northern Territory Criminal Court of Appeal quashes convictions and finds Chamberlains innocent of 'murder'.
1991-1992:	Compensation for wrongful imprisonment. Michael and Lindy divorced.
16 December 1995:	Third inquest into death of Azaria by John Lowndes, Coroner, delivers an 'open finding'.
24 February 2012:	Fourth inquest by Elizabeth Morris, Coroner, commences.

Court Trial Transcripts

The *Queen vs Chamberlain*, Supreme Court of the Northern Territory, transcript.

Northern Territory of Australia, Coroners Court at Alice Springs, no 107/1980 transcript of Proceedings before the Coroner Mr D J Barritt SM into the death of missing child Azaria Chantel Loren Chamberlain at Ayers Rock on August 17, 1980.

Northern Territory of Australia, Coroners Court at Alice Springs, no 107/1980 transcript of Proceedings before the Coroner Mr G Galvin CSM into the death of missing child Azaria Chantel Loren Chamberlain at Ayers Rock on August 17, 1980.

Findings of the High Court of Appeal of Australia – Gibbs CJ, Mason, Murphy, Brennan and Dean JJ, Alice Lyn Chamberlain and another, applicants and the Queen respondent, 22 February 1984.

Northern Territory of Australia, Coroners Court at Darwin, no 107/1980 transcript of Proceedings before the Coroner Mr J Lowndes into the death of missing child Azaria Chantel Loren Chamberlain at Ayers Rock on August 17, 1980.

Royal Commission of Inquiry into the Chamberlain Convictions, Mr Justice T R Morling Commissioner, Transcript of Proceedings, Darwin, commencing Thursday 8 May 1986.

Justice Morling, Report of the Royal Commission of Inquiry into the Chamberlain Convictions, Darwin, June 1987.

Northern Territory Criminal Court of Appeal, Ash CJ, Kearney J, Nader J, September 1988

Glossary of Main People and Terms

Adams, Michael. Council assisting Ian Barker at the Royal Commission.

Akister, John. NSW Corrective Services Minister.

Alcorta, Frank. Editor of *The Northern Territory News* 1985–86.

Allen, Bill. NSW Police Commissioner.

Allen, Dr Western. Chamberlain Innocence spokesperson.

Annable, Dr Terry. Critic of the High Court judgment.

Asche, Chief Justice Keith John Austin. One of three Northern Territory Criminal Court of Appeal Judges in the Chamberlains' successful appeal to have their verdicts quashed unanimously.

Austen Tayshus. An Australian stand-up comedian during the 1980s, who attacked mercilessly the Chamberlains.

Azaria. Means 'blessed by God.'

Azaria Newsletter. April 1984–April 1986. Bi-monthly 16 (or more) page A4 newsletter set up by Michael Chamberlain, executive editor, and Nonie Hodgson, principal journalist and editor. The goal was to inform and encourage Australian and New Zealand support groups with news, views and interviews and move towards a Royal Commission into the truth about the death of Azaria.

Azazel. The name of the goat described in the Old Testament as a 'sacrifice in the wilderness'. The mistaken rumour was that this was the meaning of Azaria festered in the media and greatly affected public opinion.

Bailey, Peter. Australian Human Rights Commissioner 1985.

Barker, Ian QC. Chamberlain trial prosecutor and Royal Commission Counsel for the Northern Territory and the police.

Barlow, Paddy. Dingo fence expert.

Barrier, Barry. Deputy Director of the Northern Territory Correctional Services.

Barritt, Denis. First inquest Coroner who requested a televised finding that Azaria was killed by a dingo and who apologised on behalf of the Australian nation to the Chamberlains for the gossip and innuendo.

Baume, Senator Peter. National Party.

Baume, Senator Michael. National Party.

Baxter, Dr Simon. Joy Kuhl's supervisor who later resigned.

Beasy, John. Found Azaria's missing matinee jacket.

Behringwerke. German manufacturer of the blood reagent used by Joy Kuhl and who described Kuhl's method of determining blood in my car as 'mistaken'.

Bentley, David. Walkley Award-winning journalist.

Berrimah Prison. Lindy's place of incarceration a few days short of three years.

Bjelke-Petersen, Joh. Premier of Queensland and supporter of an inquiry into the Chamberlains' convictions.

Blair, Barry. A forensic scientist who changed his evidence about blood.

Blanch, Ken. *Northern Territory News* journalist who ran foul of Paul Everingham after the trial.

Boettcher, Barry. Professor of Biological Sciences and Australian blood expert, University of Newcastle. Pointed out flaws in Joy Kuhl's work.

Boswell, Senator Ron. National Party, Queensland.

Bowen, Sir Lionel. Federal Government Attorney-General who supported a full Royal Commission into the death of Azaria Chamberlain, including an examination into the Northern Territory administration of justice and police evidence.

Bowhey, Jacqueline. Darwin Chamberlain support member.

Boyd, Guy (and Phyllis). Distinguished Australian sculptor and public defender of the Chamberlains. Wrote a book, *Justice in Jeopardy*, in 1984, presenting the testimony of 12 major witnesses from Ayers Rock and elsewhere supporting the Chamberlains' innocence.

Bradley, Professor. Royal Commission blood expert.

Brennan, Gerard. A Justice in the High Court who refused the Chamberlain's appeal.

Brett, David. Fell to his death at Ayers Rock late January 1986. In the subsequent search for him, Azaria's missing matinee jacket was found.

Brien, Steve. Former journalist in the Northern Territory and author of the discredited book *Azaria: Trial of the Century*. He was later hired by the NSW Police as their public relations media person.

Brinsmead, Robert. Chamberlain supporter.

Brown, Bob MP. Federal Minister for Roads and Traffic and local member for Charlton who supported Michael Chamberlain in parliament to obtain a Royal Commission.

Brown, David. Senior Lecturer at law, University of NSW, and later professor.

Brown, Pastor Graeme. Canberra National Seventh-day Adventist Church minister.

Brown, Dr Kenneth Aylesbury. Forensic odontologist who took Azaria's jumpsuit to London and gave it to pathologist James Malcolm Cameron who presented a 'slit throat' theory, later discredited.

Brown, Malcolm. *Sydney Morning Herald* senior journalist, editor and author. The longest-serving reporter to cover the Chamberlain case. He believed the Chamberlains were innocent and became increasingly frustrated at the obfuscation by the Northern Territory to admit that a dingo killed Azaria.

Brown, Neal. Federal MP.

Brunner, Dr Hans. Royal Commission dog hair expert.

Bryson, John. Lawyer and author of the book *Evil Angels*. He sold the book rights to Cinema Verity which became the basis for the film by the same name (*Evil Angels* and *A Cry in the Dark*). Bryson became a significant media legal commentator and a potent force in seeking justice for the Chamberlains.

Burnham Burnham. Aboriginal activist.

Button, Senator John. Federal Labor Senator who was highly critical of Northern Territory judicial system in 1985.

Cameron, James Malcolm. Professor of Pathology, London Medical School. Made claims about how Azaria died from a cut throat, later shown to have had no foundation.

Campbell, Ann. Women's Seventh-day Adventist ministries champion and Sydney Support Leader for the Chamberlain drive for a Royal Commission.

Carrick, Senator John. Federal Liberal Member.

Carter, Gowan. Northern Territory Police Association.

Casuarina Hospital. Darwin hospital where Lindy gave birth to Kahlia.

Catter, Bob. Knew Michael Chamberlain in Mount Isa, Queensland. Senator for the National Party and supporter of the Royal Commission into the case.

Cawood, Ian. Ranger at Ayers Rock when Azaria was killed. Owned a pet dingo named Ding but recorded in his diary six weeks before Azaria's death that he had shot it and thrown it on the Ayers Rock rubbish tip.

Cavenagh, Greg. Northern Territory solicitor for the Chamberlains at the trial. Became Chief Coroner for the Northern Territory.

Chaikin, Professor Malcolm. Regarded as an expert on dingo damage to Azaria's jumpsuit at the trial, but his evidence was discredited at the Royal Commission by an experiment showing dingoes could duplicate the act of mechanical cutting.

Chamberlain children. Sons Aidan and Reagan, daughters Azaria and Kahlia, children of Lindy and Michael Chamberlain. Zahra, daughter of Michael in second marriage to Ingrid.

Chandler, Joy. Leader of the Chamberlain support group in Christchurch and the South Island.

Chant, Ken. Pastor and author of a children's book that upset the Chamberlains.

Chapman, Ken. Scientist who assisted Les Smith in experiments on dingo teeth cuts to material.

Charlwood, Graeme. Detective Sergeant in charge of gathering information about the Chamberlains. Told Michael Chamberlain in a police interview that Azaria's clothes were found 'folded' and 'stuffed in the crevice' of a rock, which there was no evidence for.

Collins, Senator Bob. Northern Territory Federal Labor Party politician, critical of the Northern Territory injustice towards the Chamberlains and played a significant role in achieving a Royal Commission in 1985–86.

Cooney, Senator Barnabus. Federal Member.

Corbett, Dr Laurie. Northern Territory dingo expert who believed a dingo was capable of taking and killing a baby.

Cox, Dr James JC. Avondale College President before Lindy went to jail.

Cozens, Pastor Bert and Norma. Alice Springs Seventh-day Adventist minister at the time of Azaria's disappearance.

Craig, Pastor Ron. Liaison officer between the Seventh-day Adventist Church and the Chamberlains and the Union Secretary of the Trans-Tasman Seventh-day Adventist Church.

Cranwell, Phyllis and Max. Ayers Rock witnesses who criticised the police for their investigation.

Creighton-Brown, Senator Noel. West Australian Liberal.

Crispin, Dr Ken. Chamberlain Royal Commission junior counsel. Later a judge of the Australian Capital Territory.

Coulthard, Tom. Michael Chamberlain's volunteer private investigator and researcher into government management of tourism and dingoes at Fraser Island, 1995–2010.

Culliford, Dr Brian. Blood expert from England who endorsed Joy Kuhl's blood science work.

Da Costa Roque, Sylvia. Columnist for the (Brisbane) *Sunday Mail* in August 1980. Wrote derogatory comments about the Chamberlains' response to Azaria's death.

Dean, Peter. First lawyer to be used by Michael and Lindy Chamberlain at the first Alice Springs inquest on the recommendation that he was the 'most honest lawyer in town'.

Deane, Justice Sir William. High Court of Australia Judge and later Governor-General of Australia. He dissented and would have upheld the Chamberlains' Appeal with Justice Lionel Murphy.

De Luca, Geoff. First reporter for the Murdoch press' *Adelaide News* tabloid at Ayers Rock after Azaria's death who wrote a derogatory report about the Chamberlains' distressed state.

Devil's Marbles. The last tourist place before arriving at Ayers Rock/Uluru.

Dixon, Kirsty. Based at the University of Newcastle Law School, an original researcher into new dingo attacks following the Lowndes open verdict in 1995.

Donaldson, Pastor Bob. Darwin Seventh-day Adventist minister.

Donally, Bob. Northern Territory Correctional Services Director.

Doolan, Sergeant. Desk Sergeant at the Mount Isa police in 1980.

Drew, Dr Richard. GP to Michael Chamberlain in the 1980s.

Elston, Bobby (Roberta). Nurse at Ayers Rock who changed her story about the Chamberlains' behaviour.

Evans, Senator Gareth. Attorney-General Labor.

Everingham, Paul. Northern Territory Chief Minister (1978–84), Attorney-General until 1983. Announced the police invasion on the Chamberlain home, 19 September 1981.

Evil Angels, the film also called *A Cry in the Dark* starring Meryl Streep as Lindy and Sam Neill as Michael, directed by Fred Schepisi.

Fernhead, Professor. Royal Commission specialist on dingo fabric damage.

Fertility Cave. A sacred site on Ayers Rock where Lindy and Michael Chamberlain saw their first dingo, which appeared to be casing them out.

Finch, Fred. Acting Northern Territory Attorney-General.

Fischer, The Hon Tim. Deputy Prime Minister and leader of the National Party.

Fisher vs Stuart. Supreme Court case over a dingo attack, held before Azaria's death in Darwin in 1979.

Flanigan, Veronica. Chamberlain campaigner and writer.

Fogarty, Moira Beryl. Northern Territory junior police forensic investigator at the first inquest.

Forster, Justice. One of three judges in the 1988 Northern Territory Criminal Court of Appeal.

Gallagher, Justice Frank. Deputy President of the Court of Conciliation and Arbitration and Chamberlain advisor.

Gallagher, Normie. Radical left-wing activist in the Labor party.

Gallagher, Reverend Jim. Darwin Baptist Minister.

Galvin, Gerry. Second inquest Coroner.

Gibbs, Sir Harry. High Court Chief Justice in 1984 Chamberlain Appeal.

Gibson, Frank. Senior Constable, Northern Territory Police bodyguard for the Chamberlains who confessed he was a plant after recognising they were innocent and became loyal friends.

Gill, Alan. Journalist and religious commentator.

Gilroy, Michael Shamus. Inspector at Alice Springs and first to arrive at Ayers Rock with

Detective Sergeant Lincoln to interview the Chamberlains after Azaria's death.

Goodwin, Wally. First to see Azaria's bloodstained jumpsuit a week after her disappearance, some 20–30 metres away from an unknown dingo den. His description about how it was found was very different to Frank Morris' account.

Graham, Sergeant Barry William. Mount Isa policeman who examined the Chamberlains' car for blood and after two and a half hours found nothing but whose evidence was not presented at the trial.

Gustafson, Professor. Royal Commission expert on dingo teeth and fabric cuts.

Haby, Murray. School teacher and Ayers Rock witness who saw dingo tracks with Aboriginal trackers, carrying a load away from the Chamberlain tent.

Harding, Dr Les. Dingo hair expert who testified that hairs found on Azaria's jumpsuit and elsewhere in the tent, were from a dingo.

Harris, Les. President of the Australian Dingo Foundation and critical of those who didn't think a dingo could take Azaria.

Heise, Pastor Lyell. Avondale College Church Minister.

Heise, Pastor Vernon. Seventh-day Adventist minister.

Hitchcock, Kevin. Television journalist and second in charge at Channel 10. Changed his views towards the Chamberlains after his 1984 investigation into Azaria's death at Ayers Rock with private investigator Philip Ward. A documentary was produced for television that treated seriously the theory that a pet dingo may still have been alive and might have been responsible for the death of Azaria.

Hitchings, Bill. Journalist covering the majority of the Chamberlain case who, after believing them to be guilty, became very concerned, as new information emerged damning the prosecution case that the Chamberlains were in fact innocent.

Hoare, Justice MB. The Honourable CMG Retired Supreme Court Judge.

Hocking, Betty. Member of Parliament, Australian Capital Territory and driving force for a Royal Commission into the Chamberlain case.

Hodgman, Michael. Tasmanian Senator in the Federal Government critical of the Chamberlain trial verdict.

Hughes, Dr Owen and Janita. Education Chairman of Avondale College and with his wife became foster parents of Kahlia Chamberlain for 18 months.

Johnson, Dr Dianne. Journalist who was critical of the negative Australian attitudes towards the Chamberlains.

Johnstone, Commodore Eric. Administrator of the Northern Territory.

Joseit, Pastor Peter. South Pacific Seventh-day Adventist Church ministerial secretary, and Avondale College roommate.

Justice in Jeopardy. Book defending the Chamberlains' innocence, by Guy Boyd in 1984.

Kearney, Justice Sir William. Northern Territory Criminal Court of Appeal judge.

Kerr, John Fairbanks. Author of *A Presumption of Wisdom*.

Kilgariff, Senator Bernard. Northern Territory Liberal.

Killen, Senator Sir James. Federal Minister for Defence who interviewed Michael Chamberlain.

Kirby, Justice Michael. High Court Judge who agreed the Chamberlains had suffered an injustice.

Kirkham, Andrew. Junior barrister to John Winneke QC and council for the Chamberlains in the Royal Commission.

Knowles, Senator Susan. Federal Liberal Party, West Australia.

Kranz, Pastor Russell. Public Relations Director for the South Pacific Region of the Seventh-day Adventist Church during the Chamberlains' tribulation.

Kuchell, Rex. Forensic botanist attached to the South Australian police.

Kuhl, Joy. Forensic scientist for the prosecution at the trial with 18 months experience in blood identification. Discredited by the Royal Commission for her flawed opinion that Azaria's blood was present in Michael's Torana V8 hatchback car. The Royal Commission determined that she had mistaken bitumen sound deadener, copper dust and spilled milkshake as Azaria's foetal blood.

Kum, Yuen Darryl. Darwin Seventh-day Adventist Church member.

Lawrie, Delia. Northern Territory Attorney-General.

Lester, Mike. Journalist for the *Adelaide Advertiser*.

Lincoln, Kevin John. Detective Sergeant, Alice Springs and first detective to arrive at Ayers Rock after Azaria's death. Resigned soon after.

Lloyd-Jones, John. Barrister who offered his services to Lindy while she was in jail.

Lowe, Greg and Sally. Ayers Rock Camp witnesses who were present at the Chamberlains' barbecue when Azaria disappeared.

Maarten, Fritz. Dingo expert who agreed that it was inherently likely that Azaria could have been killed by a dingo.

Madigan, Dr Geoffrey. Avondale College President and friend of the Chamberlains.

Manzie, Darryl. Northern Territory Police Public Relations Officer and a police sergeant before becoming the Attorney-General in 1987. Offered the Chamberlains a 'pardon' which they firmly rejected.

Martin, Brian QC. Successor to Ian Barker in late 1981 as Solicitor-General. Denied the Chamberlains an inquiry in 1985 before being overruled in 1986 by the Federal Government Attorney-General, Lionel Bowen.

Martin Report (The). By Brian Martin QC. Denied Chamberlains an inquiry into the trial evidence, but later overthrown.

Mason, Sir Anthony. High Court Judge who did not to uphold the Chamberlains' appeal in 1984.

Mason, Senator Colin. Federal Parliament Democrat who fought for an inquiry into the Chamberlain case in 1985.

Masterman, George QC. NSW Ombudsman.

McAulay, Peter. Northern Territory Commissioner of Police during Paul Everingham's time as Chief Minister.

McHugh, Michael QC. Defended the Chamberlains in the Federal and High Court appeals, narrowly loosing the latter 3–2.

McNay, Ashleigh. Council assisting Denis Barritt at the first inquest.

McNicol, Don. Associate investigator with Phil Ward.

Mercer, Frederick. Superintendent of Berrimah Prison during Lindy's imprisonment.

Metcalfe, Jim. Senior Constable who assisted Joy Kuhl in the examination of Michael's car.

Middleweek, Dr Belinda. Author of a PhD thesis 'Dingo Media? R v Chamberlain as a model for an Australian event.' University of Sydney, 2007.

Milne, Dr Irene. Mount Isa doctor who attended the birth of Azaria.

Morling, Justice Trevor. Chamberlain Royal Commission judge.

Morris Elizabeth. Fourth Inquest Coroner, 2012.

Morris, Frank. Senior Constable Ayers Rock when Azaria died. Picked up Azaria's clothing before he photographed it.

Moorehouse, Frank. Author of first Chamberlain docudrama, 1982. Strongly criticised for his license implicating the Chamberlains in Azaria's death and incorporating the highly prejudicial and ignorant 'sacrifice in the wilderness' lie.

Mounsey, Dr. Attended Lindy at the birth of Kahlia.

Muirhead, Acting Chief Justice James Henry. Chamberlain Supreme Court trial judge in 1982.

Mulvihill, Senator James. Patron of the Native Dog (Dingo) Centre.

Murdoch, Lindsay. Northern Territory-based ABC journalist.

Murphy, Justice Lionel. High Court Judge who, with Justice Deane upheld the Chamberlain Appeal in 1984. Murphy was renowned for his quick acting to achieve fair outcomes. He became Attorney-General of Australia.

Nader, Justice John. Northern Territory Criminal Court of Appeal Judge in 1988.

Nairn, Professor Richard. Described Joy Kuhl's 'blood' investigation as crude.

Neal, David. NSW University senior law lecturer.

Neill, Sam. Actor who played Michael Chamberlain in the film *Evil Angels* (also known as *A Cry in the Dark*) with Meryl Streep.

Newsome, Dr Alan. Dingo expert and scientist with the CSIRO.

Noonan, Liz (and Dr Tony Noonan). Most effective members of the Darwin Chamberlain support group to obtain a Royal Commission into the Chamberlains' convictions. They demonstrated extreme courage facing alienation by Northern Territory Parliamentarians and the Darwin social set.

Northern Territory Conservation Commission. Denied a request by Chief Ranger Roff for .22 Hornet bullets to cull dingoes that attacked humans.

Northern Territory Criminal Court of Appeal. The three-judge appellate court that declared Michael and Lindy Chamberlain to be 'innocent', in 1988.

Nyman Trevor. Law Society president and solicitor for John Lloyd-Jones.

O'Gorman, Terry. Queensland lawyer and counsel for Civil Liberties.

O'Loughlin, Mick. Lawyer assisting the Northern Territory Coronial inquiry and trial prosecution.

Operation Ochre. New police investigation in 1981, led by Detective Sergeant Graeme Charlwood, surrounding all dingo evidence.

Orams, Dr Hector. Said that cut marks on baby blanket were consistent with dingo teeth marks.

Oram, James. Murdoch reporter who changed sides and became incensed at the Northern Territory police's treatment of the Chamberlains.

Osmond, Dr Elaine. Critic of Professor Cameron.

Otto, Pastor Billy. Seventh-day Adventist public evangelist who attacked the Roman Catholic Church's belief system while a visiting minister.

Pauling, Tom QC. Assistant prosecutor to Ian Barker and later Northern Territory Administrator.

Peddie, Dr Bill. Christchurch Boys High School friend since 1962, High School science teacher and author of several science textbooks. Peddie became a significant defender of Michael Chamberlain, writing a treatise on why the prosecution forensic science was false.

Perron, Marshall. Northern Territory Attorney-General did not support a Royal Commission in 1986.

Phillips, John Harbor QC. Chamberlains' defence lawyer at the Darwin trial. Later Chief Justice of Victoria and facilitator of a new independent forensic institution.

Piez, Steve. Ambulance driver at Tennant Creek when Chamberlains lost Azaria.

Pitjantjatjara tribe (Nation). Aboriginal tribe inhabiting the area around Uluru/Ayers Rock (Uluru).

Plueckhahn, Dr Vernon Douglas. Described Professor Cameron's interpretations at the trial as 'completely unfounded'.

Porter, Chester QC. Counsel assisting Justice Trevor Morling in the Royal Commission.

Publick, Senator Chris. Federal Liberal.

Raymond, Tony. Senior investigator at Royal Commission who gave evidence about the faulty prosecution blood and material damage evidence at the trial.

Redneck. An Australian term, meaning rogue or cowboy.

Reynolds, Senator Margaret. Federal MP Labor.

Rice, Philip QC. Chamberlain's Coronial Counsel in the first and second inquests. Later became a Supreme Court Judge in the Northern Territory.

Roberts, Webber. Owned a similar Torana V8 hatchback to Michael Chamberlain with a similar under-dash deadener spray that Joy Kuhl described as 'foetal blood'.

Robertson, Jim. Northern Territory Attorney-General who succeeded Paul Everingham.

Rodgers, Bryan. Reported seeing a dingo kill an Aboriginal child outside Tennant Creek in 1986.

Rollo, Pastor George. Agitator for a Chamberlain Royal Commission

Rose, Dr William. Royal Commission blood expert.

Rosendahl, Dr Glen. Wrote *The Dark Side of the Law*, a book critical of the forensic science of the trial prosecution

Ryan, Sheila. Radio speaker and Chamberlain Justice leader in Launceston.

Schepisi, Fred. Director of the film *Evil Angels*.

Scott, Dr Andrew. Prosecution trial expert who, after seeing the new defence evidence, was highly critical of Brian Martin's report.

Sellinger, Dr Ben. Australian National University scientist. Highly critical of Joy Kuhl's blood testing and Brian Martin's report into the Chamberlain submission to open a Royal Commission.

Seventh-day Adventist. American-based Church that grew out of an 1844 revival.

Serventy, Vincent. Animal liberationist.

Shamley, Francois. Michael Chamberlain's assistant at the fourth inquest.

Shears, Richard. Author of *Azaria* who used 'dingo woman' term.

Sholl, Sir Reginald. Supreme Court Judge (retired) and chairman of the Chamberlain Innocence committee.

Sims, Bernard. London odontologist who backed up Professor Cameron at the trial.

Simmonds, James. Author of *Azaria: Wednesday's Child*.

Smith, Les. Expert witness who helped to crack the 'blood' spatter mystery in Michael Chamberlain's car and the 'cuts' to Azaria's jumpsuit at the Royal Commission. The 'blood' was found to be 'Dufix bituminous sound deadener. The 'cuts' were consistent with the actions of dingo incisor teeth.

Spender, Stephen. Shadow Attorney-General, Federal Liberal.

Sturgess, Desmond. Well-known Queensland barrister who acted as Gerry Galvin's coronial counsel in the second inquest and an advisor to Ian Barker in the Darwin trial.

Sydney Sun. A tabloid which became infamous for its bold front-page headlines, often written by Steve Brien, setting the Chamberlains up for trial by media with evidence later shown in the Royal Commission to be almost entirely false.

Tabrett, Hillary. Witnessed what she believed to be dingo marks on Azaria's blanket.

Tarling, Lowell. Author and commentator on the Chamberlain case.

Teague, Senator Baden. Federal member.

Tedeschi, Mark QC. NSW Barrister criticised for his courtroom theatrics.

Telford Hotel, Alice Springs. The hotel that was evacuated after a bomb threat to kill the Chamberlains during the first inquest in 1981.

Tipple, Stuart William Holden. Lindy and Michael Chamberlain's solicitor since 1981 and the facilitator in bringing justice for the Chamberlain family through their exoneration. He facilitated Michael Chamberlain's submission concerning new and deadly dingo attacks. The fourth and final inquest was opened from this.

Tjikadu, Barbara. Wife of Ayers Rock Elder, Nipper Winmatti, and senior tracker of the dingo footprints which they testified was carrying Azaria.

Toohey, Justice John. The judge responsible for quashing the first inquest findings that a dingo had killed Azaria without any defence by the Chamberlains, the first inquest coroner or the Chamberlains' lawyers. Virtually all the evidence supplied was discredited at a Royal Commission five years later.

Torana hatchback V8. LX 1977 model, owned from new by Michael Chamberlain until the time of publication of this book. *Muscle Motor* magazine described it as the most famous Torana in Australia. Refurbished with $19,000 of the Northern Territory's compensation money after being partly torn apart by the Northern Territory forensic experts led by Joy Kuhl, for the prosecution. Described by Michael as a *piece de resistance* to systematic bureaucratic ineptitude and false forensic science.

Trackers. Aboriginal people who can track animal trails. Evidence at first inquest and Royal Commission confirmed a dingo in and around the Chamberlain tent, its pause in the sandhill, and their general behaviour in attacking babies and young children.

Travel Lodge Hotel. The Chamberlains' residence during the Darwin section of the Royal Commission.

Trounce, Mark. Cartoonist and satirist who illustrated *Dingo Lingo*, with Dave Hansen, in an insulting publication about the cause of Azaria's death.

Turnbull, Malcolm. Federal Member Liberal and former Leader of the Opposition.

Tuxworth, Ian. Chief Minister in the Northern Territory when Lindy was released from Berrimah Prison in 1986.

Uluru. Aboriginal name for Ayers Rock changed after 1985.

Uluru Motel. Place where the Chamberlains stayed after they lost Azaria.

Walkabout, Daisy. Key Aboriginal tracker with Barbara Tjikadu, Nipper Winmatti, Nui Minyintiri, and Chief Ranger Derek Roff, who found dingo footprints carrying a load away from the Chamberlains' tent on the night of 17 August 1980. They all agreed that this was the dingo carrying Azaria.

Walker, Sir Allan. Director for the Uniting Church.

Ward, Philip. Private investigator into the theory that a pet dingo named Ding had taken Azaria.

Watterson, Ray. Professor of Law, University of Newcastle and Latrobe and Australian reformer of the Coronial System. Michael Chamberlain's consultant at the fourth inquest.

Wendt, Jana. TV presenter. Sympathetic to the Chamberlains' call for a Royal Commission.

Wendt, Greg. *Newcastle Herald* journalist.

Wentworth, William (Bill). Federal Minister for Aboriginal Affairs. Attempted to assist Michael Chamberlain in obtaining a Royal Commission.

West, Judy and Bill. Witnesses at Ayers Rock. West Australian farmers who were angered by the accusations against the Chamberlains.

Woinarski, Brind. Junior counsel to John Winneke.

Whittacker Amy. Ayers Rock witness.

Williams, Charles P. Director of Australian Broadcasting Policy.

Wilson, Dr Douglas. Claimed he worked with Professor Cameron and validated his work.

Winmatti, Nipper. Head Elder and tracker of the dingo that took Azaria Chamberlain.

Winneke, John QC. Chamberlains' Royal Commission senior barrister and later President of the Victorian Criminal Court of Appeal.

Witten, Dr Max. CSIRO Scientist, Canberra.

Wolfgramm, Dr Robert. Monash University sociologist.

Wran, Neville. Supported an inquiry into the Chamberlains' convictions.

Wright, Geoffrey. *Bulletin* journalist.

Young, Dr Norman. Author of *Innocence Regained* and critic of the police's prejudice surrounding the Chamberlains' beliefs.

Yulara Hotel resorts. The Northern Territory Government's $150 million tourist project 11 kilometres from Ayers Rock. Work was under way in 1980 when Azaria was killed by a dingo.

About the author

Michael Leigh Chamberlain was born in Christchurch and lived in Ellesmere, Canterbury, a rich farming district in New Zealand, from 1944-65. Michael graduated with a BA in Theology from Pacific Union College and an MA in Religion from Andrews University, Michigan in 1982. He graduated with a Bachelor of Teaching from Avondale College in 2002 and with a PhD in Education from the University of Newcastle in 2002.

Formerly an ordained minister in the Seventh-day Adventist Church, he is a social historian and analyst of Seventh-day Adventist Church culture, a professional archivist and English teacher, researcher and literary analyst.

Michael is the author of three books: *Cooranbong: First Town in Lake Macquarie 1826-1996* (The Cooranbong Times, 1997); *Beyond Azaria: Black Light White Light* (Information Australia, 1999); and *Beyond Ellen White: Seventh-day Adventism in Transition* (Post Pressed, 2007). Michael is also a public speaker. Michael opened the fourth inquest in Azaria's death with his submission on new information on dingo attacks on children.

Michael is a competitive sportsman and was the successful CEO of an all Aboriginal Rugby Union team in Brewarrina. His interests include law reform, the media and Australian history and his hobbies include dry fly trout fishing, tramping, cooking, feral animal eradication and listening to classical music.

It has taken almost 32 years, 10 court cases, tens of millions of dollars, more than a dozen books, untold magazine articles and scores of television programs, movies and this book to tell the saga of Lindy and Michael Chamberlain's fight to get justice in the Northern Territory courts of law.

His second wife, Ingrid Chamberlain, describes him when faced with insurmountable adversity in getting justice for his family as having 'the raw courage and passion to pull it off'.

Index